Southern Living®

2020 Annual Recipes

KEY LIME SLAB PIE
WITH STRAWBERRY
WHIPPED CREAM
(PAGE 126)

BROWN SUGAR-
GLAZED PINEAPPLE
(PAGE 15)

CHERRY-PECAN
SWIRL BREAD
(PAGE 25)

CREAMY SPRING
VEGETABLE SLAW
(PAGE 69)

QUICK PICKLED
RADISHES WITH LEMON,
GINGER, AND MAPLE
(PAGE 69)

SMOKED-TOMATO SALSA
(PAGE 119)

The Joy of Southern Cooking

Dear Friends,

This has been a challenging year for all of us, and that includes the editorial team at *Southern Living*. Due to COVID-19, we had to shut down our Test Kitchen for several months, leaning on staffers to develop and photograph recipes at home. Like many of you, we adapted to new ways of working and communicating, but we also felt a sense of urgency and purpose, especially with food stories. We've heard from many of you who are spending more time in the kitchen—baking, grilling, and getting more creative with ingredients and techniques. Even as you have canceled the usual family gatherings and holiday celebrations, you also seem to have rediscovered the joy of Southern cooking—and so have we.

This edition of *Southern Living Annual Recipes* is special, because it represents the extraordinary efforts our editors and Test Kitchen staffers have made to bring you great dishes month after month. Despite the pandemic, we have produced some delicious new classics that taste as good as they look, from baked pastas and cornmeal desserts to the prettiest white cake you've ever seen. We've worked with some talented Southern chefs and cookbook authors to bring you plenty of new ideas and inspiration. And, as we've done for 54 years, our Test Kitchen pros fine-tuned every recipe, so you can always cook with confidence.

When it's done right, good Southern food should bring us together and sustain us during tough times. It should be nourishing, comforting, and delicious, and it should add some joy (and a little spice) to life. No matter what you're hungry for, I think you'll find it in these pages. Our "Quick Fix" Suppers are easy weeknight dishes that never skimp on flavor. Our "Southern Classic" recipes give you a fresh, updated take on a beloved regional favorite. And of course we never forget dessert, so check out the bonus section that's filled with our all-time best cakes, pies, cobblers, cookies, and bars.

A lot of care went into these recipes, so I hope you'll enjoy having them at your fingertips. Thanks for staying with us.

Sid Evans
Editor-in-Chief
Southern Living magazine

Contents

Top-Rated Recipes

We cook, we taste, we refine, we rate, and at the end of each year, our Test Kitchen shares the highest-rated recipes from each issue exclusively with *Southern Living Annual Recipes* readers.

January–February

- Tropical Granita (page 15) Pineapple is the star of this light and refreshing dessert. Store in the freezer up to 2 weeks and enjoy any day of the week.
- Pina Colada Quick Bread (page 19) This tasty treat is ready for the oven in under 20 minutes. It's perfect for breakfast, dessert, or a quick snack.
- Country Captain (page 21) You'll love our version of classic chicken and rice. Curry, coconut and bacon combine to give this dish an exotic flair. No side dishes needed!
- Slow-Cooker Buttermilk Grits (page 27) We've tried hundreds of grits recipes over the years and this one is one of our absolute favorites. You must give it a try and we think you'll agree.
- Sheet Pan Hanger Steak and Vegetables (page 33) When it's too chilly to fire up the grill, try this simple (and tasty!) recipe in the oven.

March

- Strawberry-Mint Tea (page 40) This refreshing recipe is great all on its own but if you want to add a kick, try spiking it with gin or vodka.

CHOCOLATE COBBLER

- Quick King Ranch Chicken Skillet (page 45) This casserole comes together in just 20 minutes. We add poblano chiles but if you don't want the heat, substitute small bell peppers. It's a great dish to enjoy at home or take to a casual potluck.
- Chocolate Cobbler (page 49) We took two classic Southern favorites—cobbler and chocolate and created this decadent dessert that we can't get enough of. Make a double batch—it'll disappear quickly!
- Buttermilk Alfredo Pasta with Chicken and Spinach (page 52) The beauty of this dish is that you can add or subtract any ingredients to make it your own. We love spinach with the creamy buttermilk sauce, but you can skip it or replace it with your favorite vegetable and still get great results.

April

- Warm Radish-and-Potato Salad with Smoked Trout and Radish Leaf-and-Mint Pesto (page 65) This springtime salad is as beautiful as it is delicious! It's worthy of your Easter dinner table or any other special-occasion meal. If you are not a fan of trout, you can easily leave it out or substitute with chicken or lean beef strips.
- Creamy Spring Vegetable Slaw (page 69) Forget about your usual slaw recipe and give this one a try! With only 15 minutes of prep time, it's definitely worth it. Make a large batch to keep in the fridge—it'll keep for days.

- Glazed Ham with Pineapple Chutney (page 74) Spiced pineapple chutney elevates this ham to a whole new level. You won't go back to "normal" ham again!
- Potato Salad with Dijon and Scallions (page 79) We have tested hundreds of potato salads over the years and this one stands out as one of our all-time favorites. The colorful fingerling potatoes give it a special flair worthy of any special-occasion menu.
- Macaroon Sandwich Cookies (page 84) These fancy little cookies call for strawberry jam but you can use any fruit or chocolate-flavor spread in between the delicate macaroons. Flag the recipe for your holiday baking, too!
- Baked Buttermilk French Toast (page 93) Our version of this breakfast staple is the fluffiest, tastiest, and easiest French toast you'll ever make. Our secret ingredient takes it over the top!

May

- Grilled Baby Eggplant Parmesan (page 101) We love this recipe for many reasons—mostly because they look so cute on your dinner plate. If you let them cool long enough, you can eat them by hand and serve as an appetizer. So impressive!
- Steak-and-Bell Pepper Salad (page 107) Celebrate the arrival of spring with this fresh, colorful, and hearty main-dish salad. We like to sprinkle blue cheese on top but you can use Parmesan or feta if you prefer.
- Creole Burgers (page 111) This burger will soon become your new favorite. The creole seasoning takes it to the next level. Whip up a batch of homemade chips to go alongside.

CREOLE BURGERS

- Drink-Your-Greens Smoothie (page 113) This is convenient for a meal on the go. It's packed with nutrients and tastes delicious, too!

June

- Marinated Tomatoes (page 117) Make the most of in-season tomatoes with this tangy salad—you can enjoy them on their own, or use them in several of our fresh tomato recipes starting on page 117.
- Spicy Watermelon Refresher (page 120) This big batch drink will be your signature summer beverage. Leave out the tequila if you prefer a non-alcoholic version.
- Key Lime Slab Pie with Strawberry Whipped Cream (page 126) The strawberries add the perfect amount of sweetness to complement the tanginess of the key limes. If you're short on time, you can use store-bought pie crust instead of homemade.
- Mojo Chicken Bowls (page 129) You can add steak, shrimp, or your favorite protein to the basic "bowl" base of this recipe ... or go meatless if you prefer. Any way you mix it up, you can't go wrong with this weeknight winner!
- Hot Crab-and-Artichoke Dip (page 134) Crab dip is always the hit of the buffet! We love using fresh crab but you can get the same luscious results with frozen fresh.

July

- Southern Sunrise (page 155) Shake up happy hour with this refreshing summer cocktail. It's ready to enjoy in just 10 minutes. Cheers!
- Brown Sugar Layer Cake with Peach Buttercream (page 164) This layer cake is as beautiful as it is delicious. If you have a summer birthday to celebrate, skip ordering from a fancy bakery and whip this up instead. Total active time is only 30 minutes and it looks like you baked all day!
- Mexican Street Corn Pizza (page 173) We love using a stone when we cook pizza—but if you don't have one, it's no problem! Preheat a sheet pan and you'll get the same professional results.
- Shrimp-Tomatillo Tacos (page 176) Celebrate summer with a *Southern Living* taco night. Check out our tasty variations of this weeknight staple and you'll never go back to traditional beef and cheese again!

August

- Fried Shrimp-and-Okra Po'Boys (page 183) Fresh okra is a Southern summer staple. We cook with it every chance we get and absolutely love it on a po'boy. Top these tasty sandwiches with a few fresh tomato slices.
- Freezer Breakfast Burritos (page 185) These family-pleasing burritos can be frozen for weeks. Make a big batch over the weekend and thaw and heat on those busy weekday mornings.
- Lemon-Basil Chicken Breasts (page 191) This is not your ordinary chicken recipe! Combine the ingredients into foil "packets" and cook them on the grill. It's just one of the many quick-fix foil-pack suppers you'll find starting on page 189. Dinner reinvented!
- Browned Butter Chocolate Chip Cookies (page 194) We're always trying to improve on the basic chocolate chip cookie. Brown sugar gives these treats that little something that makes them stand out above the rest.
- Pineapple-Pepper Slaw (page 195) This colorful crunchy slaw will be the star of your next backyard barbecue. We love it as a side dish or on top of a barbecue sandwich.

September

- Apple Butter Doughnuts with Salted-Caramel Glaze (page 200) Making homemade doughnuts can be intimidating but don't be afraid of these! They are easy to make, look beautiful, and melt in your mouth.
- Blackberry-Apple Butter Pie Bars (page 203) This recipe makes a big batch. Cut them into squares and freeze individual serving sizes for a quick treat. Heat in the microwave and serve with vanilla ice cream.
- Macaroni Pie (page 225) A great kid-approved meal that the grown-ups will love, too! It calls for refrigerated piecrusts making it easy to whip up in a flash.

MACARONI PIE

- Hamburger Stew with Croutons (page 227) Welcome fall with our creative spin on a traditional dish. It's hearty and a perfect meal when there's a bit of chill in the air.
- Baked Sweet Potato Fries (page 229) These oven-baked fries are just as crispy as the fried versions you enjoy eating out. And they are healthier, too!

THYME-CORNMEAL POUND CAKE

October

- Thyme-Cornmeal Pound Cake (page 234) We love this nontraditional spin on a traditional cake. The thyme adds a surprising burst of flavor and it's great for dessert, breakfast, or a tasty snack.
- Baked Ziti and Meatballs (page 240) Two of our all-time favorites in one delicious dish: meatballs and ziti. It doesn't get better than this! Be sure to make a big batch so you can enjoy leftovers.
- Chicken-and-Broccoli Skillet Pasta (page 243) When you're looking for a quick and healthy weeknight meal, look no further! We like to use Peppadew or sweet cherry peppers, but you can add any variety you choose.
- Breakfast Cookies (page 245) The name says it all! Now you can eat cookies for breakfast with zero guilt. These goodies are packed with protein and nutrients, and are a convenient and delicious way to start your day!

November

- Southern Sweet Potatoes with Brown Sugar Pecans (page 249) We cook this scrumptious side in a cast iron skillet for extra flavor and an impressive presentation. It will be the star of your Thanksgiving buffet. Don't skimp on the brown sugar pecans—they really make this stand out from your ordinary sweet potato recipe.
- Broiled Oysters with Tasso Breadcrumbs (page 252) As the holidays approach, we tend to spend more time in the kitchen to prepare those extra-special meals and snacks. This recipe will not disappoint! The presentation is just as important as the taste. Be sure to check out page 253 for ideas.
- Simple Roasted Turkey (page 254) We like to go back to the basics for the star of the Thanksgiving meal. This turkey will never fail you. And unlike some other turkey recipes, this one only calls for 15 minutes of hands-on time. You'll get to enjoy time with family instead of spending hours in the kitchen.
- Harvest Salad (page 262) This salad is filled with all of the flavors of fall. You can follow the recipe to the letter or add any of your favorites. You can also add chicken or steak to serve as a main dish meal any day of the week.

SOUTHERN SWEET POTATOES WITH BROWN SUGAR PECANS

- Mini Apple-Cinnamon Pies (page 270) It was difficult to pick our favorite from the amazing assortment of mini pies this month! You'll want to make them all and arrange a sampling to serve for your Thanksgiving dessert. Serve these warm with a dollop of vanilla ice cream.

December

- Bourbon-Praline Cheesecake (page 285) This luscious cheesecake is made even better with bourbon. The crust is a perfect combination of graham crackers, pecans, and brown sugar.
- Herb-Crusted Beef Tenderloin (page 295) This tenderloin stands out among the hundreds we've tasted over the years. It's simple, yet elegant and tastes out-of-this-world delicious!
- Pomegranate Mimosa (page 297) We love this fun spin on a traditional drink. They're festive for sipping on Christmas morning while enjoying time with your family.
- Eggs Benedict Casserole (page 298) We all rely on a good casserole during the holidays. This one will become a new favorite to enjoy on Christmas morning and for years to come.
- Slice-and-Bake Sugar Cookie Bites (page 303) These itty-bitty bites will be a nice addition for your holiday cookie swap. It's a trustworthy basic sugar cookie dough recipe that you'll want to keep on hand all year long.
- Santa's Kitchen Sink Cookies (page 305) As the name implies, we put everything we love about cookies into this one amazing recipe. They are sweet, salty, and so good! Pour a big glass of milk for Santa, too.

January–
February

TROPICAL GRANITA

Sunny Delights

The pineapple is an exotic symbol of Southern hospitality, and its tropical punch shines in these five desserts

My mother, Kent, grew up in a small town in South Carolina, but she was born in 1948 in distant Hawaii, where her parents lived when they were newlyweds and where my grandmother stayed while her husband traveled even farther afield during World War II. When my mother served anything with pineapple, my young mind assumed it was because of her glamorous Hawaiian origins.

Mom didn't love cooking and minimized her time in the kitchen accordingly. She had more exciting things to do, like practicing hula dancing. (Or so I thought. I had a very active imagination, including the ability to take one interesting tidbit and run with it.)

She made the occasional ambrosia on holidays, but was more likely to top vanilla ice cream with canned chopped pineapple or suspend a few perfectly shaped slices in lime gelatin, which was my absolute favorite.

When I grew older, I realized pineapples weren't specific to my family but a symbol of hospitality to just about everyone in the South. In years past, when fresh pineapple was particularly dear due to its inability to travel long distances, guests presented with pineapple understood they were welcomed as well as honored. Colonial hostesses who weren't wealthy enough to buy the prized fruit could rent one for the day to use as a centerpiece. They must have had incredible restraint, because who could resist cutting into the juicy fruit and devouring it?

It wasn't until I met my husband, whose parents really were rather glamorous, that I tasted fresh pineapple. While I'd love to claim a more sophisticated palate, I didn't notice that much of a difference. Thanks to my own Southern upbringing, I love the fruit in all its delicious forms: canned, fresh, candied in a fruitcake, baked into a casserole with cheese, or stirred into salsa.

These days, you can almost always find fresh pineapple at the supermarket, but that doesn't make it any less special to me. I have maintained enough of an imagination to still find the bright yellow fruit inside its prickly outer shell at least a little exciting. And when used in these dessert recipes, it's a very welcome sight. –Anne Wolfe Postic

Tropical Granita

ACTIVE 20 MIN. - TOTAL 20 MIN., PLUS 4 HOURS, 30 MIN. FREEZING
SERVES 8

- 5 cups coarsely chopped fresh pineapple (about 30 oz.)
- 1¼ cups bottled coconut water (such as Vita Coco)
- ¾ cup granulated sugar
- 1 tsp. Key lime zest plus 2 Tbsp. fresh juice (from 1 lime)
  Lime zest, for garnish

1. Process first 4 ingredients in a food processor until completely smooth, about 2 minutes. Pour mixture into a 13- x 9-inch dish. Freeze, uncovered, until just set but not completely frozen, 2½ to 3 hours.

2. Rake through granita using a fork, breaking up any large chunks. Return mixture to freezer; freeze until completely set and frozen, 2 to 3 hours. Rake through granita until it is completely broken up and no large chunks remain.

3. Transfer granita to an airtight container. Freeze up to 2 weeks. Sprinkle servings with lime zest.

Brown Sugar-Glazed Pineapple

ACTIVE 15 MIN. - TOTAL 15 MIN.
SERVES 6

- 1 (about 1¼-lb.) fresh pineapple, peeled and cored
- ¼ cup butter
- ½ cup packed light brown sugar
- 1 tsp. vanilla extract
  Vanilla ice cream, for serving
  Chopped roasted, salted macadamia nuts

Cut cored pineapple into 6 (1-inch-thick) rings. Melt butter in a large skillet over medium. Add sugar and vanilla; cook, stirring constantly, 1 minute. Add pineapple rings; cook, swirling skillet often, until pineapple is tender and sauce is smooth, about 5 minutes per side. Top with ice cream, and sprinkle with nuts.

BROWN SUGAR-GLAZED PINEAPPLE

PIÑA COLADA
QUICK BREAD
(PAGE 19)

PINEAPPLE-GINGER
UPSIDE-DOWN CAKE
(PAGE 19)

BUTTERY PINEAPPLE
CRUMBLE BARS

Piña Colada Quick Bread

(Photo, page 16)

ACTIVE 20 MIN. - TOTAL 1 HOUR, 15 MIN.,
PLUS 2 HOURS, 10 MIN. COOLING
MAKES 1 (9-INCH) LOAF

    Baking spray with flour
2   large eggs
1   cup granulated sugar
½   cup sour cream
⅓   cup butter, melted
2   Tbsp. (1 oz.) coconut rum
2   cups all-purpose flour
2   tsp. baking powder
½   tsp. baking soda
½   tsp. kosher salt
1   cup chopped fresh pineapple
      (about 6 oz.)
½   cup sweetened shredded coconut
2   cups unsifted powdered sugar
⅛   tsp. coconut extract
3   Tbsp. whole milk, as needed
      Toasted coconut chips (such as
      Dang) or toasted unsweetened
      flaked coconut

1. Preheat oven to 350°F. Coat a
9- x 5-inch loaf pan with baking spray with
flour. Beat eggs, granulated sugar, sour
cream, butter, and rum using an electric
mixer fitted with beater attachments
on medium-high speed until combined,
about 2 minutes. Whisk together flour,
baking powder, baking soda, and salt in a
medium bowl. Gradually add flour mixture
to egg mixture, beating on low speed until
just blended. Gently stir in pineapple and
shredded coconut. Spoon batter into
prepared loaf pan.
2. Bake in preheated oven until a wooden
pick inserted in center comes out clean,
55 minutes to 1 hour, 5 minutes, tenting
with aluminum foil after 45 minutes to
prevent excessive browning if needed.
Cool in pan on a wire rack 10 minutes.
Remove bread from pan, and transfer to
wire rack. Cool completely, about 2 hours.
3. Whisk together powdered sugar,
coconut extract, and 2 tablespoons of
the milk in a bowl, adding remaining
milk ½ teaspoon at a time until
desired consistency (mixture will be
thick). Spread glaze over top of cooled
bread, allowing some to drip down
sides. Immediately sprinkle top with
coconut chips.

Pineapple-Ginger Upside-Down Cake

(Photo, page 17)

ACTIVE 20 MIN. - TOTAL 1 HOUR, 10 MIN..
PLUS 40 MIN. COOLING
SERVES 8

¼   cup butter, plus ¾ cup softened
      butter, divided
1   tsp. grated fresh ginger (from
      1½-inch piece ginger)
1   cup packed light brown sugar
1   (3-lb.) fresh pineapple, peeled
1⅓ cups granulated sugar
1   tsp. vanilla extract
2   cups all-purpose flour
1   tsp. baking powder
1   tsp. kosher salt
½   tsp. baking soda
3   large eggs
¾   cup whole buttermilk

1. Preheat oven to 350°F. Melt ¼ cup
butter in a 10-inch cast-iron skillet
over medium low. Stir in grated ginger.
Remove from heat. Sprinkle evenly with
brown sugar.
2. Cut pineapple lengthwise into
8 (¼-inch-thick) planks, cutting in toward
core, and discard core. Cut larger planks
into triangles or rectangles. Arrange
triangles and smaller planks on top of
brown sugar mixture in skillet to fit snugly
together (shingling pieces as needed).
Set aside.
3. Beat granulated sugar and ¾ cup
softened butter with a heavy-duty stand
mixer fitted with a paddle attachment on
medium speed until light and fluffy, 3 to
4 minutes. Beat in vanilla. Whisk together
flour, baking powder, salt, and baking
soda in a medium bowl. Whisk together
eggs and buttermilk in a small bowl. Add
flour mixture to granulated sugar mixture
alternately with buttermilk mixture,
beginning and ending with flour mixture,
beating on medium-low speed until just
blended before next addition. Spread over
pineapple mixture in skillet.
4. Bake in preheated oven until a wooden
pick inserted in center of cake comes
out clean, 50 to 55 minutes, tenting
with aluminum foil after 40 minutes to
prevent excessive browning if needed.
Cool in skillet on a wire rack 10 minutes.
Invert cake onto a serving platter. Cool
30 minutes to serve warm, or cool
completely, about 1 hour.

Buttery Pineapple Crumble Bars

*These rich and gooey bar cookies just
might replace your usual lemon squares.
If you have one, use a stand mixer with a
paddle attachment to make the crust and
crumble topping. A hand mixer will send
flour flying.*

ACTIVE 20 MIN. - TOTAL 1 HOUR, PLUS 1 HOUR,
30 MIN. COOLING
SERVES 16

2   cups all-purpose flour
¾   cup butter, softened
½   tsp. vanilla extract
1⅓ cups granulated sugar, divided
½   tsp. kosher salt, divided
4   cups chopped fresh pineapple
      (about 22½ oz.)
¼   cup cornstarch
1½ Tbsp. fresh lemon juice
      (from 1 lemon)
¼   cup slivered almonds

1. Preheat oven to 375°F. Lightly coat a
9-inch square baking pan with cooking
spray. Beat flour, butter, vanilla, 1 cup of
the sugar, and ¼ teaspoon of the salt
with a heavy-duty stand mixer fitted with
a paddle attachment on medium-low
speed until mixture resembles coarse
crumbs, about 1 minute. Reserve 1 cup of
the crumb mixture in a small bowl for the
topping. Press remaining crumb mixture
evenly into bottom of prepared pan.
2. Bake in preheated oven until golden
brown, about 18 minutes. Transfer pan to
a wire rack, and cool crust completely,
about 30 minutes. (Do not turn off oven.)
3. Meanwhile, gently stir together
chopped pineapple, cornstarch, lemon
juice, and remaining ⅓ cup sugar and
¼ teaspoon salt in a bowl until thoroughly
combined. Spread pineapple mixture
evenly over cooled crust.
4. Stir together almonds and reserved
crumb mixture in a small bowl until
combined. Sprinkle almond mixture
evenly over pineapple mixture on crust.
Bake in preheated oven until the filling is
bubbly and the topping is lightly browned,
45 to 55 minutes. Transfer to a wire rack.
Cool completely, about 1 hour, and cut
into 16 squares.

The Exotic Country Captain

Cookbook author Cynthia Graubart explains how a curried chicken dish made it into the Southern food canon

I first tasted country captain in 1986, when I was a producer on Nathalie Dupree's television series, *New Southern Cooking.* I was in the control room as she prepared this culinary classic on camera. When we broke for crew lunch, I took a bite and instantly knew it would become a go-to in my recipe box. The flavors were reminiscent of Indian curries and Louisiana Creole cuisine. Where had this dish been all my life?

This Junior League–cookbook staple gives a nod to the culinary melting pot of the South and the burgeoning spice trade of the 1800s. Many sources say the recipe arrived on Southern shores from sea captains trading in the ports of Charleston and Savannah. But more likely, the name originated with the term "country captain," used by the English-controlled East India Company to describe someone in charge of a

"country ship," a vessel involved in trade within that region. I surmise it was a dish beloved by those very sea captains at stops along their maritime routes.

Country captain made its first appearance in an American cookbook in 1857. Eliza Leslie called it an "East India dish" in her cookbook, *Miss Leslie's New Cookery Book.* Her recipe involved boiling the chicken, seasoning it with curry powder, and frying it with onions.

Alessandro Filippini, of Delmonico's Restaurant fame in New York City, included it in *The International Cook Book of 1906,* flouring and frying the chicken and adding green peppers, garlic, and tomatoes.

But the one we recognize today is from Arie Mullins, an African American cook employed by Mrs. William Bullard of Warm Springs and Columbus, Georgia. Bullard ordered a copy of Filippini's cookbook and selected country captain to be served to future president Franklin D. Roosevelt.

Mullins deviated from the recipe by substituting two cans of whole peeled tomatoes for the fresh, which turned this dish into a year-round supper. It became one of Roosevelt's favorite meals, and Bullard (being one of the most well-known hostesses in the area) served it to many visiting dignitaries, including General George Patton.

Acknowledging the widespread affinity for this dish by so many in the military, the Army made it an MRE (meals ready to eat) in 2000, feeding our troops near and far.

Versions of country captain abound throughout the South. Rice, chicken, and a richly spiced tomato sauce are musts. The real dissent is over how you top it. Country captain is garnished with several ingredients, boosting its exotic appeal. I add the traditional mix of currants, almonds, and coconut plus chopped bacon and fresh herbs. But why pick sides? All of the additions play well together, and a dollop of chutney on top won't hurt, either.

Country Captain

ACTIVE 45 MIN. - TOTAL 1 HOUR, 10 MIN.
SERVES 4 TO 6

- 2 Tbsp. vegetable oil
- 2 Tbsp. unsalted butter
- 1 (3⅓- to 4-lb.) whole chicken, cut into 8 pieces
- 1 Tbsp. kosher salt, divided
- 1 medium yellow onion, chopped (2 cups)
- 1 small green bell pepper, chopped (about 1 cup)
- 2 medium garlic cloves, chopped (2 tsp.)
- 2 Tbsp. curry powder
- 1 tsp. black pepper
- 1 (28-oz.) can whole peeled tomatoes, undrained
- ½ cup dried currants or raisins, plus more for garnish (optional)
- 3 cups hot cooked rice (preferably Carolina Gold)
- ½ cup sliced almonds, toasted
- ½ cup unsweetened shredded coconut
- 2 bacon slices, cooked crisp and chopped (optional)
- 1 Tbsp. chopped fresh thyme leaves (optional)
- 1 Tbsp. chopped fresh flat-leaf parsley (optional)
- ½ cup apple chutney (optional)

1. Heat a large Dutch oven or deep skillet over medium-high; add oil and butter. Sprinkle chicken evenly with 1½ teaspoons of the salt.
2. Add half of the chicken, skin-side down, to Dutch oven. Cook until skin is golden brown, about 8 minutes. Turn with tongs; cook until browned on other side, about 4 minutes. Transfer chicken to a plate. Repeat process with remaining chicken.
3. Reserve 2 teaspoons drippings in Dutch oven. Add onion and bell pepper. Cook over medium-high, stirring occasionally, until soft, about 5 minutes. Stir in garlic, curry powder, black pepper, and remaining 1½ teaspoons salt. Cook, stirring constantly, until fragrant, about 30 seconds. Add tomatoes and currants, stirring well to break up tomatoes.
4. Return chicken to Dutch oven. Reduce heat to low. Cook, covered, until a thermometer inserted in thickest portion of chicken registers 165°F, about 25 minutes.
5. Transfer chicken to a plate. Bring sauce in Dutch oven to a simmer over medium-high. Simmer, uncovered, stirring occasionally, until slightly thickened, 6 to 7 minutes.
6. Serve chicken and sauce over hot rice, passing around any extra sauce at the table. Sprinkle evenly with almonds, currants, coconut, bacon, thyme, and/or parsley. Serve with chutney, if desired.

Spice, Crunch, and Flavor

Key ingredients for making this memorable dish

CURRANTS Dried currants are common in country captain recipes. In this version, they simmer in the spiced tomato sauce until plump and tender, and they also serve as a garnish. If you don't have any currants on hand, you can substitute raisins in a pinch.

CURRY POWDER There are many varieties of curry powder available to choose from. Most contain turmeric, cumin, coriander, and other spices. When choosing, make sure it is fragrant (a sign of freshness), and try different types until you find the flavor you prefer.

COCONUT Add texture and sweetness to this dish with coconut. The 1857 recipe in *Miss Leslie's New Cookery Book* calls for several tablespoons of finely grated coconut in the sauce, but we prefer to use it as a finishing touch.

ALMONDS Country captain is usually showered with a flurry of toppings including sliced almonds. They add a bit of crunch that balances out the tender chicken and vegetables. Be sure to toast the nuts before sprinkling them on top.

NO-KNEAD
BUTTERMILK BREAD
(PAGE 26)

The Beauty of Cast-Iron Baking

Is there anything cast-iron can't do? Study up on these four impressive breads, then tie on your apron and get started

CHERRY-PECAN
SWIRL BREAD
(PAGE 25)

CINNAMON SUGAR
PULL-APART LOAF

Cinnamon Sugar Pull-Apart Loaf

ACTIVE 30 MIN. - TOTAL 1 HOUR, 15 MIN.,
PLUS 1 HOUR, 45 MIN. STANDING
MAKES 1 (8- X 4½-INCH) LOAF

- 2 Tbsp. warm water (100°F to 110°F)
- 1½ tsp. active dry yeast (from 1 [¼-oz.] envelope)
- 1⅓ cups, plus ½ tsp. granulated sugar, divided
- ½ cup whole milk, warmed
- 1 large egg, beaten
- 1 tsp. kosher salt
- 7 Tbsp. unsalted butter, melted, divided
- 2½ cups bread flour, plus more for work surface
- 2 tsp. ground cinnamon

1. Stir together warm water, yeast, and ½ teaspoon of the sugar. Let stand until foamy, about 5 minutes.

2. Beat milk, egg, salt, yeast mixture, ⅓ cup of the sugar, and 4 tablespoons of the melted butter in a stand mixer fitted with a dough hook attachment on medium-low speed until well combined, about 10 seconds. Gradually add flour, beating until all flour is incorporated. Increase speed to medium; continue beating until dough is smooth and elastic, about 4 minutes. (It will be tacky.) Transfer to a medium bowl lightly coated with cooking spray. Cover with plastic wrap; let stand in a warm place until doubled in volume, 1 to 1½ hours.

3. Stir together cinnamon and remaining 1 cup sugar. Turn dough out onto a lightly floured work surface, and roll into a 20- x 12-inch rectangle. Brush with remaining 3 tablespoons melted butter; sprinkle with cinnamon sugar (reserve 1 tablespoon cinnamon sugar). Cut dough into 5 (12- x 4-inch) strips. Cut each strip into 5 (4- x 2½-inch) rectangles.

4. Lightly coat an 8- x 4½-inch cast-iron loaf pan with cooking spray. Stack dough rectangles on top of each other. Carefully transfer stack to prepared pan with rectangles standing upright (like dominoes). Cover loosely with plastic wrap. Let stand in a warm place until doubled in volume, 45 minutes to 1 hour.

5. Preheat oven to 350°F. Remove and discard plastic wrap. Sprinkle loaf with reserved 1 tablespoon cinnamon sugar. Place pan on a sheet of aluminum foil in oven. Bake until golden brown and a thermometer inserted in center of loaf registers 195°F, 38 to 42 minutes, tenting with aluminum foil after 25 minutes to prevent excessive browning, if needed.

6. Cool in pan on a wire rack 5 minutes. Run an offset spatula around edges of pan to loosen loaf; remove from pan. Serve warm, or cool completely on a wire rack, 1 hour.

Cherry-Pecan Swirl Bread

(Photo, page 23)

ACTIVE 40 MIN. - TOTAL 3 HOURS, 35 MIN., PLUS 8 HOURS CHILLING

SERVES 12

DOUGH

 1 (8-oz.) container sour cream
 6 Tbsp. unsalted butter
 1¾ tsp. kosher salt
 ¼ cup, plus 1 tsp. granulated sugar, divided
 ⅓ cup warm water (100°F to 110°F)
 1½ tsp. active dry yeast (from 1 [¼-oz.] envelope)
 2 large eggs, beaten
 2 tsp. orange zest (from 1 orange)
 3¾ to 4¼ cups bread flour, divided, plus more for work surface

FILLING

 1 cup packed light brown sugar
 ½ cup dried tart cherries, chopped
 ½ cup toasted pecans, chopped
 4 Tbsp. unsalted butter, softened
 2 tsp. ground cinnamon
 1 tsp. ground cardamom

GLAZE

 1 cup sifted powdered sugar
 2 Tbsp. fresh orange juice (from 1 orange)

1. Prepare the Dough: Cook sour cream, butter, salt, and ¼ cup of the granulated sugar in a saucepan over medium-low, stirring occasionally, until butter just melts, 4 to 5 minutes. Remove from heat. Cool to 110°F to 115°F, about 10 minutes.

2. Stir together warm water, yeast, and remaining 1 teaspoon granulated sugar in a bowl. Let stand until foamy, about 5 minutes.

3. Beat sour cream mixture, yeast mixture, eggs, and orange zest with a stand mixer fitted with a dough hook attachment on medium-low speed, gradually adding 3¾ cups of the flour, until a soft Dough forms and pulls away from sides but still adheres to bottom of bowl, 2 minutes.

4. Turn out Dough on a lightly floured work surface. Knead until smooth and elastic, 10 minutes, adding up to ½ cup remaining flour in very small increments, if needed to keep the Dough workable. (It should be tacky but not sticky.) Place in a lightly greased (with cooking spray) bowl, turning to coat all sides. Cover; chill at least 8 hours or up to 24 hours.

5. Turn out Dough on a lightly floured work surface. Roll into a 20- x 16-inch rectangle. Coat a 12-inch cast-iron skillet with cooking spray. Place a round sheet of parchment paper in bottom of skillet. Set aside.

6. Prepare the Filling: Stir together brown sugar, cherries, pecans, softened butter, cinnamon, and cardamom until mixture is well combined and the texture of wet sand.

7. Gently spread Filling over Dough, carefully pressing to adhere, leaving a 1-inch border on both long sides. Starting at 1 long side, roll up jelly-roll style. Using a serrated knife, cut log in half lengthwise. Arrange pieces side by side, cut-sides up, on the work surface. Carefully twist together, keeping cut sides facing up. Form twisted Dough into a 9-inch ring, tucking ends underneath. Place in prepared skillet, and cover loosely with plastic wrap. Let stand in a warm place until almost doubled in size, 1 to 1½ hours.

8. Preheat oven to 350°F with rack in lower third position. Remove and discard plastic wrap from Dough. Bake until golden brown and cooked through, 35 to 40 minutes, tenting with aluminum foil after 25 minutes, if needed, to prevent excessive browning. Remove from oven.

9. Prepare the Glaze: Whisk together powdered sugar and orange juice. Drizzle over bread. Serve warm, or transfer to a wire rack to cool completely, about 1 hour.

Bread Basics

FERMENTATION Once you combine the ingredients for a yeasted dough, it must rest and ferment in a warm spot. This allows the yeast to convert sugar into carbon dioxide, alcohol, and natural acids, which leaven the bread and make it flavorful and aromatic.

KNEADING When you knead dough, you develop gluten, an elastic protein that allows the dough to trap air and rise during proofing. Kneading can be sticky work, but don't overflour your work surface or the dough itself. This will make the bread tough and dense. To knead, fold the top of the dough in half toward you. Then, using the bottoms of both palms, push the dough away from you. Rotate the dough a quarter turn, and repeat the process until it becomes a smooth and stretchy ball, using little to no additional flour.

PROOFING This is the dough's chance to rise before it goes into the oven. Proofing makes the crumb light and tender and helps the bread hold its shape as it bakes. To keep the dough from drying out as it rests, cover it loosely with a kitchen towel or plastic wrap. Lightly grease the plastic wrap so it won't stick to the dough, causing it to tear and deflate.

BAKING One of the main benefits of baking with cast iron is that it gives bread a crisp and golden crust. For the best caramelization and oven-spring (the initial burst of rising that occurs in the first few minutes of baking), preheat the pan in the oven so it is hot when you add the batter or dough. If you aren't sure whether the bread is done baking, use a thermometer to check the internal temperature.

No-Knead Buttermilk Bread

(Photo, page 22)

ACTIVE 25 MIN. - TOTAL 1 HOUR, 15 MIN.,
PLUS 14 HOURS STANDING AND COOLING
SERVES 10

- 3 cups bread flour, plus more for work surface and sprinkling
- 2½ tsp. kosher salt
- ¼ tsp. active dry yeast (from 1 [¼-oz.] envelope)
- ½ cup whole buttermilk
  Fine yellow cornmeal, for sprinkling

1. Stir together flour, salt, and yeast in a large bowl. Add 1 cup water and buttermilk. Using your hand as a claw, stir together until no dry bits of flour remain and all clumps are broken up. Do not knead. Cover bowl tightly with plastic wrap; let stand at room temperature until it's very bubbly and the consistency resembles pancake batter, at least 12 hours or up to 18 hours.

2. Turn out dough on a well-floured work surface. (It will be very loose.) Incorporating as little flour from surface into dough as possible, shape it into a taut ball by folding edges in toward middle and repeating until it begins to develop structure and hold its shape, 12 to 16 times. Turn dough seam-side down on a clean (not floured) work surface. Heavily sprinkle top with flour. Using a dough scraper, pull the dough across the work surface, rotating it as you drag it, developing tension and forming a taut ball. Coat generously in flour.

3. Preheat oven to 500°F with rack in lower third position. Line an 8-inch proofing basket or bowl with a linen or cotton towel (not terry cloth). Dust the towel generously with flour; sprinkle with cornmeal. Using a dough scraper, lift and carefully invert dough ball into prepared bowl so the smooth, rounded side faces down and the seam faces up. Cover bowl with a kitchen towel. Let stand at room temperature until doubled in size, 1 to 2 hours. Meanwhile, place a cast-iron Dutch oven (5 quart or larger) with lid in oven to preheat about 20 minutes.

4. Remove hot Dutch oven from oven. Carefully invert dough ball into Dutch oven. Working quickly using a thin, sharp knife, make 3 (about 4-inch-long, ¼-inch-deep) cuts across the top of the loaf. Cover bread with Dutch oven lid; return to oven. Reduce oven temperature to 450°F.

JALAPEÑO
CORNBREAD
STICKS

Bake, covered, until loaf has increased in volume and turned a shiny, pale light brown, about 25 minutes. Remove lid. Continue baking until loaf is golden brown and a thermometer inserted in center registers 205°F, 12 to 18 minutes. Transfer to a wire rack; cool 1 hour.

Jalapeño Cornbread Sticks

ACTIVE 20 MIN. - TOTAL 35 MIN.
MAKES 14

- ½ cup all-purpose flour
- ½ cup fine yellow cornmeal
- 2 tsp. baking powder
- 1¼ tsp. kosher salt
- ¾ cup thawed frozen corn
- 1 large jalapeño chile, minced (about ¼ cup)
- 2 scallions, finely chopped (about ¼ cup)
- 10 Tbsp. unsalted butter, melted, divided
- 2 large eggs
- ¾ cup half-and-half
- 1 Tbsp. granulated sugar
- 2½ oz. shredded Mexican cheese blend (about ⅔ cup)

1. Preheat oven to 425°F. Place 2 (7-stick [5½-inch-long]) cast-iron corn stick pans on a rimmed baking sheet. Transfer baking sheet to oven. Preheat 15 minutes.

2. Meanwhile, whisk together flour, cornmeal, baking powder, and salt in a bowl; set aside.

3. Cook corn, jalapeño, scallions, and 8 tablespoons of the butter in a skillet over medium, stirring often, until mixture is softened, about 3 minutes. Set aside; cool 5 minutes.

4. Whisk together eggs, half-and-half, and sugar in a bowl. Add to flour mixture, whisking until smooth. Stir in jalapeño mixture and cheese.

5. Remove hot corn stick pans from oven. Brush molds evenly with remaining 2 tablespoons butter. Divide batter evenly among molds (about 3 tablespoons each). Bake in preheated oven until sticks are puffed and golden brown, 14 to 16 minutes. Serve warm, or turn sticks out onto a wire rack and cool completely, about 30 minutes.

Make Mini Corn Muffins: Preheat oven to 425°F. Coat 3 (12-cup) mini muffin pans with cooking spray; set aside. Proceed with Steps 2 through 4 as directed. For Step 5, divide the batter evenly among the prepared muffin pans (about 2 tablespoons each), filling 32 cavities. Working in 2 batches, bake until a wooden pick inserted in centers of muffins comes out clean, about 12 minutes. Serve warm, or remove from pans and cool completely on a wire rack, about 30 minutes. (Makes about 32 mini muffins.)

Good Grits

Three tasty ways to dress up a hearty breakfast staple

Slow-Cooker Buttermilk Grits

ACTIVE 10 MIN. - TOTAL 3 HOURS, 10 MIN.
SERVES 6

Stir together 5 cups **water**, 1½ cups **uncooked stone-ground grits**, and 2 tsp. **kosher salt** in a 5-qt. slow cooker. Let stand 2 minutes, allowing grits to settle to bottom. Tilt slow cooker slightly; skim off solids using a fine mesh strainer. Cover and cook on LOW until grits are tender and thickened, 3 to 3½ hours. Stir in ¾ cup **whole buttermilk** and 2 Tbsp. **unsalted butter**. Serve with **toppings**; add **salt** and **pepper** to taste.

CHOOSE YOUR TOPPINGS
1. Scrambled **egg**, cubed **ham**, shredded **cheddar cheese**, halved **cherry tomatoes**, chopped **fresh chives**
2. Fried **egg**, cubed **chorizo**, cubed **avocado**, crumbled **queso fresco (fresh Mexican cheese)**, **hot sauce**
3. Poached **egg**, crumbled **bacon**, sautéed **spinach**, shaved **Parmesan cheese**

It's Soup Season

Warm up weeknights with comforting recipes made with simple, whole ingredients

LEMONY CHICKEN SOUP WITH SWEET POTATOES

Lemony Chicken Soup with Sweet Potatoes

ACTIVE 15 MIN. - TOTAL 40 MIN.
SERVES 6

- 1 large lemon
- 2 Tbsp. olive oil
- 3 large shallots, thinly sliced (about 1 cup)
- 2 tsp. chopped fresh rosemary
- 8 cups unsalted chicken stock
- 2 medium sweet potatoes, peeled and cut into ¾-inch cubes (about 4 cups)
- 3 (8-oz.) boneless, skinless chicken breasts
- 2¾ tsp. kosher salt
- ¾ cup uncooked orzo
- ¼ cup chopped fresh flat-leaf parsley

1. Remove 6 (2-inch) lemon peel strips from lemon using a vegetable peeler. Squeeze lemon to equal 2 tablespoons juice. Set aside strips and juice.
2. Heat oil in a large Dutch oven over medium-high. Add shallots and rosemary. Cook, stirring occasionally, until translucent, 4 to 5 minutes. Add lemon peel strips, stock, and potatoes. Bring to a boil over high; reduce heat to medium. Add chicken and salt, and cook 10 minutes. Add orzo, and cook until a thermometer inserted in thickest part of chicken registers 165°F and potatoes and orzo are tender, about 10 minutes more.
3. Remove and discard lemon peel strips. Remove and shred chicken; return to soup. Stir in lemon juice. Ladle soup into bowls; sprinkle evenly with chopped parsley.

SMART SHORTCUT
Leftover chicken works well in this soup and makes the recipe come together even faster. As the orzo cooks, add 3 cups of shredded chicken to the pot so it heats up thoroughly.

SLOW-COOKER PEAS-
AND-GREENS SOUP WITH
TURKEY SAUSAGE

CREAMY CAULIFLOWER
SOUP WITH BACON

Slow-Cooker Peas-and-Greens Soup with Turkey Sausage

ACTIVE 15 MIN. · TOTAL 4 HOURS, 30 MIN.
SERVES 6

- 2   Tbsp. olive oil
- 1   large yellow onion, chopped (about 2 cups)
- 12 oz. Italian turkey sausage (3 links), casings removed
- 1   Tbsp. chopped fresh thyme
- 5   garlic cloves, minced (about 4 tsp.)
- 6   cups unsalted chicken stock
- 3   cups frozen black-eyed peas (from 1 [15-oz.] pkg.)
- 3   oz. chopped kale (about 4 cups)
- 1   (15-oz.) can diced tomatoes, drained
- 2   tsp. kosher salt
- 2   Tbsp. red wine vinegar
- ½   tsp. black pepper

1. Heat oil in a large skillet over medium-high. Add onion, sausage, thyme, and garlic. Cook until sausage is browned and onion is tender, stirring occasionally to break up sausage, 8 to 10 minutes. Transfer to a 6-quart slow cooker, and stir in stock and peas. Cover and cook until peas are tender, about 4 hours on HIGH or about 8 hours on LOW.
2. Stir in kale, tomatoes, and salt. Cover and cook until kale is wilted, about 10 minutes more. Stir in vinegar and pepper.

HOLD THE CREAM

Substituting a potato for the usual half-and-half or heavy cream gives this rich, full-bodied soup a velvety texture without adding more fat. To make the recipe completely dairy free, replace the butter with olive oil.

Creamy Cauliflower Soup with Bacon

ACTIVE 20 MIN. · TOTAL 40 MIN.
SERVES 4

- 3   Tbsp. butter
- 1   medium yellow onion, chopped (about 1½ cups)
- 1   Tbsp. chopped fresh thyme
- 2¾ tsp. kosher salt
- 3   garlic cloves, minced (about 1 Tbsp.)
- 2   Tbsp. all-purpose flour
- 4   cups unsalted chicken stock
- 1   (12-oz.) russet potato, peeled and diced
- 1   lb. fresh cauliflower florets (from 1 medium head)
      Pinch of cayenne pepper
- 4   thick-cut bacon slices (about 6 oz.), cooked and crumbled
- 2   Tbsp. minced fresh chives

1. Melt butter in a large Dutch oven over medium. Add onion, thyme, salt, and garlic. Cover and cook, stirring occasionally, until onion is very soft and slightly caramelized, 10 to 12 minutes. Add flour to Dutch oven, and cook, stirring constantly, 1 minute. Add stock and potato. Increase heat to high, cover, and bring to a boil. Add cauliflower, and reduce heat to medium. Cook, uncovered, until cauliflower is tender, about 20 minutes.
2. Transfer cauliflower mixture to a blender; add cayenne. Secure lid on blender, and remove center piece to allow steam to escape. Place a clean towel over opening, and process until smooth, about 1 minute. Ladle soup into bowls. Top with bacon and chives.

GO GREENER

The secret to this soup's vibrant hue? Fresh broccoli and spinach, as well as a cooking trick: After you blanch the vegetables, cool them down with cold water before pureeing them. This helps lock in the bold color.

Broccoli-Spinach Soup with Parmesan Croutons

ACTIVE 30 MIN. · TOTAL 30 MIN.
SERVES 4

2 Tbsp., plus 2¾ tsp. kosher salt, divided
2 (10-oz.) pkg. fresh broccoli florets (about 8 cups), divided
1 lb. fresh baby spinach (about 16 cups)
2 cups unsalted chicken stock
¼ cup fresh flat-leaf parsley leaves
½ cup half-and-half
¾ tsp. black pepper, divided
4 oz. French bread, torn into 1-inch pieces
2 oz. Parmesan cheese, shredded (about ½ cup)
¼ cup olive oil, divided
1 Tbsp. fresh lemon juice (from 1 small lemon)

1. Preheat oven to 425°F. Bring 4 quarts water and 2 tablespoons of the salt to a boil in a large pot over high. Set 1 cup of the broccoli aside. Add remaining broccoli to pot, and cook 3 minutes. Add spinach, pushing down to submerge in water. Cook 1 minute or until broccoli is tender and spinach is wilted. Remove 1 cup cooking liquid; set aside. Drain in a colander, discarding remaining cooking liquid. Run cold water over broccoli and spinach, draining well, until cool, 2 to 3 minutes.

2. Process cooked, cooled broccoli and spinach, 1 cup reserved cooking liquid, stock, and parsley in a blender until smooth, 1 minute. Transfer to pot; stir in half-and-half, 2½ teaspoons of the salt, and ½ teaspoon of the pepper.

3. Toss together bread, Parmesan, and 3 tablespoons of the oil. Place in 1 layer on 1 half of a greased rimmed baking sheet. Toss reserved 1 cup broccoli with remaining 1 tablespoon oil and ¼ teaspoon each of salt and pepper. Place in a single layer on other half of baking sheet. Bake in preheated oven until broccoli is tender and bread is toasted, 7 to 9 minutes.

4. Gently reheat soup over medium until steaming, 4 to 5 minutes. Stir in lemon juice. Ladle soup into bowls, and top with roasted broccoli and croutons.

Slow-Cooker Chipotle-Tomato Soup

ACTIVE 15 MIN. · TOTAL 4 HOURS, 15 MIN.
SERVES 4

- 2 Tbsp. olive oil
- 2 cups chopped yellow onion (from 1 large onion)
- 1 canned chipotle chile in adobo sauce
- 1 tsp. dried oregano
- ½ tsp. crushed red pepper
- 6 medium garlic cloves, crushed
- 6 medium plum tomatoes, chopped (about 3 cups)
- 1 (28-oz.) can whole peeled plum tomatoes
- ¾ cup Baked Tortilla Strips (recipe follows) or broken tortilla chips
- ⅓ cup sour cream
- ¼ cup fresh cilantro leaves

1. Heat olive oil in a large skillet over high. Add onion, chipotle, oregano, crushed red pepper, and garlic. Cook, stirring occasionally, until onions are translucent, 6 to 8 minutes. Place onion mixture in a 6-quart slow cooker; stir in tomatoes. Cover and cook until juices have released from fresh tomatoes and their flesh is broken down, about 4 hours on HIGH or about 8 hours on LOW.

2. Place tomato mixture in a blender. Secure lid on blender, and remove center piece to allow steam to escape. Place a clean towel over opening, and process until smooth, about 1 minute. Pour soup into bowls. Top with tortilla strips, sour cream, and cilantro.

Baked Tortilla Strips

ACTIVE 5 MIN. · TOTAL 15 MIN.
MAKES ABOUT ¾ CUP

Preheat oven to 350°F. Coat both sides of 2 (6-inch) **corn tortillas** with cooking spray. Cut into 2- x ½-inch strips. Place in a single layer on a rimmed baking sheet. Bake until browned, about 10 minutes.

Perfect Pork Tenderloin

Juicy meat teams up with a flavorful whole grain salad in this 20-minute skillet supper

Pork Tenderloin with Farro Salad

ACTIVE 20 MIN. - TOTAL 20 MIN.
SERVES 4

- 2 Tbsp. apple cider vinegar
- 1 tsp. finely chopped garlic (from 1 medium garlic clove)
- 5 Tbsp. olive oil, divided
- 4 tsp. pure maple syrup, divided
- 3 tsp. Dijon mustard, divided
- 1½ tsp. kosher salt, divided
- ½ tsp. black pepper, divided
- 1 (8-oz.) pkg. precooked microwavable farro (about 1½ cups)
- 1 lb. pork tenderloin, trimmed and cut crosswise into 12 pieces
- ½ cup (4 oz.) dry white wine
- 2 Tbsp. unsalted butter
- 3 cups baby arugula (3 oz.)
- 1 small unpeeled Fuji apple, sliced

1. Whisk together vinegar, garlic, 3 tablespoons of the oil, 2 teaspoons of the maple syrup, 2 teaspoons of the mustard, ¾ teaspoon of the salt, and ¼ teaspoon of the pepper in a large bowl until combined. Stir in farro; let stand 5 to 10 minutes.

2. Meanwhile, heat remaining 2 tablespoons oil in a large skillet over medium-high. Flatten pork pieces slightly using the palm of your hand. Sprinkle evenly with remaining ¾ teaspoon salt and ¼ teaspoon pepper. Working in 2 batches, if needed, add pork to skillet. Cook until browned on both sides and just cooked through, about 2 minutes per side. Transfer to a plate; cover to keep warm.

3. Add wine to skillet; stir (using a wooden spoon) over medium-high to release any browned bits from bottom of pan. Cook, stirring often, until wine reduces by half, 1 to 2 minutes. Whisk in remaining 2 teaspoons maple syrup and 1 teaspoon mustard. Remove from heat. Add butter, stirring until butter melts, about 1 minute.

4. Add arugula and apple to farro mixture in bowl, and toss to coat. Divide salad and pork evenly among 4 plates, and spoon sauce over pork.

CALORIES: **453** – CARBS: **26G** – FAT: **26G**

Let's Make Steak

When it's too chilly to grill, try this easy recipe in the oven

Sheet Pan Hanger Steak and Vegetables

ACTIVE 20 MIN. · TOTAL 45 MIN.
SERVES 4

1½ lb. hanger steak (about 3 [8-oz.] steaks)

1 large sweet potato, peeled and cut into ½-inch cubes (about 2½ cups)

12 oz. French green beans (haricots verts) or green beans, trimmed

3 Tbsp. olive oil, divided

1½ tsp. kosher salt, divided

½ tsp. black pepper, divided

¼ cup butter, softened

1 tsp. chopped fresh thyme

1 tsp. lemon zest (from 1 lemon)

1 tsp. Dijon mustard

1. Preheat oven to high broil with rack positioned 6 inches from heat source. Let steaks stand at room temperature 20 minutes.

2. Meanwhile, toss together sweet potatoes, green beans, 2 tablespoons of the oil, and ¾ teaspoon of the salt on a large rimmed baking sheet. Spread in an even layer. Place a wire rack on top.

3. Rub steaks evenly with remaining 1 tablespoon oil; sprinkle with ¼ teaspoon

of the pepper and remaining ¾ teaspoon salt. Arrange on rack over vegetables. Broil in preheated oven until steaks are lightly browned on 1 side, 5 to 6 minutes. Turn steaks over; broil until lightly browned on other side and cooked to medium-rare doneness (130°F), 4 to 5 minutes. Remove wire rack from baking sheet. Transfer steaks to a cutting board; rest 10 minutes.

4. Meanwhile, return vegetables to oven; broil until tender, 5 to 10 minutes.

5. Stir together butter, thyme, lemon zest, mustard, and remaining ¼ teaspoon pepper. Slice steak against the grain. Serve steak and vegetables alongside butter.

Have a Heart

Test Kitchen professional and *Hey Y'all* star Ivy Odom shares cookies that are as fun to make as they are to give

There's no better way to spread love than with a homemade chocolate treat on Valentine's Day. Whenever I'm baking batches of individual sweets for gifting, I like to keep things simple and use some store-bought components to save time. These adorable heart-shape linzer cookies are made with basic chocolate shortbread and filled with ready-made marshmallow crème—no icing or special filling required! They're fun to decorate, too. You can tint the marshmallow pink or red with a little food coloring and then top it with sprinkles or sparkly sanding sugar. Best of all, the cookies are so cute that you don't need to spend a fortune on fancy packaging. Wrap them in cellophane bags tied up with ribbon, and add a note for each of your Valentines.

Chocolate–Marshmallow Linzer Cookies

ACTIVE 40 MIN. · TOTAL 2 HOURS, PLUS 2 HOURS CHILLING

MAKES 1 DOZEN

- 1 cup butter, softened
- 1 cup unsifted powdered sugar
- 1 tsp. vanilla extract
- 2 cups all-purpose flour, plus more for work surface
- ⅓ cup unsweetened cocoa
- ½ tsp. kosher salt
- ⅔ cup marshmallow crème
  Pink food coloring gel
  Assorted pink and red candy sprinkles and/or sanding sugar

1. Beat softened butter and sugar with a heavy-duty stand mixer fitted with a paddle attachment on medium speed until creamy, about 2 minutes. Add vanilla, and beat until just blended. Stir together flour, cocoa, and salt in a bowl; gradually add to butter mixture, beating on low speed until just combined, about 1 minute.
2. Divide dough in half; pat each half into a 5-inch disk. Wrap each disk in plastic wrap; chill 2 hours.
3. Preheat oven to 325°F. Unwrap 1 dough disk; place on a lightly floured work surface. Roll disk to ¼-inch thickness. Using a 2½-inch heart-shaped cutter, cut 12 cookies from dough, rerolling scraps as needed. Using a 1-inch heart-shape cutter, cut holes in centers of 6 of the cookies (leaving remaining 6 cookies whole).

4. Arrange the 6 whole cookies on a baking sheet lined with parchment paper. Arrange the 6 cut-out cookies on a separate baking sheet lined with parchment. Bake in preheated oven until bottoms are slightly browned, 9 to 11 minutes (cut-out cookies will bake a little quicker). Cool on baking sheets 2 minutes; transfer to wire racks to cool completely, 20 minutes. (You can bake the unused centers from the cut-out hearts 6 to 8 minutes.)
5. Meanwhile, repeat Steps 3 and 4 using remaining dough disk.
6. Divide marshmallow crème evenly between 2 small bowls. Tint crème in 1 bowl with 2 drops of pink food coloring, and stir to incorporate. Leave crème in second bowl untinted. Spread pink crème evenly among the centers of 6 of the whole cookies; spread untinted crème over remaining 6 whole cookies. Place crème-covered cookies on a baking sheet; decorate with sprinkles or sanding sugar as desired. Top crème-covered cookies with cut-out cookies to make 12 cookie sandwiches.

COOKING SL SCHOOL

The Right Way to Roast

Follow this basic method for tender, caramelized vegetables

Preheat the oven to 425°F. High heat ensures the vegetables won't steam and turn soggy.

Make sure the veggies are cut roughly the same size. Coat them generously with olive oil, and season with salt and pepper.

Spread them out on a sheet pan, making sure not to overcrowd. Roast until they are charred around the edges.

Stone-Ground Picks

Two of our favorite brands

SUPERMARKET:
We like these grits because they're a bargain and cook up nice and thick with plenty of toothsome texture. Stone Ground White Grits; traderjoes.com

SOUTHERN MADE:
With a robust corn flavor, this South Carolina product has a creamy consistency that's just right—not too thick or thin. White Grits; geechieboymill.com

---

3 Secrets to Great Grits

How to take your next pot from dull to delicious

Robby Melvin
Test Kitchen Director

ADD RICHNESS: Cook grits in a mixture of water and heavy cream (or milk) for the tastiest results. When they're done cooking, stir in a bit more cream and, of course, butter.

SEASON WELL: Add salt to the cooking liquid before you whisk in the grits to make sure they are flavored through and through. Taste cooked grits, and add more salt if necessary.

SKIM: Once you add the grits to the liquid, use a spoon or a small mesh strainer to remove the bits of husk that float to the top. They will not soften as they cook and can ruin the texture.

March

GILLIARD FARMS IS RUN BY
PARTNERS JOVAN SAGE (LEFT)
AND MATTHEW RAIFORD AS
WELL AS ALTHEA RAIFORD.

Seasons of Change

An entrepreneurial farming family in Brunswick, Georgia, plots their next steps

Eight years have passed since chef and farmer Matthew Raiford and herbalist Jovan Sage met and started a life together. But it's still easy to catch them in an adorable, winding cycle of recollection. Was it he who approached her? Was she the one who invited him for coffee?

Forget about determining who made the first move; Theirs was a quick match.

The auspicious meeting place was Turin, Italy, at Terra Madre, the Slow Food International biennial gathering. For many food professionals, the festival is destination-worthy not just for the gorgeous locale but for the chance to come together with thousands of independent food producers from more than 100 countries. It's probably a miracle they even crossed paths at the busy event, but then it seems 2012 offered a dash of perfect timing. Raiford had just recently jump-started his family's coastal Georgia land back to its farming origins, and Sage (then living in New York and serving as director of network engagement for Slow Food USA) was eager to become more hands-on in her work. They instantly recognized each other as kindred spirits.

Sage started visiting Gilliard Farms, the historic acreage that had belonged to Raiford's family for six generations. They hosted wine tastings, cooking classes, and pop-up dinners. She planted an herb garden. In brainstorming sessions, they envisioned a life of partnership, with Gilliard Farms as their base.

Time can be funny. As a kid growing up in Brunswick, Raiford never imagined launching a career in his hometown. He left as soon as he could sign on the Army's dotted line. When he was a toddler, his family moved from Bridgeport, Connecticut, to Brunswick to be closer to his maternal relatives and all that land (his great-great-great-grandfather Jupiter Gilliard bought 476 acres in 1874, not long after emancipation).

Raiford has fond memories of growing up on Gilliard, of the tomatoes, okra, peas, peppers, and muscadine grapes. He recalls passing time in the swing under the giant oak that still marks the center of the property. "I didn't know that people shopped at the grocery store for fruits and vegetables until I was an adult because we grew everything," he says. "I thought the store was where you went for flour and sugar, those kinds of things."

But segregation and its slow thaw through the 1970s made a mark on Raiford. His mother was a domestic worker out on Jekyll Island. His father had trained to be a baker in New England, but Raiford recalls that white business owners in Brunswick were not impressed by a "colored" man who seemed to know too much, so his father got work as a longshoreman. By

the time Raiford was a teenager in the eighties, he'd decided not to stay.

He spent nine years in the armed services and then trained as a chef at The Culinary Institute of America. After working in hotel kitchens, he led catering at the House of Representatives in Washington, D.C. All the while, he'd steeped in more than a decade of inquiries from Nana, his family matriarch, who wondered who would take the reins of Gilliard. Raiford always demurred, but eventually, the timing seemed to be right—he wanted to step up. "Finally, I was like: 'I'll do it. I'll do it,'" he says. In 2010, he returned to farming with his sister and co-owner, Althea. The remaining 28 acres of the original property would be plenty.

While Raiford was figuring out how to be a farmer, Sage was looking for ways to put her vast knowledge into practice. Born and raised in Kansas City, Missouri, she'd developed a career in community activism. Sage understood how the complex systemic issues of race, class, and gender could impact the ways people buy, grow, and consume food. She learned about herbal healing and became a health coach. She and Raiford wanted to combine their knowledge and skills and impact their community.

When they first set out, Nana was 90 years old and very much at home on the farm. It was one thing to host one-off events, but launching an open-door business practically out of her front yard didn't feel right. Plus, downtown Brunswick was making a push for its own revitalization, and locals were encouraging them to create a brick-and-mortar restaurant. "People were recruiting us. They asked us to open on St. Simons Island," Sage says. But the couple wanted to be in Brunswick.

In 2015, they opened The Farmer & The Larder in a narrow storefront on Newcastle Street downtown. The restaurant's seasonal menu evoked the city's port influences and Raiford's fine-dining background with dishes like pork belly atop a black-eyed pea fritter and fresh-catch wahoo. Sage sold custom tea blends and made sauerkraut, kimchi, and pickled vegetables sourced from the farm. Locals who yearned for creative dining without having to drive to Jekyll Island or St. Simons fell in love. In fall 2018, they opened a second restaurant, Strong Roots Provisions, a block down the street.

A few months later, almost a year after Raiford earned a James Beard Award semifinalist nod for Best Chef Southeast, he and Sage made the tough decision to shutter The Farmer & The Larder. Soon afterward, Strong Roots Provisions closed as well. Their effort to build outward was suddenly unsustainable. "Everything we were doing was taking us farther and farther away from the farm," Sage says. "We really had to ask ourselves: 'What are the things that are feeding us?'"

The land was the impetus for Raiford's return to Brunswick. For Sage, it was the prospect of building a life with her partner where she could live out the principles that she held dear. "I wasn't sure if I could recoup from closing two restaurants in one year," Raiford says of the experience. But once they began to walk through a pared-down business model for the farm, some tension dissipated. They envisioned a different plan.

"We had good help this past year, and it opened our eyes to how much more we could accomplish if we lived and worked here," Raiford says. Nana had passed on. Maybe it was time to not just keep the farm in operation but to bring people back to the land.

The future looks promising. Last spring, the couple hosted and prepared a ticketed farm dinner for 130 people with chefs including Carla Hall. Restaurant regulars are signing up for cooking classes, seed starters, composting and

fermentation training, chef's dinners, and tea and herbal-healing workshops.

Owning more than 100 chickens has made egg sales a part of the farm's business, and there will be hogs soon. Sage's hibiscus, deerberries, and culantro (an herb) are harvested and dried as part of a collaboration with local gin maker Simple Man Distillery. Sage has also ramped up her herbal-products business, Sage's Larder.

Cooking, farming—it's all about timing, making the best of what you've got. This farm has weathered many seasons of change. Raiford and Sage stand ready to embrace whatever comes next.

Strawberry-Mint Tea

This family recipe is great on its own or spiked with gin for a sparkling cocktail.

ACTIVE 15 MIN. - TOTAL 30 MIN.
SERVES 6

Place 2 cups hulled and chopped **fresh strawberries** and 1 cup **sugar** in a saucepan; muddle using a wooden spoon. Cook over low, stirring occasionally, until sugar dissolves, 5 minutes. Place 1 **peppermint sprig** in the palm of your hand. Give it a good slap (this brings out the volatile oils). Repeat with 7 more peppermint sprigs. Stir sprigs into strawberry mixture; remove from heat. Cool to room temperature, 15 minutes. Remove and discard mint. Pour mixture through a fine mesh strainer into a half-gallon pitcher. Stir in 6 cups **chilled sparkling water**. Serve over **ice**.

Morning, Sunshine!

Sticky-sweet, citrusy rolls are worth waking up for

Orange Rolls

ACTIVE 35 MIN. - TOTAL 1 HOUR,
PLUS 2 HOURS, 15 MIN. RISING
MAKES 1 DOZEN

- 3¾ cups all-purpose flour, plus more for work surface
- ½ cup whole milk
- ½ cup sour cream
- 6 Tbsp. unsalted butter, melted
- 2 tsp. kosher salt
- 1 large egg, lightly beaten
- 1 (¼-oz.) envelope instant or quick-rising yeast (such as Fleischmann's RapidRise)
- 1 cup granulated sugar, divided
- ½ cup unsalted butter, softened
- 2 oranges (to make 3 Tbsp., plus 1 tsp. grated zest, divided, and 3 to 4 Tbsp. juice)
- 2 cups powdered sugar

1. Combine flour, milk, sour cream, melted butter, salt, egg, yeast, and ⅓ cup of the granulated sugar in bowl of a stand mixer fitted with paddle attachment. Beat on medium speed until dough forms, 1 minute. Turn off mixer. Switch to dough hook attachment. Beat on medium speed until dough is smooth and elastic, about 6 minutes. (Dough should pull away from sides of bowl but stick to bottom.)

2. Spray a large bowl with cooking spray. Place dough in bowl, turning to coat all sides. Cover and let rise in a warm, draft-free place (about 75°F) until dough has doubled in size, about 1 hour and 30 minutes.

3. Lightly punch down dough. Roll dough out on a lightly floured surface into a 19- x 13-inch rectangle. Spread softened butter over dough.

4. Stir together 3 tablespoons of the orange zest and remaining ⅔ cup granulated sugar. Sprinkle sugar mixture over buttered dough, gently pressing to adhere. Starting with 1 long side, roll dough into a log, and pinch seam to seal. Turn log seam-side down, and cut into 12 rolls.

5. Spray a 12-cup muffin pan with cooking spray. Using your thumb, push upward slightly beneath bottom center of each roll, and place rolls into prepared pan. Cover with plastic wrap, and let rise in a warm, draft-free place (about 75°F) until almost doubled in size, 45 minutes.

6. Preheat oven to 350°F. Uncover rolls. Bake until golden brown and cooked through, about 20 minutes. Transfer pan to a wire rack; let stand in pan 5 minutes. Remove rolls to wire rack.

7. Whisk together powdered sugar, 3 tablespoons of the orange juice, and remaining 1 teaspoon orange zest in a bowl, adding remaining 1 tablespoon juice 1 teaspoon at a time, if needed, for desired consistency. Drizzle glaze over warm rolls.

ROOKIE MISTAKE
Don't head to the dairy aisle and buy American cheese slices. Your grocery store's deli counter sells (cheaper) bricks of cheese instead of individually wrapped slices.

Liquid Gold

Is there an art to making cheese dip? We asked the queen of queso herself

One night long ago in Austin, Texas, I ended up at a friend's house enjoying queso straight from the slow cooker. It was the standard party recipe—a can of tomatoes with green chiles and a melted 1-pound brick of processed cheese. Perhaps you know what I'm talking about and agree that this is indeed fine stuff. Food snobs may turn up their noses, but that's their loss.

After a while, I observed that most of us were gathered around the slow cooker in the kitchen. And as we took turns dipping tortilla chips into the golden elixir, there was much connecting, sharing, and laughter among this group of old friends and new. This is the power of queso.

For the uninitiated, queso (or chile con queso, as it is more formally known) is a crowd-favorite dip that's made from chile peppers and melted cheese and is ubiquitous in the Southwest. Like all Texans, I grew up eating it, but that initial spark was fully ignited when I moved away from home and learned that it's not nearly as common outside that part of the country.

When I first left Texas to live in New York City, I discovered it was a challenge to find the traditional building blocks of classic slow-cooker queso, so I had to improvise with what was available. As I researched recipes for my book *Queso!*, I learned there was a whole world of chile con queso beyond spicy canned tomatoes and brick cheese.

For instance, the kind you would find in El Paso and the northern Mexican state of Chihuahua, which is in the region where the dish originated, is a thicker concoction made with white cheese and large handfuls of roasted green chiles. As you travel across Texas, you will discover vegan versions made with nuts and vegetables and unique ones featuring kimchi or Indian chutney.

This recipe for Austin Diner-Style Queso is one of my favorites. Restaurants that are open all night long are popular spots for people to get their melted-cheese fix in Austin. While this recipe is not specific to any place, it is an easy, smooth queso that will remind you of late nights and good friends. — Lisa Fain

Three Keys to Queso

CHEESE Queso can be made with many different types of cheeses, but American and brick processed cheese (such as Velveeta) are the most popular because they easily melt to a liquid state.

CHILES While canned green chiles are fine to use, we recommend also including fresh jalapeños. Either roasted or raw ones will add brightness and cut the richness of the cheese.

THICKENER Queso that's made with American cheese (or anything other than brick processed cheese) needs a little cornstarch or flour to give the dip its thick and smooth texture.

Austin Diner-Style Queso

ACTIVE 25 MIN. - TOTAL 25 MIN.
SERVES 8

- 2 Tbsp. unsalted butter
- ¼ cup diced yellow onion (from 1 small onion)
- 4 jalapeño chiles, seeded and finely diced (¼ cup)
- 1 (4½-oz.) can chopped green chiles (undrained)
- 2 small garlic cloves, minced (2 tsp.)
- 1 cup whole milk
- 2 Tbsp. cornstarch
- 1 lb. white American cheese, shredded (about 4 cups)
- 2 Tbsp. chopped fresh cilantro, plus more for topping
- 1 tsp. ground cumin
- 1 tsp. kosher salt
- ¼ tsp. cayenne pepper
  Tortilla chips, guacamole, and pico de gallo

1. Melt butter in a medium saucepan over medium-low. Add onion and jalapeños. Cook, stirring occasionally, until softened, about 5 minutes. Add green chiles and garlic. Cook, stirring occasionally, 30 seconds.
2. Whisk together milk, 1 cup water, and cornstarch in a bowl until well combined. Add to chile mixture in saucepan. Bring to a simmer over medium-low, stirring constantly. Continue cooking, stirring constantly, until mixture thickens, 5 to 7 minutes. Add cheese; reduce heat to low, and cook, stirring occasionally, until cheese is melted, about 2 minutes. Stir in cilantro, cumin, salt, and cayenne. (Add additional seasoning, if desired.)
3. Transfer queso to a serving bowl, small slow cooker, or chafing dish set over a flame. Sprinkle with cilantro. Serve queso warm with tortilla chips, guacamole, and pico de gallo.

Tex–Mex Tonight

Tacos! Enchiladas! Five recipes to fire up dinner

QUICK KING RANCH
CHICKEN SKILLET

ON THE MILD SIDE
Two poblano chiles give this casserole a nice amount of heat. If you want to make it less spicy, substitute small bell peppers for one or both of the poblanos.

Quick King Ranch
Chicken Skillet

ACTIVE 20 MIN. - TOTAL 35 MIN.
SERVES 4

- 1 Tbsp. canola oil
- 1 medium yellow onion, chopped
     (about 1½ cups)
- 2 large poblano chiles, stemmed,
     seeded, and chopped
     (about 1½ cups)
- 1 (10-oz.) can diced tomatoes and
     green chiles (such as Ro*Tel),
     undrained
- 1 (10 ½-oz.) can cream of
     mushroom soup
- 4 cups chopped, cooked chicken
     (from 1 rotisserie chicken)
- ½ cup lower-sodium chicken broth
- 1½ tsp. ground cumin
- ½ tsp. kosher salt
- ½ tsp. black pepper
- 8 oz. sharp cheddar cheese,
     shredded (about 2 cups), divided
- 8 (5½-inch) white corn tortillas,
     each cut into eighths
     Fresh cilantro leaves, chopped

1. Preheat oven to 425°F. Heat oil in a
12-inch ovenproof skillet over medium-
high. Add onion and poblanos, and cook,
stirring often, until softened, about
6 minutes. Stir in tomatoes and green
chiles, mushroom soup, chicken, broth,
cumin, salt, and pepper. Bring to a boil,
and boil, stirring often, about 3 minutes.
Stir in half of the shredded cheese.
Arrange cut tortillas over top, and sprinkle
with remaining cheese.
2. Bake in preheated oven until cheese
is melted and mixture is bubbling, about
15 minutes. Sprinkle with cilantro.

CHEESE ENCHILADAS
WITH CHILI GRAVY

TWICE THE TOMATO
Double-concentrated tomato paste, which is sold in
squeeze tubes at the grocery store, makes this spicy
sauce extra rich and tangy.

Cheese Enchiladas
with Chili Gravy

ACTIVE 15 MIN. - TOTAL 35 MIN.
SERVES 4

- 3 Tbsp. canola oil
- 3 Tbsp. all-purpose flour
- 3 Tbsp. chili powder
- 5 tsp. double-concentrated tomato
     paste
- 1 tsp. ground cumin
- ¾ tsp. garlic powder
- ½ tsp. kosher salt
- 2¼ cups lower-sodium chicken broth
- 13 (5½-inch) corn tortillas
- 1 (16-oz.) block Colby Jack cheese,
     shredded (about 4 cups), divided
- ½ cup thinly sliced red onion
- ⅓ cup crema or sour cream

1. Preheat oven to 425°F. Heat oil in a
large skillet over medium-high. Whisk
in flour, and cook, whisking constantly,
until light brown, about 2 minutes.
Whisk in chili powder, tomato paste,
cumin, garlic powder, and salt. Cook,
whisking constantly, until fragrant, about
30 seconds. Gradually whisk in broth until
smooth. Bring to a boil, stirring often, until
sauce is thick enough to coat the back of
a spoon, about 2 minutes. Remove from
heat; let cool 5 minutes.
2. Spread ½ cup sauce in bottom of a
13- x 9-inch baking dish.
3. Dip each tortilla in sauce, letting excess
drip off. Place ¼ cup shredded cheese
in center of each dipped tortilla, and roll
up. Place seam-side down in baking dish.
Drizzle with remaining sauce. Sprinkle top
with remaining ¾ cup shredded cheese.
4. Bake in preheated oven until sauce
begins to bubble and cheese melts, about
12 to 15 minutes. Top with onion slices,
and drizzle with crema.

Slow-Cooker Carnitas Tacos

ACTIVE 25 MIN. · TOTAL 8 HOURS, 25 MIN.
SERVES 6

- 3 lb. boneless pork shoulder
- ¾ cup lower-sodium chicken broth
- ¼ cup fresh orange juice (from 1 orange)
- 4 garlic cloves, smashed
- 1 tsp. black pepper
- 1 Tbsp., plus 1 tsp. kosher salt, divided
  Warm corn tortillas, shredded cabbage, diced avocado, queso fresco (fresh Mexican cheese), lime wedges, for serving

1. Combine pork, chicken broth, orange juice, garlic, pepper, and 1 tablespoon of the salt in a 6- to 7-quart slow cooker. Cover and cook on LOW until pork is fork-tender, about 8 hours.
2. Preheat broiler to high with oven rack 6 inches from heat. Shred pork in slow cooker. Remove pork from liquid, and transfer to a large rimmed baking sheet. Spread into an even layer. Broil until pork begins to brown and crisp, about 8 minutes. Stir and broil 2 minutes more. Sprinkle with remaining 1 teaspoon salt, and toss well. Transfer to a serving platter.
3. Serve pork with tortillas, shredded cabbage, diced avocado, queso fresco, and lime wedges.

THICKENING TIP
This recipe makes tender beans in a nice soupy broth. For a thicker consistency, mash 1 cup of cooked beans in a bowl; then stir the beans back into the slow cooker.

Slow-Cooker Cowboy Beans

ACTIVE 15 MIN. · TOTAL 6 HOURS, 15 MIN., PLUS 8 HOURS SOAKING

SERVES 6

- 1 lb. dried pinto beans
- 6 thick-cut bacon slices, chopped
- 2 garlic cloves, smashed
- 1 canned chipotle chile in adobo sauce, chopped
- 4 cups lower-sodium chicken broth
- 2 Tbsp. kosher salt
- 1 large white onion, diced, divided (about 2 cups)
- 2 Tbsp. fresh lime juice (from 1 lime)
- 1½ Tbsp. fresh oregano leaves, plus more for garnish
- 1 tsp. ground cumin
  Hot cooked rice, for serving

1. Combine beans and water to cover by 2 inches in a large bowl. Cover and let soak at room temperature 8 hours or overnight. Drain and rinse beans; set aside.

2. Cook bacon in a medium skillet over medium until crispy, about 10 minutes. Pour bacon and drippings into a 6-quart slow cooker. Add 2 cups water to skillet, and scrape up browned bits from bottom. Pour into slow cooker. Add drained beans, garlic, chopped chipotle, broth, salt, and 1½ cups of the chopped onion; stir to combine. Cover and cook on LOW until beans are tender, about 6 hours.

3. Stir in lime juice, oregano, and cumin. Serve over hot cooked rice. Garnish with remaining ½ cup chopped onion and oregano leaves.

HOT STUFF
The beef filling should still be bubbling when you pour the cornbread batter over it. This will ensure that the cornbread will bake evenly without overbrowning.

Beef Tamale Pie

ACTIVE 20 MIN. · TOTAL 40 MIN.
SERVES 6

1 Tbsp. canola oil
1 lb. lean ground beef
1 medium yellow onion, chopped (about 1½ cups)
1 (14.5-oz.) can diced fire-roasted tomatoes, undrained
1 (15-oz.) can black beans, drained and rinsed
½ cup bottled chili sauce
1 Tbsp. chili powder
1½ tsp. kosher salt
2 large jalapeño chiles, divided
6 oz. sharp cheddar cheese, shredded (about 1½ cups), divided
1 (8.5-oz.) pkg. corn muffin mix
½ cup whole milk
1 large egg

1. Preheat oven to 425°F. Heat oil in a 10-inch cast-iron skillet over high. Add beef and onion; cook, stirring often, until beef is browned and crumbly, 5 to 7 minutes. Stir in tomatoes, beans, chili sauce, ¼ cup water, chili powder, salt, and 1 finely chopped and seeded jalapeño. Bring to a boil, and remove from heat. Sprinkle top with 1 cup of the cheese.
2. Whisk together corn muffin mix, milk, egg, and remaining ½ cup cheese. Pour batter over hot filling in skillet, spreading batter to edges of skillet. Thinly slice remaining jalapeño; sprinkle slices over top of batter.
3. Bake in preheated oven until cornbread is golden brown, 18 to 22 minutes.

Memories of Chocolate

Three old-fashioned desserts ready for a comeback

Chocolate Cobbler

ACTIVE 15 MIN. - TOTAL 45 MIN.
SERVES 8

- ¾ cup butter
- 1 cup self-rising flour
- ½ cup semisweet chocolate chips
- ¾ cup packed light brown sugar, divided
- 1 cup granulated sugar, divided
- 7 Tbsp. unsweetened cocoa, divided
- ½ cup whole milk
- 2 tsp. vanilla extract
- 1½ cups boiling water
  Vanilla ice cream

1. Preheat oven to 350°F. Place butter in an 11- x 7-inch baking dish. Place dish in oven (the oven does not need to be fully preheated). Heat until butter melts, about 10 minutes. Remove from oven.
2. Stir together flour, chocolate chips, ½ cup of the brown sugar, ⅓ cup of the granulated sugar, and 2 tablespoons of the cocoa in a medium bowl. Stir together milk and vanilla in a separate bowl. Stir milk mixture into flour mixture until batter is smooth. Pour batter evenly over melted butter in baking dish (do not stir).
3. Stir together remaining 5 tablespoons cocoa, ¼ cup brown sugar, and ⅔ cup granulated sugar in a small bowl. Sprinkle evenly over batter in baking dish (do not stir). Gently pour boiling water over mixture in dish (do not stir).
4. Bake in preheated oven until edges are golden brown and mixture is set on top, 30 to 35 minutes. Serve cobbler warm with vanilla ice cream.

TAKE TIME TO TOAST

Thoroughly toast the oats to bring out their nutty flavor.

Chocolate-Oatmeal Pie

ACTIVE 40 MIN. · TOTAL 6 HOURS
SERVES 8

CRUST

- 1½ cups all-purpose flour, plus more for work surface
- 1 Tbsp. granulated sugar
- ¾ tsp. kosher salt
- ½ cup cold butter, cubed
- 4 to 5 Tbsp. ice-cold water
- 1 large egg white

FILLING

- 1½ cups uncooked old-fashioned regular rolled oats
- 1 (4-oz.) bittersweet chocolate baking bar, chopped
- ¼ cup heavy cream
- ¾ cup packed light brown sugar
- 6 Tbsp. butter, melted
- 1 Tbsp. unsweetened cocoa
- ½ tsp. kosher salt
- ½ tsp. ground ginger
- ⅓ cup cane syrup
- ⅓ cup dark corn syrup
- 2 tsp. vanilla extract
- 2 tsp. apple cider vinegar
- 4 large eggs

1. Prepare the Crust: Pulse flour, sugar, and salt in a food processor 3 to 4 times. Add butter; pulse until mixture resembles coarse meal, 8 to 10 times. Drizzle 4 tablespoons of the cold water over flour mixture; pulse until moist clumps just form, 4 to 5 times. If needed, add up to remaining 1 tablespoon water 1 teaspoon at a time, pulsing 1 to 2 times after each addition, until mixture clumps. Gather into a ball; flatten into a disk. Wrap in plastic wrap; chill dough 30 minutes or up to 3 days.

2. Place a rimmed baking sheet in oven; preheat oven to 400°F. Unwrap chilled dough disk. Roll dough into a 12-inch circle (about ⅛ inch thick) on a lightly floured surface. Fit into a 9-inch pie plate. Fold edges under; crimp. Prick bottom and sides using a fork. Line dough with parchment paper; fill with pie weights or dried beans. Bake on hot baking sheet 20 minutes.

3. Whisk together egg white and 1 teaspoon tap water in a bowl. Remove Crust from oven (leave baking sheet in oven). Place Crust on a wire rack; remove pie weights and parchment. Let stand 1 minute. Brush bottom and sides with egg mixture. Return to oven (on baking sheet); bake at 400°F for 5 minutes. Place Crust on wire rack; cool completely, 30 minutes.

4. Prepare the Filling: Reduce oven temperature to 350°F. Spread oats on rimmed baking sheet. Bake, stirring occasionally, until toasted, 10 to 12 minutes. Transfer baking sheet to a wire rack; cool about 10 minutes.

5. Reduce oven temperature to 325°F. Stir together chocolate and heavy cream in a small microwavable bowl. Microwave at MEDIUM (50%) power until melted and smooth, 1½ to 2 minutes, stopping to stir every 30 seconds. Pour mixture into cooled Crust; spread in an even layer. Freeze until ganache is firm, about 10 minutes.

6. Whisk together brown sugar, melted butter, cocoa, salt, and ginger in a medium bowl. Whisk in cane and corn syrups, vanilla, and vinegar. Add eggs 1 at a time, whisking well after each addition. Stir in cooled oats until well combined. Remove Crust from freezer, and pour in Filling.

7. Bake on baking sheet at 325°F until edges are set and center is firm to the touch, 50 to 55 minutes, covering edges with aluminum foil after 30 to 35 minutes, if needed. Transfer to a wire rack; cool completely, about 3 hours.

Wacky Cake

ACTIVE 20 MIN. · TOTAL 2 HOURS, 45 MIN.

SERVES 6

CAKE

1½	cups all-purpose flour
¾	cup granulated sugar
⅓	cup unsweetened cocoa
1	tsp. baking soda
½	tsp. kosher salt
⅓	cup canola oil
1	Tbsp. distilled white vinegar
2	tsp. vanilla extract

ICING

⅓	cup butter
¼	cup whole milk
3	Tbsp. unsweetened cocoa
2¾	cups powdered sugar, sifted
1	tsp. vanilla extract

ADDITIONAL INGREDIENT

¼	cup chopped toasted pecans

1. Prepare the Cake: Preheat oven to 350°F. Sift flour, sugar, cocoa, baking soda, and salt into an ungreased 8- x 8-inch baking pan; spread mixture evenly in pan. Make 1 large well and 2 small wells in mixture in pan. Carefully pour oil into the large well; vinegar into 1 small well, and vanilla into remaining small well. Pour 1 cup water evenly over entire mixture in pan. Stir everything together using a fork until combined.

2. Bake in preheated oven until a wooden pick inserted in center comes out clean, 25 to 30 minutes. Transfer to a wire rack.

3. Prepare the Icing: Cook butter, milk, and cocoa in a small saucepan over medium-low, stirring often, until mixture comes to a simmer. Remove from heat; gradually whisk in powdered sugar and vanilla until completely smooth.

4. Pour Icing over warm Cake. Sprinkle with chopped pecans. Cool completely, about 2 hours.

NO BOWL REQUIRED

The batter for this quirky old-school cake is stirred together right in the baking pan, which is how it earned its name.

Better with Buttermilk

Make a lightened-up sauce that's still rich and creamy

Buttermilk Alfredo Pasta with Chicken and Spinach

ACTIVE 15 MIN. - TOTAL 20 MIN.

SERVES 6

- 8 oz. uncooked rigatoni pasta
- 2 Tbsp. unsalted butter
- ¼ cup all-purpose flour
- 1½ cups whole milk
- ½ cup whole buttermilk
- ¾ tsp. kosher salt
- ½ tsp. black pepper
- 4 oz. Parmesan cheese, finely shredded (about 1½ cups), divided
- 1 (5-oz.) pkg. fresh baby spinach
- 4 cups shredded rotisserie chicken

1. Cook pasta according to package directions. Drain and set aside.
2. Melt butter in a large skillet over medium. Whisk in flour until smooth. Cook, whisking constantly, 1 minute. Slowly whisk in milk. Cook, whisking constantly, until mixture is thickened and bubbly, 3 to 4 minutes. Remove from heat.
3. Whisk buttermilk, salt, pepper, and 1 cup of the cheese into flour mixture, whisking until cheese is melted. Stir in spinach, 1 cup at a time, stirring until wilted before the next addition. Add chicken and pasta; stir until coated and warmed through. Sprinkle with remaining ½ cup cheese.

CALORIES: **460** – CARBS: **38G** – FAT: **15G**

SMOOTH MOVE
Take the pan off the heat before you whisk in the buttermilk so the sauce will remain creamy and won't break.

Hold the Beans

Even die-hard Texans will approve of this bowl of red

Slow-Cooker Texas Chili

ACTIVE 20 MIN. · TOTAL 9 HOURS, 50 MIN.
SERVES 8

- 3 whole dried ancho chiles, stems and seeds removed
- 2 whole dried guajillo chiles, stems and seeds removed
- 3 Tbsp. all-purpose flour
- 1 Tbsp. chipotle chile powder
- 1 Tbsp. ground cumin
- 1 tsp. dried oregano
- 1 Tbsp., plus 1 tsp. kosher salt, divided
- 2 lb. beef brisket, trimmed and cut into ½-inch cubes
- 2 large yellow onions, chopped (about 4 cups)
- ¾ cup beef broth
- 5 Tbsp. minced garlic (from 8 large garlic cloves)
- 1 (28-oz.) can tomato puree
- 1 (14.5-oz.) can fire-roasted tomatoes
- 1 jalapeño chile, seeded and minced (about 1½ Tbsp.)
- 1 Tbsp. granulated sugar
   Toppings: sour cream, shredded cheese, cilantro, thinly sliced scallions

1. Place dried ancho and guajillo chiles in a blender, and cover with 1 cup hot tap water; soak 30 minutes. Drain and discard half of the liquid, reserving remaining ½ cup soaking liquid in blender. Process mixture until smooth, about 5 seconds. Set aside chile puree.

2. Stir together flour, chipotle chile powder, cumin, dried oregano, and 1 tablespoon of the salt in a medium bowl. Add beef cubes to flour mixture; toss to coat evenly. Set aside.

3. Stir together onion, beef broth, garlic, tomato puree, fire-roasted tomatoes, jalapeño, and chile puree in a 6-quart slow cooker. Add beef mixture to slow cooker; stir to combine. Cover and cook on LOW until beef is very tender, about 9 hours. Stir in sugar and remaining 1 teaspoon salt; serve with desired toppings.

MAKE IT AHEAD
This chili is best prepared a day or two in advance. It tastes even better after all the flavors have had time to come together.

COOKING ⓈⓁ SCHOOL

PANTRY PRIMER

Pick a (Dried) Pepper

Four varieties that add complex flavor and heat

DE ÁRBOL
Flavor profile: Small in size but big in color and spice, with a distinctive nutty taste
Heat level: Hot to very hot
Best for: Stir-fries and curries

CHIPOTLE
Flavor profile: Jalapeños that are smoked before they are dried for a deep, earthy taste
Heat level: Medium to hot
Best for: Salsas and other sauces

GUAJILLO
Flavor profile: Long, narrow chiles with bright, berrylike, undertones
Heat level: Mild to moderate
Best for: Spice rubs

ANCHO
Flavor profile: Sweet with notes of dried fruit (like raisins)
Heat level: Mild
Best for: Sauces, chili, and stews

Robby Melvin
Test Kitchen Director

"I love cooking with dried chiles, but I also keep my pantry stocked with San Marcos chipotle peppers. The fiery chiles and smoky-sweet adobo sauce are a faster way to add heat to a dish."

Signs of Freshness

Tips for choosing the best dried chiles

SHINE: The skin should be glossy and vivid, not dull.

FLEXIBILITY: As a test, try to gently twist or bend the pepper.

AROMA: It should smell spicy and a little like dried fruit.

KNOW-HOW

Rehydrate Right

Simple steps for using dried chiles in recipes

1

TRIM: Snip off each stem with kitchen shears, and open the chiles. Discard the seeds and stems.

2

SOAK: Submerge chiles in hot water for 30 minutes. This step can be done in a blender if you plan to puree them.

3

BLEND: Place them in the blender or food processor with half of the soaking liquid. Process until a smooth paste forms, about 30 seconds.

April

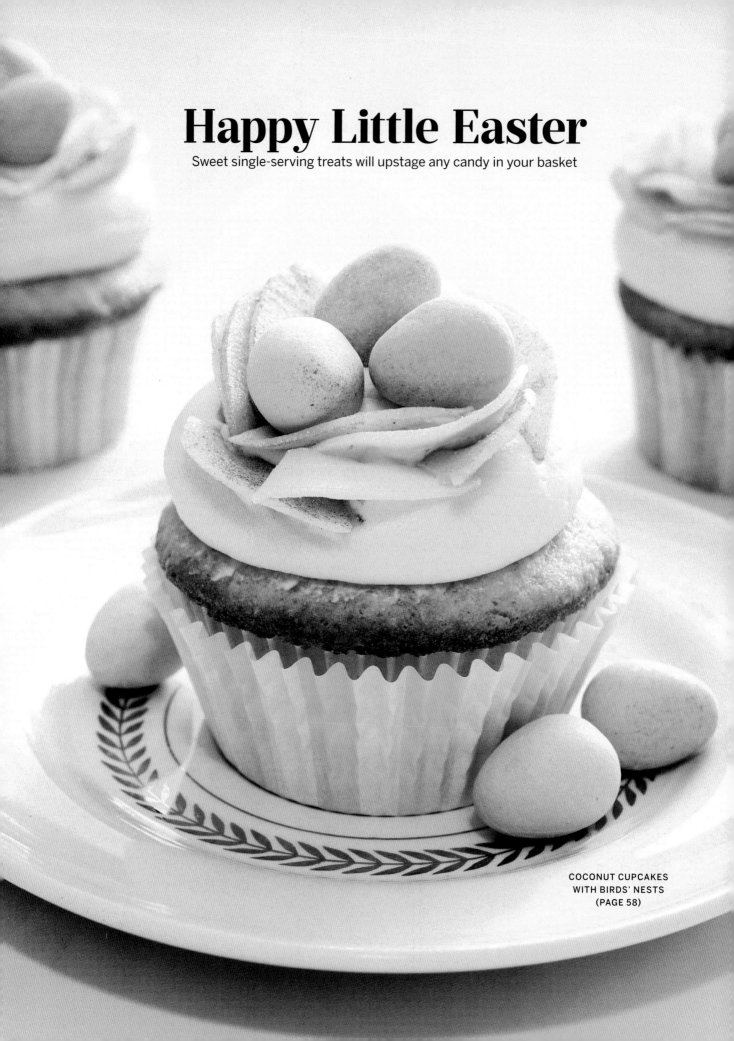

Happy Little Easter

Sweet single-serving treats will upstage any candy in your basket

COCONUT CUPCAKES
WITH BIRDS' NESTS
(PAGE 58)

CARROT-PINEAPPLE
MINI BUNDT CAKES WITH
BUTTERMILK-VANILLA GLAZE
(PAGE 58)

Coconut Cupcakes with Birds' Nests

(Photo, page 56)

ACTIVE 40 MIN. - TOTAL 1 HOUR, 30 MIN.
MAKES 2 DOZEN

COCONUT CUPCAKES
- 1 cup butter, softened
- 2 cups granulated sugar
- 4 large eggs
- 3 cups bleached cake flour
- 1 Tbsp. baking powder
- ½ tsp. kosher salt
- 1 cup well-shaken and stirred coconut milk
- 1 tsp. vanilla extract
- ½ tsp. coconut extract

COCONUT-CREAM CHEESE FROSTING
- 1 (8-oz.) pkg. cream cheese, softened
- ½ cup butter, softened
- 1 Tbsp. well-shaken and stirred coconut milk
- 1 tsp. vanilla extract
- ¼ tsp. coconut extract
- ⅛ tsp. kosher salt
- 1 (16-oz.) pkg. powdered sugar

NEST GARNISH
- 2 cups unsweetened shaved coconut, divided
- 1 Tbsp. powdered sugar, divided
  Pastel-colored edible luster dust in two hues
  Small candy eggs (such as Cadbury Mini Eggs)

1. Prepare the Cupcakes: Preheat oven to 350°F. Beat butter with a heavy-duty stand mixer on medium speed until creamy. Gradually add sugar, beating until light and fluffy. Add eggs, 1 at a time, beating just until blended after each addition.
2. Stir together cake flour, baking powder, and salt in a medium bowl. Add flour mixture to butter mixture alternately with coconut milk, beginning and ending with flour mixture, beating at low speed just until blended after each addition. Beat in vanilla and coconut extracts.
3. Spoon batter into 2 (12-cup) muffin pans lined with paper baking cups, filling each about three-fourths full. Bake in preheated oven until a wooden pick inserted in center comes out clean, 15 to 18 minutes. Cool in pans on wire racks 5 minutes. Remove cupcakes from muffin pans to wire racks, and cool completely, about 30 minutes.

4. Prepare the Frosting: Beat together cream cheese, butter, coconut milk, vanilla, coconut extract, and salt with a heavy-duty stand mixer on medium speed until creamy and smooth. Gradually add powdered sugar on low speed until well blended. Increase speed to medium-high, and beat until light and fluffy. Evenly frost Cupcakes.
5. Prepare the Nest Garnish: Place about one-third of the shaved coconut and ½ tablespoon of the powdered sugar in a zip-top plastic bag. Add a small amount of luster dust to bag, and seal. Shake bag to coat coconut. Add more luster dust, if desired, until preferred color is reached. Transfer coconut to a fine mesh strainer, and sift off excess powdered sugar. Transfer coconut to a small bowl until ready to use. Repeat process with half of remaining shaved coconut, remaining powdered sugar, and another color of luster dust. Reserve rest of coconut to leave uncolored. Transfer all coconut to a medium bowl, and gently stir to create a multicolored mixture.
6. Top each Cupcake with 1 to 2 teaspoons coconut, and lightly press an indention in center. Add 2 or 3 candy eggs to each nest.

Carrot-Pineapple Mini Bundt Cakes with Buttermilk-Vanilla Glaze

(Photo, page 57)

ACTIVE 25 MIN. - TOTAL 1 HOUR, 25 MIN.
MAKES 1 DOZEN

MINI BUNDT CAKES
- 1 cup granulated sugar
- 1 cup firmly packed light brown sugar
- ½ cup butter, softened
- ½ cup canola oil
- 3 large eggs
- 2½ cups all-purpose flour
- 2 tsp. baking soda
- 1½ tsp. ground cinnamon
- ½ tsp. kosher salt
- ¼ tsp. ground nutmeg
- ¾ cup whole buttermilk
- 2 tsp. vanilla extract
- 3 large carrots, grated (about 1¾ cups)
- 1 (8-oz.) can crushed pineapple, drained
- ¾ cup sweetened flaked coconut
- ¾ cup chopped toasted pecans

BUTTERMILK-VANILLA GLAZE
- 2 cups powdered sugar
- 2 Tbsp. butter, melted
- 2 tsp. vanilla extract
- 2 to 3 Tbsp. whole buttermilk

GARNISH
  Pineapple Flowers (recipe follows)

1. Prepare the Cakes: Preheat oven to 350°F. Beat together granulated sugar, brown sugar, and butter with a heavy-duty stand mixer on medium speed until well blended. Add oil, and beat until blended. Add eggs, 1 at a time, beating just until blended after each addition.
2. Whisk together flour, baking soda, cinnamon, salt, and nutmeg in a medium bowl. Add flour mixture to sugar mixture alternately with buttermilk, beginning and ending with flour mixture. Beat in vanilla at low speed just until blended. Fold in carrots, drained pineapple, coconut, and pecans. Spoon batter into 2 heavily greased (with cooking spray) 6-cup mini-Bundt pans, filling each about three-fourths full.
3. Bake in preheated oven until a wooden pick inserted in center comes out clean, 18 to 23 minutes. Cool in pans on wire racks for 10 minutes. Gently run a knife around edges. Remove from pans; cool completely, about 30 minutes.
4. Prepare the Glaze: Stir together powdered sugar, melted butter, vanilla, and 2 tablespoons of the buttermilk in a medium bowl. Gradually add remaining buttermilk, 1 teaspoon at a time, as needed for desired consistency. Spoon glaze over tops of cooled cakes, allowing to drip down sides. Garnish with Pineapple Flowers.

Pineapple Flowers

ACTIVE 15 MIN. - TOTAL 2 HOURS, PLUS 8 HOURS DRYING
MAKES 1 DOZEN

Preheat oven to 225°F. Using a very sharp knife, cut the top off of 1 **fresh pineapple**. Then remove the skin, slicing very close to the fruit and leaving the eyes (seeds). Using a ⅛-teaspoon measure, scoop out the eyes (you will have little round holes all over the pineapple). Lay pineapple on its side, and cut 12 very thin (about ⅛-inch-thick) slices. Blot pineapple slices dry with paper towels. Place on parchment paper-lined baking sheets. Bake 30 minutes. Using tongs, carefully turn slices over, return pan to oven, and bake 30 more minutes. Continue to bake in 15 minute increments, turning each time, until they are dried and beginning to turn golden brown around edges (watch very carefully to prevent overbrowning). When slices are done baking, place them in the cups of a 12-cup muffin pan, gently shaping petals so they curve upward. Let flowers dry, uncovered, at room temperature 8 hours or overnight.

Raspberry-Rhubarb Bars

(Photo, page 60)

ACTIVE 30 MIN. - TOTAL 1 HOUR, 30 MIN., PLUS 1 HOUR COOLING

MAKES 16

CRUST

- 2½ cups all-purpose flour
- ¾ cup toasted slivered almonds
- ⅔ cup powdered sugar
- ½ tsp. kosher salt
- 1 cup butter, cubed

FILLING

- 1½ cups toasted sliced almonds
- 1 cup granulated sugar
- 2 Tbsp. all-purpose flour
- ¼ tsp. kosher salt
- 10 Tbsp. butter, cubed
- 2 large eggs
- ½ tsp. almond extract
- 2 large fresh rhubarb stalks
- 1 pt. fresh raspberries
  Powdered sugar

1. Prepare the Crust: Preheat oven to 350°F. Pulse flour, slivered almonds, powdered sugar, and salt in a food processor until thoroughly combined and almonds are finely chopped, 8 to 10 times. Add butter; pulse until mixture resembles coarse meal, 8 or 9 times.
2. Line bottom and sides of a 13- x 9-inch pan with aluminum foil, allowing 2 to 3 inches to extend over sides; lightly coat foil with cooking spray. Press flour mixture evenly in bottom of prepared pan. Bake in preheated oven until beginning to brown around edges, about 20 minutes. Cool completely on a wire rack, about 20 minutes.
3. Prepare the Filling: Pulse sliced almonds, granulated sugar, flour, and salt in a food processor until nuts are very finely ground, 10 to 12 times. Add butter, and pulse until fully incorporated, 10 to 12 times. Add eggs and almond extract, and pulse just until mixture is combined, 5 or 6 times. Spread almond mixture evenly over cooled Crust.

4. Trim rhubarb, and slice into 1½- x 2-inch pieces. Slice in half horizontally, and cut into ½-inch-wide strips. Place strips of rhubarb, color-side up, and raspberries evenly on top of almond mixture.
5. Bake at 350°F until a wooden pick inserted into center comes out clean and mixture is golden brown on top, 45 to 50 minutes. Cool completely in pan on a wire rack, about 1 hour. Using aluminum foil as handles, remove bars from pan. Dust with powdered sugar, cut into squares, and serve.

Strawberry Chiffon Mini Pies

(Photo, page 61)

ACTIVE 50 MIN. - TOTAL 1 HOUR, 10 MIN., PLUS 5 HOURS, 15 MIN. CHILLING

MAKES 6

- 2 Tbsp. powdered sugar, divided
- 1 (14.1-oz.) pkg. refrigerated piecrusts
- 1 qt. fresh strawberries, hulled, plus more small halved strawberries, for garnish
- 1¼ cups granulated sugar, divided
- 1½ tsp. unflavored gelatin
- 2 Tbsp. strawberry-flavored gelatin (such as Jell-O)
- 2 large pasteurized eggs, separated
- 2 Tbsp. fresh lemon juice (from 1 lemon)
- ¼ tsp. kosher salt
- 2 cups heavy cream, divided

1. Preheat oven to 400°F. Lightly dust work surface with 1 tablespoon of the powdered sugar. Unroll 1 piecrust on top of powdered sugar, and roll into a 12-inch circle. Use a 6-inch round cutter to cut 2 (6-inch) circles. Reroll the scraps once, and cut 1 more circle. Repeat procedure with remaining piecrust and powdered sugar to have a total of 6 mini piecrusts. Fit each circle into a 5-inch round mini pie pan; fold edges under, and crimp. Prick bottom and sides with a fork. Chill 15 minutes.
2. Place pie pans on a cookie sheet. Line each crust with a small square of parchment paper, and fill with pie weights or dried beans. Bake in preheated oven until crust is set and edges are lightly browned, 12 to 15 minutes. Carefully remove weights and parchment, and continue baking until crusts are golden brown, about 5 minutes. Remove to a wire rack, and cool until ready to use.

3. Process strawberries in a food processor until very smooth, 1 to 2 minutes. Strain pureed strawberries through a fine mesh strainer into a 2-cup glass measuring cup to get 1½ cups juice (reserve any extra juice for another use). Discard solids. Stir together 1½ cups strawberry juice and ½ cup of the granulated sugar in a small saucepan over medium. Bring mixture to a boil, and reduce heat to medium-low. Cook, stirring often, until mixture is reduced to 1 cup, 8 to 10 minutes.
4. Sprinkle unflavored gelatin over ¼ cup cool water in a small bowl, and set aside. Whisk together egg yolks in a medium bowl, and slowly add about half of cooked strawberry juice mixture to yolks, whisking constantly. Slowly whisk yolk mixture back into strawberry juice mixture in pan. Cook, whisking constantly, until mixture has thickened slightly, 3 to 4 minutes. Whisk in unflavored gelatin mixture to combine. Whisk in strawberry gelatin, lemon juice, and salt to combine completely. Remove from heat, and transfer mixture to a large bowl. Chill mixture until thickened slightly, 1 hour to 1 hour and 15 minutes, stirring after 30 minutes.
5. Beat egg whites with an electric mixer on high speed, until soft peaks form, about 8 minutes. (Pasteurized eggs take longer to whip up than regular eggs.) Gradually add ¼ cup of the granulated sugar, and beat until stiff peaks form, 2 to 3 minutes. Gently whisk strawberry mixture to incorporate any lumps. Gradually fold egg white mixture into strawberry mixture until thoroughly combined.
6. Beat 1 cup of the heavy cream with a heavy-duty stand mixer on high speed, using the whisk attachment, until foamy. Gradually add ¼ cup of the granulated sugar, beating until stiff peaks form. Gradually fold whipped cream into strawberry mixture. Spoon mixture evenly (about ¾ cups) into prepared piecrusts. Chill at least 4 hours or overnight.
7. Beat remaining 1 cup heavy cream with a heavy-duty stand mixer on high speed, using the whisk attachment, until foamy. Gradually add remaining ¼ cup granulated sugar, and beat until stiff peaks form. Dollop or pipe whipped cream on top of pies, and garnish with small halved strawberries.

RASPBERRY-RHUBARB
BARS (PAGE 59)

STRAWBERRY CHIFFON
MINI PIES (PAGE 59)

CHOCOLATE-PEANUT
BUTTER EGGS &
DAFFODIL COOKIES

Chocolate–Peanut Butter Eggs

ACTIVE 30 MIN. · TOTAL 1 HOUR, 30 MIN.,
PLUS 3 HOURS, 30 MIN. CHILLING
MAKES 2 DOZEN

- ¼ cup butter
- 3 Tbsp. honey
- 2 cups creamy peanut butter
- 1½ cups powdered sugar
- 2 tsp. vanilla extract
- 1 (10-oz.) pkg. dark chocolate melting wafers (such as Ghirardelli)
  Royal Icing (recipe follows)
  Mint green and lavender food coloring gel

1. Lightly grease an 8-inch square pan with cooking spray. Place butter and honey in a small saucepan over medium. Cook, stirring often, until melted, about 1 minute. Stir in peanut butter; cook, stirring often, until smooth, about 1 minute. Remove from heat; whisk in powdered sugar and vanilla. Spread mixture in prepared pan. Chill, covered, until firm, about 2 hours.
2. Using an oval 1-tablespoon measure (or serving spoon) lightly sprayed with cooking spray, scoop peanut butter mixture and pack into spoon, leveling with hand. Gently push leveled scoops onto a parchment paper-lined baking sheet. Repeat procedure with remaining mixture. Chill 1 hour.
3. Melt dark chocolate wafers according to package directions. Dip each peanut butter egg into melted chocolate using a fork, allowing excess chocolate to drip back into bowl. Place dipped eggs on parchment paper-lined baking sheet. Chill until set, about 30 minutes.
4. Divide Royal Icing between 2 small bowls, and add desired amount of food coloring to each. Spoon into piping bags fitted with small round tips (such as Wilton #3). Remove peanut butter eggs from refrigerator, and pipe icing designs as desired. Let stand until set, about 1 hour. Store in an airtight container at room temperature up to 3 days.

Royal Icing

ACTIVE 10 MIN. · TOTAL 10 MIN.
MAKES 2 CUPS

- 3 cups powdered sugar
- 2 tablespoons meringue powder
- ½ tsp. vanilla extract
- ½ tsp. almond extract

Combine powdered sugar, ¼ cup water, meringue powder, and vanilla and almond extracts in the bowl of a stand mixer fitted with the paddle attachment. Beat on medium speed until blended, smooth, and stiff, scraping down sides as needed, about 1 minute (mixture should hold stiff peaks). Thin mixture as needed for recipe by gradually stirring in additional water ½ teaspoon at a time. Store in an airtight container for up to 2 weeks.

Daffodil Cookies

ACTIVE 1 HOUR · TOTAL 1 HOUR, 30 MIN.,
PLUS 1 HOUR CHILLING AND 2 HOURS,
30 MIN. STANDING
MAKES 18

- 1 cup butter, softened
- ⅔ cup granulated sugar
- 2 large egg yolks
- ½ tsp. vanilla extract
- 2¼ cups all-purpose flour, plus more for work surface
- ½ tsp. kosher salt
  Royal Icing (recipe above)
  Orange and yellow food coloring gel
  Assorted orange nonpareils and sprinkles

1. Beat butter with a heavy-duty stand mixer on medium speed until creamy. Gradually add sugar, beating until light and fluffy. Add egg yolks, 1 at a time, beating until well incorporated after each addition. Beat in vanilla.
2. Stir together flour and salt in a medium bowl, and gradually add to butter mixture, beating at low speed just until blended. Shape dough into a 1-inch-thick disk. Wrap in plastic wrap, and chill until firm, about 1 hour.
3. Preheat oven to 300°F. Roll dough to ⅓-inch thickness on a lightly floured surface. Using a 2½-inch round cookie cutter, cut out cookies. Place about 2 inches apart on a large parchment paper-lined baking sheet. Gather dough scraps, and reroll once to get a total of 18 cookies.
4. Using a small paring knife, cut 6 small triangular slits (¾ inch long and ⅛ inch wide at the base) around perimeter of each cookie to mimic flower petals. Bake until golden brown around the edges, 20 to 22 minutes.
5. Cool cookies on baking sheet 5 minutes. Transfer to a wire rack to cool completely, about 30 minutes.
6. Prepare the Royal Icing, and divide among 3 small bowls. Tint 1 bowl with orange food coloring, tint another bowl with yellow food coloring, and leave remaining bowl white. Spoon orange icing into a piping bag fitted with a small star tip (such as Wilton #16). Spoon half of yellow icing and half of white icing into separate piping bags fitted with small round tips (such as Wilton #3 or #4).
7. Pipe yellow and white icings on cookies in an outline of daffodil petals. Keep tips of piping bags covered with a damp paper towel or plastic wrap when not using so icing doesn't dry out.
8. Stir water, ½ teaspoon at a time, into bowls of remaining yellow and white icing until "flooding" consistency (about as thick as honey). Spoon icings into separate piping bags fitted with small round tips. Pipe icing inside petal outlines to fill them in. Let cookies stand at room temperature until icing is slightly hardened, about 30 minutes.
9. When icing petals have hardened, pipe small stars of orange icing in a ring in centers of cookies. Fill rings with additional white or yellow icing. Carefully fill centers of rings with orange nonpareils and/or sprinkles. Let cookies stand at room temperature until icing has completely hardened, about 2 hours. Then serve cookies, or store in an airtight container up to 3 days.

Relish the Radish

It's time to give this seasonal gem a fresh new spin

Crisp, colorful radishes are early risers, one of the first things to pop up in our gardens and at farmers' markets each spring, giving us the first good crunch of the season.

They are eager to please cooks and eaters, yet they are so often underestimated. Meant for more than just a supporting role in a nice salad or plate of crudités, radishes are versatile root vegetables, which means they taste great when cooked, too—especially when roasted or quickly sautéed. The best way to reap their rewards is to explore selections beyond the familiar round and red ones. They come in all sorts of colors, shapes, and sizes. Some are spicy and sharp while others are buttery and tender.

No matter the shape, select well-formed, unblemished ones that feel firm when gently squeezed. There is no need to peel radishes, but their flavor is concentrated in the skin, so doing so will reduce their pungency when they pack too much of a punch.

The freshest ones come with their perky, peppery greens still attached, and the leaves are an unexpected bonus to enjoy raw or cooked. If you plan to eat them within a day or two, leave the greens attached. If you need to store them for a while, the roots will keep better if you remove the greens, which are delicate and go bad much faster. When storing, place loose ones in a clean, dry plastic bag in the crisper drawer of the refrigerator for up to one week.

Any way you slice (or pickle or roast or puree) them, radishes add a welcome dose of color and heat.

Warm Radish-and-Potato Salad with Smoked Trout and Radish Leaf-and-Mint Pesto

If your radishes don't have greens or if there aren't enough for this recipe, substitute or supplement with watercress or baby arugula. Rinse the radish greens in cool water to remove any grit.

ACTIVE 20 MIN. - TOTAL 50 MIN.
SERVES 4

RADISHES
- 1 lb. small round radishes with greens attached

PESTO
- 1 oz. Parmesan cheese, shredded (¼ cup)
- 2 Tbsp. toasted slivered almonds
- 1 medium garlic clove
- 1 Tbsp. lemon zest plus 2 Tbsp. fresh juice (from 1 large lemon)
- ½ tsp. kosher salt
- ¼ tsp. black pepper
- ½ cup lightly packed fresh mint leaves
- ¼ cup olive oil, plus more as needed

SALAD
- 1 lb. multicolored baby new potatoes
- 8 medium garlic cloves
- 2 Tbsp. olive oil
- ½ tsp. kosher salt
- ¼ tsp. black pepper
- 8 oz. hot-smoked trout or salmon, skin removed and discarded, fish broken into large pieces
- 1 oz. Parmesan cheese, shaved (½ cup)
- ¼ cup lightly packed fresh mint leaves
- 1 small shallot, cut into thin rounds (about ¼ cup)
- 2 (¾- x 3-inch) lemon peel strips, cut into ¼- x ¼- x 3-inch strips

1. Prepare the Radishes: Remove the greens. Trim Radishes, and set aside. Discard any tough stems from greens. Rinse greens, and blot dry. Set aside ½ cup lightly packed greens for Pesto, and set aside ¼ cup lightly packed greens for Salad. (Discard any remaining greens, or reserve for another use.)

2. Prepare the Pesto: Pulse together Parmesan, almonds, garlic, lemon zest and juice, salt, and pepper in a food processor until finely chopped, 7 to 8 times. Add mint leaves and reserved ½ cup radish greens; pulse until finely chopped, 6 to 7 times. Add oil; pulse until mixture forms a loose paste with a bit of texture, 6 to 7 times. Store, tightly covered, in refrigerator up to 1 week.

3. Prepare the Salad: Preheat oven to 375°F. Halve any Radishes or potatoes that are larger than a golf ball; leave the rest whole. Place on a rimmed baking sheet. Add garlic; drizzle with oil, and sprinkle with salt and pepper. Toss to coat; spread mixture in a single layer. Roast in preheated oven until vegetables are tender and browned in spots, about 30 minutes.

4. Divide roasted vegetable mixture evenly among 4 plates; top with trout, Parmesan, mint leaves, and reserved ¼ cup radish greens. Sprinkle with shallot and lemon peel strips. Top each Salad with 2 tablespoons Pesto. Serve immediately.

RADISH, AVOCADO, AND CITRUS
SALAD WITH ORANGE-POPPY SEED
DRESSING (PAGE 68)

CHILLED RADISH-AND-
AVOCADO SOUP (PAGE 68)

The Most Elegant Snack Ever

Serve raw radishes with flavored butters, flaky salt, and baguette slices to make a deliciously easy snack. To prepare each compound butter, combine the ingredients below with ½ cup butter at room temperature. Salted butter works, but velvety European-style cultured butter is even better. Chill, covered, up to 1 week. Serve at room temperature.

- -

ORANGE-TARRAGON BUTTER
- 1 Tbsp. orange zest (from 1 small orange)
- 2 tsp. finely chopped fresh tarragon
- ⅛ tsp. kosher salt

HONEY-MUSTARD-CHIVE BUTTER
- 1 Tbsp. honey
- 2 tsp. whole grain Dijon mustard
- 2 tsp. finely chopped fresh chives
- ⅛ tsp. kosher salt

HERBED CHÈVRE BUTTER
- ¼ cup goat cheese, softened
- 1 tsp. finely chopped fresh dill
- 1 tsp. finely chopped fresh flat-leaf parsley
- 1 tsp. finely chopped fresh thyme
- ⅛ tsp. kosher salt

Chilled Radish-and-Avocado Soup

(Photo, page 67)

This refreshing dish has a bite from radishes, hot sauce, and chile powder that is balanced out by creamy avocados and buttermilk. You can prepare it up to one day in advance and store it, covered, in the refrigerator.

ACTIVE 25 MIN. - TOTAL 25 MIN., PLUS 1 HOUR CHILLING
SERVES 4

- 12 oz. radishes, trimmed, divided
- 3 ripe avocados, divided
- 1 bunch scallions, divided
- 3 cups whole buttermilk, chilled, plus more as needed
- ¼ cup lime zest plus ¼ cup fresh juice (from 2 limes)
- 2 Tbsp. honey, plus more to taste
- 1 Tbsp. green pepper hot sauce (such as Cholula Green Pepper), plus more to taste
- 1¼ tsp. kosher salt, plus more to taste
- ½ tsp. ancho chile powder, plus more for garnish

1. Set aside 6 radishes for serving. Coarsely chop remaining radishes, and place in a blender.
2. Set aside 1 of the avocados for serving. Peel and pit remaining 2 avocados; add to blender.
3. Set aside 2 of the scallions for serving. Coarsely chop remaining scallions (white and tender green parts only) to equal ½ cup; add to blender.
4. Add buttermilk, lime zest and juice, honey, hot sauce, salt, ancho chile powder, and 2 tablespoons water to blender. Process until mixture is mostly smooth and consistency is similar to a smoothie (it will have bits of finely chopped radishes and scallions remaining), 1½ to 2 minutes, adding more buttermilk if the soup is too thick.
5. Refrigerate until chilled, at least 1 hour or up to overnight.
6. Stir well, and taste. Add more honey, hot sauce, and/or salt to taste. Divide evenly among 4 bowls.
7. Thinly slice reserved radishes and scallions, and cut reserved avocado into small cubes. Top bowls evenly with radishes, scallions, and avocado. Sprinkle with ancho chile powder. Pass the bottle of hot sauce at the table.

Radish, Avocado, and Citrus Salad with Orange-Poppy Seed Dressing

(Photo, page 66)

Rich in color, flavor, and texture, this salad makes a fabulous side or lunchtime main dish. Watermelon radishes can be hard to find in supermarkets, but they are worth seeking out at the farmers' market.

ACTIVE 25 MIN. - TOTAL 25 MIN.
SERVES 4

DRESSING
- ¼ cup mayonnaise
- 2 Tbsp. orange blossom honey or other floral honey
- 1 Tbsp. orange zest plus ¼ cup fresh juice (from 1 orange)
- ½ tsp. dry mustard (such as Colman's)
- ½ tsp. poppy seeds
- ⅛ tsp. kosher salt
- ⅛ tsp. black pepper

SALAD
- 1 large watermelon radish, peeled and cut into very thin rounds (about 2 cups)
- 1 medium orange, peeled and cut into thin rounds (about 1 cup)
- 1 medium grapefruit, peeled and cut into segments (about 1 cup)
- 6 oz. small radishes, trimmed and cut into thin wedges (about 2 cups)
- 2 small avocados, peeled, pitted, and diced (about 2 cups)
- ½ cup pomegranate arils
- 3 Tbsp. salted roasted pistachios
- 2 Tbsp. chopped scallions (white and tender green parts only)
- ¼ tsp. kosher salt
- ⅛ tsp. black pepper

1. Prepare the Dressing: Whisk together all ingredients in a small bowl. Refrigerate until ready to use.
2. Prepare the Salad: Arrange watermelon radish, orange, grapefruit, small radishes, and avocados on a serving platter (or divide evenly among 4 plates). Sprinkle evenly with pomegranate arils, pistachios, scallions, salt, and pepper.
3. When ready to serve, drizzle the Salad with a little of the Dressing. Pass the remaining Dressing at the table.

Creamy Spring Vegetable Slaw

(Photo, page 4)

Swap out your usual cabbage slaw for this colorful version made with seasonal vegetables and a tangy sour cream-dill dressing. To prevent the grated vegetables from releasing too much water into the dressing, salt them and let them drain in a colander for one hour.

ACTIVE 15 MIN. - TOTAL 15 MIN.,
PLUS 1 HOUR CHILLING
SERVES 4

  6 oz. radishes, trimmed and greens
       removed
  2 mini seedless cucumbers,
       unpeeled
  2 small carrots
  ¾ tsp. kosher salt, divided
  2 oz. sugar snap peas, thinly sliced
       at an angle (about 1 cup)
  ¼ cup sour cream or plain whole-
       milk Greek yogurt
  1 Tbsp. chopped fresh dill
  2 tsp. granulated sugar
  1 medium garlic clove, minced
       (1½ Tbsp.)
  ¼ tsp. black pepper

1. Grate radishes, cucumbers, and carrots using the coarse grater disk on a food processor (or the largest holes on a box grater). Transfer grated vegetables to a colander set over a medium-size bowl, and toss with ½ teaspoon of the salt. Refrigerate 1 hour. Discard drained liquid in bowl, blot vegetables dry with paper towels, and place in bowl.
2. Stir sliced sugar snap peas into vegetables in bowl. Add sour cream, dill, sugar, garlic, pepper, and remaining ¼ teaspoon salt, and stir to combine. Serve immediately.

Quick Pickled Radishes with Lemon, Ginger, and Maple

(Photo, page 5)

These tangy-sweet pickles make a great burger topping, but you'll be tempted to eat them straight from the jar. For the thinnest radish slices, use a mandoline or a very sharp chef's knife.

ACTIVE 30 MIN. - TOTAL 30 MIN.,
PLUS 8 HOURS CHILLING
MAKES 2 PT.

**SAUTÉED RADISHES
WITH BACON**

  1 lb. radishes, trimmed and
       sliced very thinly into rounds
       (using a mandoline)
  2 (½-inch-wide) lemon peel strips
  ½ tsp. mustard seeds
  ½ tsp. coriander seeds
  1 cup rice vinegar
  3 Tbsp. pure maple syrup or honey
  2 tsp. kosher salt
  2 tsp. grated fresh ginger

1. Divide radishes, lemon peel strips, mustard seeds, and coriander seeds evenly between 2 sterilized lidded pint jars.
2. Stir together 1 cup water, vinegar, maple syrup, kosher salt, and ginger in a small saucepan. Bring mixture to a boil over high.
3. Remove vinegar mixture from heat; slowly pour evenly into the jars, making sure radishes are submerged in liquid. (If not submerged, push radishes into liquid using a spoon, and gently shake jar to distribute.)
4. Seal jars with lids; let stand until cooled to room temperature, about 15 minutes. Chill pickles 8 hours or overnight before eating.

Sautéed Radishes with Bacon

This simple-yet-flavorful side dish proves that cooked radishes are just as tasty as raw ones. You can make this recipe with or without the greens. Serve it alongside fish, chicken, or pork.

ACTIVE 25 MIN. - TOTAL 25 MIN.
SERVES 4

  2 thick-cut hickory-smoked bacon
       slices, cut into small cubes
  1 lb. radishes, halved (if small) or
       quartered (if large) with greens
       separated
  1½ Tbsp. light brown sugar
  ½ tsp. kosher salt
  ¼ tsp. black pepper
  1 Tbsp. fresh thyme leaves
  1½ Tbsp. fresh lemon juice
       (from 1 lemon)

1. Cook bacon in a large heavy skillet (preferably cast iron) over medium-high, stirring often, until it begins to brown and crisp, about 6 minutes.
2. Add radishes; stir to coat in bacon drippings. Stir in sugar, salt, and pepper. Cook, stirring often, until bacon is crisp and radishes are tender-crisp with a few browned, caramelized edges, about 10 minutes. Add the radish greens; stir until slightly wilted.
3. Sprinkle mixture with thyme, and drizzle with lemon juice. Serve warm.

DAO FAMILY
CRAWFISH BOIL
(PAGE 72)

VIETNAMESE
CAJUN FRIED RICE
(PAGE 72)

Beauty of the Boil

Houston-born food writer Dan Q. Dao shares his family's favorite Viet-Cajun crawfish tradition

"You just don't look like someone from Texas," some people can't help but inform me when I tell them I was born and raised in the Lone Star State. "But, people," I respond, with a bless-your-heart smile, "I'm from Houston."

The implication of my un-Texan-ness, even in appearance, used to bother me, but now I relish the chance to enlighten those who have come from other places. By many measures, Houston is one of the most ethnically diverse major cities in the country—something obvious to anyone who has tried the food. Here in Space City, fancy steak houses sit comfortably beside soul food canteens and Japanese soba dens. Grocery stores carry Chinese snacks, Indian spices, and Mexican produce. It's a colorful, sprawling culinary landscape.

My visits home from New York City, where I live now, are less frequent these days, but I do my best to make it back for my family's annual crawfish boils—because Vietnamese-Cajun crawfish is what my Texas looks like. It's dozens of parents, uncles, aunties, cousins, and friends clearing 70 pounds of crawfish—and a couple coolers of beer—in the afternoon sun. It's my aunt Van Dao, our family's designated crawfish master, obsessing over the perfect amount of spice. It's loud conversations, sticky hands, burning lips, and heaps of discarded shells.

It's worth noting that Vietnamese-Cajun crawfish doesn't have any actual roots in Vietnam; it's a Southern food through and through. Like Tex-Mex or Creole cuisine, it was born on American soil through a specific set of circumstances at a particular moment in time. When tens of thousands of Vietnamese refugees landed on the Gulf Coast, it was Louisiana's "boiling points" that most resembled the casual, social outdoor stalls in Vietnam where you'd

go to throw back a few beers while snacking on fish, shellfish, or snails.

For my family, it began when I was in elementary school: Every year from April until August, my parents and their friends would get together on weekends for backyard boils. They'd take turns hosting, and while the kids ran around the house, the adults spent hours on end outside—washing, cooking, mixing, and eating those seemingly alien critters.

"We started making crawfish about 20 years ago when we would take short trips to Louisiana," says Auntie Van. "The first time we tried it the Vietnamese way was actually at a wedding—we sat there

and picked apart the ingredients. There was some garlic, a little orange. Around that time, your Auntie Trinh came up with the recipe we use today."

Although all Vietnamese families have their own (typically unwritten) boil recipe, the sauce she describes is emblematic of the Vietnamese-Cajun style. Like in Cajun or Low-Country versions, the crawfish starts off boiled in a spice blend. The difference is that it's cooled and then thrown into an ice chest or container filled with a chunky sauce, usually involving lots of butter, diced garlic cloves, orange wedges, and peppers. The result is

high-intensity flavor on the inside and outside—a simple tweak that launched an unprecedented crawfish craze spreading from Houston's Chinatown to Los Angeles and the Midwest.

Two decades into this tradition, we've refined the process to a science. The day begins with prep: The crawfish are hosed down before going into a large pot of boiling water with corn and potatoes. Around the time folks arrive to start on appetizers, the first of the mudbugs have been tossed in the magic sauce and set out on serving trays. One thing that is different every time around? New faces.

"I remember the first time I invited my non-Vietnamese friends to my mom's house to try our version of crawfish," says Auntie Van's son, my cousin Khang Tran. "They were blown away. It's always exciting to introduce people to this recipe we have fallen in love with. Now, when summer rolls around, everyone here knows that means crawfish. It has its own season."

For Vietnamese people, food—and even more importantly, entertaining—is perhaps the most salient expression of love. I can see it in the way my parents pull out all the stops setting up the backyard the night before a boil or how my father labors over a pot of seafood gumbo to accompany the crawfish. And no one embodies this idea more than Auntie Van, who works feverishly on new recipes for weeks in advance.

"My mom is a mad scientist. She loves to try new things," says Khang. "That crawfish is basically perfect already, but she's always thinking about how to make it better. That's where you see how much she loves everyone in the family."

Of course, there's also some friendly inter-family competition. One of my fondest memories was a contest between Auntie Van (my father's sister) and my mother's brother, Uncle Son. "We did a very careful blind tasting," says Auntie Van. "It was really close, but I won and made your Uncle Son bow down and recognize that my recipe is the best!"

It's not clear exactly whom to credit for the "invention" of Vietnamese-Cajun crawfish. Nor is it clear what the official recipe should be—as with many other dishes created and riffed on by Vietnamese cooks, who rarely utilize recipes, Viet-Cajun crawfish is a moving target. But there's no denying the fact that Houston's many crawfish restaurants (now a crowded field of contenders) have evolved the dish into its next iteration, building off that original seasoning technique with tasty innovations in both ingredients and forms.

Restaurants like James Beard Award semifinalist Crawfish & Noodles; the 15-year-old pioneer, Cajun Kitchen; and Kau Ba Kitchen are frequented by locals and sought out by visitors. That has led to people trying other forms of Vietnamese food, after having first been introduced to the gateway drug of crawfish.

"People hear about this Vietnamese-Cajun restaurant thing, and they come out to Chinatown to try it," says Cajun Kitchen chef-owner John Nguyen. "But then they see the rest of the menu and want to try other kinds of seafood like clams and snails, too. Our customers here are white, black, Latino—everyone is so open-minded."

Even after living in New York City for 10 years, I still find Houston to be one of the most magical places in America. Maybe that's because it's one of the most clear-cut examples of a spot where food has been the defining factor in rewriting a stereotypical narrative. This Texas city is leading the conversation about a dynamic South—a living, evolving place that is at once informed by and informing the world.

When I went home last May for a boil, we cooked up our crawfish with a side of Cajun fried rice and my dad's signature gumbo. For dessert, we had blueberry pie. The guests were as varied as the food, yet nothing and no one felt out of place. What could look more like Texas, more like America, than that?

Dao Family Crawfish Boil

(Photo, page 70)

ACTIVE 30 MIN. - TOTAL 45 MIN.
MAKES 8 LB.

- 1½ cups kosher salt
- 2 (3-oz.) pkg. crawfish boil seasoning (such as Zatarain's)
- 8 lb. live crawfish

Dao Family Crawfish Sauce (recipe follows)

Fill a very large stockpot about one-third full of water. Stir in salt and crawfish boil seasoning. Bring mixture to a boil over high. Add crawfish; cover and cook until crawfish are done (they will turn red and float to the surface), 5 to 7 minutes. Transfer cooked crawfish to a cooler using tongs. Pour Dao Family Crawfish Sauce into cooler. Mix well using tongs, and let stand 5 minutes. Serve.

Dao Family Crawfish Sauce

ACTIVE 15 MIN. - TOTAL 1 HOUR, 15 MIN.
MAKES ABOUT 2½ QT.

- 2 large oranges
- 1¼ lb. yellow onions, minced (4½ cups)
- ⅓ lb. peeled garlic cloves (from 2 large heads)
- ½ cup granulated garlic
- ½ cup lemon pepper
- ¼ cup black pepper
- ¼ cup unsalted butter
- 2 Tbsp. cayenne pepper, or to taste
- 1 (3-oz.) pkg. spicy crawfish boil seasoning (such as Zatarain's)

Peel oranges using a vegetable peeler; place orange peel strips in a large stockpot. (Reserve remaining oranges for another use.) Add remaining ingredients to the pot. Add enough water to cover mixture by 1 inch. Cover, and bring to a simmer over medium-high. Reduce heat to medium-low, and simmer 1 hour. Use immediately, or cover and refrigerate up to 2 days. (Reheat over high until hot, about 5 minutes.)

Vietnamese-Cajun Fried Rice

ACTIVE 1 HOUR - TOTAL 2 HOURS, 50 MIN., PLUS 8 HOURS CHILLING
SERVES 14

BROTH
- ½ Tbsp. canola oil
- 2 medium shallots, thinly sliced (about ¼ cup)
- 6 medium garlic cloves, chopped (3 Tbsp.)
- 1 (4½-oz.) fresh Cajun andouille sausage link, casing removed
- 1 green bell pepper, coarsely chopped (about ½ cup)

1 stalk celery, coarsely chopped (about ½ cup)
  1 plum tomato, coarsely chopped (about ½ cup)
  1 tsp. fish sauce
  ½ tsp. dried basil
  ⅛ tsp. dried thyme
  ⅛ tsp. dried oregano
  ⅛ tsp. ground cumin
  4 cups unsalted chicken broth

FRIED RICE

  3 cups uncooked sushi rice
  4 small (3 oz.) smoked Cajun andouille sausages (from 1 [12-oz.] pkg.)
  3 Tbsp. unsalted butter, divided
  8 medium garlic cloves, chopped (about 4 Tbsp.), divided
  12 oz. medium peeled, deveined raw shrimp, cut into ½-inch pieces
  2 medium stalks celery, chopped (about 1 cup)
  1 Tbsp., plus ¼ tsp. Dao Family Cajun Blend, divided, (recipe follows)
  ¼ tsp. kosher salt, divided
  6 oz. fresh sugar snap peas, chopped (about 1½ cups)
  4 small shallots, diced (about 1 cup)
  ½ to 1 Tbsp. soy sauce, to taste
  6 large eggs, beaten
  2 plum tomatoes, diced (about ⅔ cup)
  4 scallions, sliced (about ½ cup)
  Hot sauce, for serving

1. Prepare the Broth: Heat oil in a medium nonstick pot over medium-high. Add sliced shallots and chopped garlic. Cook, stirring occasionally, until fragrant, 1 to 2 minutes. Add fresh sausage. Cook, stirring with a spoon to break up sausage, until slightly browned and fragrant, about 2 minutes. Add bell pepper, celery, tomato, fish sauce, basil, thyme, oregano, and cumin. Cook, stirring often, 3 minutes. Add chicken broth; bring to a boil over high.

2. Reduce heat to medium-low; simmer, undisturbed, 20 minutes. Pour mixture through a fine mesh strainer into a large heatproof bowl, pressing mixture with a spoon to extract as much liquid as possible. Discard solids. Store strained Broth, covered, in refrigerator until ready to use or up to 3 days. (If desired, refrigerate strained Broth overnight; skim and discard fat that rises to the top.)

3. Prepare the Fried Rice: Rinse rice in a colander under cold water until water runs clean; drain. Cook rice and 2¼ cups of the Broth in a rice cooker according to manufacturer's instructions. Reserve remaining Broth for another use. (Alternative stove-top method: Place rice and 3½ cups of the Broth in a medium saucepan; bring to a boil over medium-high. Reduce heat to low; cover and cook, undisturbed, 20 minutes. Remove from heat; let stand, covered, 10 minutes.)

4. Spread out cooked rice in a single layer on a baking sheet. Let cool completely, 1 to 2 hours. Cover and refrigerate at least 8 hours or up to overnight.

5. Remove rice from refrigerator. Lightly separate grains using your hands until no clumps remain. Set aside.

6. Bring ½ cup water to a boil in a medium saucepan over high. Add smoked sausages, and boil until water evaporates, about 6 minutes. Continue cooking sausages in dry saucepan, shaking pan to roll sausages around, until they turn slightly brown, about 1 minute. Remove from saucepan, and let cool 5 minutes. Slice thinly into rounds, or cut into cubes. Set aside.

7. Melt ½ tablespoon of the butter in a very large nonstick pan over high. Add 2 tablespoons of the chopped garlic. Cook, stirring often, until fragrant, about 1 minute. Stir in shrimp. Cook, stirring often, until shrimp are cooked through, 2 to 3 minutes. Remove from heat, and quickly transfer mixture to a large bowl. Set aside.

8. Add ½ tablespoon of the butter to saucepan over high. Add chopped celery and ⅛ teaspoon each of the Cajun seasoning and salt. Cook, stirring occasionally, until celery starts to soften, about 1 minute. Transfer celery mixture to shrimp mixture in bowl. Repeat process using ½ tablespoon of the butter, chopped sugar snap peas, ⅛ teaspoon of the Cajun seasoning, and remaining ⅛ teaspoon salt.

9. Wipe saucepan clean, and add remaining 1½ tablespoons butter over high. Add diced shallots, and cook, stirring occasionally, 1 minute. Add rice and remaining 2 tablespoons chopped garlic, and cook, stirring often, 5 minutes. Add soy sauce and remaining 1 tablespoon Cajun seasoning, and stir well to combine. Taste, and add more salt or Cajun seasoning if desired.

VIETNAMESE-CAJUN FRIED RICE

10. Move rice mixture to sides of saucepan using a spatula, leaving an empty spot in middle of saucepan. Add half of the beaten eggs. Cook over high, stirring after eggs begin to set and scraping eggs from the outside inward, until eggs are cooked and scrambled, 2 to 3 minutes. Break up eggs, and fold into rice mixture, stirring well to mix. Repeat process using remaining beaten eggs.

11. Stir cooked sausage pieces into rice mixture, and cook over high, stirring until incorporated, 1 minute. Add cooked vegetable-shrimp mixture, diced tomatoes, and sliced scallions, and stir to combine. Remove Fried Rice from heat. Serve hot with hot sauce.

Dao Family Cajun Seasoning Blend

MAKES ABOUT ½ CUP

Combine 2 Tbsp. **garlic powder**, 1½ Tbsp. **paprika**, 1 Tbsp. **onion powder**, 1 Tbsp. **dried oregano**, ½ Tbsp. **black pepper**, ½ Tbsp. **ground white pepper**, ½ Tbsp. **cayenne pepper**, ½ Tbsp. **dried thyme**, and ⅛ tsp. **ground cumin** in a small bowl.

Easter Made Easy

Choose from two impressive main dishes and four go-with-anything sides
to design a memorable holiday menu

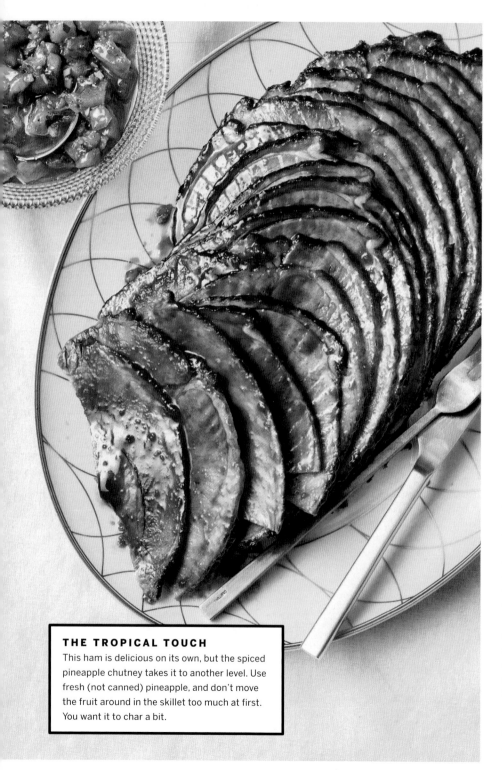

THE TROPICAL TOUCH

This ham is delicious on its own, but the spiced pineapple chutney takes it to another level. Use fresh (not canned) pineapple, and don't move the fruit around in the skillet too much at first. You want it to char a bit.

Glazed Ham with Pineapple Chutney

ACTIVE 40 MIN. - TOTAL 3 HOURS
SERVES 12

- ¼ cup (2 oz.) bourbon
- 1¼ cups pineapple preserves, divided
- ⅓ cup, plus 2 Tbsp. packed dark brown sugar, divided
- 1 (8- to 9-lb.) fully cooked bone-in spiral-cut ham half
- 2 fresh pineapples, peeled, cored, and cut into ½-inch cubes (6 cups)
- 2 Tbsp. coconut oil
- 1 red Fresno chile, seeded, and finely chopped (2 Tbsp.)
- 1 (2½-inch) piece fresh ginger, peeled and minced (2 Tbsp.)
- ¼ tsp. kosher salt
- ⅛ tsp. ground allspice
- 2 tsp. fresh lime juice (from 1 small lime)

1. Preheat oven to 350°F. Line a rimmed baking sheet with aluminum foil; set a wire rack inside the baking sheet. Stir together bourbon, 1 cup of the preserves, and ⅓ cup of the brown sugar in a small bowl. Place ham on a large piece of aluminum foil big enough to cover entire ham; brush with ½ cup of the bourbon glaze. Wrap tightly in aluminum foil. Place, cut-side down, on prepared wire rack. Add 3 cups water to baking sheet under rack. Bake ham 2 hours.

2. Meanwhile, heat a large cast-iron skillet over high until very hot. Add pineapple; cook, stirring occasionally, until browned on 2 to 3 sides, about 10 minutes. Reduce heat to medium; add coconut oil, chile, and ginger. Cook, stirring often, until softened and fragrant, about 2 minutes. Add salt, allspice, remaining ¼ cup preserves, and 2 tablespoons brown sugar. Cook, stirring often, until liquid has mostly evaporated, about 4 minutes. Remove from heat; stir in lime juice. Transfer mixture to a bowl; cool to room temperature, about 20 minutes.

3. Remove ham from oven; remove foil. Increase oven temperature to 425°F. Baste ham with ½ cup of the bourbon glaze, brushing in between slices. Return to oven; bake, uncovered, at 425°F for 15 minutes. Remove from oven; brush with remaining ½ cup glaze. Continue baking, uncovered, until a thermometer inserted in thickest portion of ham registers 140°F, about 15 minutes. Remove from oven; rest 10 minutes. Slice and serve with pineapple chutney.

Herb-Crusted Leg of Lamb with Parsley-Mint Sauce

ACTIVE 20 MIN. · TOTAL 3 HOURS. PLUS 1 HOUR STANDING
SERVES 10 TO 12

- 1 (6- to 7-lb.) bone-in leg of lamb, trimmed and patted dry
- 1 Tbsp. finely chopped fresh rosemary
- 1 Tbsp. chopped fresh thyme
- 1¼ cups olive oil, divided
- 1 Tbsp., plus ½ tsp. grated garlic (from 4 cloves), divided
- 1 tsp. black pepper
- 6 tsp. kosher salt, divided
- 2 cups loosely packed fresh flat-leaf parsley leaves
- 1 cup loosely packed fresh mint leaves
- 2 Tbsp. red wine vinegar

1. Set a wire rack inside a rimmed baking sheet lined with aluminum foil. Score the fatty top of the lamb 5 times (¼ inch deep and 4 inches long). Stir together rosemary, thyme, ¼ cup of the oil, and 1 tablespoon of the garlic. Rub mixture all over lamb. Season with pepper and 5 teaspoons of the salt. Place on wire rack on baking sheet. Let stand at room temperature 1 hour.
2. Preheat oven to 325°F. Cook lamb until a thermometer inserted in thickest portion of meat registers 125°F to 130°F for medium doneness, 1 hour, 45 minutes.

Remove from oven; rest 30 minutes.
3. Meanwhile, increase oven temperature to 450°F. Return lamb to oven; cook until meat is browned and a crust has formed, 10 to 15 minutes. Rest on wire rack 15 minutes.
4. Process parsley, mint, vinegar, and remaining ½ teaspoon garlic in a food processor 20 seconds. With machine running, pour remaining 1 cup oil into mixture until blended, 20 seconds. Stir in remaining 1 teaspoon salt.
5. Slice lamb against the grain; serve with sauce.

THE RIGHT WAY TO ROAST
This flavorful lamb is wonderfully crisp on the outside and tender on the inside. The secret is to cook it low and slow and then turn up the heat so the exterior can brown and form a crust.

Asparagus with Cheese Sauce and Herb Breadcrumbs

ACTIVE 25 MIN. - TOTAL 25 MIN.
SERVES 8

- 2 Tbsp. unsalted butter
- ½ cup panko breadcrumbs
- ½ tsp. crushed red pepper
- ¼ tsp. plus ⅛ tsp. kosher salt, divided
- 3 Tbsp. finely chopped fresh flat-leaf parsley
- 1 Tbsp. finely chopped fresh tarragon
- 2 lb. medium fresh asparagus spears, trimmed
- 1 Tbsp. olive oil
- ½ cup heavy cream
- 4 oz. Parmigiano-Reggiano cheese, finely shredded (about 1½ cups)
- 1 tsp. lemon zest (from 1 small lemon)

1. Melt butter in a small skillet over medium-high. Add panko, crushed red pepper, and ⅛ teaspoon of the salt. Cook, stirring often, until toasted, 2 to 3 minutes. Stir in parsley and tarragon; set aside.

2. Preheat oven to high broil with rack in middle position. Place asparagus on a rimmed baking sheet, and drizzle with olive oil; toss to coat. Sprinkle with remaining ¼ teaspoon of the salt, and broil until asparagus is tender-crisp, about 5 minutes (do not stir).

3. While asparagus broils, place heavy cream in a small skillet. Bring to a gentle simmer over medium, stirring occasionally. Add Parmigiano-Reggiano ¼ cup at a time, stirring until completely melted and smooth after each addition.

4. Arrange broiled asparagus on a platter. Spoon cheese sauce over asparagus, and sprinkle with panko mixture and lemon zest.

Strawberry-Spinach Salad with Sweet Vidalia Onion Dressing

ACTIVE 15 MIN. · TOTAL 15 MIN.
SERVES 10

- ½ cup chopped Vidalia onion (1 small onion)
- ½ cup light olive oil
- 3 Tbsp. white balsamic vinegar
- 1 Tbsp. plus 2 tsp. granulated sugar
- 1 Tbsp. mayonnaise
- ½ tsp. Dijon mustard
- ¼ tsp. kosher salt
- 1 (10-oz.) pkg. fresh spinach
- 1 lb. fresh strawberries, stemmed and halved (2½ cups)
- 4 oz. blue cheese, crumbled (1 cup)
- 1 cup chopped candied pecans

1. Process onion, oil, vinegar, sugar, mayonnaise, mustard, and salt in a blender until creamy and smooth, about 50 seconds.
2. Arrange spinach, strawberries, blue cheese, and pecans on a large platter. Drizzle with dressing.

Sugar Snap Peas with Orange Zest and Buttery Almonds

ACTIVE 25 MIN. - TOTAL 25 MIN.
SERVES 8

- 6 Tbsp. unsalted butter, divided
- 1½ lb. fresh sugar snap peas, trimmed and halved at an angle (about 8 cups)
- ½ tsp. kosher salt
- ½ tsp. black pepper
- ½ cup sliced almonds
- ¼ tsp. Creole seasoning (such as Tony Chachere's)
- 1 tsp. orange zest, plus ¼ cup fresh juice (from 1 large orange), divided

1. Melt 1 tablespoon of the butter in a large skillet over high until foamy. Add 4 cups of the snap peas, ¼ teaspoon of the salt, and ¼ teaspoon of the pepper. Cook, stirring often, until tender-crisp, 3 to 4 minutes. Transfer peas to a large serving platter. Repeat process with 1 tablespoon of the butter and remaining 4 cups peas, ¼ teaspoon salt, and ¼ teaspoon pepper.

2. Reduce heat under skillet to medium; melt remaining 4 tablespoons butter. Add almonds and Creole seasoning. Cook, stirring constantly, until butter browns, about 3 minutes. Stir in orange juice. Cook, stirring constantly, until sauce is glossy and thickened slightly, about 1 minute. Spoon over peas on platter; sprinkle with orange zest.

Potato Salad with Dijon and Scallions

ACTIVE 20 MIN. · TOTAL 40 MIN.
SERVES 8

3 lb. multicolored fingerling potatoes, halved lengthwise

2 Tbsp., plus 2 tsp. kosher salt, divided

1 bunch scallions

1 small red onion, thinly sliced

⅓ cup apple cider vinegar

¼ cup plus 2 Tbsp. olive oil

¼ cup whole grain mustard

3 Tbsp. fresh lemon juice (from 1 large lemon)

2 Tbsp. Dijon mustard

2 tsp. honey

1. Place potatoes, 8 cups water, and 2 tablespoons of the salt in a large saucepan, and bring to a boil over high. Reduce heat to medium. Simmer, uncovered, until potatoes are fork-tender, 12 to 14 minutes. Drain and rinse with cold water until potatoes are room temperature, and transfer to a large bowl.

2. While potatoes boil, slice scallions into ½-inch pieces, keeping green and white parts separate. Set aside the green parts. Place white parts in a small microwavable bowl; add red onion, apple cider vinegar, and ½ teaspoon of the salt. Microwave on HIGH for 90 seconds. Stir mixture; press down on onion slices to submerge in vinegar. Let stand at room temperature 15 minutes; drain.

3. Whisk together oil, whole grain mustard, lemon juice, Dijon mustard, honey, and remaining 1½ teaspoons salt in a large bowl until blended. Add potatoes; toss to coat. Transfer mixture to a platter; sprinkle with scallion greens and pickled onion mixture.

It's Tee Time!

Test Kitchen professional and *Hey Y'all* host Ivy Odom's annual Masters parties
are a tradition unlike any other

My favorite week of the year is when the azaleas and dogwoods are in full bloom at Augusta National Golf Club. I grew up watching the tournament with my grandparents, and the picturesque scenes of pink and white flowers, the sounds of golf claps and hushed announcers, and the taste of my nana's pimiento cheese fill my head every April. Although I've never been to the Masters,

I celebrate by hosting a string of get-togethers with plenty of food and drink. While regulated game play doesn't technically start until Thursday, my festivities tee off on Wednesday, in time for the annual par 3 contest. Each day, I plan a special menu inspired by classic masters fare, like pimiento cheese and Arnold Palmers. Even though the traditional drink doesn't contain alcohol, I make a spiked version for adults to sip on while they watch their favorite players. Arnold probably would have preferred vodka, but my recipe gets an extra punch from bourbon.

My pimiento cheese is different from the famous Augusta National recipe and the one Nana made because I gussy it up with gouda cheese, Worcestershire sauce, sweet onion, and paprika. I like to serve it on slider buns with fried chicken tenders and pickled okra, topped with toothpicks fashioned after the iconic Augusta yellow tee flag. They're so good that your guests will want to stay long after the green jacket ceremony is over.

Big-Batch Arnold Palmers

ACTIVE 10 MIN. - TOTAL 2 HOURS, 10 MIN.
MAKES ABOUT 13 CUPS

Stir together 6 cups **unsweetened iced tea**, 4 cups **bottled lemonade**, 2¼ cups **bourbon**, and ⅔ cup **simple syrup** in a large bowl or pitcher. Thinly slice 3 **medium lemons**; add to pitcher. Refrigerate until chilled, at least 2 hours or up to 24. Serve over **ice**, and garnish with **mint sprigs** and **lemon slices**.

Ivy's Favorite Pimiento Cheese

ACTIVE 15 MIN. - TOTAL 15 MIN.,
PLUS 4 HOURS CHILLING
MAKES ABOUT 3 CUPS

Grate 8 oz. **sharp cheddar cheese**, 4 oz. **mild cheddar cheese (such as hoop cheese)**, and 4 oz. **creamy unsmoked gouda cheese** on large holes of a box grater into a large bowl. Stir together 1 cup **mayonnaise**, 2 (4-oz.) jars drained sliced **pimientos**, 2 Tbsp. finely grated **sweet onion**, 1½ tsp. **Worcestershire sauce**, 1 tsp. **black pepper**, ½ tsp. **kosher salt**, and ¼ tsp. each **cayenne** and **smoked paprika** in a medium bowl. Fold mayonnaise mixture into cheese until well combined. Cover and refrigerate at least 4 hours. Serve with **crackers** and **crudités**.

Fried Chicken Sliders

ACTIVE 10 MIN. - TOTAL 10 MIN.
SERVES 12

Spread ¼ cup **Ivy's Favorite Pimiento Cheese** on bottom half of each of 12 **slider buns or dinner rolls**. Top each with ½ of a prepared **fried chicken tender**, sliced **pickled okra**, and top half of bun. Skewer with wooden picks to hold in place.

FRIED CHICKEN
SLIDERS

IVY'S FAVORITE PIMIENTO CHEESE

BIG-BATCH ARNOLD PALMERS

MASHED POTATOES
WITH CARAMELIZED
VIDALIA ONIONS

BRISKET WITH
CARROTS AND
HORSERADISH-
PARSLEY
GREMOLATA

A Passover to Remember

A savory slow-cooker brisket is the centerpiece of this elegant Seder meal

Brisket with Carrots and Horseradish–Parsley Gremolata

ACTIVE 30 MIN. - TOTAL 30 MIN., PLUS 7 HOURS SLOW-COOKING

SERVES 8

BRISKET

- 3 Tbsp. olive oil
- 1 (5-lb.) beef brisket, fat trimmed to ¼ inch thick
- 1 Tbsp. kosher salt
- 1 tsp. black pepper
- 2 large red onions, cut into 1-inch slices
- 1 cup kosher dry red wine
- 1 lb. small carrots, peeled
- 1 cup dried pitted plums (about 5 oz.)
- 3 fresh thyme sprigs

GREMOLATA

- 1½ cups packed fresh flat-leaf parsley leaves
- ½ cup olive oil
- 1½ Tbsp. prepared or grated fresh horseradish
- ½ tsp. lemon zest plus 1 Tbsp. fresh juice (from 1 lemon)
- ½ tsp. kosher salt
- ⅛ tsp. black pepper

1. Prepare the Brisket: Heat oil in a large skillet over high until just smoking. Sprinkle meat with salt and pepper. Cook in hot oil until browned on all sides, about 12 minutes total. Transfer to a 6- to 8-quart slow cooker; set aside.
2. Reduce heat under skillet to medium-high. Add onions to skillet. Cook, stirring occasionally, until browned and beginning to wilt, about 2 minutes. Add wine; cook, stirring and scraping bottom of skillet to loosen browned bits, until liquid is reduced by about half, about 2 minutes. Add to slow cooker. Place carrots, dried plums, thyme, and 1 cup water in slow cooker. Cover and cook on LOW until Brisket is tender, about 7 hours.
3. Prepare the Gremolata: Combine parsley, olive oil, horseradish, lemon zest and juice, salt, and pepper in a food processor, and pulse until very finely chopped, about 10 times. Cover and refrigerate until ready to use.
4. Transfer Brisket to a cutting board to rest; transfer carrots to a platter. Pour cooking juices from slow cooker through a fine mesh strainer into a large bowl, discarding solids. Let strained liquid stand 10 minutes for fat to rise to the surface; skim and discard fat. Whisk liquid vigorously; transfer 1½ cups to a small bowl. Discard remaining liquid. Slice Brisket against the grain; transfer to platter with carrots. Top with Gremolata, and serve with reserved liquid.

Mashed Potatoes with Caramelized Vidalia Onions

ACTIVE 45 MIN. - TOTAL 45 MIN.

SERVES 6 TO 8

- ⅓ cup olive oil
- 2 medium Vidalia onions, thinly sliced (about 3 cups)
- 3 lb. russet potatoes, peeled and halved
- 2 Tbsp., plus 2½ tsp. kosher salt, divided
- 1½ cups chicken broth
- ¼ tsp. black pepper
- 2 Tbsp. finely chopped fresh chives

1. Heat oil in a large skillet over medium. Add onions to skillet, and cook, stirring often, until onions begin to caramelize, about 40 minutes. (You should have about 1 cup caramelized onions.)
2. Meanwhile, place potatoes in a large saucepan. Fill with cold water to cover by 2 inches. Add 2 tablespoons of the salt, and bring to a boil over high. Reduce heat to medium-high, and gently boil until potatoes are tender, about 12 minutes. Remove from heat, and drain. Return cooked potatoes to saucepan.
3. Mash potatoes to desired degree of smoothness. Stir in chicken broth, caramelized onions, pepper, and remaining 2½ teaspoons salt. Transfer to a bowl or platter, and sprinkle with chives.

The Seder Plate

On Passover, families gather around the table to retell the story of the Jewish people's escape from Egypt's rule. Items on the Seder plate bring their journey to freedom to life.

ROASTED EGG (BEITZAH) An egg is a symbol of an ancient sacrifice made at the Holy Temple. Hard-cooked eggs are usually eaten before the meal.

PARSLEY (KARPAS) This represents the hard work Jewish people endured under the Egyptian pharaoh's rule.

SALT WATER The parsley is dipped into salt water and eaten in remembrance of tears shed.

BITTER HERBS (MAROR) Horseradish, paired with matzah, signifies the bitterness of slavery.

ROASTED SHANK BONE (ZEROAH) A lamb (or chicken) bone represents the lamb sacrificed the night before the Jewish people made their journey out of Egypt.

CHAROSET This sweet mix of apples, nuts, wine, and spices is a reminder of the mortar and bricks Jews were forced to make.

Macaroon Sandwich Cookies

ACTIVE 15 MIN. · TOTAL 1 HOUR, 30 MIN.
MAKES 16

- 3 large egg whites
- ⅓ cup granulated sugar
- ¼ tsp. kosher salt
- 8 oz. sweetened flaked coconut (about 2½ cups)
- ½ cup finely chopped walnuts (2½ oz.)
- ½ cup kosher-for-Passover strawberry jam

1. Preheat oven to 350°F. Line 2 large baking sheets with parchment paper; set aside.

2. Whisk together egg whites, sugar, and salt in a large bowl until frothy. Stir in coconut and walnuts. Drop coconut mixture in 1-tablespoon mounds 2 inches apart on prepared baking sheets. Flatten each to ½-inch thickness.

3. Bake both baking sheets at the same time in preheated oven until golden brown, about 12 minutes, rotating baking sheets (top rack to bottom rack and front to back) halfway through baking. Cool completely on baking sheets, about 45 minutes.

4. Turn half of cookies over (flat-side up), and spread each with about 1 teaspoon jam. Top with remaining cookies, flat-side down, to form sandwiches. Chill until set, about 15 minutes. Store, covered, at room temperature up to 3 days.

FUN WITH FILLINGS

Replace the strawberry jam with another fruit flavor, or spread the cookies with melted (kosher-for-Passover) chocolate.

Spring on a Plate

Herbed goat cheese makes this salad sing

Spring Salad with Herbed Goat Cheese

ACTIVE 20 MIN. - TOTAL 20 MIN.
SERVES 4

- 5 Tbsp. chopped mixed fresh herbs (such as chives, dill, and tarragon)
- 1 (8-oz.) plain goat cheese log
- 10 oz. fresh thick asparagus (from 1 [1-lb.] bunch), trimmed and shaved into thin strips using a vegetable peeler
- 8 oz. fresh sugar snap peas, strings removed
- 3 medium radishes, thinly sliced on a mandoline
- 2 oz. mixed spring greens (about 2 cups)
- 1 cup thawed frozen sweet peas
- 1 cup loosely packed fresh mint leaves
- 3 Tbsp. fresh lemon juice (from 1 lemon)
- 2 Tbsp. extra-virgin olive oil
- ½ tsp. kosher salt
- ¼ tsp. black pepper
- ¼ cup chopped roasted salted almonds

1. Spread chopped mixed herbs in an even layer on a medium plate. Roll goat cheese log in herbs until evenly coated, pressing lightly to adhere. Chill 10 minutes.
2. Gently toss together asparagus, sugar snap peas, radishes, spring greens, sweet peas, and mint leaves in a large bowl until well combined. Drizzle mixture with lemon juice and olive oil, and sprinkle with salt and pepper. Gently toss to coat.
3. Using a sharp knife, slice the goat cheese log into 12 (¼-inch-thick) rounds. Arrange goat cheese rounds on top of salad. Sprinkle with almonds, and serve.

PEEL IT PRETTY
To make asparagus strips, hold each spear by the cut end on a flat surface; shave away from your hand with a vegetable peeler.

Cracking the Code on Egg Salad

Like deviled eggs, this recipe has Southern roots and modern smarts

Southern cooks have always had a deft touch with eggs. We are, after all, experts with the deviled kind, knowing just how to make them extraordinary. It pays to use those same strategies for the salad: Start with perfectly hard-cooked eggs, season them generously, and finish with a dab of your favorite mayo. Beyond that, it's much easier than making deviled eggs because you don't have to fret over ragged yolks or runny filling.

There's nothing wrong with simply devouring it straight from the bowl, though it's easy to spoon onto a lettuce leaf or a pile of tender greens. Egg salad is also de rigueur for elegant tea sandwiches, those two-bite delights made with thinly sliced bread, crusts optional. If you moisten the perfectly cut edges of the sandwiches with mayonnaise and dip them in minced herbs, they are worthy of a tearoom or bridal shower.

Countless Southern meals and recipes rely on eggs because they're so easy and plentiful that we consider them a staple. Back when many families lived on farms or in rural communities, chickens usually pecked about the barnyard, so they were a reliable homegrown protein. As more and more people moved into town, we turned to mom-and-pop markets and shiny grocery stores to keep us supplied with fresh dozens. These days, some of us do both—buying them at the market and collecting them from our own backyard birds.

Whether eaten as a workday lunch or special-occasion fare, this tasty recipe will come together in minutes and keep for days. It's not fast food; it's quick food—and homemade to boot. – Sheri Castle

Just-Fancy-Enough Egg Salad

ACTIVE 10 MIN. - TOTAL 1 HOUR, 10 MIN.
MAKES ABOUT 3 CUPS

- ¼ cup mayonnaise
- 2 Tbsp. Dijon mustard
- 2 Tbsp. chopped fresh dill
- 1 tsp. lemon zest plus 2 tsp. fresh juice (from 1 lemon)
- 1 tsp. seasoned salt
- 1 tsp. granulated sugar
- ½ tsp. black pepper
- ½ tsp. paprika
- ½ tsp. hot sauce
- 8 hard-cooked eggs, peeled
- 2 small stalks celery, finely diced (about ½ cup)
- 4 chopped scallions (about ⅓ cup)

1. Whisk together mayonnaise, mustard, dill, lemon zest and juice, salt, sugar, pepper, paprika, and hot sauce in a bowl. Coarsely crumble hard-cooked eggs into mayonnaise mixture; gently fold together using a spatula to coat. Fold in celery and scallions. Taste salad, and adjust seasonings. Refrigerate, tightly covered, until chilled, at least 1 hour or up to 3 hours.
2. Stir salad. Taste, and adjust seasonings before serving. Store, covered, in refrigerator up to 3 days.

ROOKIE MISTAKE

We commonly use the term hard-boiled eggs, but hard-cooked eggs is more accurate because you shouldn't leave them in boiling water long. Arrange the eggs in a single layer in a saucepan; add water to submerge them by 2 inches. Cover and cook over medium-high heat. As soon as the water comes to a boil, remove the pan from the heat, and let stand for 10 minutes. Immediately transfer the eggs to a bowl of ice water, and let cool before peeling.

Mastering Egg Salad

Four tips that will improve any recipe

1 CRUMBLE, DON'T MASH
For a salad with hearty texture that won't turn gummy or pasty, use your hands to crumble the eggs instead of chopping the whites and mashing the yolks with a fork.

2 DON'T OVERDO THE MAYO
Use a light hand with mayonnaise and other binders to keep it from turning gloppy. The mixture might seem dry at first, but continue folding gently (to avoid overworking the eggs) just until it comes together.

3 PLAY WITH FLAVORS
Be creative with variations, as long as the proportions remain the same. Replace the finely diced celery with seedless cucumbers or radishes. Fresh chives, parsley, or tarragon can stand in for the dill.

4 SEASON WELL
No matter what else you put in your egg salad, be sure to use a generous touch with the seasonings because refrigeration can dull those flavors.

Pork, Meet Your Match

Chops, cutlets, roasts—pair your favorite cuts with fresh in-season produce

**PORK TENDERLOIN
WITH SHAVED
VEGETABLE SALAD**

A PROPER SHAVE
Use a sharp paring knife or a Y-shape
peeler to thinly shave the carrots and
zucchini for the salad. A mandoline works
best on the radishes and fennel bulb.

Pork Tenderloin with Shaved Vegetable Salad

ACTIVE 25 MIN. - TOTAL 25 MIN.
SERVES 4

- ¼ cup olive oil, divided
- 1 (1½-lb.) pork tenderloin, trimmed
- 2 tsp. kosher salt, divided
- 1 tsp. black pepper, divided
- 2 Tbsp. fresh lemon juice (from 1 medium lemon)
- 1 small shallot, chopped (1 Tbsp.)
- 1 Tbsp. Dijon mustard
- 2 tsp. honey
- 1 medium bulb fennel, thinly shaved (2 cups)
- 2 large carrots, shaved
- 2 medium zucchini, thinly shaved
- 4 large radishes, thinly shaved
- ½ cup fresh flat-leaf parsley leaves

1. Preheat oven to 400°F. Heat 1 tablespoon of the oil in a large ovenproof skillet over medium-high. Sprinkle pork with 1½ teaspoons of the salt and ½ teaspoon of the pepper, and cook, turning occasionally, until well browned on all sides, about 8 minutes. Place skillet in oven, and bake until a thermometer inserted in thickest portion of pork registers 140°F, about 10 minutes. Remove pork from skillet, and let stand 10 minutes.

2. Meanwhile, whisk together lemon juice, shallot, mustard, honey, and remaining ½ teaspoon each of salt and pepper in a large bowl. Whisk in remaining 3 tablespoons oil until emulsified. Add fennel, carrots, zucchini, radishes, and parsley, and toss until evenly coated.

3. Thinly slice pork, and serve with salad.

PORK CHOPS WITH SPRING ONIONS, FARRO, AND ASPARAGUS

Pork Chops with Spring Onions, Farro, and Asparagus

ACTIVE 10 MIN. - TOTAL 35 MIN.
SERVES 4

- 2 Tbsp. olive oil
- 4 (12-oz., 1½-inch-thick) bone-in pork chops
- ½ tsp. black pepper
- 2 tsp. kosher salt, divided
- 1½ cups uncooked semipearled farro
- 4 large spring onions, split lengthwise
- 12 oz. medium asparagus, trimmed and cut into 3-inch pieces
- 1¼ cups unsalted chicken stock
- 1 Tbsp. white wine vinegar
- 2 Tbsp. chopped fresh dill

1. Preheat oven to 375°F. Heat oil in a large skillet over high. Sprinkle pork chops with pepper and 1 teaspoon of the salt and add to skillet. Cook until deeply browned on 1 side, about 4 minutes. Turn pork, and cook 1 minute.

2. Place farro in a 13- x 9-inch baking dish. Arrange pork chops (browned-side up), spring onions, and asparagus on top of farro.

3. Add stock, vinegar, and remaining 1 teaspoon salt to hot skillet, and bring to a boil, stirring and scraping up browned bits from bottom. Pour stock mixture over pork. Cover dish with aluminum foil. Transfer to preheated oven, and bake until farro, onions, and asparagus are tender and a thermometer inserted in pork registers 140°F, 20 to 25 minutes. Remove from oven, and let stand 5 minutes. Sprinkle with dill.

SLOW-COOKER
PORK ROAST WITH
CARROTS, TURNIPS,
AND POTATOES

Oven-Baked Risotto with Ham, Leeks, and Peas

ACTIVE 15 MIN. - TOTAL 45 MIN.
SERVES 4

- 1 Tbsp. olive oil
- 6 oz. diced ham
- 1 large leek, white part only, chopped (2 cups)
- 4 garlic cloves, minced
- 2 Tbsp. fresh thyme leaves, divided
- 1½ cups uncooked Arborio rice
- ½ cup dry white wine
- 2½ tsp. kosher salt
- 3½ cups unsalted chicken stock, divided
- 1 cup frozen sweet peas, thawed
- 2 Tbsp. unsalted butter
- 3 oz. Parmesan cheese, grated (about ¾ cup), divided

1. Preheat oven to 400°F. Heat oil in a large ovenproof Dutch oven over medium-high. Add ham, and cook, stirring often, until crispy, about 3 minutes. Remove half of ham and set aside. Add leeks, garlic, and 1 tablespoon of the thyme to Dutch oven, and cook, stirring occasionally, until softened, 4 to 5 minutes. Add rice, and cook, stirring, 1 minute. Add wine, and cook until almost evaporated, about 30 seconds. Stir in 3 cups water, salt, and 2 cups of the chicken stock, and bring mixture to a boil.
2. Cover Dutch oven, and place in preheated oven. Bake in preheated oven until rice is cooked through, 20 to 25 minutes.
3. Remove from oven. Stir in peas, butter, ½ cup of the Parmesan, and remaining 1½ cups stock. Spoon risotto into shallow bowls. Top with reserved ham, remaining 1 tablespoon fresh thyme, and ¼ cup Parmesan. Serve immediately.

Slow-Cooker Pork Roast with Carrots, Turnips, and Potatoes

ACTIVE 20 MIN. - TOTAL 4 HOURS, 30 MIN.
SERVES 6

- 1 cup unsalted chicken stock
- 5 medium Yukon Gold potatoes, quartered
- 3 medium carrots, peeled and cut into 2-inch pieces
- 1 large turnip, cut into 8 wedges
- 2 Tbsp. chopped fresh rosemary
- 1 Tbsp. chopped fresh thyme
- 2½ tsp. kosher salt
- 1 tsp. black pepper
- 1 (2-lb.) boneless pork loin roast
- 2 Tbsp. olive oil, divided
- ¼ cup finely chopped fresh flat-leaf parsley
- 1 Tbsp. finely grated lemon zest (from 1 lemon)
- 3 garlic cloves, finely minced

1. Place stock, potatoes, carrots, and turnip in a 6-quart slow cooker. Cover and cook on HIGH 1 hour.
2. Meanwhile, stir together rosemary, thyme, salt, and pepper in a small bowl. Rub pork with 1 tablespoon of the oil. Sprinkle pork all over with 2 tablespoons rosemary mixture, pressing to adhere. Heat remaining tablespoon oil in a large skillet over medium-high. Add pork, and cook until well browned, about 10 minutes, turning once halfway through.
3. Sprinkle vegetables in slow cooker with remaining rosemary mixture; add pork. Reduce heat to LOW, cover, and cook until a thermometer inserted in thickest portion of pork registers 135°F and vegetables are tender, about 3 hours. Remove to a cutting board, and let stand 10 minutes (pork temperature will rise as it stands). Place vegetables on a platter. Cut pork into ½-inch-thick slices, and arrange over vegetables. Stir together parsley, zest, and garlic; sprinkle over pork. Serve with juices from slow cooker.

OVEN-BAKED RISOTTO
WITH HAM, LEEKS,
AND PEAS

STEP AWAY FROM THE STOVE
This oven-baked risotto requires only a little stirring at the stovetop. Make sure the rice mixture is boiling before covering the pot and putting it in the oven.

Crispy Pork Cutlets with Creamy Spring Slaw

ACTIVE 30 MIN. - TOTAL 30 MIN.
SERVES 4

4 (4-oz.) boneless pork chops
1 cup all-purpose flour
1 Tbsp., plus 1 tsp. kosher salt, divided
2 large eggs, lightly beaten
1 cup panko breadcrumbs
1 cup peanut oil
1 small head cabbage, thinly sliced (3 cups)
6 oz. fresh snow peas, thinly sliced (about 2 cups)
1 small red onion, thinly sliced
⅓ cup mayonnaise
3 Tbsp. apple cider vinegar
1 tsp. granulated sugar
½ tsp. black pepper

1. Working with 1 at a time, place a pork chop between 2 sheets of plastic wrap on a cutting board. Pound to ½-inch thickness using flat side of a meat mallet.
2. Stir together flour and 1 tablespoon of the salt in a shallow dish. Place eggs in a second shallow dish. Place panko in a third shallow dish. Dredge pork chops in flour, dip in beaten eggs, and then coat in breadcrumbs, shaking off excess each time.
3. Heat oil in a large skillet over medium-high until shimmering, 2 to 3 minutes. Add 2 pork chops to hot oil in skillet, and fry until golden brown, about 3 minutes per side. Remove from skillet, and sprinkle evenly with ¼ teaspoon of the salt. Repeat with ¼ teaspoon of the salt and remaining 2 pork chops.
4. Toss together cabbage, snow peas, and onion in a large bowl. Stir together mayonnaise, vinegar, sugar, pepper, and remaining ½ teaspoon salt and add to cabbage mixture. Toss well to coat, and serve with pork.

Fluffier French Toast

Buttermilk is the secret to this light and lemony breakfast casserole

Baked Buttermilk French Toast

ACTIVE 15 MIN. · TOTAL 2 HOURS
SERVES 8

- 4 large eggs
- 1½ cups whole buttermilk
- 1 cup heavy cream
- ½ cup granulated sugar
- 1 tsp. lemon zest plus 1 Tbsp. fresh juice (from 1 lemon)
- ½ tsp. vanilla extract
- ¼ tsp. kosher salt
- 27 (½-inch-thick) French bread slices (from about 12 oz. bread)
  Pure maple syrup, powdered sugar, and fresh berries

1. Lightly coat a 13- x 9-inch baking dish with cooking spray. Whisk together eggs, buttermilk, cream, granulated sugar, lemon zest and juice, vanilla extract, and salt in a large bowl. Working with 1 slice at a time, dip bread in egg mixture to completely saturate on both sides. Shingle soaked bread slices in prepared baking dish. Let stand at room temperature 1 hour.
2. Preheat oven to 325°F. Meanwhile, pour out and discard any egg mixture that has accumulated in bottom of baking dish. Transfer baking dish to oven, and bake French toast until top is golden brown, about 30 minutes.
3. Remove dish from oven; let stand 15 minutes. Serve with maple syrup, powdered sugar, and berries.

MAKE IT AHEAD
Hosting weekend brunch? Let the bread slices soak, covered, in the baking dish one day before serving. As the oven preheats, allow the casserole dish to come to room temperature.

COOKING (SL) SCHOOL

TIPS AND TRICKS FROM THE SOUTH'S MOST TRUSTED KITCHEN

Buttermilk Backup

In a pinch? Try this two-ingredient mixture

NOTHING beats the tangy richness of buttermilk, but if there isn't any left in your refrigerator, you can make a decent stand-in by mixing liquid dairy with an acid. Our Test Kitchen tasted several combinations of milk, half-and-half, or yogurt mixed with fresh lemon juice or vinegar. The clear winner was half-and-half and lemon juice. This thick and creamy combo works well in recipes like pies, pancakes, and biscuits. But if you're pouring a glass to drink, we recommend going with the real thing.

Quick and Simple Substitute
MAKES 1 CUP

Stir together 14 Tbsp. (1 cup minus 2 Tbsp.) **half-and-half** and 2 Tbsp. **fresh lemon juice** in a small bowl. Let stand 10 minutes before using.

"Buttermilk freezes well, though it will separate when defrosted. Whisk it, or pulse in a food processor a few times until the liquid comes together."

Pam Lolley
Test Kitchen Professional

WASTE NOT

Polish It Off

From breakfast to dessert, four ways to use up any leftover buttermilk

▶ Blend a few tablespoons into your favorite smoothie.

▶ Use it to replace heavy cream in soups.

▶ Add a splash to oatmeal.

▶ Swap out the milk in a buttercream frosting recipe.

May

DEEP-DISH
BERRY COBBLER
(PAGE 98)

Berry Good Cobbler

Soft and cakelike, topped with biscuits, or bubbling under a lattice top—these desserts are delicious

BLUEBERRY-ORANGE-
GINGER COBBLERS
(PAGE 98)

Deep-Dish Berry Cobbler

(Photo, page 96)

A lattice crust gives any fruit cobbler a fancy upgrade, which is why it's often reserved for church suppers and other special meals where you want dessert to look its best. Our version is still relatively fuss-free thanks to refrigerated piecrust, though you can also use homemade pastry. Make sure the filling is bubbling before you remove the dish from the oven. This is a sign that the cornstarch has been activated, so the filling will be nice and thick.

ACTIVE 15 MIN. · TOTAL 1 HOUR, 30 MIN.
SERVES 8

- 4 cups fresh raspberries (about 21 oz.)
- 2 cups fresh blackberries (about 9 oz.)
- 2 cups fresh blueberries (about 9 oz.)
- ½ cup granulated sugar
- ¼ cup cornstarch
- 2 Tbsp. butter, cut into small cubes
- 1 Tbsp. lemon zest (from 2 lemons)
- 2 tsp. vanilla extract
- ½ tsp. kosher salt
- ½ tsp. ground cinnamon
- ¼ tsp. ground nutmeg
- ½ (14.1-oz.) pkg. refrigerated piecrusts (1 crust)
- 1 large egg
- 1 to 2 Tbsp. turbinado sugar
  Sweetened whipped cream

1. Preheat oven to 375°F. Stir together berries, granulated sugar, cornstarch, butter, lemon zest, vanilla, salt, cinnamon, and nutmeg in a large bowl. Let stand 15 minutes, gently stirring occasionally. Spoon berry mixture into a 2-quart baking dish.
2. Roll piecrust out on a lightly floured surface into a 14-inch circle. Using a fluted cutter, cut piecrust into 1-inch-wide strips, and arrange in a lattice pattern on top of berries. Whisk together egg and 1 tablespoon water in a small bowl. Brush piecrust strips with egg mixture, and sprinkle with turbinado sugar.
3. Bake in preheated oven until filling is bubbly and crust is golden brown, about 55 minutes, covering with aluminum foil after 45 to 50 minutes to prevent excessive browning. Serve warm with whipped cream.

Blueberry-Orange-Ginger Cobblers

(Photo, page 97)

The first cobbler many of us attempted was likely biscuits baked atop a layer of fruit, whether you use refrigerated biscuits and canned pie filling or started from scratch.

ACTIVE 15 MIN. · TOTAL 1 HOUR, PLUS 30 MIN. COOLING
SERVES 6

- 2 cups all-purpose flour
- 1 Tbsp. baking powder
- ½ tsp. kosher salt
- ⅓ cup, plus 1 Tbsp. granulated sugar, divided
- ½ cup butter, cut into ½-inch cubes
- 1 cup, plus 1 Tbsp. heavy cream, divided
- 6 cups fresh blueberries (from 3 [9-oz.] containers)
- ½ cup packed light brown sugar
- 2 Tbsp. cornstarch
- 1 Tbsp. orange zest (from 1 orange)
- 2 tsp. grated fresh ginger (from 1 [1-in.] piece)
  Vanilla ice cream

1. Preheat oven to 400°F. Stir together flour, baking powder, salt, and ⅓ cup of the granulated sugar in a large bowl. Cut butter into flour mixture with a pastry blender until crumbly and mixture resembles small peas. Freeze 5 minutes. Add 1 cup of the cream, stirring just until dry ingredients are moistened.
2. Turn dough out onto parchment paper; gently press or pat dough into a ¾-inch-thick, 9- x 6-inch rectangle. (Mixture will be a little crumbly.) Cut into 6 (3- x 2-inch) rectangles. Place biscuits in a single layer on a baking sheet. Brush tops with remaining 1 tablespoon cream, and sprinkle with remaining 1 tablespoon granulated sugar. Refrigerate until ready to use.
3. Stir together blueberries, brown sugar, cornstarch, orange zest, and grated ginger in a large bowl until well blended. Spoon berry mixture evenly into 6 (7- to 8-ounce) ramekins, about 1 cup in each. Place on an aluminum foil-lined rimmed baking sheet.
4. Bake in preheated oven 20 minutes. Remove from oven, and place 1 biscuit on each ramekin. Return to oven, and bake at 400°F until biscuits are golden brown and done, about 18 more minutes. Cool on baking sheet on a wire rack at least 30 minutes. Serve with ice cream.

Cakey Strawberry Cobbler

In this dessert—sometimes called a batter cobbler—batter is poured over melted butter and then the strawberries are scattered on top. As it bakes, the batter rises around the fruit, creating a golden, cakelike topping with crispy edges and tender center.

ACTIVE 10 MIN. · TOTAL 1 HOUR, 30 MIN, PLUS 15 MIN. COOLING
SERVES 6

- 2 qt. fresh strawberries, hulled and halved, with larger ones quartered (about 2 lb. strawberries)
- 1 Tbsp. lemon zest plus 2 Tbsp. fresh lemon juice (from 1 large lemon)
- 1 cup granulated sugar, divided
- ½ cup butter
- 1 cup all-purpose flour
- 1½ tsp. baking powder
- ½ tsp. kosher salt
- ¼ tsp. baking soda
- 1 cup whole buttermilk
- 1 tsp. vanilla extract
  Sweetened whipped cream or vanilla ice cream

1. Preheat oven to 350°F. Gently stir halved strawberries, lemon zest and juice, and ¼ cup of the sugar in a large bowl until totally combined. Let strawberry mixture stand, stirring occasionally, until juicy, about 15 minutes.
2. Place butter in a 13- x 9-inch baking dish and put dish in preheated oven until butter is melted, 8 to 10 minutes. Remove dish from oven.
3. Whisk together flour, baking powder, salt, baking soda, and remaining ¾ cup sugar in a medium bowl until combined. Whisk together buttermilk and vanilla in a glass measuring cup. Whisk buttermilk mixture into flour mixture, and continue to whisk until batter is smooth. Pour mixture evenly over melted butter in hot baking dish. (Do not stir.) Using a slotted spoon, scatter strawberry mixture evenly over batter. Drizzle 3 tablespoons of accumulated juice from bottom of bowl over strawberries. Discard any remaining juice, or reserve for another use.
4. Bake in preheated oven until batter is puffed and slightly golden in the center and dark golden brown around edges, 40 to 45 minutes. Cool on a wire rack at least 15 minutes. Serve warm with whipped cream or ice cream.

CAKEY
STRAWBERRY
COBBLER

GRILLED WEDGE SALADS WITH BUTTERMILK-BLUE CHEESE DRESSING

Garden to Grill

When the freshest vegetables meet the heat, magic happens

Grilled Wedge Salads with Buttermilk-Blue Cheese Dressing

Unlike kale or romaine, iceberg lettuce is made for the grill because its high water content keeps it from drying out and shriveling over the flames. Oil the cut sides of the lettuce wedges, and keep a close eye on them as they cook—they can go from nicely charred to burnt in minutes.

ACTIVE 20 MIN. - TOTAL 20 MIN.
SERVES 4

2½ oz. blue cheese, crumbled
(about ⅔ cup)
¼ cup mayonnaise
¼ cup sour cream
¼ cup whole buttermilk
1½ tsp. white wine vinegar
1½ tsp. fresh lemon juice
(from 1 lemon)
¾ tsp. kosher salt, divided
½ tsp. black pepper, divided
1 small (about 6 oz.) head iceberg
lettuce, outer leaves removed,
head quartered through the core
2 Tbsp. olive oil
3 thick-cut bacon slices, cooked and
cut into 1-inch pieces
2 Tbsp. chopped fresh chives

1. Preheat a gas grill to medium (350°F to 400°F). Meanwhile, mash cheese in a medium bowl using a whisk. Whisk in mayonnaise, sour cream, buttermilk, vinegar, lemon juice, and ¼ teaspoon each of the salt and pepper. Set aside dressing.
2. Brush lettuce wedges evenly with oil, and sprinkle with remaining ½ teaspoon salt and ¼ teaspoon pepper. Place wedges, cut-sides down, on oiled grates. Grill, uncovered, until lettuce edges are browned and grill marks form, about 3 minutes per cut side.
3. Transfer grilled wedges to a serving platter. Drizzle wedges evenly with dressing, and sprinkle with bacon and chives before serving.

Grilled Baby Eggplant Parmesan

Baby eggplant is ideal for grilling because it has tender skin and is less fibrous and tough than the larger kind.

ACTIVE 20 MIN. - TOTAL 30 MIN.
SERVES 4

4 small (10 to 12 oz. each)
eggplants, halved lengthwise
1 tsp. kosher salt, divided
2 Tbsp. extra-virgin olive oil
¼ tsp. black pepper
1 cup jarred marinara sauce
2 oz. Parmigiano-Reggiano cheese,
grated (about ½ cup)
8 oz. fresh mozzarella cheese,
thinly sliced
¼ cup small fresh basil leaves

1. Preheat a gas grill to medium-high (400°F to 450°F) on 1 side. Sprinkle cut sides of eggplants evenly with ½ teaspoon of the salt, and let stand 10 minutes. Pat dry with paper towels.
2. Brush cut sides of eggplants evenly with oil, and sprinkle with pepper and remaining ½ teaspoon salt. Place eggplants, cut-sides down, on oiled grates over lit side of grill. Grill, covered, until eggplants are tender and grill marks appear, 4 to 6 minutes. Turn eggplants. Cook, covered, 5 minutes.
3. Move eggplants to oiled grates over unlit side of grill, and top evenly with marinara, Parmigiano-Reggiano, and mozzarella. Grill, covered, until cheeses are melted and bubbling, 3 to 5 minutes. Transfer to a serving platter, and sprinkle evenly with basil leaves. Serve immediately.

GRILLED BABY
EGGPLANT
PARMESAN

Grilled Hot-Pepper Sauce

ACTIVE 10 MIN. · TOTAL 20 MIN.
MAKES ABOUT 1 CUP

Preheat grill to medium-high (400°F to 450°F). Place 2 **medium jalapeño chiles**, 2 **medium serrano chiles**, and 1 stemmed and seeded **medium red bell pepper** on oiled grates. Grill, uncovered, turning occasionally, 7 minutes. Transfer chiles and bell pepper to a heavy-duty zip-top plastic bag; seal and let stand 10 minutes. Remove and discard skins from chiles and bell pepper. Place chiles and bell pepper, ⅓ cup **red wine vinegar**, 2 Tbsp. **light brown sugar**, 2 Tbsp. **water**, 1 tsp. **kosher salt**, and 1 **small garlic clove** in a blender or food processor. Process until smooth, 1 to 2 minutes. Use immediately, or store pepper sauce in an airtight container in refrigerator up to 2 weeks.

PEPPER SAUCE SPIN-OFFS
Substitute these pepper combos in the recipe to make a new blend
For a green sauce: 2 jalapeños, 2 serranos, and 1 poblano
For a red sauce: 2 red Fresno chiles, 1 habanero, and 1 red bell pepper

---

HOT AND SWEET PEPPERS
The secret to great grilled peppers is in the peeling. Unless you're making kebabs, grilled peppers (large or small, mild or spicy) taste better without their skins. Char them on all sides, and then place the hot cooked peppers in a heavy-duty zip-top plastic bag for 10 minutes. The trapped steam will loosen the skins so they can be easily peeled away from the flesh.

Grilled Bell Pepper Caprese

ACTIVE 20 MIN. · TOTAL 30 MIN.
SERVES 4

- 5 large multicolor bell peppers
- 4 Tbsp. extra-virgin olive oil, divided
- 1 tsp. kosher salt
- ½ tsp. black pepper
- 8 oz. fresh small mozzarella cheese balls (such as pearls)
- 2 Tbsp. fresh lime juice (from 1 lime)
- ½ cup torn fresh basil leaves

1. Preheat grill to medium (350°F to 400°F). Trim and discard tops and bottoms from bell peppers; remove and discard seeds and white membranes using a paring knife. Slice each bell pepper in half lengthwise. Brush evenly with 2 tablespoons of the oil. Place bell peppers, skin-sides down, on oiled grates. Grill, uncovered, until charred, about 7 minutes. Turn bell peppers; grill until tender, about 5 minutes. Transfer to a large heavy-duty zip-top plastic bag. Seal and let stand 10 minutes.
2. Remove bell peppers from bag. Remove and discard skins. Chop bell peppers into ¾- to 1-inch pieces. Transfer to a serving platter, and sprinkle with salt and black pepper. Top bell peppers with mozzarella, and drizzle with lime juice and remaining 2 tablespoons oil. Sprinkle with basil before serving.

Grilled Stuffed Poblanos

ACTIVE 45 MIN. · TOTAL 45 MIN.
SERVES 4

- 8 medium poblano chiles
- 5 ears fresh yellow corn, shucked
- 2 Tbsp. butter
- 1 (15-oz.) can black-eyed peas, drained and rinsed
- 2 medium garlic cloves, minced (2 tsp.)
- 1½ tsp. kosher salt
- 1 tsp. ground cumin
- ¼ tsp. black pepper
- ¼ cup chopped fresh cilantro
- 1 Tbsp. chopped fresh oregano
- 8 oz. Monterey Jack cheese, shredded (about 2 cups)
  Pico de gallo

1. Preheat a gas grill to medium-high (400°F to 450°F) on 1 side. Place poblano chiles and corn on oiled grates over lit side of grill. Cover grill. Grill poblanos, turning once, until skins are charred, about 5 minutes per side. Grill corn, turning occasionally, until charred, about 5 minutes per side. Remove poblanos and corn from grill.
2. Transfer poblanos to a heavy-duty zip-top plastic bag. Seal and let stand 10 minutes.
3. Meanwhile, let corn cool 5 minutes. Cut kernels from cobs, discarding cobs. Set aside kernels.
4. Remove poblanos from plastic bag. Remove and discard skins, keeping stems intact. Working with 1 at a time, make a lengthwise slit down side of poblano, starting at the stem and being careful to not cut through the other side of the pepper. Carefully remove and discard seeds and membrane. Set aside poblanos.
5. Heat butter in a large skillet over medium-high until melted and foamy. Add peas. Cook, stirring often, until hot, about 2 minutes. Stir in reserved corn kernels, garlic, salt, cumin, and black pepper. Cook, stirring often, 2 minutes. Stir in cilantro and oregano. Remove from heat; stir in cheese.
6. Spoon pea mixture evenly into poblanos, pulling sides of each chile around the filling to enclose. Transfer poblanos to a baking sheet lightly coated with cooking spray. Place on unlit side of grill. Grill, covered, until cheese is melted and bubbling, about 5 minutes. Serve immediately with pico de gallo on the side for topping.

GRILLED
HOT-PEPPER
SAUCE

GRILLED STUFFED
POBLANOS

GRILLED BELL PEPPER
CAPRESE

GRILLED YELLOW
SQUASH ROLL-UPS

GRILLED BABY ZUCCHINI-
AND-TOMATO SALAD

GRILLED SHRIMP-AND-SQUASH
PASTA WITH SUMMER HERBS

Grilled Baby Zucchini-and-Tomato Salad

ACTIVE 25 MIN. · TOTAL 25 MIN.
SERVES 4

- ¼ cup red wine vinegar
- 1 Tbsp. minced shallot (from 1 small shallot)
- 1 tsp. Dijon mustard
- 1 tsp. honey
- 2 tsp. fresh thyme leaves
- 5 Tbsp. extra-virgin olive oil, divided
- 1½ tsp. kosher salt, divided
- ½ tsp. black pepper, divided
- 10 to 12 baby zucchini (about 12 oz.), cut in half lengthwise
- 3 oz. day-old sourdough bread, sliced ¾ inch thick
- 1 medium garlic clove, halved crosswise
- 1 pt. multicolor cherry tomatoes, halved
- ½ cup torn fresh mixed basil and flat-leaf parsley

1. Preheat a gas grill to medium-high (400°F to 450°F). Stir together vinegar, shallot, mustard, and honey in a small bowl, and let stand 10 minutes. Whisk in thyme, 3 tablespoons of the oil, 1 teaspoon of the salt, and ¼ teaspoon of the pepper until combined.
2. Toss together zucchini, 1 tablespoon of the oil, and remaining ½ teaspoon salt and ¼ teaspoon pepper in a large bowl. Place zucchini on oiled grates. Grill, uncovered, until zucchini are tender and grill marks appear, about 2 minutes per side. Transfer to a medium bowl.
3. Brush remaining 1 tablespoon oil evenly over both sides of bread slices. Place bread on grates; grill until slightly charred and crispy, 1 to 2 minutes per side. Rub grilled bread on both sides with garlic halves. Discard garlic, or reserve for another use. Tear bread into 1-inch pieces.
4. Add tomatoes and 2 tablespoons of the vinegar-shallot mixture to zucchini in bowl, and gently toss to coat. Spoon tomato-zucchini mixture onto a serving platter. Top with torn grilled bread, and sprinkle with basil and parsley. Serve immediately alongside remaining vinegar-shallot mixture.

Grilled Shrimp-and-Squash Pasta with Summer Herbs

ACTIVE 30 MIN. · TOTAL 30 MIN.
SERVES 4

- 8 oz. uncooked casarecce (or penne) pasta
- 2¾ tsp. kosher salt, divided
- 3 small zucchini, sliced into ½-inch-thick rounds
- 3 small yellow squash, sliced into ½-inch-thick rounds
- 3 Tbsp. olive oil, divided
- 1 tsp. black pepper, divided
- 1½ lb. large peeled, deveined raw shrimp
- ½ cup loosely packed fresh flat-leaf parsley leaves, chopped
- ½ cup loosely packed fresh basil leaves, chopped
- ½ cup loosely packed fresh mint leaves, chopped
- 2 Tbsp. thinly sliced fresh chives
- 2 Tbsp. butter, softened

1. Prepare pasta in boiling water with 1 teaspoon salt according to package directions. Drain, reserving ½ cup cooking water.
2. Meanwhile, preheat grill to medium-high (400°F to 450°F). Toss together zucchini, squash, 1 tablespoon of the oil, ¾ teaspoon of the salt, and ¼ teaspoon of the pepper in a large bowl. Toss together shrimp and remaining 2 tablespoons oil, 1 teaspoon salt, and ¾ teaspoon pepper in a separate bowl. Arrange zucchini and squash in a single layer in a metal grilling basket. Place grilling basket on unoiled grates. Grill, covered, until slightly charred and tender, about 3 minutes per side.
3. Place shrimp directly on oiled grates. Grill, uncovered, until slightly charred and pink, about 2 minutes per side. Set aside.
4. Toss together zucchini, squash, shrimp, pasta, reserved pasta cooking water, parsley, basil, mint, and chives in a large bowl. Add butter, and toss until butter is melted. Serve immediately.

Grilled Yellow Squash Roll-Ups

ACTIVE 25 MIN. · TOTAL 25 MIN.
SERVES 8

- 2 large yellow squash (about 1 lb.)
- 1 Tbsp. olive oil
- ¼ tsp. black pepper
- 1¼ tsp. kosher salt, divided
- 3 oz. goat cheese
- 2 tsp. lemon zest (from 1 lemon)
- 2 tsp. chopped fresh tarragon
- 30 fresh basil leaves (about 1 cup loosely packed)

1. Preheat a gas grill to medium-high (400°F to 450°F). Cut squash lengthwise into 30 (¼-inch-thick) slices total using a mandoline or a sharp knife. (Discard remaining squash, or reserve for another use.) Brush squash slices evenly with oil on both sides, and sprinkle both sides with pepper and 1 teaspoon of the salt.
2. Place slices on oiled grates; grill, uncovered, until slices are tender and grill marks appear, about 3 minutes per side. Remove from grill.
3. Stir together goat cheese, lemon zest, tarragon, and remaining ¼ teaspoon salt in a small bowl.
4. Spoon ½ teaspoon cheese mixture onto 1 grilled squash slice about ½ inch from 1 end. Top cheese with 1 basil leaf, and roll up the squash slice. Place roll-up, seam-side down, on a serving platter. Repeat process with remaining cheese mixture, squash slices, and basil leaves. Serve chilled or at room temperature.

SUMMER SQUASH

Two rules apply for zucchini or yellow squash: Cook it fast, and serve it quickly. Whether you're grilling in a basket or straight on the grate, it needs only a few minutes over the flames, so pull it off before it gets too charred. Then serve it soon to keep it from turning soggy.

It's Salad Season

Toss together one of these fresh, flavorful warm-weather suppers

GRILLED CORN-AND-
SALMON SALAD WITH
TOMATOES

NO-STICK SALMON
Skinless salmon fillets are less likely to stick
to the grill and easier to separate into chunks.
If you prefer your fish well done, cook it until
the center registers 140°F.

Grilled Corn-and-Salmon Salad with Tomatoes

ACTIVE 35 MIN. - TOTAL 35 MIN.
SERVES 4

- 3 Tbsp. extra-virgin olive oil
- 2 Tbsp. white wine vinegar
- ½ tsp. black pepper
- 1½ tsp. kosher salt, divided
- 1 large (9-oz.) orange or yellow heirloom tomato, cut into 10 wedges
- 2 cups cherry tomatoes, halved
- 4 (6-oz.) skinless salmon fillets
- 1 Tbsp. Dijon mustard
- 3 large ears fresh yellow corn
- 3 oz. fresh baby spinach (4 cups)
- ½ cup torn fresh basil
- ¼ cup chopped fresh chives

1. Whisk together oil, vinegar, pepper, and 1 teaspoon of the salt in a large bowl. Add heirloom and cherry tomatoes, and toss to coat. Let stand 10 minutes.

2. Meanwhile, coat a grill pan with cooking spray; heat over medium-high. Rub salmon evenly with mustard, and sprinkle with remaining ½ teaspoon salt. Place salmon on grill pan, and cook until a thermometer inserted in thickest portion of fish registers 125°F for medium-rare doneness, 9 to 10 minutes, turning once halfway through cook time. Remove salmon from pan.

3. Coat corn with cooking spray. Add to grill pan, and cook over medium-high, turning occasionally, until charred on several sides, about 15 minutes. Remove corn from pan. Cut kernels off cobs, and discard cobs.

4. Add corn, spinach, and basil to tomato mixture in bowl; toss to coat. Break salmon into pieces. Arrange tomato mixture on a large platter. Top with salmon pieces, and sprinkle with chives.

STEAK-AND-BELL PEPPER SALAD

Steak-and-Bell Pepper Salad

ACTIVE 20 MIN. - TOTAL 40 MIN.
SERVES 4

- 6 oz. sourdough bread, torn into ¾-inch pieces
- 9 Tbsp. extra-virgin olive oil, divided
- ½ tsp. black pepper
- ½ tsp. paprika
- ¼ tsp. garlic powder
- 1½ tsp. kosher salt, divided
- 1 (1-lb.) flank steak
- 4 multicolor baby bell peppers
- 2 large shallots, halved lengthwise
- 2 Tbsp. red wine vinegar
- 4 oz. baby arugula (4 cups)
- 3 oz. blue cheese, crumbled (½ cup) (optional)

1. Preheat oven to 400°F. Toss together bread and 3 tablespoons of the oil on a rimmed baking sheet. Bake until toasted, 10 to 12 minutes.

2. Meanwhile, heat a grill pan coated with cooking spray over medium-high. Stir together black pepper, paprika, garlic powder, and 1 teaspoon of the salt in a small bowl; sprinkle evenly over steak. Coat bell peppers with cooking spray. Add steak, bell peppers, and shallots to pan. Cook steak to desired degree of doneness, about 7 minutes per side for medium. Cook bell peppers, turning occasionally, until char marks appear, 10 to 15 minutes. Cook shallots until tender, 4 to 5 minutes per side. Remove steak, bell peppers, and shallots from pan as they finish cooking. Let stand 5 minutes. Cut steak thinly across the grain. Cut bell peppers into strips, discarding stems and seeds. Cut shallots vertically into slices.

3. Whisk together vinegar, remaining 6 tablespoons oil, and remaining ½ teaspoon salt in a large bowl. Add toasted bread; toss to coat. Add steak, bell peppers, shallots, and arugula; toss gently to coat. Divide salad evenly among 4 plates. Sprinkle with cheese, if desired.

Crispy-Shrimp Salad with Avocado Dressing

ACTIVE 20 MIN. - TOTAL 20 MIN.
SERVES 4

- 1 lb. large peeled, deveined raw shrimp
- ½ tsp. black pepper
- 1 tsp. kosher salt, divided
- 2 large eggs, beaten
- ½ cup panko breadcrumbs
- 6 Tbsp. extra-virgin olive oil, divided
- ¼ cup packed fresh cilantro leaves
- 2 Tbsp. plain whole-milk Greek yogurt
- 2 Tbsp. fresh lime juice (from 1 lime)
- 1 large avocado, pitted and halved, divided
- 1 (5-oz.) pkg. mixed baby greens
- 1 cup sliced English cucumber (from 1 [5-oz.] cucumber)
- 2 medium radishes, thinly sliced

1. Sprinkle shrimp evenly with pepper and ½ teaspoon of the salt. Place eggs in a shallow dish. Place panko in a separate shallow dish. Dredge shrimp in egg, shaking off excess. Dredge shrimp in panko, pressing to adhere. Heat 2 tablespoons oil in a large nonstick skillet over medium-high. Add shrimp; cook until opaque and crispy, 5 minutes, turning once halfway through cook time. Remove from pan; cover to keep warm.
2. Process cilantro, 3 tablespoons water, yogurt, lime juice, 2 tablespoons oil, half of the avocado, and remaining ½ teaspoon salt in a food processor until smooth, about 15 seconds, stopping to scrape down sides as needed.
3. Cut remaining avocado into cubes. Toss together mixed greens and remaining 2 tablespoons oil in a large bowl; transfer to a platter. Top with cucumber, radishes, avocado cubes, and shrimp. Drizzle with dressing.

Field Pea Fattoush

ACTIVE 15 MIN. · TOTAL 25 MIN.
SERVES 4

⅓ cup extra-virgin olive oil

3 Tbsp. fresh lemon juice (from 1 lemon)

1½ tsp. kosher salt

½ tsp. ground sumac

½ tsp. black pepper

2 (6-inch) pita bread rounds, torn into 1-inch pieces

1 pt. heirloom cherry tomatoes, halved

2 Persian cucumbers, sliced (about 1 cup)

¾ cup cooked fresh field peas, cooled

2 romaine lettuce hearts, chopped (about 6 cups)

⅓ cup packed small mint leaves

1. Preheat oven to 400°F. Whisk together oil, lemon juice, salt, sumac, and pepper in a large bowl. Arrange torn pita rounds on a rimmed baking sheet. Drizzle evenly with 3 tablespoons of the oil mixture, and toss to coat. Bake until browned and crisp, 5 to 6 minutes.

2. Add tomatoes, cucumbers, and peas to remaining oil mixture in bowl; toss to coat. Let stand 10 minutes. Add lettuce, mint, and toasted pita chips, and toss to coat. Arrange salad on a platter.

Kale-and-Chicken Salad with Jalapeño-Lime Dressing

ACTIVE 20 MIN. · TOTAL 20 MIN.
SERVES 4

- 1 Tbsp., plus ¼ cup olive oil, divided
- 1 (5-oz.) bunch curly kale, destemmed and chopped (about 6 cups)
- 2 Tbsp. fresh lime juice (from 1 large lime)

- 2 Tbsp. chopped seeded jalapeño chile (from 1 medium chile)
- 1½ Tbsp. honey
- ¾ tsp. kosher salt
- ½ tsp. black pepper
- 2 cups sliced green cabbage (from 1 small cabbage)
- ½ cup packed fresh cilantro leaves
- ¼ cup packed fresh mint leaves
- 2 cups coarsely shredded rotisserie chicken
- ½ cup honey-roasted peanuts

1. Massage 1 tablespoon of the oil into kale in a bowl until kale softens, about 30 seconds.
2. Process lime juice, jalapeño, honey, salt, pepper, and remaining ¼ cup oil in a mini food processor until blended, 30 seconds.
3. Add lime dressing, cabbage, cilantro, and mint to kale in bowl; toss to coat. Stir in chicken. Arrange salad on a platter, and sprinkle with peanuts.

Kicked-Up Burgers

Creole spices and a tangy sauce add bold new flavor

Creole Burgers

ACTIVE 30 MIN. - TOTAL 30 MIN.
SERVES 4

- 1½ lb. ground chuck
- 3 thinly sliced scallions (about ⅓ cup)
- 2 Tbsp. Creole seasoning (such as Zatarain's)
- ¼ tsp. cayenne pepper
- ½ cup mayonnaise
- 2 Tbsp. chopped fresh flat-leaf parsley
- 1 tsp. Creole mustard
- 1 tsp. hot sauce
- 1 tsp. fresh lemon juice (from 1 lemon)
- 1 medium red onion, sliced into ¼-inch rounds
- 1 Tbsp. olive oil
- 4 brioche hamburger buns, lightly toasted
- 1 large romaine lettuce heart, sliced (about 1 cup)

1. Preheat a grill to medium (350°F to 400°F). Place ground chuck, scallions, Creole seasoning, and cayenne in a medium bowl. Using hands, gently combine. Shape mixture into 4 patties and place on a plate. Clean bowl thoroughly. Stir together mayonnaise, parsley, mustard, hot sauce, and lemon juice in cleaned bowl; set aside.

2. Place patties on oiled grates. Grill, covered, until no longer pink, about 5 minutes per side. Remove from grill; loosely cover patties with aluminum foil. Place onion slices on grates; brush with oil. Grill, covered, until slightly charred and tender, about 3 minutes per side.

3. Spread 1 tablespoon of mayonnaise mixture on bottom half of each bun. Top each with romaine lettuce, 1 patty, and grilled onions. Cover with bun tops.

PATTY POINTER
For juicy, tender burgers, don't overmix the meat. Form the patties loosely without pressing too much.

Bowled Over

One zingy sauce is used two flavorful ways in this salmon supper

Sweet-and-Spicy Glazed Salmon Bowls

ACTIVE 30 MIN. - TOTAL 30 MIN.

SERVES 4

- ⅓ cup unsalted chicken stock
- ½ tsp. cornstarch
- 2 Tbsp. rice vinegar
- 1½ Tbsp. honey
- 2 tsp. Sriracha chile sauce
- 2½ Tbsp. toasted sesame oil, divided
- 1½ tsp. kosher salt, divided
- 4 (5-oz.) skinless salmon fillets (about 1½ inches thick)
- 2 (8.8-oz.) pkg. precooked microwavable brown rice
- 6 oz. fresh snow peas, trimmed (about 2 cups)
- 3 scallions, diagonally sliced (½ cup)
- 1 small English cucumber, diced (about ¾ cup)
- 3 medium radishes, cut into matchsticks (½ cup)
- 1 tsp. toasted sesame seeds

1. Whisk together stock and cornstarch in a small saucepan. Add vinegar, honey, Sriracha, ½ tablespoon of the oil, and ¼ teaspoon of the salt; bring to a simmer over medium, whisking constantly. Cook, whisking occasionally, until reduced to ½ cup, about 4 minutes. Remove from heat. Place 2 tablespoons of the sauce in a medium bowl, and let cool slightly. Set aside remaining sauce. Add salmon to bowl, toss to coat, and let stand 5 minutes.

2. Meanwhile, microwave rice according to package directions.

3. Heat 1 tablespoon of the oil in a large skillet over medium-high. Add snow peas. Cook, stirring often, until tender, about 4 minutes. Stir in rice, scallions, and ½ teaspoon of the salt; cook, stirring occasionally, 1 minute. Remove mixture from skillet; keep warm.

4. Add remaining 1 tablespoon oil to skillet. Sprinkle fish with remaining ¾ teaspoon salt. Add salmon to

skillet. Cook until lightly charred and a thermometer registers 130°F (medium doneness), 3 to 4 minutes per side. Divide rice mixture and salmon evenly among 4 shallow bowls. Top evenly with cucumber, radishes, and sesame seeds. Drizzle with remaining sauce.

CALORIES: **489** – CARBS: **44G** – FAT: **4G**

SALMON SMARTS

This recipe is best made with fillets that are about 1½ inches thick. Avoid pieces from the tail, which are too thin and will overcook.

Sip, Sip, Hooray!

Simple, satisfying smoothies get your day started on a bright note

DROP THE DAIRY
Coconut yogurt can replace whole-milk yogurt, and coconut water or almond milk can sub for milk.

Drink Your Greens Smoothie

ACTIVE 10 MIN. · TOTAL 10 MIN.
SERVES 2

Combine 1½ cups loosely packed **spinach leaves**, ⅔ cup **vanilla whole-milk yogurt**, ⅔ cup **bottled coconut water**, ½ cup **ice cubes**, 1 small **banana**, and ½ **ripe avocado** in a blender. Process until smooth, 45 to 60 seconds.

Sunshine Smoothie

ACTIVE 10 MIN. · TOTAL 10 MIN.
SERVES 2

Combine 1½ cups **matchstick carrots**, 1 cup **frozen mango chunks**, 1 cup **vanilla whole-milk yogurt**, ½ cup **fresh orange juice**, ½ cup **ice cubes**, and 1 Tbsp. **honey** in a blender. Process until smooth, 45 to 60 seconds.

Nutty Strawberry Smoothie

ACTIVE 10 MIN. · TOTAL 10 MIN.
SERVES 2

Combine 3 cups hulled and halved **fresh strawberries**, ½ cup **almond milk**, ½ cup **ice cubes**, 2 Tbsp. **creamy peanut butter**, 1 Tbsp. **honey**, and 1 small **ripe frozen banana** in a blender. Process until smooth, 45 to 60 seconds.

COOKING  SCHOOL

GREAT GEAR

Mini & Mighty

A cool new tool for smoothie lovers

This compact yet powerful machine cranks out single-serving fruit or green smoothies quickly, with less mess and noise. The 20-ounce jar has a travel lid and is marked with a guide telling in which order to add the ingredients.

Hamilton Beach Power Blender Plus, bedbathandbeyond.com

MAKE IT AHEAD

Smoothies in Seconds

Stock your freezer with bags of ready-to-blend ingredients

Satisfy snack cravings or make a grab-and-go breakfast with easy frozen smoothie packs. Place cut-up fruits, vegetables, and other ingredients (such as peanut butter and protein powder) in zip-top plastic freezer bags. Label each pouch with the amount of liquid that needs to be added to the blender when you're ready to mix. A good ratio for each serving is 1 part liquid to 1½ parts frozen fruits and vegetables.

"If you're making a smoothie, use whole-milk yogurt. Nonfat or low-fat yogurt will have a chalky texture when blended."

Pam Lolley
Test Kitchen Professional

SPICE IT UP

Special Sauces

Ketchup has some new competition

BARBECUE THOUSAND ISLAND DRESSING

Stir together 1 cup **mayonnaise**, ½ cup **barbecue sauce**, ½ cup **dill pickle relish**, 1 tsp. **red wine vinegar**, and ½ tsp. **paprika.**

CLASSIC DIJONNAISE

Stir together 1 cup **mayonnaise**, 2 Tbsp. **Dijon mustard**, 2 Tbsp. **coarse-grain mustard**, 1 tsp. **apple cider vinegar**, and ½ tsp. **granulated sugar.**

AVOCADO-LIME SAUCE

Place 1 chopped **large avocado**, 3 Tbsp. **plain yogurt**, 2 Tbsp. **fresh lime juice**, 2 Tbsp. **fresh cilantro leaves**, and ½ tsp. **kosher salt** in a food processor. Process until smooth, 1 minute.

June

SLOW-ROASTED CHERRY
TOMATO BRUSCHETTA

How to Eat a Tomato

With a bounty like this, it's time to get creative

ROAST 'EM

This recipe is the easiest way to make use of an overabundance of cherry tomatoes. Roasting concentrates the sweetness and makes the fruit jammy and rich. You don't want the tomatoes to break down completely in the oven; they should still hold their shape. Once they have cooled a bit, you can easily remove and discard the skins. Or leave them on, and serve as is.

Slow-Roasted Cherry Tomato Bruschetta

ACTIVE 15 MIN. - TOTAL 55 MIN.
MAKES 8

- 1½ lb. cherry tomatoes (about 4 cups)
- 6 medium garlic cloves
- 5 thyme sprigs
- 1 tsp. fennel seeds
- 1 tsp. kosher salt
- 1 Tbsp. sherry vinegar
- ¾ cup extra-virgin olive oil, divided
- ½ (8-oz.) baguette, sliced diagonally (about 8 slices)
- 4 oz. goat cheese log, softened
   Small fresh basil leaves

1. Preheat oven to 350°F. Toss together tomatoes, garlic, thyme, fennel seeds, salt, vinegar, and ¼ cup of the oil in an 11- x 7-inch baking dish. Roast; stirring once, until tomatoes are tender and skins blister, 25 to 30 minutes. Cool 10 minutes.
2. Meanwhile, place baguette slices in a shallow baking pan, and drizzle with ¼ cup of the oil. Bake in preheated oven until slightly browned, 8 to 10 minutes. Carefully remove and discard blistered peels from cooled tomatoes, if desired. Spread goat cheese on warm baguette slices, and place on a serving platter. Top with tomatoes, drizzle with remaining ¼ cup oil, and sprinkle with basil leaves.

MARINATE 'EM

These tangy tomatoes can be enjoyed solo, in a salad with torn summer herbs, or with hot cooked pasta for a lighter and brighter take on marinara sauce. However you serve them, let the tomatoes sit in the vinaigrette at room temperature for the full 20 minutes. This allows them to release their juices, absorb the flavors of the garlic and red wine vinegar, and break down a bit to become more tender.

Marinated Tomatoes

ACTIVE 10 MIN. - TOTAL 30 MIN.
SERVES 4

Whisk together ¼ cup **red wine vinegar**, ¼ cup **extra-virgin olive oil**, 1 Tbsp. minced **shallot** (from 1 small shallot), 1 tsp. **kosher salt**, ½ tsp. **black pepper**, and 3 minced **garlic cloves**. Gently stir in 1 lb. **mixed heirloom tomatoes**, cut into 1-inch-thick wedges; let stand 20 minutes. Serve as is, or use as directed in recipes below.

Pasta with Marinated Tomatoes

ACTIVE 10 MIN. - TOTAL 20 MIN., PLUS TIME TO PREPARE MARINATED TOMATOES
SERVES 4

Cook 8 oz. **penne pasta** according to package directions; drain. Place one-fourth of **Marinated Tomatoes** with marinade in a blender; pulse until tomatoes are very finely chopped, 3 to 4 times. Coarsely chop remaining Marinated Tomatoes, reserving marinade. Combine finely and coarsely chopped tomatoes and reserved marinade with hot cooked pasta, and toss to coat. Stir in 1 cup loosely packed chopped **fresh basil** and 8 oz. torn **fresh mozzarella cheese**.

Marinated Tomato-and-Herb Salad

ACTIVE 10 MIN. - TOTAL 10 MIN., PLUS TIME TO PREPARE MARINATED TOMATOES
SERVES 4

Gently remove **Marinated Tomatoes** from marinade, reserving marinade. Arrange Marinated Tomatoes on a serving platter with 1 large **beefsteak tomato** (7 oz.), cut into ½-inch-thick slices, and 1 cup halved **heirloom cherry tomatoes**. Drizzle with reserved marinade, sprinkle with ½ tsp. **flaky sea salt**, and top with ½ cup loosely packed torn **mixed fresh herbs** (such as parsley, basil, dill, and chives).

MARINATED TOMATO-AND-HERB SALAD

FRIED GREEN
TOMATO SALAD WITH
BUTTERMILK DRESSING

We're not going to lie—the crisp, golden-brown breading is the tastiest part of a fried green tomato. Yellow cornmeal (use fine, not coarse ground) has good flavor, texture, and color, but the secret to a great crust is to add a little all-purpose flour to the breading mixture. This helps coat the tomato slices evenly without clumping or caking.

Fried Green Tomato Salad with Buttermilk Dressing

ACTIVE 30 MIN. · TOTAL 30 MIN.
SERVES 4

- 3 Tbsp. mayonnaise
- 1½ Tbsp. sour cream
- 1½ Tbsp. thinly sliced fresh chives
- 1 Tbsp. fresh lemon juice (from 1 lemon)
- 1 Tbsp. Dijon mustard
- 2 tsp. extra-virgin olive oil
- 1 cup whole buttermilk, divided
- 2½ tsp. kosher salt, divided
- 1½ tsp. black pepper, divided
  Vegetable oil
- 1 large egg, lightly beaten
- ¾ cup fine yellow cornmeal
- ¼ tsp. cayenne pepper
- 1 cup all-purpose flour, divided
- 1 lb. green tomatoes (about 3), cut into ⅓-inch slices (12 slices)
- 8 cups assorted mixed lettuces (such as arugula and butter lettuce)
- 1 small red onion, thinly sliced (about ½ cup)

1. Whisk together mayonnaise, sour cream, chives, lemon juice, mustard, oil, ½ cup of the buttermilk, 1 teaspoon of the salt, and ½ teaspoon of the black pepper. Cover; chill buttermilk dressing until ready to serve.

2. Pour vegetable oil to a depth of 3 inches in a large cast-iron Dutch oven; heat over high to 350°F. Whisk together egg and remaining ½ cup buttermilk in a shallow dish. Combine cornmeal, cayenne, ½ cup of the flour, 1 teaspoon of the salt, and ½ teaspoon of the black pepper in a second shallow dish. Combine remaining ½ cup flour, ½ teaspoon salt, and ½ teaspoon black pepper in a third shallow dish. Working with 1 slice at a time, dredge tomato in flour mixture, then in egg mixture, and then in cornmeal-flour mixture.

3. Fry tomato slices, in 2 batches, in hot oil until browned, about 3 to 4 minutes total, turning slices halfway through frying. Drain on paper towels.

4. Combine lettuces and red onion in a large bowl. Toss lettuce mixture with ¼ cup of the buttermilk dressing, reserving the rest. Divide salad among 4 plates, top each with 3 fried green tomatoes. Drizzle evenly with remaining dressing.

This simple salsa has an incredible depth of flavor that can be achieved only by smoking the tomatoes and jalapeños. Plum tomatoes are perfect for this cooking method because they are meaty but still contain a lot of moisture. We like the mild flavor of applewood chips, but other types of wood will work–except for hickory, which can be overpowering.

Smoked-Tomato Salsa

(Photo, page 6)

ACTIVE 30 MIN. · TOTAL 2 HOURS
SERVES 8

- 2 cups applewood chips
- 1½ lb. plum tomatoes, cut in half lengthwise (6 tomatoes)
- 2 jalapeño chiles
- 1 medium red onion, coarsely chopped (1 cup)
- ⅓ cup fresh cilantro leaves
- 2 Tbsp. fresh oregano leaves
- 2 garlic cloves
- 2 Tbsp. fresh lime juice (from 1 lime)
- 1 Tbsp. honey
- 1¼ tsp. kosher salt

1. Soak wood chips in water 30 minutes. Drain well. Meanwhile, prepare a charcoal fire in a smoker according to manufacturer's instructions. Maintain temperature at 200°F to 225°F for 15 to 20 minutes. Place wood chips on coals. Smoke tomatoes and jalapeños, covered with smoker lid, until tender, about 45 minutes. Remove tomatoes and jalapeños from smoker; discard stems from jalapeños.

2. Place onion, cilantro, oregano, and garlic in a food processor; pulse until finely chopped, about 5 times. Transfer to a medium bowl. Place tomatoes, jalapeños, lime juice, honey, and salt in food processor; process until smooth, 1 minute. Transfer to bowl with onion mixture; stir to combine. Cover; chill at least 45 minutes before serving.

Enjoy tomatoes well past summer with a few jars of these tangy pickles stored in your pantry. When purchasing green selections for pickling, choose ones that are about the size of a baseball or smaller. Larger tomatoes tend to be tough and bitter and won't absorb the brine as well.

Pickled Green Tomatoes

ACTIVE 15 MIN. · TOTAL 24 HOURS, 15 MIN., INCLUDING 24 HOURS CHILLING
SERVES 8

- 1¼ cups rice vinegar
- ½ cup granulated sugar
- 2 Tbsp. kosher salt
- 3 basil sprigs
- ¼ cup thinly sliced shallot (from 1 medium shallot)
- ¼ tsp. crushed red pepper
- 1 lb. small green tomatoes (about 4), cored and cut into ⅓-inch-thick slices (about 4 slices each)

Stir together 1 cup water, vinegar, sugar, and salt in a medium saucepan. Bring to a boil over high, stirring until sugar dissolves. Remove from heat; cool 10 minutes. Place basil, shallots, crushed red pepper, and green tomatoes in a 32-ounce canning jar. Pour vinegar mixture over green tomato mixture in jar. Cover with a tight-fitting lid; chill 24 hours. Store in refrigerator up to 2 months.

PICKLED GREEN TOMATOES

The House Cocktail

Six refreshing big-batch drinks that will be your signature beverages all summer long

Lemon–Basil Spritzer

ACTIVE 15 MIN. - TOTAL 1 HOUR, 45 MIN., INCLUDING 1 HOUR, 30 MIN. COOLING
SERVES 6

Prepare two batches **Simple Syrup** (recipe follows). Remove from heat; stir in 3 (1-inch-long) **lemon peel strips** and 3 **large fresh basil leaves**. Cover and steep 30 minutes. Pour mixture through a fine mesh strainer into a bowl; discard solids. Cool to room temperature, 1 hour. Pour cooled syrup into a 2- to 3-qt. pitcher. Stir in 1 (750-ml) bottle chilled **Champagne** or **dry sparkling wine**. (For a mocktail, substitute 1 liter **lemon-flavored seltzer water**.) Fill 6 stemless wineglasses with **ice**. Pour cocktail evenly into glasses; garnish with **basil leaves and lemon peel twists**.

Spicy Watermelon Refresher

ACTIVE 30 MIN. - TOTAL 2 HOURS, INCLUDING 1 HOUR COOLING
SERVES 8

Prepare one-half batch **Simple Syrup** (recipe follows); remove from heat. Stir in ½ seeded and chopped **serrano chile** (about 1 Tbsp.). Cover and steep 30 minutes. Pour mixture through a fine mesh strainer into a bowl; discard solids. Cool to room temperature, 1 hour. While syrup cools, process 3 cups cubed **seedless watermelon** (about 2 lb.) in a blender until smooth, 2 to 3 minutes. Working in batches, pour watermelon puree through a fine mesh strainer into a bowl; discard solids. Pour watermelon juice into a 2- to 3-qt. pitcher. Stir in ¾ cup (6 oz.) **tequila reposado**, 1 (12-oz.) can **watermelon-flavor or plain seltzer water**, and cooled syrup. Salt the rims of 8 Collins glasses, and fill with **ice**. Pour cocktail evenly into glasses; garnish with **chile slices and watermelon wedges**.

Sweet Tea Mule

ACTIVE 15 MIN. - TOTAL 15 MIN.
SERVES 8

Stir together 2 (12-oz.) bottles **ginger beer**, 4½ cups **unsweetened tea**, ¾ cup (6 oz.) **bourbon**, ⅓ cup Simple Syrup (recipe follows), and ¼ cup **fresh lime juice** (from 2 limes) in a 2- to 3-qt. pitcher. Fill 8 large highball glasses or Moscow mule mugs with **ice**. Pour cocktail evenly into glasses; garnish with thinly sliced **lime**.

LEMON-BASIL SPRITZER

SPICY WATERMELON REFRESHER

SWEET TEA MULE

MAKE IT A MOCKTAIL

They're also delicious as mocktails! Unless noted below, you can omit the alcohol in these drinks with great results

Pineapple-Coconut Fizz

ACTIVE 20 MIN. - TOTAL 20 MIN.
SERVES 8

Process 4 cups peeled, cored, and cubed **fresh pineapple** (from 1 [3 lb.] pineapple) in a blender until smooth and frothy, 2 to 3 minutes. Pour into a 2- to 3-qt. pitcher, and stir in 1 liter **coconut-flavored seltzer water** and 1 cup (8 oz.) **white rum**. Fill 8 Collins glasses with **crushed ice**, and add 2 **pineapple leaves** to each glass. Pour cocktail evenly into glasses. Garnish with **pineapple wedges**.

PINEAPPLE-
COCONUT
FIZZ

Blackberry-Mint Sparkler

ACTIVE 20 MIN. - TOTAL 1 HOUR, 50 MIN., INCLUDING 1 HOUR COOLING
SERVES 8

Bring 4 (6-oz.) pkg. **fresh blackberries**, 2 cups **granulated sugar**, and 2 cups **water** to a simmer in a saucepan over medium-low, stirring occasionally. Cook, stirring occasionally, until the blackberries start to soften, about 5 minutes. Remove from heat; stir in 1 packed cup **fresh mint leaves**. Cover; steep 30 minutes. Pour berry mixture through a fine mesh strainer into a bowl; discard solids. Cool to room temperature, 1 hour. Pour 3 cups of the cooled syrup into a 2- to 3-qt. pitcher. Stir in 1 liter **plain seltzer water** or **club soda** and 1½ cups (12 oz.) **vodka**. Taste; add more syrup, if desired. Fill 8 highball glasses with **ice**. Working with 1 **mint sprig** at a time, hold sprig in 1 hand and gently smack with your palm to release its essential oils. Add a sprig to each glass. Pour cocktail evenly into glasses; garnish with **blackberries**.

Cucumber-Honeydew Cooler

ACTIVE 30 MIN. - TOTAL 30 MIN.
SERVES 8

Process about 4 cups chopped **English cucumbers** (2 medium cucumbers), 1½ cups cubed **honeydew melon** (about 1 lb.), 1 cup **water**, and 2 Tbsp. **granulated sugar** in a blender until smooth, 2 to 3 minutes. Working in batches, pour puree through a fine mesh strainer into a bowl; discard solids. Pour cucumber-honeydew juice into a 2- to 3-qt. pitcher. Stir in 1 cup (8 oz.) **floral gin** (such as Hendrick's). (For a mocktail, substitute 1 (12-oz.) can **lime-flavored seltzer water**.) Slice 1 **English cucumber** very thinly with a mandoline. Loop cucumber ribbons around insides of 8 small stemless wineglasses. Fill with **ice**; pour cocktail evenly into glasses.

Simple Syrup

ACTIVE 10 MIN. - TOTAL 1 HOUR, 10 MIN., INCLUDING 1 HOUR COOLING
MAKES ¾ CUP

Bring ½ cup **granulated sugar** and ½ cup **water** to a boil in a small saucepan over medium-low, stirring occasionally. Remove from heat, and cool to room temperature, 1 hour.

CUCUMBER-
HONEYDEW COOLER

BLACKBERRY-
MINT SPARKLER

BLUEBERRY-ORANGE
BLOSSOM HONEY SLAB PIE

Easy as Slab Pie

Turn your farmers' market haul into sweet seasonal desserts

Blueberry-Orange Blossom Honey Slab Pie

ACTIVE 30 MIN. - TOTAL 2 HOURS, 15 MIN., PLUS 1 HOUR, 30 MIN. COOLING

SERVES 12

   Slab Pastry Crust (recipe, p. 126)
   All-purpose flour, for work surface
- ¾ cup granulated sugar
- ¼ cup orange blossom honey
- 3 Tbsp. uncooked quick-cooking tapioca, ground in a spice grinder or food processor
- 3 Tbsp. cornstarch
- 2 Tbsp. fresh lemon juice (from 1 lemon)
- 1 Tbsp. orange zest plus 2 Tbsp. fresh juice (from 1 orange)
- 1 tsp. vanilla extract
- ½ tsp. kosher salt
- 10 cups fresh blueberries (from 5 pt. blueberries)
- 1 large egg
   Sparkling sugar (optional)

1. Preheat oven to 375°F. Unwrap the larger Slab Pastry Crust disk; roll out on a lightly floured work surface into an 18- x 13-inch rectangle. Wrap dough around rolling pin, and gently fit inside a 15- x 10-inch jelly-roll pan. Turn dough edges under; crimp. Prick bottom and sides of dough with a fork. Line with parchment paper, leaving a 3- to 4-inch overhang around edges of pan. Fill with pie weights or dried beans. Bake 10 minutes. Remove parchment and pie weights. Return crust to oven; bake 5 minutes. Transfer to a wire rack; cool completely, about 30 minutes.
2. Stir together granulated sugar, honey, ground tapioca, cornstarch, lemon juice, orange zest and juice, vanilla, and kosher salt in a large bowl until combined. Gently stir in blueberries until completely coated. Let mixture stand 15 minutes, stirring occasionally.
3. Meanwhile, unwrap the remaining smaller Slab Pastry Crust disk; roll out on a lightly floured work surface to ¼-inch thickness. Cut out blooms in various shapes and sizes using assorted flower-shape cookie cutters. Refrigerate until ready to assemble pie.
4. Spoon blueberry mixture evenly into prepared crust. Arrange assorted flower cutouts over top of pie. Whisk together egg and 1 tablespoon water in a small bowl. Brush mixture over cutouts. If desired, sprinkle flower cutouts with sparkling sugar.
5. Bake in preheated oven until crust and flowers are browned and filling is bubbly, 45 to 50 minutes, covering crust edges with aluminum foil during final 15 minutes of baking to prevent excessive browning, if needed. Transfer to a wire rack; cool completely, about 1 hour.

Triple-Berry Slab Pie

(Photo, page 125)

ACTIVE 30 MIN. - TOTAL 1 HOUR, 10 MIN., PLUS 1 HOUR, 30 MIN. COOLING

SERVES 12

   Slab Pastry Crust (recipe, p. 126)
   All-purpose flour, for work surface
- 3 (6-oz.) pkg. fresh raspberries (about 4 cups)
- 3 (6-oz.) pkg. fresh blackberries (about 4 cups)
- 9 oz. fresh blueberries (2 cups)
- 1 Tbsp. lemon zest plus 2 Tbsp. fresh juice (from 1 lemon)
- ⅔ cup granulated sugar
- ⅔ cup packed light brown sugar
- ½ cup all-purpose flour
- 1 Tbsp. chopped fresh thyme
- ½ tsp. kosher salt
- 2 Tbsp. butter, cut into small cubes
- 1 large egg

1. Preheat oven to 375°F. Unwrap the larger Slab Pastry Crust disk, and roll dough out on a lightly floured work surface into an 18- x 13-inch rectangle. Wrap dough around rolling pin; gently fit inside a 15- x 10-inch jelly-roll pan. Turn edges under; crimp. Prick bottom and sides of dough with a fork. Line with parchment paper, leaving a 3- to 4-inch overhang around pan edges. Fill with pie weights or dried beans. Bake 10 minutes. Remove parchment and pie weights. Return crust to oven; bake 5 minutes. Transfer to a wire rack; cool completely, about 30 minutes.
2. Gently stir together berries, lemon zest, and lemon juice in a large bowl. Stir together granulated sugar, brown sugar, flour, thyme, and salt in a small bowl. Sprinkle over berry mixture; stir gently to incorporate. Spoon berry mixture into prepared crust. Sprinkle evenly with cubed butter.
3. Unwrap remaining smaller Slab Pastry Crust disk; roll dough out on a lightly floured work surface into a 12- x 6- x ¼-inch rectangle. Cut 15 (12-inch-long, ¼-inch-wide) strips from dough rectangle. (Discard dough scraps, or reserve for another use.) Whisk together egg and 1 tablespoon water in a small bowl.
4. Braid 3 dough strips together, keeping the braid as snug as possible. Carefully place dough braid crosswise on top of pie about 2 inches from 1 short side of pan. Brush top of crimped crust where dough braid overlaps with it, and press together to adhere. Brush top of dough braid with some of the egg mixture. Repeat process with remaining 12 dough strips and egg mixture, making 5 dough braids total, each spaced 2 to 3 inches apart on top of pie.
5. Bake in poreheated oven until crust is golden brown and filling is bubbly, 45 to 50 minutes, covering crust edges with aluminum foil during final 15 minutes of baking to prevent excessive browning, if needed. Transfer to a wire rack, and cool completely, about 1 hour.

STONE FRUIT LATTICE-
TOPPED SLAB PIE
(PAGE 126)

TRIPLE-BERRY SLAB PIE
(PAGE 123)

Stone Fruit Lattice-Topped Slab Pie

(Photo, page 124)

ACTIVE 20 MIN. - TOTAL 2 HOURS, 10 MIN.,
PLUS 1 HOUR, 30 MIN. COOLING
SERVES 12

> Slab Pastry Crust (recipe follows)
> 2 lb. firm ripe peaches, peeled, pitted, and sliced (about 6 cups)
> 1 lb. fresh Bing cherries, pitted (about 4 cups)
> 1½ lb. firm ripe nectarines, peeled and sliced (about 2 cups)
> 2 tsp. vanilla extract
> ¾ cup granulated sugar
> ½ cup packed light brown sugar
> ⅓ cup all-purpose flour, plus more for work surface
> ½ tsp. kosher salt
> ¼ cup butter, melted
> 1 large egg
> Turbinado sugar (optional)

1. Preheat oven to 375°F. Unwrap the larger Slab Pastry Crust disk; roll dough out on a lightly floured work surface into an 18- x 13-inch rectangle. Wrap dough around rolling pin, and gently fit inside a 15- x 10-inch jelly-roll pan. Turn dough edges under; crimp. Prick bottom and sides of dough with a fork. Line with parchment paper, leaving a 3- to 4-inch overhang around edges of pan. Fill with pie weights or dried beans. Bake 10 minutes. Remove parchment and pie weights. Return crust to oven, and bake 5 minutes. Transfer to a wire rack, and cool completely, about 30 minutes.

2. Place peaches, cherries, nectarines, and vanilla in a large bowl. Stir together granulated sugar, brown sugar, flour, and salt in a medium bowl. Sprinkle over peach mixture; stir gently to combine. Spoon mixture into prepared crust, and drizzle evenly with melted butter.

3. Unwrap the remaining smaller Slab Pastry Crust disk, and roll dough out on a lightly floured work surface into a 12- x 16-inch rectangle. Cut lengthwise into 7 (1½-inch-wide) strips, and arrange in a lattice pattern over peach mixture in crust. Press dough strips to edges to adhere. Whisk together egg and 1 tablespoon water in a small bowl, and brush mixture over dough strips. If desired, sprinkle dough strips with turbinado sugar.

4. Bake in preheated oven until crust is deep golden and peach mixture is bubbly, 45 to 50 minutes, covering pie with aluminum foil during final 15 minutes of bake time to prevent excessive browning. Transfer to a wire rack, and cool completely, about 1 hour.

Key Lime Slab Pie with Strawberry Whipped Cream

ACTIVE 30 MIN. - TOTAL 1 HOUR, 40 MIN.,
PLUS 1 HOUR, 30 MIN. COOLING AND
3 HOURS CHILLING
SERVES 12

> Slab Pastry Crust (recipe follows)
> All-purpose flour, for work surface
> 2 (14-oz.) cans sweetened condensed milk
> 6 large egg yolks
> 2 tsp. Key lime zest plus 1 cup fresh juice (from about 1 lb. Key limes), plus additional zest for garnish
> 7 fresh strawberries, halved lengthwise, plus more for garnish
> 2 cups heavy whipping cream
> 1 tsp. vanilla extract
> 6 Tbsp. powdered sugar
> Soft pink food coloring gel (optional)

1. Preheat oven to 375°F. Unwrap the larger Slab Pastry Crust disk; roll dough out on a lightly floured work surface into an 18- x 13-inch rectangle. Wrap dough around rolling pin; gently fit inside a 15- x 10-inch jelly-roll pan. Turn dough edges under; crimp. Prick bottom and sides of dough with a fork. Line with parchment paper, leaving a 3- to 4-inch overhang around pan edges. Fill with pie weights or dried beans. Bake 10 minutes. Remove parchment paper and pie weights. Return crust to oven; bake until lightly browned, 8 to 10 minutes. Transfer to a wire rack; cool completely, about 30 minutes. (Reserve remaining smaller Slab Pastry Crust disk for another use.)

2. Reduce oven temperature to 350°F. Whisk together condensed milk, yolks, and lime zest and juice in a large bowl. Gently pour into prepared crust. Return to oven, and bake until center is almost set, 11 to 13 minutes. (The center will not be firm but will set up as it chills.) Transfer to a wire rack; cool completely, about 1 hour. Cover and chill at least 3 hours or up to 24 hours.

3. Process strawberries in a food processor or blender until completely smooth, about 30 seconds. Pour through a fine mesh strainer into a small bowl; discard solids.

4. Beat heavy cream, vanilla, and 3 tablespoons of the strained strawberry mixture in a stand mixer fitted with a whisk attachment on medium-high speed until foamy, about 30 seconds. Gradually add powdered sugar and, if desired, food coloring gel, beating until soft peaks form, about 1 minute. (Reserve any remaining strained strawberry mixture for another use.)

5. Spoon whipped cream mixture over pie filling, gently swirling to cover and leaving some of the filling showing underneath. Garnish the pie with additional lime zest and strawberries.

Slab Pastry Crust

ACTIVE 10 MIN. - TOTAL 40 MIN.
MAKES 2 DOUGH DISKS

> 4 cups all-purpose flour
> 2½ Tbsp. granulated sugar
> 1¼ tsp. salt
> 1 cup cold butter, cubed
> 8 Tbsp. cold shortening, cubed
> 6 to 8 Tbsp. ice water, as needed

1. Pulse flour, sugar, and salt in a food processor until combined, 3 to 4 times. Add butter and shortening; pulse until mixture resembles coarse meal, 8 to 10 times. Drizzle in 6 tablespoons of the ice water, 1 tablespoon at a time, pulsing after each addition, until mixture clumps together. If needed, add remaining 2 tablespoons water, 1 teaspoon at a time, pulsing after each addition, until mixture clumps together. Gently divide dough into thirds. Shape one-third of the dough into a flat rectangle, and shape the other two-thirds together into a larger flat rectangle. Wrap dough disks individually in plastic wrap; chill at least 30 minutes or up to 24 hours. (Dough may be stored in freezer, wrapped tightly with plastic wrap, up to 1 month. To use from frozen, let dough thaw 8 hours or overnight in refrigerator.)

2. Follow shaping and baking instructions for each individual pie.

KEY LIME SLAB PIE
WITH STRAWBERRY
WHIPPED CREAM

Peach-Plum Crumble Slab Pie

ACTIVE 20 MIN. · TOTAL 2 HOURS,
PLUS 40 MIN. COOLING
SERVES 12

    Slab Pastry Crust (recipe, p. 126)
2 lb. firm ripe peaches, peeled,
    pitted, and sliced (about 6 cups)
1½ lb. firm ripe red plums, sliced
    (about 4 cups)
1 cup all-purpose flour, divided, plus
    more for work surface
1 cup granulated sugar, divided
6 Tbsp. butter, melted
1 tsp. ground cinnamon

½ tsp. kosher salt
    Vanilla ice cream (optional)

1. Preheat oven to 375°F. Unwrap the larger Slab Pastry Crust disk; roll dough out on a lightly floured work surface into an 18- x 13-inch rectangle. Wrap dough around rolling pin; gently fit inside a 15- x 10-inch jelly-roll pan. Turn edges under; crimp. Prick bottom and sides of dough with a fork. Line with parchment paper, leaving a 3- to 4-inch overhang around pan edges. Fill with pie weights or dried beans. Bake 10 minutes. Remove parchment and pie weights. Return crust to oven; bake minutes. Transfer to a wire

rack; cool completely, about 30 minutes. (Reserve smaller Slab Pastry Crust disk for another use.)
2. Gently toss together peaches, plums, and ½ cup each of the flour and sugar in a large bowl. Spoon mixture into prepared crust. Stir together butter, cinnamon, salt, and remaining ½ cup each flour and sugar in a medium bowl. Sprinkle over peach mixture in crust.
3. Bake in preheated oven until lightly browned and bubbly, 35 to 40 minutes. Let stand at least 10 minutes or up to 2 hours. Serve warm with vanilla ice cream, if desired.

Hot off the Grill

Winner! Winner! Five flavorful chicken dinners

Mojo Chicken Bowls

ACTIVE 30 MIN. - TOTAL 1 HOUR, 35 MIN.
SERVES 4

- 1   cup refrigerated orange juice
- 1/3 cup loosely packed fresh oregano leaves, chopped
- 1/3 cup olive oil
- 1/4 cup fresh lemon juice (from 2 lemons)
- 1/4 cup fresh lime juice (from 2 limes)
- 10 medium garlic cloves, finely chopped (about 1/4 cup)
- 1   medium jalapeño chile, unseeded and thinly sliced (about 1/4 cup)
- 2   tsp. kosher salt, divided
- 8   (4-oz.) boneless, skinless chicken thighs
- 2   medium red onions, sliced into 1/2-inch-thick rings
- 1   (10-oz.) pkg. yellow rice, prepared according to pkg. directions
- 2   medium (6 oz. each) avocados, diced (about 2 1/2 cups)
      Chopped fresh cilantro, for garnish
      Lime wedges

1. Stir together orange juice, oregano, oil, lemon juice, lime juice, garlic, jalapeño, and 1 teaspoon of the salt in a large bowl. Add chicken; toss to coat. Cover bowl with plastic wrap; chill 1 hour.

2. Preheat a gas grill to medium-high (400°F to 450°F). Place onion rings on oiled grates. Grill, uncovered, until charred on both sides, 6 to 8 minutes total. Coarsely chop charred onions. Transfer to a medium bowl; cover with plastic wrap, and set aside.

3. Using tongs, transfer chicken from marinade to a plate, letting excess drip off (discard marinade). Sprinkle chicken evenly with remaining 1 teaspoon salt. Using tongs, transfer chicken to oiled grates. Grill, uncovered, until a thermometer inserted in thickest portion of thigh registers 165°F, 6 to 7 minutes per side. Transfer chicken to a clean plate; let rest 5 minutes.

4. Divide rice, avocados, onions, and chicken among 4 bowls. Garnish with cilantro, and serve with lime wedges.

Curried Chicken Thighs with Charred-Vegetable Rice

ACTIVE 30 MIN. - TOTAL 45 MIN.
SERVES 4

1½ tsp. curry powder
½ tsp. garlic powder
½ tsp. paprika
3 tsp. kosher salt, divided
8 (6-oz.) bone-in, skin-on chicken thighs
4 medium (6 oz. each) shucked ears fresh bicolored corn
1 large (12-oz.) zucchini, halved lengthwise
1 large (9-oz.) yellow squash, halved lengthwise
1 large (8-oz.) red bell pepper
1 medium (8-oz.) red onion, sliced into quarters
3 Tbsp. olive oil, divided

1 (8.8-oz.) pkg. precooked microwavable white rice, prepared according to pkg. directions
¼ cup coarsely chopped fresh cilantro
1 tsp. fresh lime juice (from 1 lime)
½ tsp. black pepper

1. Whisk together curry powder, garlic powder, paprika, and 2 teaspoons of the salt in a small bowl. Sprinkle evenly over chicken thighs.
2. Preheat a gas grill to medium (350°F to 400°F). Place chicken, skin-side down, on unoiled grates. Grill, uncovered, until grill marks appear and skin is golden brown and slightly charred, 8 to 10 minutes. Turn chicken; cover grill. Grill until a thermometer inserted in thickest portion of meat registers 165°F, 10 to 12 minutes. Transfer chicken to a plate or cutting

board. Tent with aluminum foil, and rest about 10 minutes.
3. Meanwhile, toss together corn, zucchini, squash, bell pepper, red onion, and 2 tablespoons of the olive oil in a large bowl. Place vegetables on unoiled grates. Grill, uncovered, turning occasionally, until charred on all sides, 6 to 8 minutes. Transfer vegetables to a baking sheet; let stand until cool enough to handle, 6 to 8 minutes.
4. Cut corn kernels from cobs; place kernels in a large bowl, and discard cobs. Roughly chop zucchini, squash, and onion; add to bowl. Chop bell pepper, discarding seeds and membrane; add to bowl. Add rice, cilantro, lime juice, black pepper, and remaining 1 teaspoon salt and 1 tablespoon oil; toss to coat. Divide vegetable mixture and chicken among 4 plates.

Grilled Lemon Chicken with Herb Couscous

ACTIVE 45 MIN. - TOTAL 45 MIN.,
PLUS 1 HOUR CHILLING

SERVES 4

- 1 (4-lb.) whole chicken, cut into 6 pieces (leg quarters, breasts, and wings)
- 2 medium garlic cloves, minced
- 2 Tbsp. Dijon mustard
- 1 Tbsp. honey
- 2 tsp. lemon zest plus ½ cup fresh juice (from 3 lemons)
- ¾ cup plus 2 Tbsp. olive oil
- 1 tsp. black pepper
- 2 tsp. kosher salt, divided
- 2 cups uncooked Israeli couscous
- 2 lemons, halved crosswise
- 2 small cucumbers, chopped (2 cups)
- ¼ cup chopped fresh flat-leaf parsley
- 2 Tbsp. chopped fresh mint

1. Cut chicken wings at joints, separating flats, drumettes, and tips. Discard tips. Set aside 8 remaining chicken pieces. Stir together garlic, mustard, honey, and lemon zest and juice. Whisk in oil until emulsified. Whisk in pepper and 1 teaspoon of the salt.

2. Place chicken in a large bowl. Add ¾ cup garlic-lemon mixture (reserving remaining mixture in a separate bowl); toss to coat. Cover bowl with plastic wrap; chill 1 hour.

3. Meanwhile, bring a large pot of water to a boil over high. Add couscous, and return to a boil. Reduce heat to medium. Simmer, stirring occasionally, until couscous is tender, about 10 minutes. Drain; transfer to a large bowl. Cool 10 minutes. Add remaining ¾ cup garlic-lemon mixture to couscous; toss to coat. Cover; chill until ready to serve or up to 1 day.

4. Preheat a gas grill to medium (350°F to 400°F). Using tongs, transfer chicken from marinade to a plate, letting excess drip off (discard marinade). Sprinkle evenly with ½ teaspoon of the salt. Using tongs, transfer chicken to unoiled grates, skin-sides down. Grill, uncovered, until a thermometer inserted in thickest portion of thighs registers 165°F (13 to 14 minutes per side for legs and breasts and 10 minutes per side for wings). Add lemon halves, cut-sides down, to grates while chicken cooks; grill until charred, 2 minutes. Let chicken rest 10 minutes.

5. Stir cucumbers, parsley, mint, and remaining ½ teaspoon salt into couscous mixture. Divide couscous, chicken, and charred lemons among 4 plates.

MAKE IT AHEAD

Prepare the couscous and marinade a day in advance, and chill. Add the remaining garlic-lemon mixture to the chicken an hour before you plan to grill it. Stir in the cucumbers, herbs, and extra salt just before serving.

Greek Chicken Pita Sandwiches

ACTIVE 25 MIN. - TOTAL 25 MIN.,
PLUS 1 HOUR MARINATING
SERVES 6

¼ cup olive oil
3 medium garlic cloves, finely chopped (about 1 Tbsp.)
2 tsp. chopped fresh oregano
1½ tsp. kosher salt
½ tsp. black pepper
½ tsp. lemon zest, plus 1 Tbsp. fresh juice (from 1 lemon), divided
4 (8-oz.) boneless, skinless chicken breasts
6 (8-in.) pita rounds
¾ cup refrigerated tzatziki
6 romaine lettuce leaves (from 1 small head)
1½ cups multicolor cherry tomatoes, halved
1 small red onion, thinly sliced (about 1 cup)

1. Stir together oil, garlic, oregano, salt, pepper, and lemon zest in a large bowl. Add chicken, and turn to coat. Cover and refrigerate 1 hour.
2. Preheat grill to medium-high (400°F to 450°F). Remove chicken from marinade; discard marinade. Place on unoiled grates. Grill, uncovered, until a thermometer inserted in thickest portion of meat registers 165°F, 6 to 8 minutes per side. Transfer chicken to a cutting board; drizzle with lemon juice. Rest 5 minutes or up to 20 minutes. Cut crosswise into ¾-inch slices.
3. While chicken rests, place pita rounds on unoiled grates. Grill, uncovered, over medium-high until warmed and slightly charred, about 2 minutes per side. Remove from grill; spread 2 tablespoons tzatziki over each pita.
4. Divide lettuce, tomatoes, onion, and sliced chicken evenly among pitas.

SUPERMARKET SHORTCUT

Look for refrigerated tzatziki in the produce section of your grocery store near the hummus. Our Test Kitchen recommends the Cedar's brand, a deliciously thick and creamy blend of yogurt, cucumber, garlic, and dill.

Grilled Chicken Salad with Blueberries, Goat Cheese, and Pickled Onion

ACTIVE 35 MIN. · TOTAL 40 MIN.
SERVES 4

- 1 cup red wine vinegar
- ½ cup packed light brown sugar
- 3 whole cloves
- 1 Tbsp. plus 1½ tsp. kosher salt, divided
- 1 small red onion, thinly sliced (about 1½ cups)
- ½ tsp. black pepper
- 7 Tbsp. olive oil, divided
- 4 (8-oz.) boneless, skinless chicken breasts
- 1 tsp. Dijon mustard
- ½ tsp. fresh lemon juice (from 1 lemon)
- 8 oz. spring mix salad greens
- 8 oz. goat cheese, crumbled (about 2 cups)
- 1 (6-oz.) pkg. fresh blueberries
- 1 cup candied pecans

1. Whisk together vinegar, sugar, cloves, and 1 tablespoon of the salt in a medium saucepan. Bring to a boil over medium-high. Continue boiling, stirring occasionally, until sugar and salt dissolve, about 5 minutes. Place onion slices in a medium-size heatproof bowl, and pour hot vinegar mixture over onion. Let cool completely to room temperature, about 30 minutes.

2. Meanwhile, stir together pepper, 2 tablespoons of the oil, and remaining 1½ teaspoons salt in a small bowl. Brush mixture evenly over chicken breasts. Preheat a gas grill to medium-high (400°F to 450°F). Place chicken on unoiled grates. Grill, uncovered, until a thermometer inserted in thickest portion of meat registers 165°F, 7 to 8 minutes per side. Transfer chicken to a cutting board, and rest 10 minutes. Cut into ¾-inch slices.

3. Measure 3 tablespoons onion-pickling liquid into a medium bowl. Add mustard, lemon juice, and remaining 5 tablespoons oil; whisk until smooth. Place salad greens in a large bowl; add mustard mixture, goat cheese, blueberries, and pecans. Toss to coat. Drain remaining pickling liquid from onion; discard liquid and cloves. Add onion to salad; toss to combine. Divide evenly among 4 bowls; top with sliced chicken.

BRING ON THE BERRIES
Fresh blueberries add a pop of color and sweetness to this salad, but for extra tang, you can substitute homemade Pickled Berries (recipe, p. 138).

This Calls for Crab

Elevate happy hour with a rich and creamy dip

Hot Crab-and-Artichoke Dip

ACTIVE 15 MIN. - TOTAL 45 MIN.
SERVES 4

- 2 oz. cream cheese
- ¼ cup mayonnaise
- 2 scallions, chopped (about 3 Tbsp.)
- ¾ tsp. Old Bay seasoning
- ¾ tsp. Worcestershire sauce
- ¾ tsp. hot sauce (optional)
- 1 tsp. lemon zest, plus 1 Tbsp. fresh juice (from 1 lemon), divided
- ½ cup finely chopped artichoke hearts (from 1 [14-oz.] can)
- 4 oz. lump crabmeat, drained, picked over, and squeezed dry
- 1 oz. low-moisture mozzarella cheese, shredded (about ¼ cup)
- ¾ cup shredded Parmesan cheese (2 oz.), divided
  Crackers and Belgian endive leaves, for serving

1. Preheat oven to 350°F. Lightly coat a 1-quart gratin baking dish with cooking spray. Microwave cream cheese in a large microwavable bowl on HIGH until very soft, about 20 seconds. Stir in mayonnaise, scallions, Old Bay, Worcestershire sauce, hot sauce (if desired), and lemon zest until well blended. Gently fold in lemon juice, artichokes, crabmeat, mozzarella, and ⅔ cup of the Parmesan. Spread mixture evenly in prepared baking dish; sprinkle with remaining Parmesan (about 1½ tablespoons).

2. Bake in preheated oven until dip is hot throughout and bubbly around edges, about 25 minutes. Let stand 5 minutes. Serve with crackers and endive leaves.

SEAFOOD SMARTS

For the best-tasting dip, look for freshly picked unpasteurized crabmeat at your local seafood counter. Your second-best option is frozen fresh crabmeat. Avoid the canned kind; it is pasteurized to have a longer shelf life and doesn't have as much flavor or aroma as the fresh stuff.

Skillet Shrimp

There's no catch—this seafood supper is easy and delicious

One-Pan Shrimp Destin with Orzo

ACTIVE 35 MIN. · TOTAL 35 MIN.
SERVES 4

- 1 bunch scallions
- 12 oz. medium peeled, deveined raw shrimp
- 2 tsp. lemon zest (from 1 lemon)
- 1½ tsp. kosher salt, divided
- 2 Tbsp. olive oil
- 3 garlic cloves, minced (about 1 Tbsp.)
- 2 cups uncooked orzo (1 lb.)
- ⅔ cup (5⅓ oz.) dry white wine
- 3½ cups vegetable stock
- 2 Tbsp. chopped fresh flat-leaf parsley
- 2 Tbsp. chopped fresh dill

1. Slice dark green scallion tops to equal ¼ cup; slice light green and white bottoms to equal ½ cup. Set aside, keeping scallion parts separate. (Reserve the remaining scallions for another use.) Toss together shrimp, lemon zest, and ½ teaspoon of the kosher salt in a large bowl.

2. Heat oil in a large, deep skillet over medium. Add garlic and scallion bottoms. Cook, stirring often, until translucent, 3 minutes. Add orzo; cook, stirring often, until lightly toasted, 2 minutes. Stir in wine. Cook, stirring constantly, 1 minute. Add stock and remaining 1 teaspoon salt; bring to a simmer over medium-high.

3. Cover and reduce heat to low. Cook, undisturbed, until orzo is tender, about 12 minutes, adding shrimp during final 3 minutes of cook time. Remove pan from heat. Sprinkle evenly with scallion tops, parsley, and dill.

Twirl Up Your Pasta Salad

Pair your favorite noodles with seasonal fresh produce

Pasta Salad with Lemon Vinaigrette, Herbs, and Field Peas

ACTIVE 15 MIN. · TOTAL 30 MIN.
SERVES 8

Whisk together ¼ cup **fresh lemon juice** plus 1 tsp. **lemon zest**, 1 Tbsp. **Dijon mustard**, 2 tsp. **honey**, 1½ tsp. **kosher salt**, ½ tsp. **black pepper**, and 1 pressed **garlic clove** in a small bowl; slowly whisk in ⅓ cup **extra-virgin olive oil**. Stir together 8 oz. **pasta** (cooked, drained, and rinsed with cold water), 3 cups **fresh or frozen field peas** (cooked, drained, and cooled), 1 cup halved **cherry tomatoes**, and 3 Tbsp. each chopped **fresh basil**, **chives**, **dill**, and **flat-leaf parsley** in a large bowl. Add vinaigrette, and gently toss to combine. Serve at room temperature, or cover and chill.

CALORIES: **250** – CARBS: **34G** – FAT: **10G**

Three More Salad Spin-Offs

Tangy Chickpea
Prepare vinaigrette and pasta as directed. Combine with 1 cubed and roasted **eggplant**, 4 oz. **feta cheese**, 1 (15½-oz.) can **chickpeas** (drained and rinsed), and 1 cup chopped **Peppadew peppers**.

CALORIES: **342** – CARBS: **43G** – FAT: **14G**

Pintos and Peppers
Prepare vinaigrette and pasta as directed. Combine with 1 charred and chopped **poblano chile**, 1 cup charred **corn kernels**, 1 (15½-oz.) can **pinto beans** (drained and rinsed), and 3 Tbsp. each chopped **scallions** and **cilantro**.

CALORIES: **284** – CARBS: **33G** – FAT: **11G**

Dilly Bean
Prepare vinaigrette and pasta as directed. Combine with 2 cups blanched **green and wax beans**, ¼ cup sliced toasted **almonds**, and 2 Tbsp. chopped **dill**.

CALORIES: **221** – CARBS: **39G** – FAT: **11G**

Fritta-da!

Enjoy this two-bite fix-and-freeze breakfast on the go

Mini Hash Brown Frittatas

ACTIVE 15 MIN. · TOTAL 1 HOUR, 15 MIN.
MAKES 12

Baking spray with flour

1 (20-oz.) pkg. refrigerated shredded hash browns

10 oz. sharp cheddar cheese, shredded (about 2½ cups), divided

1 (10-oz.) pkg. frozen chopped spinach, thawed

1 Tbsp. unsalted butter

1 small onion, minced (about 1 cup)

6 large eggs

¾ cup half-and-half

2½ tsp. kosher salt

½ tsp. black pepper

½ cup quartered cherry tomatoes (from 1 pint tomatoes)

1. Preheat oven to 375°F. Coat a 12-cup muffin pan with baking spray. Toss together hash browns and 2 cups of the cheese in a large bowl until combined. Spoon hash brown mixture evenly into prepared pan, filling all cavities (about ½ cup each), pressing up and around sides to form a cup. Bake until edges are golden and crispy, about 30 minutes.
2. Meanwhile, place spinach in a clean kitchen towel; squeeze to remove liquid. Melt butter in a medium skillet over medium-high. Add onion. Cook, stirring occasionally, until translucent and tender, about 5 minutes. Reduce heat to low. Add spinach, and cook, stirring occasionally, just until spinach is warmed and combined with onion, about 1 minute. Remove from heat and set aside until ready to use.
3. Remove baked hash brown cups from oven, and spoon 1 heaping tablespoon onion-spinach mixture into bottom of each cup. Whisk together eggs, half-and-half, salt, and pepper in a large bowl until eggs are beaten and mixture is well combined. Carefully pour evenly into hash brown cups to cover onion-spinach mixture. Top evenly with tomatoes, and sprinkle with remaining ½ cup cheese.
4. Bake in preheated oven until eggs are set and hash browns are crispy and browned, about 30 minutes. Remove from oven; cool on a wire rack 5 minutes. Serve warm.

MAKE THEM AHEAD

Place cooked, cooled frittatas in a zip-top plastic bag, and press out air before sealing and freezing. To reheat, thaw in the refrigerator; then remove from the bag, and microwave 1 minute or bake at 350°F until heated through, 5 minutes.

IN SEASON

A Fresh Idea for Fruit

Sweet-tart Pickled Berries brighten up salads, cocktails, and cheese boards

Pickled Berries

ACTIVE 15 MIN. - TOTAL 35 MIN., PLUS 4 HOURS CHILLING
MAKES ABOUT 8 CUPS

Stir together 2½ cups **white distilled vinegar**, 1⅓ cups **water**, 2 Tbsp. **honey**, 2 tsp. **kosher salt**, 1 tsp. **black peppercorns**, and 4 (2-inch) **lemon peel strips** in a medium saucepan over high. Bring to a boil, stirring often until honey is dissolved. Boil 1 minute. Remove from heat; stir in 3 cups **ice cubes**. Cool 20 minutes. Divide 8 cups **fresh berries** (such as blackberries, raspberries, or hulled and halved strawberries) between 2 (1-quart) canning jars or 4 pint jars. Pour room-temperature vinegar mixture evenly over fruit. Cover; refrigerate at least 4 hours or up to 2 days.

KITCHEN TIPS

Pasta Salad Pointers

Three secrets to the best summer side

KEEP NOODLES COOL (NOT COLD)

Rinse the just-cooked pasta under cold water until it's lukewarm. Hot pasta will absorb too much of the dressing. If it's cold, it won't absorb enough.

DRESS IT NOW AND LATER

If you're preparing dinner in advance, toss the noodles in half of the dressing and reserve the rest in the refrigerator. Add the remaining dressing when you are ready to serve it.

CHECK THE SEASONING

Pasta salad that's served straight from the fridge often needs a little extra flavor, so you might want to taste it and add more salt.

TASTE TEST

Spice Up Your Chicken

Southern-made seasoning blends make poultry extra flavorful

CITRUSY
This all-purpose seasoning salt is jazzed up with onion, garlic, and a hint of citrus. White Magic Seasoning; misrubins.com

TANGY
The rich, zesty blend is made with tomato and balsamic vinegar powders and garlic. Modena Balsamic Rub; spicewalla.com

SPICY
Chipotle peppers, smoked paprika, sugar, and fennel add savory-sweet heat. Fire & Smoke Society Wicked Winona; walmart.com

Our Favorite Grilling Recipes

Where there's fire, there's smoke, and that means flavor. There's something magical about the effect fire has on food–whether it's a juicy burger with a beautiful caramelized exterior, a crisp-crusted pizza cooked in the style of a wood-fired oven (without having to have one!), or a batch of fresh oysters, bubbling in a briny and delicious poaching liquid of oyster liquor, butter, garlic, and herbs. A bonus: Cooking in the outdoors works up an appetite, so light a fire and get grilling!

GRILLED CHIPOTLE CHICKEN
(PAGE 143)

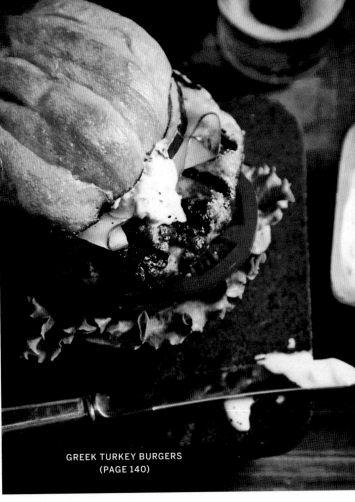

GREEK TURKEY BURGERS
(PAGE 140)

Burgers

Bacon-Wrapped Barbecue Burgers

Don't skip the step to precook the bacon in the microwave. It helps crisp it up to perfection on the grill.

ACTIVE 45 MIN. · TOTAL 1 HOUR
SERVES 4

8 center-cut bacon slices
1 (4.5-oz.) jar sliced mushrooms, drained and chopped
1 small Vidalia or sweet onion, chopped (about ½ cup)
2 tsp. olive oil
½ cup bottled honey barbecue sauce, divided
1½ lb. ground beef
Wooden picks
¼ tsp. table salt
4 sesame-seed hamburger buns, toasted

1. Arrange bacon on a paper towel-lined microwave-safe plate; cover with a paper towel. Microwave bacon at HIGH 2 minutes or until edges begin to crinkle and bacon is partially cooked.
2. Sauté mushrooms and onion in hot oil in a small nonstick skillet over medium heat 4 to 5 minutes, or until tender and liquid is absorbed. Remove from heat, and stir in 2 tablespoons barbecue sauce.
3. Preheat grill to medium-high (350°F to 400°F). Shape ground beef into 8 (5-inch) thin patties. Place 2 tablespoons mushroom mixture in center of each of 4 patties. Top with remaining patties, pressing edges to seal. Shape into 4-inch patties. Wrap sides of each patty with 2 bacon slices, overlapping ends. Secure bacon using wooden picks. Sprinkle patties with salt. Cover and chill 10 minutes.
4. Grill patties, covered with grill lid, 5 to 6 minutes on 1 side. Turn and baste with half of remaining barbecue sauce. Grill 5 to 6 minutes or until beef is no longer pink in center. Turn and baste with remaining barbecue sauce. Remove from grill, and let stand 5 minutes. Remove wooden picks. Serve burgers on buns topped with remaining mushroom mixture.

Carolina Chicken Burgers with Ancho Slaw

Try this healthy burger option at your next backyard barbecue. Your guests will love it.

ACTIVE 20 MIN. · TOTAL 1 HOUR, 5 MIN., INCLUDING SAUCE AND SLAW
SERVES 6

2 lb. lean ground chicken breast
⅓ cup mayonnaise
1 Tbsp. coarse-grain Dijon mustard
1 tsp. kosher salt
½ tsp. freshly ground black pepper
6 sesame-seed hamburger buns
Carolina Burger Sauce (recipe follows)
Creamy Ancho Slaw (recipe follows)
Dill pickle slices

1. Preheat grill to medium-high (350°F to 400°F). Gently combine ground chicken, mayonnaise, mustard, salt, and pepper in a large bowl. Shape mixture into 6 patties.
2. Grill patties, covered with grill lid, 5 to 6 minutes on each side or until a meat thermometer inserted into thickest portion registers 165°F. Grill buns 1 minute on each side or until toasted. Spread Carolina Burger Sauce on bottom half of each bun. Top with patties, Creamy Ancho Slaw, pickles, and top halves of buns.

Carolina Burger Sauce

ACTIVE 20 MIN. · TOTAL 20 MIN.
MAKES ABOUT 1 CUP

Stir together ¾ cup **ketchup**; ⅓ cup **apple cider vinegar**; ¼ cup **coarse-grain Dijon mustard**; 1 large **shallot**, minced; 1 tablespoon **dark brown sugar**; and ¼ teaspoon **crushed red pepper** in a medium saucepan. Bring to a boil over medium; reduce heat to low, and simmer, stirring occasionally, 8 to 10 minutes or until thickened. Season with **kosher salt** and **freshly ground black pepper**. Refrigerate in an airtight container up to 2 weeks.

Creamy Ancho Slaw

ACTIVE 10 MIN. · TOTAL 25 MIN.
SERVES 6

Whisk together ½ cup **mayonnaise**, 2 tablespoons **apple cider vinegar**, 1¼ teaspoons **ancho chile powder**, and 1 teaspoon **granulated sugar** in a large bowl. Add ½ small head **savoy cabbage**, shredded or finely chopped; 1 **large celery rib**, chopped; and ½ cup grated **carrot**. Toss to coat, and add **kosher salt** and **freshly ground black pepper** to taste. Let stand 15 minutes before serving, tossing occasionally.

Greek Turkey Burgers

(Photo, page 139)

Traditional Greek flavors make this burger a real winner!

ACTIVE 25 MIN. · TOTAL 25 MIN.
SERVES 4

1⅓ lb. ground turkey breast
1 (4-oz.) package crumbled feta cheese
¼ cup finely chopped red onion
1 tsp. dried oregano
1 tsp. lemon zest (from 1 lemon)
1 tsp. table salt, divided
½ cup grated English cucumber
1 (6-oz.) container fat-free Greek yogurt
1 Tbsp. chopped fresh mint
4 French bread hamburger buns, split and toasted
Toppings: lettuce leaves, tomato slices, thinly sliced cucumber, sliced red onion rings

1. Stir together ground turkey, feta, onion, oregano, lemon zest, and ½ teaspoon salt. Shape mixture into 4 (½-inch-thick) patties.
2. Heat a grill pan over medium-high heat. Coat grill pan with cooking spray. Add patties; cook 5 minutes on each side or until done.
3. Stir together cucumber, yogurt, mint, and the remaining ½ teaspoon salt in a small bowl. Serve burgers on buns with cucumber sauce and desired toppings.

CLOCKWISE FROM TOP LEFT:

- BACON-WRAPPED
BARBECUE BURGERS (LEFT)

- CAROLINA CHICKEN BURGERS WITH
ANCHO SLAW (LEFT)

- GRILLED CHICKEN WINGS (PAGE 142)

- SWEET TEA-BRINED CHICKEN (PAGE 143)

- GRILLED CHICKEN THIGHS WITH WHITE
BARBECUE SAUCE (PAGE 142)

- GREEK PIZZA WITH CHICKEN
AND ARTICHOKES (PAGE 144)

- GRILLED SAUSAGE SALAD PIZZA
(PAGE 143)

- GRILLED TOMATO-PEACH PIZZA
(PAGE 143)

Chicken

Ginger "Beer Can" Chicken

Spray the aluminum cans with vegetable cooking spray for easy removal.

ACTIVE 15 MIN. - TOTAL 2 HOURS, 10 MIN., INCLUDING GLAZE
SERVES 8 TO 10

- 1 (13- x 9-inch) disposable aluminum baking pan
- 2 Tbsp. kosher salt
- 2 tsp. paprika
- 2 tsp. granulated sugar
- 1 tsp. black pepper
- ¾ tsp. ground ginger
- ½ tsp. cayenne pepper
- 2 (3½- to 4-lb.) whole chickens
- 2 (12-oz.) cans ginger ale
  Ginger Ale Glaze (recipe follows)

1. Light 1 side of grill, heating to medium-high to high (400°F to 475°F); leave other side unlit, placing disposable baking pan under grate. Stir together salt and next 5 ingredients; sprinkle mixture inside cavity and on outside of each chicken.
2. Reserve ¾ cup ginger ale from each can to contribute to the 2 cups needed in the Ginger Ale Glaze. Place chickens upright onto each can, fitting can into cavity. Pull legs forward.
3. Pour water to a depth of 1 inch into disposable pan. Place chickens upright on unlit side of grill above pan. Grill, covered with grill lid and rotating chickens occasionally, 1 hour and 20 minutes to 1 hour and 30 minutes or until golden and a meat thermometer inserted in thickest portion registers 165°F. Let stand 10 minutes. Remove chickens from cans, and carve. Serve with Ginger Ale Glaze.

Ginger Ale Glaze

ACTIVE 10 MIN. - TOTAL 25 MIN.
MAKES ABOUT ¼ CUP

- 2 cups ginger ale
- 2 Tbsp. light brown sugar
- 2 Tbsp. grated fresh ginger
- ⅛ tsp. cayenne pepper

Stir together all ingredients in a saucepan. Bring to a boil over high; reduce heat to medium. Cook, stirring occasionally, 15 to 20 minutes or until reduced to ¼ cup.

Grilled Chicken Thighs with White Barbecue Sauce

(Photo, page 141)

The secret that takes this dish to the next level is the white barbecue sauce, an Alabama original.

ACTIVE 10 MIN. - TOTAL 30 MIN., PLUS 4 HOURS CHILLING AND BARBECUE SAUCE
SERVES 5

- 1 Tbsp. dried thyme
- 1 Tbsp. dried oregano
- 1 Tbsp. ground cumin
- 1 Tbsp. paprika
- 1 tsp. onion powder
- ½ tsp. table salt
- ½ tsp. freshly ground black pepper
- 10 bone-in, skin-on chicken thighs (about 3 lb.)
  White Barbecue Sauce (recipe follows)

1. Combine first thyme, oregano, cumin, paprika, onion powder, salt, and pepper until blended. Rinse chicken, and pat dry; rub seasoning mixture over chicken. Place chicken in a zip-top plastic freezer bag. Seal and chill 4 hours.
2. Preheat grill to medium-high (350°F to 400°F). Remove chicken from bag, discarding bag.
3. Grill chicken, covered with grill lid, 8 to 10 minutes on each side or until a meat thermometer inserted into thickest portion registers 165°. Serve with White Barbecue Sauce.

White Barbecue Sauce

The famous creamy and tangy sauce from Big Bob Gibson's barbecue restaurant in north Alabama is the best way to spice up smoked chicken.

ACTIVE 5 MIN. - TOTAL 5 MIN.
MAKES 1½ CUPS

- 1 cup mayonnaise
- ⅓ cup apple cider vinegar
- 1 tsp. Worcestershire sauce
- ½ tsp. kosher salt
- ½ tsp. garlic powder
- ½ tsp. onion powder
- ½ tsp. freshly ground black pepper
- ¼ tsp. hot sauce

Stir together mayonnaise, vinegar, and 1 tablespoon water and the remaining ingredients in a small bowl. Serve immediately, or refrigerate in an airtight container for up to 3 days.

Grilled Chicken Wings

(Photo, page 141)

Choose a Honey Drizzle to suit any taste.

ACTIVE 35 MIN. - TOTAL 35 MIN.
SERVES 6 TO 8

- 2 lb. chicken wings
- 2 Tbsp. olive oil
- 1½ tsp. kosher salt
- ½ tsp. freshly ground black pepper
  Honey Drizzle of choice (recipes follow)

1. Preheat grill to medium-high (350°F to 400°F). Toss together wings and oil in a large bowl. Sprinkle with salt and pepper; toss to coat.
2. Grill wings, covered with grill lid, 25 to 30 minutes or until skin is crisp and wings are done, turning occasionally. Toss with desired Honey Drizzle.

Cider Vinegar–Brown Butter Honey Drizzle

ACTIVE 15 MIN. - TOTAL 15 MIN.
MAKES ABOUT ¾ CUP

- ¼ cup butter
- ½ cup honey
- 1 Tbsp. apple cider vinegar

1. Cook butter in a saucepan over medium-high 5 minutes or until brown and fragrant. Transfer to a small bowl, and cool 5 minutes.
2. Cook honey and vinegar in a saucepan over medium heat, stirring often, 2 minutes or until thoroughly heated. Whisk in browned butter.

Horseradish–Honey Mustard Drizzle

ACTIVE 5 MIN. - TOTAL 5 MIN.
MAKES ABOUT ¾ CUP

- ½ cup honey
- 3 Tbsp. prepared horseradish
- 2 Tbsp. coarse-grain mustard

Cook honey, horseradish, and mustard in a small saucepan over medium, stirring often, 2 minutes or until thoroughly heated.

Cracked Pepper-Rosemary Honey Drizzle

ACTIVE 5 MIN. - TOTAL 5 MIN.
MAKES ABOUT ½ CUP

- ½ cup honey
- 1 tsp. cracked black pepper
- 1 (3-inch) fresh rosemary sprig

Cook honey, 2 tablespoons water, pepper, and rosemary sprig in a saucepan over medium, stirring often, 2 minutes or until thoroughly heated. Discard rosemary.

Chili-Lemon Honey Drizzle

ACTIVE 5 MIN. - TOTAL 5 MIN.
MAKES ABOUT 1 CUP

- ½ cup honey
- ¼ cup bottled chili sauce
- 2 Tbsp. fresh lemon juice

Cook honey, chili sauce, and lemon juice over medium, stirring often, 2 minutes or until thoroughly heated.

Grilled Chipotle Chicken

(Photo, page 139)
You'll never want plain grilled chicken again!

ACTIVE 10 MIN. - TOTAL 20 MINUTES
SERVES 4

- 2 lb. skinned and boned chicken thighs
- 2 Tbsp. firmly packed light brown sugar
- ½ tsp. dried oregano
- ½ tsp. ground chipotle chile pepper
- ½ tsp. kosher salt

1. Preheat grill to medium-high (350°F to 400°F). Place each chicken thigh between 2 sheets of heavy-duty plastic wrap, and flatten to ¼-inch thickness, using a rolling pin or flat side of a meat mallet. Combine sugar, oregano, chile pepper, and salt; rub over chicken.
2. Grill chicken, covered with grill lid, 2 to 3 minutes on each side or until done. Remove from grill, and cover with aluminum foil until ready to serve.

Sweet Tea-Brined Chicken

(Photo, page 141)
This just might be the finest chicken ever to come off our Test Kitchen grill.

ACTIVE 30 MIN. - TOTAL 1 DAY, 2 HOURS, 35 MIN., INCLUDING 1 DAY CHILLING
SERVES 6 TO 8

- 2 family-size tea bags
- ½ cup packed light brown sugar
- ¼ cup kosher salt
- 1 Tbsp. black pepper
- 1 small sweet onion, thinly sliced
- 1 lemon, thinly sliced
- 3 garlic cloves, halved
- 2 rosemary sprigs
- 2 cups ice cubes
- 1 (3½- to 4-lb.) whole chicken, cut up

1. Bring 4 cups water to a boil in a 3-quart heavy saucepan over medium-high; add tea bags. Remove from heat; cover and steep 10 minutes.
2. Discard tea bags. Add brown sugar, salt, pepper, onion, lemon, garlic, and rosemary sprigs; stir until sugar dissolves. Cool completely, about 45 minutes. Stir in ice.
3. Place chicken and tea mixture in a large zip-top plastic freezer bag; seal. Place bag in a shallow baking dish, and chill 24 hours, turning occasionally.
4. Preheat grill to low (300°F to 350°F) with an area cleared of coals or a burner turned off. Remove chicken from marinade; discard marinade. Pat chicken dry with paper towels. Grill chicken, covered, over indirect heat until done, 40 to 50 minutes. Transfer chicken, skin-side down, to direct heat area, and grill until skin is crispy, 2 to 3 minutes. Let stand 5 minutes.

Pizza

Grilled Sausage Salad Pizza

(Photo, page 141)
Dinner is complete with this equal parts salad and pizza combo.

ACTIVE 10 MIN. - TOTAL: 45 MIN.
MAKES 1 (12-INCH) PIZZA

- 1 medium sweet onion, cut into ¼-inch-thick slices
- 3 Tbsp. olive oil, divided

- ½ lb. smoked link sausage
- 1 (12-inch) prebaked Italian pizza crust
- 6 oz. mozzarella cheese, freshly shredded (1½ cups)
- 1¼ tsp. kosher salt, divided
- 1 cup firmly packed arugula
- ½ cup fresh flat-leaf parsley
- ½ tsp. freshly ground black pepper
- 1 lemon, halved

1. Preheat grill to medium-high (350°F to 400°F). Brush onion with 1 tablespoon oil. Grill onion, covered with grill lid, 6 minutes on each side. Grill sausage 4 minutes on each side; slice.
2. Brush pizza crust with 1 tablespoon oil. Grill crust, oil-side down, 2 minutes. Turn crust over, and brush with remaining 1 tablespoon oil; sprinkle with cheese and ¼ teaspoon salt. Grill 2 minutes or until cheese melts.
3. Toss together arugula, parsley, pepper, sausage, onion, and remaining 1 teaspoon salt. Top pizza with salad; squeeze lemon juice over salad. Serve immediately.

Grilled Tomato-Peach Pizza

(Photo, page 141)
This fresh-tasting pizza uses convenient store-bought dough to get dinner on the table in a flash.

ACTIVE 10 MIN. - TOTAL 30 MIN.
MAKES 1 (14-INCH) PIZZA

- 2 tomatoes, sliced
- ½ tsp. table salt
- 1 large peach, peeled and sliced
- 1 lb. bakery pizza dough
- ½ (16-oz.) pkg. fresh mozzarella, sliced
- 6 to 7 fresh basil leaves

1. Coat cold cooking grate of grill with cooking spray, and place on grill. Preheat grill to medium (300°F to 350°F).
2. Sprinkle tomatoes with salt; let stand 15 minutes. Pat tomatoes dry with paper towels.
3. Grill peach slices, covered with grill lid, 2 to 3 minutes on each side or until grill marks appear.
4. Place dough on a large baking sheet coated with cooking spray; lightly coat dough with cooking spray. Roll dough to ¼-inch thickness (about 14 inches in diameter). Slide pizza dough from baking sheet onto cooking grate.

Recipe continued on page 144

Recipe continued from page 143

5. Grill, covered with grill lid, 2 to 3 minutes or until lightly browned. Turn dough over, and reduce temperature to low (250°F to 300°F); top with tomatoes, grilled peaches, and mozzarella. Grill, covered with grill lid, 5 minutes or until cheese melts. Arrange basil leaves over pizza. Serve immediately.

Greek Pizza with Chicken and Artichokes

(Photo, page 141)

Bypass the pizza parlor and grill up your own. This calls for homemade dough, but you can also pick up some from the bakery.

ACTIVE 20 MIN. · TOTAL 1 HOUR, 15 MIN., INCLUDING DOUGH

MAKES 1 (14-INCH) PIZZA

- 1 (6-oz.) jar marinated artichoke hearts, drained and coarsely chopped
- 1 (4-oz.) jar roasted red peppers, drained and cut into strips
- 10 Kalamata olives, drained, pitted, and thinly sliced
- 1 Tbsp. olive oil
- 1½ Tbsp. chopped fresh oregano
- ½ tsp. freshly ground black pepper
- ½ recipe Brick Oven Pizza Dough (recipe follows)
- 4 oz. mozzarella cheese, shredded, divided (1 cup)
- 2 cups chopped cooked chicken
- 4 oz. feta cheese, crumbled (²/₃ cup)

1. Coat cold cooking grate of grill with cooking spray. Preheat grill to medium (300°F to 350°F).
2. Combine artichoke hearts, red peppers, olives, oil, oregano, and black pepper in a bowl; toss gently.
3. Place dough on a large baking sheet coated with cooking spray; lightly coat dough with cooking spray. Roll dough to ¼-inch thickness (about 14 inches in diameter). Slide pizza dough from baking sheet onto cooking grate.
4. Grill, covered with grill lid, 2 to 3 minutes or until lightly browned. Turn dough over, and reduce temperature to low (250°F to 300°F); top with ¾ cup mozzarella cheese and chicken.
5. Spoon artichoke mixture evenly over chicken. Sprinkle with remaining ¼ cup mozzarella cheese; top with feta cheese. Grill, covered with grill lid, 5 minutes or until cheese melts. Serve immediately.

Brick Oven Pizza Dough

ACTIVE 20 MIN. · TOTAL 1 HOUR

MAKES 2 (14-INCH) PIZZA CRUSTS

- 3 tsp. active dry yeast (from 2 [¼-oz.] envelopes)
- 2 cups warm water (100° to 110°)
- 5 cups all-purpose unbleached flour, divided
- 1 cup coarse-ground whole wheat flour
- 2 tsp. table salt
- 2 tsp. granulated sugar
- 1½ tsp. dried thyme
- 1 oz. Parmesan cheese, grated (¼ cup) (optional)
- ½ cup plus 3 Tbsp. extra-virgin olive oil, divided

1. Combine yeast and 2 cups warm water in a liquid measuring cup, and let stand 5 minutes.
2. Combine yeast mixture, 3 cups all-purpose flour, whole wheat flour, salt, sugar, thyme, and, if desired, cheese in a large mixing bowl; add ½ cup olive oil. Beat at low speed with an electric mixer until blended, stopping to scrape down sides as necessary. Stir in enough remaining all-purpose flour to make a stiff dough. (Dough will be smooth.)
3. Place dough and 1 tablespoon oil in a large lightly greased bowl, turning to coat top. Cover and let rise in a warm place for 45 minutes or until dough is doubled in bulk. Punch dough down.
4. Turn dough out onto a lightly floured surface, and knead 4 or 5 times. Divide dough in half, and shape into balls. Roll each ball into a 14-inch circle on a lightly floured surface. Place one 14-inch circle onto a lightly floured pizza peel; brush with remaining 1 tablespoon oil, and prick with a fork. Add desired toppings and bake or grill until browned and bubbly.

Pork

Grilled Pork Tenderloin Sandwiches

(Photo, page 146)

ACTIVE 10 MIN. · TOTAL 45 MIN.

SERVES 6

- 1 tsp. garlic powder
- 1 tsp. table salt

- 1 tsp. dry mustard
- ½ tsp. coarsely ground black pepper
- 2 (¾-lb.) pork tenderloins
- 6 whole wheat hamburger buns
- 6 Tbsp. Vidalia Onion Barbecue Sauce (recipe follows)

1. Preheat grill to medium-high (350°F to 400°F). Stir together garlic powder, salt, dry mustard, and pepper; rub pork tenderloins with seasoning mixture. Lightly coat pork with cooking spray.
2. Grill, covered with grill lid, 10 to 12 minutes on each side or until a meat thermometer inserted into thickest portions registers 145°F. Remove from grill, and let stand 10 minutes. Chop or slice, and serve on hamburger buns. Drizzle each sandwich with 1 tablespoon Vidalia Onion Barbecue Sauce.

Vidalia Onion Barbecue Sauce

Sweet, succulent Vidalia onions hail from the namesake, Vidalia, Georgia.

ACTIVE 10 MIN. · TOTAL 30 MIN.

MAKES ABOUT 2½ CUPS

- 1 medium sweet onion, finely chopped (about ½ cup)
- 1 cup ketchup
- 2 Tbsp. firmly packed brown sugar
- 2 Tbsp. fresh lemon juice (from 1 lemon)
- 2 Tbsp. apple cider vinegar
- 2 Tbsp. Worcestershire sauce
- 1 Tbsp. olive oil
- 1 garlic clove, minced
- ½ tsp. table salt
- ½ tsp. freshly ground black pepper

Stir together all ingredients and ½ cup water in a large saucepan; bring to a boil over medium. Reduce heat to low, and simmer, stirring occasionally, 20 minutes. Refrigerate in an airtight container for up to a week.

Brown Sugar Pork Chops with Peach Barbecue Sauce

(Photo, page 146)

These pork chops caramelize beautifully when they hit the hot grill.

ACTIVE 30 MIN. · TOTAL 1 HOUR, 10 MIN.

SERVES 4

- ¾ cup packed dark brown sugar
- ¼ cup kosher salt

2 cups boiling water
3 cups ice cubes
4 bone-in pork loin chops
(about 2 lb.)
1 medium sweet onion, finely
chopped (about ½ cup)
1 Tbsp. canola oil
1 garlic clove, minced
1 (1-inch) piece fresh ginger, peeled
and grated
1½ cups ketchup
½ cup peach preserves or jam
2 large peaches (about 1 lb.), peeled
and cut into ¾-inch chunks
2 Tbsp. apple cider vinegar
Fresh thyme

1. Combine sugar and salt in a large bowl; add boiling water, stirring until sugar and salt dissolve. Stir in ice cubes to cool mixture. Add pork chops; cover and chill 30 minutes.
2. Meanwhile, sauté onion in hot oil in a medium saucepan over medium 2 minutes or until tender. Add garlic and ginger; cook, stirring constantly, 45 to 60 seconds or until fragrant. Add ketchup, peach preserves, and peaches. Reduce heat to low, and simmer, stirring occasionally, 30 minutes or until sauce thickens. Add vinegar. Remove from heat.
3. Remove pork from brine, discarding brine. Rinse pork well, and pat dry with paper towels.
4. Preheat grill to medium-high (350°F to 400°F). Pour half of peach mixture into a bowl; reserve remaining mixture. Season both sides of pork with desired amount of table salt and freshly ground pepper.
5. Grill pork, covered with grill lid, 5 to 6 minutes on each side or until a meat thermometer inserted into thickest portion of each chop registers 145°F, basting pork occasionally with peach mixture in bowl. Remove pork from grill; let stand 5 minutes before serving. Serve with reserved peach mixture.

Sweet Chili-and-Mustard Baby Back Ribs

(Photo, page 146)

ACTIVE 45 MIN. - TOTAL 4 HOURS, 50 MIN.
SERVES 6

2 (2½- to 3-lb.) slabs baby back
pork ribs
¼ cup kosher salt
2 Tbsp. ground cumin

2 Tbsp. dry mustard
2 tsp. cayenne pepper
½ cup sweet chili sauce
½ cup Dijon mustard
¼ cup honey
¼ cup rice vinegar
2 Tbsp. soy sauce

1. Pat both sides of slabs dry with paper towels. Using a sharp knife, remove thin membrane from back of each slab by slicing into it and pulling it off with a paper towel. (This will make ribs more tender and allow meat to absorb the rub better.) Combine salt, cumin, dry mustard, and cayenne in a small bowl; rub over both sides of slabs, and let stand at room temperature 30 minutes. Combine sweet chili sauce, Dijon mustard, honey, vinegar, and soy sauce.
2. Prepare a charcoal fire on bottom grate of a large charcoal grill. When coals are covered with gray ash, push to one side of grill. Maintain an inside temperature of about 300°F. Brush both sides of ribs with ¼ cup sweet chili sauce mixture. Place ribs on top oiled grate of grill directly over hot coals, and grill, covered, 10 minutes per side. Brush both sides of ribs again with ¼ cup sweet chili sauce mixture, and place on grate over side without the coals. Grill, covered, 40 minutes.
3. Brush both sides again with ¼ cup sweet chili sauce mixture, and grill, covered, until meat is tender to the touch and pulls away from bones on the ends, about 2 hours, brushing with ¼ cup sweet chili sauce mixture after 1 hour. Remove ribs from grill, and brush with remaining sweet chili sauce mixture.

Seafood

Grilled Salt-Crusted Red Snapper

Salt-crusting the snapper ensures a moist and flaky texture.

ACTIVE 15 MIN. - TOTAL 40 MIN.
SERVES 4

4 lb. kosher salt
1 lemon
1 Tbsp. chopped fresh dill
2 (1½-lb.) whole red snappers,
cleaned and scaled

1 cup thinly sliced fennel
4 dill sprigs

1. Preheat grill to medium-high (350°F to 400°F). Combine salt and 1½ cups water (mixture should resemble slushy wet sand). Grate zest from lemon to equal 1 tsp. Cut lemon into 6 slices. Stir lemon zest and chopped dill into salt mixture.
2. Place 2 large sheets of heavy-duty aluminum foil on a large baking sheet. Spread 2 cups salt mixture into a 13- x 7-inch rectangle on each piece of foil.
3. Top each salt portion with 1 fish. Place 3 lemon slices, ½ cup fennel, and 2 dill sprigs inside the cavity of each fish. Pat remaining 4 cups salt mixture evenly over both fish to cover completely.
4. Carefully slide foil with fish onto grill. Grill, covered with grill lid, 25 to 30 minutes, or until a meat thermometer inserted into thickest part of fish reaches 145°F. Remove fish from grill.
5. Crack salt crust away from fish, and serve immediately.

Grilled Oysters with Horseradish-Garlic Panko Topping

(Photo, page 146)

When buying oysters, look for those that are similar in size so they'll all cook in the same amount of time.

ACTIVE 10 MIN. - TOTAL 35 MIN.
MAKES 2 DOZEN

¼ cup butter
2 garlic cloves, minced
1 cup panko breadcrumbs
1 tsp. lemon zest (from 1 lemon)
2 Tbsp. prepared horseradish
2 Tbsp. chopped fresh flat-leaf
parsley
2 dozen oysters in the shell

1. Preheat grill to medium (300°F to 350°F). Melt butter in a large skillet over medium. Add garlic and panko. Cook 3 to 4 minutes, stirring constantly, until breadcrumbs are toasted.
2. Remove pan from heat, and stir in lemon zest, horseradish, and parsley.
3. Place oysters in single layer on grill rack. Grill oysters, covered with grill lid, 15 minutes or until oysters open. Top with crumb mixture before serving.

CLOCKWISE FROM TOP LEFT:

- GRILLED PORK TENDERLOIN SANDWICHES (PAGE 144)

- BROWN SUGAR PORK CHOPS WITH PEACH BARBECUE SAUCE (PAGE 144)

- SWEET CHILI-AND-MUSTARD BABY BACK RIBS (PAGE 145)

- GRILLED SEA BASS WITH MANGO SALSA (RIGHT)

- GRILLED OYSTERS WITH HORSERADISH-GARLIC PANKO TOPPING (PAGE 145)

- LOW-COUNTRY BOIL KABOBS WITH SPICY OLD BAY BUTTER (RIGHT)

- GRILLED SQUASH AND SALSA VERDE (RIGHT)

- GRILLED MEXICAN-STYLE STREET CORN (PAGE 148)

Grilled Sea Bass with Mango Salsa

Keep some fresh fruit salsa in the fridge to snack on with tortilla chips.

ACTIVE 15 MIN. - TOTAL 2 HOURS, 25 MIN., INCLUDING CHILLING

SERVES 4

- 1 diced fresh mango (about 1 cup)
- ½ cup diced red bell pepper
- 2 scallions, chopped (about ¼ cup)
- 1 jalapeño chile, seeded and minced
- ¼ cup chopped fresh cilantro
- 1 garlic clove, minced
- ⅛ tsp. table salt
- 2 Tbsp. fresh lime juice (from 1 lime)
- 4 (6-oz.) sea bass or halibut fillets (about 1¼ inches thick)

1. Combine mango, bell pepper, scallions, jalapeño, cilantro, garlic, salt, and lime juice in a bowl. in a bowl. Cover and chill at least 2 hours.
2. Preheat grill to medium (300°F to 350°F).
3. Coat fish lightly with cooking spray.
4. Place fish on grill rack coated with cooking spray. Grill, covered with grill lid, 5 minutes on each side or just until fish flakes with a fork. Serve with mango salsa.

Low-Country Boil Kabobs with Spicy Old Bay Butter

Enjoy this coastal Georgia favorite with all the elements skewered on kabobs.

ACTIVE 10 MIN. - TOTAL 35 MIN.

SERVES 6

- 12 (12-inch) wooden or metal skewers
- 1 lb. small new potatoes
- 3 ears fresh corn
- 1½ lb. peeled large raw shrimp
- 1 lb. smoked sausage, cut into 1-inch pieces
- 2 lemons, cut into wedges
- ½ cup butter, melted
- 2 Tbsp. Old Bay seasoning
- ½ tsp. cayenne pepper

1. Soak wooden skewers in water 30 minutes. Preheat grill to medium-high (350°F to 400°F). Bring potatoes and water to a boil in a large Dutch oven. Boil 8 minutes. Add corn. Cook 5 more minutes or until potatoes are tender and corn is almost done. Drain.
2. Cut each ear of corn into 1-inch pieces. Thread potatoes, corn, shrimp, sausage, and lemon wedges onto skewers.
3. Combine melted butter, Old Bay, and cayenne pepper.
4. Grill skewers 5 to 6 minutes, turning occasionally and basting with butter mixture.

Grilled Sides

Grilled Balsamic-Molasses Bacon

(Photo, page 151)

Serve this bacon for breakfast, on top of your favorite burger, or just all by itself.

ACTIVE 10 MIN. - TOTAL 1 HOUR

SERVES 6 TO 8

- 14 (8-inch) wooden skewers
- 6 Tbsp. molasses
- 3 Tbsp. balsamic vinegar
- ¼ tsp. ground red pepper
- 14 thick applewood-smoked bacon slices
- 3 fresh rosemary sprigs
  Freshly ground black pepper for seasoning

1. Soak wooden skewers in water 30 minutes. Preheat grill to low (250°F to 300°F).
2. Stir together molasses and next 2 ingredients. Thread 1 bacon slice onto each skewer.
3. Grill bacon, covered with grill lid, 15 to 18 minutes or until bacon begins to brown, turning every 6 minutes. Baste with half of molasses mixture, using rosemary sprigs as a brush; grill, covered with grill lid, 5 minutes. Turn bacon, and baste with remaining molasses mixture, using rosemary sprigs. Grill, covered with grill lid, 5 minutes or until browned and crisp. Remove from grill. Sprinkle with freshly ground black pepper to taste. Serve bacon immediately.

Grilled Squash and Salsa Verde

Choose an assortment of summer squash and zucchini at your local farmers' market or grocery store to make this simple and tasty dish.

ACTIVE 10 MIN. - TOTAL 20 MIN., INCLUDING SALSA

SERVES 4 TO 6

- 4 or 5 assorted medium squash (about 3½ lb.)
- 3 Tbsp. olive oil
- ¼ tsp. kosher salt
- 1 cup raw, unsalted, shelled pepitas (pumpkin seeds), toasted
  Salsa Verde (recipe follows)
- 1½ oz. goat cheese, crumbled (¼ cup)

1. Preheat grill to medium (300°F to 350°F).
2. Cut squash lengthwise into ¼-inch-thick slices. Toss with olive oil and salt.
3. Grill 10 minutes or until lightly caramelized.
4. Place squash on a serving platter. Top with pepitas, Salsa Verde, and goat cheese.

Salsa Verde

This slightly chunky green salsa adds a zing to grilled vegetables, meats, and even plain-Jane tortilla chips. Process the tomatillos to your desired thickness.

ACTIVE 10 MIN. - TOTAL 10 MIN.

MAKES ABOUT 1 CUP

- 7 fresh tomatillos, husks removed
- ½ small onion
- 2 tsp. kosher salt, divided
- 2 Tbsp. chopped fresh cilantro
- 2 Tbsp. fresh lime juice (from 1 lime)
  Garnish: fresh cilantro sprigs

1. Combine tomatillos, onion, 1 teaspoon salt, and water to cover in a deep saucepan. Bring to a boil; boil 3 to 5 minutes or until tender. Drain and cool.
2. Process tomatillo mixture, cilantro, lime juice, and remaining 1 teaspoon salt in a blender 10 to 20 seconds or until slightly chunky.

Grilled Fingerling Potato Salad

(Photo, page 151)

ACTIVE 20 MIN. - TOTAL 3 HOURS, INCLUDING
VINAIGRETTE AND PICKLED SHALLOTS
SERVES 8

- 3 lb. fingerling potatoes (about 6 cups), halved lengthwise
- 2 Tbsp. extra-virgin olive oil
- 1 tsp. kosher salt
- ½ tsp. freshly ground black pepper
- 3 Tbsp. Whole Grain Mustard Vinaigrette (recipe follows)
- 3 Tbsp. Pickled Shallots (recipe follows)
- 2 Tbsp. chopped fresh chives
- 2 Tbsp. chopped fresh flat-leaf parsley
- 1 tsp. chopped fresh thyme
- 3 Tbsp. cooked and crumbled bacon slices (optional)

1. Preheat grill to medium-high (350°F to 400°F). Toss potatoes in olive oil; sprinkle with the salt and black pepper. Place, cut-sides down, on cooking grate; grill, covered with grill lid, 2 minutes or until grill marks appear.
2. Remove from grill. Place potatoes in a single layer in center of a large piece of heavy-duty aluminum foil. Bring up foil sides over potatoes; double-fold top and side edges to seal, making a packet. Grill potatoes, in foil packet, covered with grill lid, 15 minutes on each side.
3. Remove packet from grill. Carefully open packet, using tongs. Cool 5 minutes. Toss together potatoes, vinaigrette, next 4 ingredients, and, if desired, bacon.

Whole Grain Mustard Vinaigrette

ACTIVE 5 MIN. - TOTAL 5 MINUTES
MAKES ⅔ CUP

- ¼ cup white wine vinegar
- 1 Tbsp. firmly packed light brown sugar
- 3 Tbsp. whole grain mustard
- ½ tsp. freshly ground black pepper
- ⅛ tsp. table salt
- ⅓ cup olive oil

Whisk together vinegar, sugar, mustard, pepper, and salt in a small bowl. Add olive oil in a slow, steady stream, whisking constantly until smooth. Store in an airtight container in refrigerator for up to one week.

Pickled Shallots

ACTIVE 20 MIN. - TOTAL 1 HOUR, 20 MIN.,
INCLUDING CHILLING
MAKES 1½ CUPS

- ¾ cup red wine vinegar
- ⅓ cup granulated sugar
- 2 Tbsp. kosher salt
- ½ tsp. dried crushed red pepper
- 1½ cups thinly sliced shallots

Bring ¾ cup water, vinegar, sugar, kosher salt, and dried crushed red pepper to a boil, whisking until sugar and salt are dissolved. Pour over shallots in a sterilized canning jar. Cool to room temperature. Cover and chill 1 hour. Store in an airtight container in refrigerator for up to a week.

Grilled Mexican-Style Street Corn

(Photo, page 146)

ACTIVE 10 MIN. - TOTAL 20 MIN.
SERVES 8

- 8 ears fresh corn
- ½ cup mayonnaise
- ½ cup crema
- ⅓ cup chopped fresh cilantro
- 2 garlic cloves, minced
- 1 Tbsp. smoked paprika
- 6 oz. Cotija cheese, crumbled (1 cup)
    Lime wedges

1. Preheat grill to medium-high (350°F to 400°F). Pull husks back from corn; remove silks and replace husks.
2. Grill corn 12 to 15 minutes, turning occasionally. Shuck corn.
3. Combine mayonnaise, crema, cilantro, garlic, and smoked paprika. Brush mixture over corn. Roll corn in cheese. Serve with lime wedges.

Grilled Stuffed Sweet Peppers

(Photo, page 151)

If the weather outside is less than ideal, you can also cook these on a baking pan in the oven.

ACTIVE 35 MIN. - TOTAL 45 MIN.
SERVES 8

- 2 (8-oz.) pkg. mini bell peppers
- 1 (8-oz.) pkg. cream cheese, softened
- 6 oz. feta cheese, crumbled (1 cup)
- ¼ cup sun-dried tomatoes in oil

- 2 garlic cloves, minced
- 2 Tbsp. chopped fresh basil
- ½ tsp. freshly ground black pepper
- 2 Tbsp. olive oil

1. Preheat grill to medium-high (350°F to 400°F). Carefully cut the stems from the top of the peppers, reserving tops, and remove membranes and seeds.
2. Pulse cream cheese, feta, sun-dried tomatoes, garlic, basil, and pepper in a food processor until smooth.
3. Place cream cheese mixture in a zip-top plastic bag. Snip the corner with scissors and pipe mixture into peppers. Replace pepper tops. Brush with oil.
4. Place a sheet of aluminum foil on grill. Grill peppers 7 minutes or until peppers are blistered and filling is warm.

Steaks

Bulgogi Flank Steak

This Korean barbecue steak gets its tenderness and flavor from a long marinating time.

ACTIVE 10 MIN. - TOTAL 12 HOURS, 45 MIN.,
INCLUDING MARINATING
SERVES 6

- ½ cup soy sauce
- ¼ cup packed light brown sugar
- 2 scallions, chopped (¼ cup)
- ¼ cup dark sesame oil
- 2 Tbsp. dry sherry
- 2 Tbsp. minced fresh garlic
- 1 Tbsp. grated fresh ginger
- 1 tsp. dried crushed red pepper
- 1 (2-lb.) flank steak

1. Combine soy sauce, sugar, scallions, oil, sherry, garlic, ginger, and crushed red pepper in a 2-gallon zip-top plastic freezer bag; add steak. Seal bag, and chill 12 hours. Remove steak from marinade, discarding marinade.
2. Preheat grill to high (400°F to 450°F). Grill steak, covered with grill lid, 9 minutes on each side or to desired degree of doneness. Let stand 10 minutes. Cut diagonally across the grain into thin slices.

Herb-Marinated Flank Steak

The herb marinade is also great on chicken. Substitute boneless, skinless breasts, and grill 7 minutes on each side or until done.

ACTIVE 10 MIN. - TOTAL 1 HOUR, INCLUDING MARINATING
SERVES 6

- ½ small sweet onion, minced
- 3 garlic cloves, minced
- ¼ cup olive oil
- 2 Tbsp. chopped fresh basil
- 1 Tbsp. chopped fresh thyme
- 1 Tbsp. chopped fresh rosemary
- 1 tsp. table salt
- ½ tsp. dried crushed red pepper
- 1¾ lb. flank steak
- 1 lemon, halved

1. Place onion, garlic, basil, thyme, rosemary, salt, and crushed red pepper in a 2-gallon zip-top plastic freezer bag, and squeeze bag to combine. Add steak; seal bag, and chill 30 minutes to 1 hour and 30 minutes. Remove steak from marinade, discarding marinade.
2. Preheat grill to high (400°F to 450°F). Grill steak, covered with grill lid, 9 minutes on each side or to desired doneness. Remove from grill; squeeze juice from lemon over steak. Let stand 10 minutes. Cut across the grain into thin slices.

Flank Steak Sandwiches with Blue Cheese

(Photo, page 151)

ACTIVE 15 MIN. - TOTAL 30 MIN.
SERVES 6

- 2 large sweet onions, cut into ¼-inch-thick slices
- 4 Tbsp. olive oil, divided
- ½ tsp. table salt
- ½ tsp. freshly ground black pepper
- 3 red bell peppers, cut into 1-inch-wide strips
- 6 (2- to 3-oz.) ciabatta rolls, split
- 5 oz. soft-ripened blue cheese
- 1½ cups loosely packed arugula
  Herb-Marinated Flank Steak (recipe, above)
- 6 Tbsp. mayonnaise

1. Preheat grill to high (400°F to 450°F). Brush onions with 1 tablespoon olive oil, and sprinkle with ¼ teaspoon each salt and pepper. Place pepper strips in a large bowl, and drizzle with 1 tablespoon olive oil. Sprinkle with remaining salt and pepper; toss to coat.

2. Grill onions and bell pepper strips, covered with grill lid, 7 to 10 minutes on each side or until lightly charred and tender.
3. Brush cut sides of rolls with remaining 2 tablespoons olive oil, and grill, cut-sides down, without grill lid, over high (400°F to 450°F) 1 to 2 minutes or until lightly browned and toasted.
4. Spread blue cheese on cut sides of roll bottoms; top with steak, bell pepper strips, onion, and arugula. Spread mayonnaise on cut sides of roll tops. Place roll tops, mayonnaise-sides down, on top of arugula, pressing lightly.

Grilled Flat Iron Steak with Charred Tomato Relish

(Photo, page 151)

ACTIVE 20 MIN. - TOTAL 20 MIN.
SERVES 4

- 6 medium plum or campari tomatoes, halved lengthwise
- 3 Tbsp. olive oil, divided
- 2 tsp. kosher salt, divided
- 1¼ tsp. black pepper, divided
- 1½ lb. flat iron steak
- ¼ cup firmly packed fresh flat-leaf parsley leaves, coarsely chopped
- 1 Tbsp. red wine vinegar
- 1 garlic clove, finely chopped
- 1 tsp. granulated sugar
- ¼ tsp. crushed red pepper

1. Preheat grill to medium-high (about 450°F), or heat a grill pan over medium-high. Toss together tomatoes, 1 tablespoon of the oil, ½ teaspoon of the salt, and ¼ teaspoon of the black pepper in a medium bowl; set aside. Rub steak with 1 tablespoon of the oil and remaining 1½ teaspoons salt and 1 teaspoon black pepper.
2. Grill tomatoes, turning often, until charred and softened, 4 to 6 minutes. Remove from grill, and let cool until ready to use. Grill steak, turning occasionally, until lightly charred and medium-rare, 8 to 10 minutes. Transfer to a board, and let rest, 5 to 10 minutes.
3. Chop tomatoes coarsely, and transfer to a medium bowl. Add parsley, vinegar, garlic, sugar, crushed red pepper, and remaining 1 tablespoon olive oil, and toss to combine.
4. Slice steak against the grain, and spoon tomato relish over top.

Grilled Tri-Tip

(Photo, page 151)

Tri-tip is a relatively inexpensive cut of beef ideal for quick grilling.

ACTIVE 10 MIN. - TOTAL 40 MIN., INCLUDING CITRUS-CHILE BUTTER
SERVES 8 TO 10

- 2 (2-lb.) tri-tip steaks
- 2 tsp. table salt, divided
- 1¼ tsp. freshly ground black pepper, divided
  Citrus-Chile Butter (recipe follows)
- 3 bunches baby Vidalia or scallions, trimmed
- 3 Tbsp. olive oil

1. Preheat grill to medium-high (350°F to 400°F). Sprinkle steaks with 1½ teaspoons of the salt and 1 teaspoon of the pepper. Grill steaks, covered with grill lid, 9 to 12 minutes on each side or to desired degree of doneness.
2. Remove from grill, and rub 3 tablespoons Citrus-Chile Butter onto steaks. Cover steaks with aluminum foil; let stand 5 minutes.
3. Meanwhile, toss onions with olive oil; season with remaining ½ teaspoon salt and ¼ teaspoon pepper. Grill onions, without grill lid, 2 minutes; turn and grill 1 more minute.
4. Uncover steaks, and cut diagonally across the grain into thin slices. Serve with grilled onions and remaining Citrus-Chile Butter.

Citrus-Chile Butter

ACTIVE 10 MIN. - TOTAL 10 MIN.
MAKES 1 CUP

- 1 cup butter, softened
- 2 Tbsp. lime zest
- 2 Tbsp. lemon zest
- 3 garlic cloves, minced
- 1 Tbsp. seeded and minced jalapeño pepper
- 1 tsp. chopped fresh thyme

1. Stir together butter, lime zest and juice, garlic, jalapeño, and thyme in a bowl.
2. Cover and chill until ready to serve, or shape into a log with plastic wrap and freeze up to 1 month.

Coffee-Rubbed Skirt Steak

Serve this tender, flavor-packed skirt steak with grilled corn and sliced tomatoes.

ACTIVE 10 MIN. · TOTAL 50 MIN.
SERVES 6 TO 8

- 2 Tbsp. chili powder
- 1 Tbsp. granulated sugar
- 1 Tbsp. kosher salt
- 1 Tbsp. finely ground chicory coffee
- 1 tsp. coarsely ground black pepper
- 2 (1½-lb.) boneless skirt, flank, or tri-tip steaks
  Fresh fruit salsa
  Lime wedges

1. Preheat grill to high (400°F to 450°F). Stir together chili powder, sugar, salt, ground coffee, and pepper in a bowl; rub over steaks. Let stand 30 minutes.
2. Grill, covered with grill lid, 3 to 5 minutes on each side or to desired degree of doneness. Let stand 5 minutes. Cut across the grain into thin strips; serve with salsa and lime wedges.

Sides

Beer-Batter Fried Pickles

ACTIVE 25 MIN. · TOTAL 30 MIN., INCLUDING SAUCE
SERVES 8 TO 10

- 2 (16-oz.) jars dill pickle chips, drained
- 1 large egg
- 1 (12-oz.) can beer
- 1 Tbsp. baking powder
- 1 tsp. seasoned salt
- 1½ cups all-purpose flour
  Vegetable oil
  Spicy Ranch Dipping Sauce (recipe follows)

1. Pat the pickles dry with paper towels.
2. Whisk together the egg beer, baking soda, salt, and flour in a large bowl; add the flour, and whisk until smooth.
3. Pour the oil to a depth of 1½ inches into a large heavy skillet or Dutch oven; heat over medium-high (375°F).
4. Dip pickle slices into the batter, allowing excess batter to drip off. Fry pickles, in batches, 3 to 4 minutes or until golden. Drain and pat dry on paper towels; serve with the Spicy Ranch Dipping Sauce.

Spicy Ranch Dipping Sauce

ACTIVE 10 MIN. · TOTAL 10 MIN.
MAKES ABOUT 1 CUP

- ¾ cup (6 oz.) buttermilk
- ½ cup mayonnaise
- 2 Tbsp. minced scallions
- 1 garlic clove, minced
- 1 tsp. hot sauce
- ½ tsp. seasoned salt

Whisk together all the ingredients in a small bowl. Store in an airtight container in refrigerator up to 2 weeks.

Fried Green Tomatoes with Buttermilk-Feta Dressing

The dressing elevates these tasty tomatoes to a new level of flavor.

ACTIVE 36 MIN. · TOTAL 1 HOUR, 6 MIN.
SERVES 4

- 3 green tomatoes, sliced ½ inch thick
- 1¼ tsp. kosher salt, divided
- ½ cup (2 oz.) all-purpose flour
- 2 large eggs, beaten
- ⅓ cup plain yellow cornmeal
- ⅓ cup fine, dry breadcrumbs
- 3 cups vegetable oil
- 2 Tbsp. buttermilk
- 2 Tbsp. mayonnaise
- 2 Tbsp. sour cream
- 1 Tbsp. fresh dill, chopped, plus more for serving
- 1 Tbsp. fresh lemon juice (from 1 lemon)
- ¼ tsp. black pepper
- 4 oz. feta cheese, crumbled, divided (1 cup)

1. Set a wire rack in a rimmed baking sheet. Place tomato slices on wire rack, and sprinkle with ½ teaspoon of the salt. Turn slices over, and sprinkle with another ½ teaspoon of the salt. Let stand 30 minutes. Blot tomatoes dry with paper towels.
2. Place flour in a shallow dish. Place eggs in a second shallow dish. Stir together cornmeal and breadcrumbs in a third shallow dish. Working with 1 slice at a time, dredge tomato slices in flour; dip in eggs, shaking off excess. Dredge slices in breadcrumb mixture, pressing gently to adhere. Place tomatoes in a single layer on wire rack.

3. Heat oil in a large, heavy skillet, preferably cast-iron, over medium-high. (When a few breadcrumbs dropped in the oil sizzle, it's ready for frying.) Fry tomatoes, in batches, until golden brown and crisp, turning halfway through, about 2 minutes per side. (Be careful not to overcrowd the skillet.) Transfer to wire rack to drain. Top each tomato with a pinch of salt.
4. Whisk together buttermilk, mayonnaise, sour cream, dill, and lemon juice in a small bowl. Whisk in black pepper, ½ cup of the feta, and remaining ¼ teaspoon salt. Spoon about 3 tablespoons of the dressing onto each plate; add 3 or 4 tomato slices. Sprinkle with dill and remaining ½ cup feta.

Pan-Fried Okra with Cornmeal

Using two medium skillets gives the okra plenty of room to cook up extra crispy.

ACTIVE 10 MIN. · TOTAL 28 MIN.
SERVES 4

- 6 Tbsp. canola oil, divided
- 2 lb. fresh okra, stems trimmed, cut into ½-inch pieces
- 1½ tsp. coarse sea salt
- 1 tsp. black pepper
- ⅔ cup fine yellow cornmeal
- ⅛ tsp. cayenne pepper

Place 1½ tablespoons of the canola oil in each of 2 medium nonstick skillets, and heat over medium-high. Divide okra pieces between skillets, and stir well to coat. Cover and cook, stirring occasionally, until okra is bright green, about 10 minutes. Sprinkle okra in each skillet with ¾ teaspoon of the salt and ½ teaspoon of the black pepper. Divide yellow cornmeal and cayenne pepper evenly between skillets; stir well to coat. Drizzle remaining 1½ tablespoons oil over mixture in each skillet, and cook, uncovered, stirring occasionally, until okra is tender and browned, about 6 minutes.

CLOCKWISE FROM TOP LEFT:

• GRILLED FINGERLING POTATO SALAD
(PAGE 148)

• GRILLED BALSAMIC-MOLASSES BACON
(PAGE 147)

•GRILLED STUFFED SWEET PEPPERS
(PAGE 148)

• FLANK STEAK SANDWICHES WITH BLUE
CHEESE (PAGE 149)

• GRILLED TRI-TIP (PAGE 149)

• GRILLED FLAT IRON STEAK WITH
CHARRED TOMATO RELISH (PAGE 149)

• FRIED GREEN TOMATOES WITH
BUTTERMILK-FETA DRESSING (LEFT)

• BEER-BATTER FRIED PICKLES (LEFT)

Rum Baked Beans

You'll love this creative spin on traditional baked beans.

ACTIVE 20 MIN. - TOTAL 1 HOUR, 20 MIN.
SERVES 10

- 6 thick-cut bacon slices, chopped
- 1 large Vidalia onion, chopped (about 1 cup)
- 2 garlic cloves, minced
- 1 (28-oz.) can baked beans with bacon and brown sugar
- 1 (16-oz.) can navy beans, drained and rinsed
- 1 (16-oz.) can dark red kidney beans, drained and rinsed
- 1 (16-oz.) can light red kidney beans, drained and rinsed
- 1 (15-oz.) can black beans, drained and rinsed
- ½ cup packed dark brown sugar
- ½ cup ketchup
- ½ cup gold rum
- ¼ cup apple cider vinegar

1. Preheat oven to 350°F. Cook bacon in a large skillet over medium until crisp; remove, reserving 2 tablespoons drippings in skillet. Add onion, and cook, stirring often, until tender, about 5 minutes; add garlic, and cook 1 minute.
2. Stir together bacon, onion mixture, all of the beans, sugar, ketchup, rum, and vinegar in a large bowl. Spoon into a lightly greased 13- x 9-inch baking dish.
3. Bake, covered with aluminum foil, 30 minutes; uncover and bake 30 more minutes.

Easy Coleslaw

This slaw is great on its own, but it's also a great topping for sandwiches.

ACTIVE 5 MIN. - TOTAL 5 MIN.
SERVES 4

- ⅓ cup mayonnaise
- ⅓ cup sour cream
- 1 Tbsp. apple cider vinegar
- ½ tsp. kosher salt
- ¼ tsp. freshly ground black pepper
- 1 (16-oz.) pkg. tri-color deli coleslaw mix

Whisk together mayonnaise, sour cream, apple cider vinegar, salt, and pepper in a large bowl. Add coleslaw mix; toss to coat. Cover and chill until ready to serve.

Sweet, Salty, and Spicy Watermelon Refresher

A healthy, colorful and tasty side dish you'll love all summer long.

ACTIVE 30 MIN. - TOTAL 50 MIN.
SERVES 10 TO 12

- ¼ cup fresh lime juice (from 1 lime)
- 1 Tbsp. turbinado sugar
- 2 Tbsp. fresh orange juice (from 1 orange)
- 1 jalapeño or 2 serrano chiles, seeded and minced
- ½ tsp. sea or kosher salt
- ¼ tsp. dried crushed red pepper
- 1 small red onion, diced (about ⅓ cup)
- ½ cup coarsely chopped fresh cilantro
- 2 Tbsp. coarsely chopped fresh mint
- 1 small seedless watermelon
- 1 small cantaloupe
- 2 English cucumbers
- 1 jicama
- 2 mangoes

1. Combine lime juice and next 5 ingredients in a small bowl.
2. Place red onion, cilantro, and mint in a large bowl. Dice watermelon and cantaloupe into 1-inch pieces; add to bowl. Peel and dice cucumbers, jicama, and mangoes; add to bowl. Stir in lime juice mixture. Cover and chill 20 minutes.

Tangy Tzatziki Pasta Salad

This incredible pasta salad will steal the show at your next cookout!

ACTIVE 35 MIN. - TOTAL 2 HOURS, 35 MIN.
SERVES 10

- 1 (16-oz.) container low-fat plain Greek yogurt
- ¼ cup olive oil
- 1 Tbsp. chopped fresh dill
- 1 Tbsp. lemon juice (from 1 lemon)
- 1 tsp. sea salt
- ½ tsp. freshly ground pepper
- 3 garlic cloves
- 1 (16-oz.) pkg. penne pasta
- 1 cup pitted Kalamata olives, sliced
- 2 cucumbers, peeled, seeded, and diced
- ¾ cup sun-dried tomatoes in oil, drained and chopped

- 1 (9.9-oz.) jar marinated artichoke hearts, drained and chopped
- 9 oz. feta cheese, crumbled (1½ cups)

1. Process yogurt, oil, dill, lemon juice, salt, pepper, and garlic in a food processor 30 seconds or until thoroughly blended. Transfer to a bowl, and cover and chill 1 to 24 hours.
2. Cook pasta according to package directions; drain and rinse with cold water.
3. Place cooled pasta in a large bowl. Stir in olives cucumbers, sun-dried tomatoes, and artichoke hearts until well blended. Add yogurt mixture, and stir just until well coated. Gently stir in feta cheese. Cover and chill 1 hour.

Wilber's Potato Salad

Boil the potatoes with skins on so they hold their shape; the skins peel off easily after cooking.

ACTIVE 1 HOUR, 5 MIN. - TOTAL 1 HOUR, 20 MIN.
SERVES 6

- 3 lb. russet potatoes (about 4 potatoes)
- 1 cup mayonnaise
- 1 Tbsp. yellow mustard
- 1 Tbsp. kosher salt
- 1 Tbsp. apple cider vinegar

1. Bring the potatoes and water to cover to a boil in a large stockpot over high. Boil potatoes until tender, 45 to 50 minutes. Drain the potatoes, and let stand until potatoes are cool to the touch, about 15 minutes.
2. Peel and dice potatoes, and place in a large bowl. Add the mayonnaise, mustard, salt, and vinegar. Using a potato masher or whisk, mash the potatoes until they reach a smooth and incorporated consistency, with some potato chunks remaining. Serve immediately, or cover and chill until ready to serve.

July

BOURBON-PEACH
ICED TEA

Raise Your Spirits

Shake up happy hour with seven refreshing, summery cocktails

Bourbon-Peach Iced Tea

ACTIVE 20 MIN. · TOTAL 40 MIN.
SERVES 10

- 2 cups chopped fresh peaches (from 2 ripe peaches)
- 1½ cups granulated sugar
- 8 black tea bags
- 1 cup (8 oz.) bourbon
  Ice
  Peach slices, for garnish

Bring chopped peaches, sugar, and 1 cup water to a boil in a saucepan over medium-high. Reduce heat to low, and simmer, stirring often, about 10 minutes. Cool slightly; process in a blender 30 seconds. Pour through a fine mesh strainer into a 1-gallon container. Bring 3 cups water to a boil over high heat in a saucepan. Add tea bags, and boil 1 minute. Remove from heat. Cover; steep 10 minutes. Discard tea bags. Stir the tea, bourbon, and 6 cups cold water into peach mixture. Serve in highball glasses over ice, and garnish with peach slices.

Southern Sunrise

ACTIVE 10 MIN. · TOTAL 10 MIN.
SERVES 2

- 6 oz. fresh orange juice (from 2 oranges)
- 3 oz. tequila
  Ice
- 1 oz. grenadine, divided
  Maraschino cherries and Sparkling Orange Wheels (recipe follows), for garnish

Stir together the orange juice and tequila in a pitcher. Pour mixture into 2 ice-filled highball glasses. Slowly add ½ ounce grenadine to each glass. Do not stir. Top each with a cherry and a Sparkling Orange Wheel.

SOUTHERN SUNRISE

Sparkling Orange Wheels

ACTIVE 10 MIN. · TOTAL 40 MIN.
MAKES 6

- 1 small orange
- 1 Tbsp. light corn syrup
  Sparkling sugar

Cut orange into 6 (⅛-inch-thick) rounds, and discard the seeds. Microwave corn syrup in a microwavable bowl on HIGH until warm, 5 seconds. Using a small brush, coat both sides and edges of rounds with corn syrup. Sprinkle with sugar. Place wheels on a wire rack to dry for 30 minutes; use within 2 hours.

RUM
SWIZZLES

Rum Swizzles

ACTIVE 10 MIN. - TOTAL 10 MIN.
SERVES 2

> Shaved ice
> 5 oz. light rum
> 3 Tbsp. fresh lime juice
>   (from 2 limes)
> 4 tsp. granulated sugar
> 2 dashes Angostura bitters
>   Orange slices, fresh mint sprigs,
>   and lime zest strips, for garnish

Combine ice, rum, lime juice, sugar, and bitters in a pitcher. Stir vigorously until foamy, 20 seconds. Pour into 2 rocks glasses. Top with orange slices, mint, and lime zest.

Big-Batch Cajun Lemonade

ACTIVE 10 MIN. - TOTAL 10 MIN.
MAKES ABOUT 8 CUPS

> 2 cups (16 oz.) light rum
> 2 cups (16 oz.) citron vodka
> 1 (12-oz.) can frozen lemonade
>   concentrate, thawed
> 1 tsp. hot sauce
> 1 liter club soda, chilled
>   Crushed ice
>   Lemon slices and sugarcane
>   sticks, for garnish

Stir together rum, vodka, concentrate, and hot sauce in a pitcher. Add club soda just before serving. Pour mixture into 8 highball glasses filled with crushed ice. Garnish with lemon slices and sugarcane.

Blackberry Bramble Pisco Sours

ACTIVE 15 MIN. - TOTAL 15 MIN.
SERVES 4

> 1 cup fresh blackberries
> 1 cup pisco (grape brandy), chilled
> ⅓ cup fresh lime juice (from 3 limes)
> 3 large pasteurized egg whites
> 5 Tbsp. Blackberry Simple Syrup
>   (recipe follows)
>   Ice
>   Angostura bitters
>   Fresh blackberries and basil
>   leaves, for garnish

1. Process blackberries in a blender until smooth. Pour through a fine mesh strainer into a 1-quart jar with a tight-fitting lid, discarding solids.
2. Add pisco and the next 3 ingredients to jar. Cover with lid; shake 30 seconds or until foamy. Pour mixture into 4 rocks glasses filled with ice. Top each with a dash of bitters, blackberries, and basil.

Blackberry Simple Syrup

TOTAL 15 MIN.
MAKES 1½ CUPS

Bring 4 cups **fresh blackberries**, 1 cup **granulated sugar**, and ½ cup **water** to a boil in a saucepan over medium-high, stirring often, until sugar dissolves. Reduce heat to medium-low. Simmer, stirring occasionally, until fruit is soft and liquid is syrupy, 10 minutes. Press mixture through a fine mesh strainer into a jar with a lid, discarding solids. Store in refrigerator up to 1 week.

Key Lime Daiquiris

ACTIVE 10 MIN. - TOTAL 10 MIN.
SERVES 2

> 3 tsp. grenadine
> 2 Tbsp. fresh Key lime juice
>   (from 2 Key limes)
> 3 oz. light rum
> ½ cup crushed ice
>   Key lime slices, for garnish

Stir together grenadine and lime juice until dissolved; transfer to a blender. Add rum and ice to blender. Process until smooth, about 30 seconds. Pour mixture into 2 hurricane glasses; garnish with lime slices.

Watermelon Slushies

ACTIVE 10 MIN. - TOTAL 4 HOURS, 10 MIN.,
INCLUDING 4 HOURS FREEZING
SERVES 2

> 4 cups cubed seedless watermelon
> ¼ cup grenadine
> 2 Tbsp. fresh lime juice (from
>   2 limes)
> 2 tsp. Key Lime-Mint Sugar
>   (recipe follows)
>   Watermelon wedges, for garnish

1. Process cubed melon in a juicer or blender. Strain through a fine mesh strainer, discarding solids. (You should have 1½ cups juice.) Pour into ice cube trays; freeze 4 hours or overnight.
2. Combine watermelon ice cubes, grenadine, and lime juice in a blender; pulse until slushy, about 15 times.
3. Rim 2 Collins glasses with Key Lime-Mint Sugar. Pour the mixture into prepared glasses. Top with watermelon wedges.

Key Lime–Mint Sugar

ACTIVE 10 MIN. - TOTAL 2 HOURS, 10 MIN.,
INCLUDING 2 HOURS STANDING
MAKES ½ CUP

Process 1 Tbsp. finely chopped **fresh mint**, 2 Tbsp. **Key lime zest (from 10 Key limes)**, and ¼ cup **granulated sugar** in a mini food processor until sugar is finely ground, 10 seconds. Place in a bowl, and stir in additional ¼ cup sugar. Spread mixture on a rimmed baking sheet; let stand at room temperature until dry, 2 hours. Return mixture to food processor, and pulse until finely ground, about 4 times. Store in an airtight container in the refrigerator up to 3 months.

BLACKBERRY
BRAMBLE
PISCO SOURS

WATERMELON
SLUSHIES

KEY LIME
DAIQUIRIS

BIG-BATCH
CAJUN
LEMONADE

Celebrating Her Roots

South Carolina native and Food Network star Kardea Brown honors Gullah cuisine and her family's traditions

GULLAH CHEF KARDEA BROWN WITH HER GRANDMOTHER JOSEPHINE AT CHARLES TOWNE LANDING STATE HISTORIC SITE IN SOUTH CAROLINA

At first blush, *Delicious Miss Brown* might seem like your average, glossed-up Food Network cooking show. The house, located just outside picturesque Charleston, South Carolina, is beautiful. The host, former caterer Kardea Brown, is polished. The dinner parties, featuring Brown's friends and family, are enviable. But look a little closer.

The Charleston that you see on the show isn't the fancy hotels and seafood towers often spotlighted in magazines. It's the Sea Islands, an area where West Africans arrived in America as slaves and formed what is known as the Gullah community. Brown, who is Gullah, tells it like it is. She'll describe how fish fries were started by slaves who had no choice but to take what was available from the land and water and turn that into sustenance. And when describing her use of garlic powder in a recipe, she'll explain that her ancestors didn't always have access to the fresh stuff. Her guests—who include her thrifty Aunt TC and her brassy mother, Patricia—are bold, fun, and refreshingly unfiltered.

This is a show that is comfortable with itself, one that is not afraid to dig a little deeper to teach us something about our history. It's a breath of fresh air on a network whose slate of stars hasn't always reflected the diversity of our country. But Brown, whose show is now going into its third season, followed anything but a straight path to get here, and her fight for representation is far from over.

It's a sunny and slightly breezy Friday in Charleston. Brown, sporting a sharp bob and a shiny manicure, has posted up at her grandmother Josephine's house, a homey spot in the residential neighborhood of West Ashley, filled with old issues of *Ebony* magazine and ceramic animals. Brown knows every inch of her matriarch's kitchen, from where she keeps the garlic powder to where you'll find the stash of local okra. Family members stream in and out of the house—her mother, her aunt, her cousin Mikey—as Brown prepares okra stew.

It's a Gullah tradition to make okra stew on Fridays, Brown says, so everyone can gather around and eat a hearty meal after a long week. She grabs a big pot from under the stove; browns some beef until it fills the kitchen with a rich, irresistible scent; and then adds crushed tomatoes, stock, ginger, and fat slices of okra. Her grandmother playfully inquires as to why she didn't use homemade stock. "We don't always have time for that!" she responds bluntly.

Brown doesn't seem to mind the steady buzz of relatives. She was raised by her single mother and grandmother and spent a significant portion of her childhood on Wadmalaw Island, surrounded by the large Gullah community.

It was there that her grandmother insisted on teaching her about Gullah foodways. For that generation, keeping their culture alive involves cooking. Slaves weren't taught to read or write, so that was one of the few means they had of passing down their traditions. That's how Brown learned to prepare okra stew, shrimp and grits, stewed lima beans, and pimiento cheese—dishes that are often associated with Charleston's distinct brand of Low-country cuisine but aren't always credited to the Gullah people.

After college, Brown got a job in social work, and cooking became a way to get through the mental strains of the job. On a whim, in 2014, her boyfriend at the time submitted a tape of her to the Cooking Channel, and she was soon contacted about being a guest for a pilot. The show never got picked up, but the Food Network executives loved her. They said she should go find her unique culinary point of view, and then they would talk.

> "The food is at the center of it all, like little branches that connect everything else."

That's how The New Gullah Supper Club was born. Brown quit her social work job, raised money through GoFundMe, and created a traveling dinner series to showcase her heritage. Soon, word spread wide about her pimiento cheese-buttered crostini and sweet-potato-pie cheesecake.

Then in 2018, she got another call. Her producers had pitched a series to the Food Network that would focus on Brown, her family, and her life in Charleston. This time, they wanted to film a pilot.

Delicious Miss Brown premiered in July 2019. It takes place at Brown's family estate on Edisto Island. She hosts shrimp boils and fish fries with many of her relatives and puts her Gullah heritage front and center. The food is geared toward comfort rather than Instagram perfection. Kardea Brown bursts with heart.

Gullah cuisine, she proudly explains, is a food of survival. It's what slaves cooked when they were given only scraps. "This is such a colorful and rich and deep community," she says. "The food is at the center of it all, like little branches that connect everything else."

That's why she takes issue with the growing notion that Gullah cuisine is disappearing due to the lack of written documentation and the destruction of the Sea Islands caused by climate change. Brown insists that her generation is committed to keeping these traditions alive. She points to chefs like BJ Dennis, who are championing this cuisine on a national level. In reality, *Delicious Miss Brown* is probably the biggest stage Gullah food has ever been given, and Brown understands the responsibility that comes with that.

"I hope to bridge the gap between what people know of Charleston and what is actually represented here," she says. "I want people to come here and go to the Sea Islands."

Still, even with a show that averages just over 1 million viewers an episode, Brown, the network's new kid, feels like she has to work a little harder, whether that's pushing for advertising dollars to promote the show or asking to be featured at Food Network events alongside her colleagues.

She was filming an episode of her show where she was hosting a supper club and discussing the origins of her dishes. "I started talking about slavery, and people said, 'We don't know if we can say this,'" she recalls. "I was like, 'Why not? It's the truth!'"

"Sadly, it is 2020, and we are still not ready to have that conversation," she adds with a sigh.

So her goal for the next season, which begins filming soon, is to have those in-depth conversations and give people an even more thorough education on Gullah cuisine, African American history, and yes, slavery. Getting her message across in a network-friendly way may not be so easy or straightforward, but she's up for the challenge.

Sometimes it's slow going, she says with a chuckle, slurping a spoonful of okra stew, "but we're getting there."

KARDEA'S OKRA SOUP WITH SHRIMP

Kardea's Okra Soup with Shrimp

ACTIVE 30 MIN. - TOTAL 1 HOUR, 30 MIN.
SERVES 10

SHRIMP BROTH
- 12 oz. unpeeled raw shrimp
- 1 large carrot, coarsely chopped (1 cup)
- 3 stalks celery, coarsely chopped (1 cup)
- 1 small yellow onion, coarsely chopped (about ½ cup)
- 1 Tbsp. unsalted butter
- 1 tsp. kosher salt
- 1 bay leaf

OKRA SOUP
- 2 Tbsp. olive oil
- 2 medium garlic cloves, minced (2 tsp.)
- 1 large yellow onion, chopped (about 2 cups)
- 1 medium green bell pepper, chopped (about 1 cup)
- 2 Tbsp. unsalted butter, divided
- 4 tsp. kosher salt, divided
- 2 cups fresh or thawed frozen corn kernels
- 2 cups thawed frozen lima beans
- 2 fresh plum tomatoes, diced (1 cup)
- 1 (28-oz.) can diced tomatoes

- ¼ tsp. black pepper
- 2½ cups sliced fresh or thawed frozen okra
- 1 tsp. ground ginger
- 2 Tbsp. fresh lemon juice (from 1 lemon)
  Hot cooked white rice (optional)

1. Prepare the Shrimp Broth: Peel and devein raw shrimp, reserving shells. Cover and refrigerate shrimp until ready to use. Rinse shells with cold water until clean. Place shrimp shells, 5 cups water, chopped carrot, celery, onion, butter, salt, and bay leaf in a large stockpot. Bring to a boil over high, and boil, stirring occasionally, about 5 minutes. Reduce heat to medium-low, and simmer, covered with lid slightly ajar, until reduced to about 3 cups, about 45 minutes; skim off and discard any foam or other impurities that rise to the top. Pour broth through a fine mesh strainer into a bowl; discard solids.
2. Prepare the Okra Soup: Heat a large gumbo pot or 5- to 6-quart Dutch oven over medium-high. Add olive oil, garlic, onion, bell pepper, 1 tablespoon of the butter, and 1 teaspoon of the salt. Cook,

stirring often, until vegetables soften, 4 to 6 minutes. Stir in corn, lima beans, and plum tomatoes until well combined. Stir in canned diced tomatoes, reserved Shrimp Broth, and 2 teaspoons of the salt; bring to a boil. Reduce heat to medium-low, and simmer until mixture is slightly thickened, about 20 minutes.
3. Meanwhile, melt remaining 1 tablespoon butter in a medium skillet over medium-high heat. Add the reserved shrimp, and season with pepper and ½ teaspoon of the salt. Cook, stirring occasionally, until the shrimp begin to turn pink, about 2 minutes. Add sliced okra, ground ginger, and fresh lemon juice. Continue cooking, stirring occasionally, until okra and shrimp are cooked through, about 2 minutes. Remove from heat.
4. After soup has simmered 20 minutes, add shrimp-and-okra mixture. Cook until shrimp are heated through, 1 to 2 minutes. Season with remaining ½ teaspoon salt, and stir. Ladle into individual bowls. (If desired, spoon rice evenly into bowls before adding soup.)

Let's Take It Outside

A simple drink and snacks made for long summer afternoons on the porch

Pineapple-Sweet Tea Punch

ACTIVE 15 MIN. - TOTAL 30 MIN.,
PLUS 20 MIN. COOLING
SERVES 4

Bring 1 cup **pineapple juice** and ½ cup **granulated sugar** to a boil in a small saucepan over medium-high. Boil, undisturbed, until mixture reduces to ½ cup and becomes syrupy, 12 to 16 minutes. Remove from heat; cool completely, about 20 minutes. Stir together 2½ cups chilled **unsweetened iced tea**, ¾ cup (6 oz.) **vodka (optional)**, 1 Tbsp. **fresh lime juice** (from 1 lime), and cooled pineapple syrup in a small pitcher. Pour evenly into 4 **ice**-filled glasses; garnish each with 1 **pineapple wedge**.

Creamy Avocado Dip

ACTIVE 10 MIN. - TOTAL 10 MIN.
SERVES 8

- 2 medium avocados, chopped
- ½ cup sour cream
- ½ cup mayonnaise
- 2 Tbsp. fresh lime juice (from 1 lime)
- 1 medium jalapeño chile, seeded and minced (2 Tbsp.)
- 1 tsp. kosher salt
- ⅓ cup chopped fresh cilantro
  Tortilla chips, bell pepper strips, celery sticks, and small carrots

Process avocados, sour cream, mayonnaise, fresh lime juice, jalapeño, and salt in a food processor until smooth, 2 to 3 minutes. Transfer to a serving bowl; stir in cilantro. Serve with tortilla chips and vegetables.

Chile-Lime Honey-Roasted Peanuts

ACTIVE 5 MIN. - TOTAL 40 MIN.
SERVES 8

- ¼ cup honey
- 2 tsp. fresh lime zest, plus 3 Tbsp. juice (from 2 limes), divided

CHILE-LIME
HONEY-ROASTED
PEANUTS

PINEAPPLE-
SWEET TEA
PUNCH

CREAMY
AVOCADO DIP

- 2 Tbsp. ancho chile powder
- 1 Tbsp. kosher salt
- ⅛ tsp. cayenne pepper
- 4 cups unsalted peanuts

Preheat oven to 250°F. Whisk together honey, lime juice, chile powder, salt, and cayenne in a large bowl until combined.

Add peanuts; stir to coat evenly. Spread in a single layer on a rimmed baking sheet. Bake until fragrant, dry, and slightly browned, about 30 minutes, stirring once halfway through cook time. Remove peanuts from oven, and cool on baking sheet 5 minutes. Transfer to a serving bowl; stir in lime zest, and serve.

BUTTERMILK-
PEACH POPS
(PAGE 168)

Peaches + Cream

Not much improves this juicy, sun-ripened fruit, other than a scoop of ice cream,
a rich buttercream frosting, or a swirl of tangy buttermilk.
In any form, it makes an unbeatable combination

PEACH SHORTCAKE
TRIFLE (PAGE 164)

Peach Shortcake Trifle

(Photo, page 163)

This showstopping dessert with its layers of juicy peaches, mascarpone whipped cream, and tender vanilla cake can be served immediately or prepared a day ahead. Mascarpone, a thick, rich Italian cheese made from cow's milk, gives the whipped cream a slight tang and extra-smooth texture.

ACTIVE 30 MIN. - TOTAL 1 HOUR, 35 MIN., PLUS 1 HOUR COOLING

SERVES 12

- ½ cup butter, softened, plus more for greasing pan
- 1½ cups granulated sugar, divided
- 2 large eggs, separated
- 1½ cups all-purpose flour, plus more for pan
- 1½ tsp. baking powder
- ⅛ tsp. table salt
- ½ cup whole milk
- 3 tsp. vanilla extract, divided
- 8 cups sliced ripe peaches (about 2½ lb.)
- 1 Tbsp. chopped fresh mint
- 2 (8-oz.) containers mascarpone cheese
- ¾ cup powdered sugar, sifted
- 2 cups heavy cream

1. Preheat oven to 350°F. Beat butter with a heavy-duty stand mixer on medium speed until creamy. Gradually add 1 cup of the granulated sugar, and beat until light and fluffy, 3 to 5 minutes. Add egg yolks, 1 at a time, beating just until blended after each addition.

2. Whisk together flour, baking powder, and salt in a medium bowl. Add to butter mixture alternately with milk, beginning and ending with flour mixture. Beat on low speed just until blended after each addition. Beat in 1 teaspoon of the vanilla extract.

3. Beat egg whites with an electric mixer on high speed until stiff peaks form. Fold about one-third of the egg whites into batter; fold in remaining egg whites in 2 batches. Spoon batter into a greased (with butter) and floured 9-inch square baking pan.

4. Bake in preheated oven until a wooden pick inserted in center comes out clean, 25 to 28 minutes. Cool in pan on a wire rack 10 minutes. Remove cake from pan, and cool completely on wire rack, about 1 hour.

5. Stir together peaches and remaining ½ cup granulated sugar in a large bowl. Let stand, stirring occasionally, 30 minutes. Stir in mint.

6. Gently whisk together mascarpone cheese, powdered sugar, and remaining 2 teaspoons vanilla in a large bowl. Beat heavy cream with a heavy-duty stand mixer, fitted with a whisk attachment, on medium-high speed until stiff peaks form. Gently fold whipped cream into mascarpone mixture.

7. To assemble trifle: Cut cooled cake into 1-inch cubes. Layer one-third of the cake cubes in bottom of a 4-quart trifle dish. Top with one-third each of peach slices with juice and whipped cream mixture. Repeat layers twice. Serve immediately, or cover and chill up to 24 hours.

Brown Sugar Layer Cake with Peach Buttercream

You'll love the lightly spiced cake layers, but the real star of this dessert is the frosting, which is made with peach puree and rich browned butter. Cook the butter in a light-color pan so you can watch it change shades as the water evaporates and golden brown flecks (toasted milk solids) appear.

ACTIVE 30 MIN. - TOTAL 1 HOUR, PLUS 1 HOUR COOLING

SERVES 12

- 1 cup butter, softened, plus more for greasing pans
- 1 cup granulated sugar
- 1 cup packed light brown sugar
- 4 large eggs
- 3 cups all-purpose flour, plus more for pans
- 2 tsp. baking powder
- ½ tsp. ground cinnamon
- ½ tsp. table salt
- ½ tsp. baking soda
- 1¼ cups whole buttermilk
- 2 tsp. vanilla extract
  Peach Buttercream (recipe follows)
  Fresh peach slices

1. Preheat oven to 350°F. Beat butter with a heavy-duty stand mixer on medium speed until creamy. Gradually add granulated sugar and brown sugar, beating until light and fluffy, 3 to 5 minutes. Add eggs, 1 at a time, beating just until blended after each addition.

2. Whisk together flour, baking powder, cinnamon, salt, and baking soda in a medium bowl until well blended. Add flour mixture to butter mixture alternately with buttermilk, beginning and ending with flour mixture. Beat on low speed just until blended after each addition. Beat in vanilla extract. Pour batter into 3 greased (with butter) and floured 9-inch round pans.

3. Bake in preheated oven until a wooden pick inserted in center comes out clean, 19 to 24 minutes. Cool in pans on wire racks 10 minutes, and remove from pans. Cool completely on wire racks, about 1 hour.

4. Use a small offset spatula to spread Peach Buttercream between layers and on top and sides of cake. Garnish top with peach slices.

Peach Buttercream

ACTIVE 30 MIN. - TOTAL 50 MIN., PLUS 1 HOUR CHILLING

MAKES ABOUT 7 CUPS

- 1½ cups butter
- 5 peaches, peeled and coarsely chopped (about 1½ lb.)
- ½ tsp. table salt
- 3 (16-oz.) pkg. powdered sugar
- 3 tsp. vanilla extract
- 8 to 9 Tbsp. whole milk

1. Cook butter in a small heavy saucepan over medium, stirring constantly, until butter begins to turn golden brown, 8 to 10 minutes. Immediately remove pan from heat, and pour butter into a small freezer-proof bowl. Cover and chill until butter is cool and begins to solidify, about 1 hour.

2. Meanwhile, process peaches in a food processor until completely smooth. Pour peaches through a fine mesh strainer into a bowl, and discard solids. Place strained peaches in a small heavy saucepan over medium. Cook, stirring often, until reduced to ½ cup, 10 to 15 minutes. Cool completely, about 20 minutes.

3. Beat together cooled butter and salt with a heavy-duty stand mixer on medium speed until creamy. Gradually add powdered sugar alternately with reduced peaches (about 6 tablespoons), vanilla, and 8 tablespoons milk, beating well after each addition. If needed, add up to 1 additional tablespoon milk, 1 teaspoon at a time, and beat until desired consistency is reached.

**BROWN SUGAR LAYER CAKE
WITH PEACH BUTTERCREAM
(PAGE 164)**

PEACH CUSTARD PIE
(PAGE 168)

SKILLET-FRIED PEACHES
À LA MODE (PAGE 168)

Peach Custard Pie

(Photo, page 166)

This smooth and creamy custard-filled pie tastes great chilled or at room temperature. Bake it a day ahead of time, or prepare the dough two days in advance. Wrap it tightly in plastic wrap, and store it, covered, in the refrigerator. However you make it, let the pie cool completely before slicing so the filling has time to firm up.

ACTIVE 25 MIN. - TOTAL 2 HOURS,
PLUS 2 HOURS COOLING
SERVES 8

CRUST
- 1½ cups all-purpose flour, plus more for work surface
- 1 Tbsp. granulated sugar
- ¾ tsp. table salt
- ¼ cup cold butter, cubed
- ¼ cup cold shortening, cubed
- 4 to 5 Tbsp. ice-cold water

FILLING
- ¾ cup granulated sugar
- ¾ cup heavy cream
- ¼ cup butter, melted
- 3 Tbsp. all-purpose flour
- ¼ tsp. table salt
- ¼ tsp. ground ginger
- 3 large eggs
- 4 medium (about 1¼ lb. total), firm-ripe peaches, sliced

1. Prepare the Crust: Pulse flour, granulated sugar, and salt in a food processor until combined, 3 or 4 times. Add butter and shortening, and pulse until mixture resembles coarse meal, 8 to 10 times. Drizzle in water, 1 tablespoon at a time, and pulse until dough begins to clump together. Gather dough into a ball, and flatten into a disk. Wrap in plastic wrap, and chill 30 minutes.
2. Preheat oven to 375°F. Roll dough into a 12-inch circle (about 1/8 inch thick) on a lightly floured work surface. Fit dough into a 9-inch pie plate. Fold edges under, and crimp. Prick bottom and sides with a fork. Line dough with parchment paper; fill with pie weights or dried beans. Bake 20 minutes. Remove weights and parchment paper; bake until lightly browned, 5 to 10 minutes. Transfer to a wire rack, and cool piecrust completely, about 30 minutes.

3. Prepare the Filling: Whisk together sugar, heavy cream, butter, flour, salt, ginger, and eggs in a medium bowl until completely smooth. Place peaches in cooled piecrust, and pour sugar-cream mixture evenly over peaches.
4. Bake in preheated oven until almost set in the middle, 40 to 45 minutes, covering edges with aluminum foil during the last 10 to 15 minutes, if needed, to prevent excessive browning. Transfer pie to a wire rack. Cool completely, about 2 hours, before serving.

Skillet-Fried Peaches à la Mode

(Photo, page 167)

Apples aren't the only fruit that can be fried in a skillet. These buttery peaches make an amazing topper for ice cream, pound cake, or both. A dash of peach schnapps deepens the flavor of the fruit and adds a little kick. (Bourbon, rum, or brandy will also work well.) Or skip the alcohol completely and use the same amount of vanilla extract.

ACTIVE 15 MIN. - TOTAL 15 MIN.
SERVES 6

- 5 medium peaches, sliced into ½-inch-thick wedges (about 6 cups)
- 1 Tbsp. fresh lemon juice (from 1 lemon)
- ½ tsp. ground cinnamon
- ¼ tsp. ground nutmeg
- ¼ tsp. kosher salt
- ½ cup packed light brown sugar
- ¼ cup butter
- 1 Tbsp. peach schnapps
  Vanilla ice cream

1. Toss together peaches, lemon juice, cinnamon, nutmeg, and salt in a medium bowl; set aside.
2. Melt sugar and butter in a large skillet over medium-high, stirring often, until mixture is bubbly, about 2 minutes. Stir in peach mixture. Cook, stirring occasionally, until softened and sauce is thickened, about 6 minutes. Stir in peach schnapps, and cook 1 minute. Remove peach mixture from heat, and let stand 5 minutes. Serve warm over vanilla ice cream.

Buttermilk-Peach Pops

(Photo, page 162)

This is a delicious way to use up any overripe or less-than-perfect peaches. Taste the fruit before adding honey—you might need less, depending on the sweetness of the peaches.

ACTIVE 15 MIN. - TOTAL 15 MIN.,
PLUS 6 HOURS FREEZING
MAKES 10

- ¾ cup whole buttermilk
- ½ cup honey
- ¼ cup heavy cream
- ¼ tsp. table salt
- 3 ripe peaches, peeled and diced (about 2½ cups), divided
- 10 wooden craft sticks

1. Process buttermilk, honey, cream, salt, and 1½ cups of the peaches in a blender or food processor until completely smooth, about 1 minute.
2. Finely chop remaining 1 cup peaches; stir into buttermilk mixture. Divide peach mixture among plastic frozen pop molds, leaving some room at top to allow for expansion. Cover with lids, and insert wooden craft sticks. Freeze until pops are completely firm and sticks are set, 6 to 8 hours. To remove pops, run outside of molds under hot water for a few seconds and remove lids.

Eat Like You're at the Beach

This goes-with-anything condiment is as essential at the shore as sunscreen

Growing up, I'd go with my family to our beach house on St. George Island, Florida. We would make the three-hour drive from Moultrie, Georgia, down to the Gulf any chance we got. Our first stop as we crossed the bridge onto the island was Doug's Fresh Seafood Market, a bright yellow trailer stocked with the best selection of fish in town. After picking up Mr. Doug's catch of the day, we'd unpack the car and head straight for the beach to soak in the last few hours of sun before dinner.

Our supper always featured goodies we'd bought from the seafood truck served with a few ingredients Mama had brought from home. My recipe for Old Bay Rémoulade with Crudités and Shrimp is an ode to those getaways we took years ago. Stir together Old Bay seasoning, mayonnaise, and a few pantry staples for an easy sauce that tastes amazing served with steamed peel 'n' eat shrimp or any other fresh seafood.

It's the perfect first-day-at-the-beach supper, which, now that I'm an adult, is ideal paired with rosé spritzers and enjoyed with my friends.

Old Bay Rémoulade with Crudités and Shrimp

ACTIVE 30 MIN. · TOTAL 30 MIN.
SERVES 8

- 1 small garlic clove
- 1½ cups mayonnaise
- 2 Tbsp. ketchup
- 2 tsp. drained capers, finely chopped
- 2 tsp. stone-ground mustard
- 2 tsp. Worcestershire sauce
- 2 tsp. prepared horseradish
- 1½ tsp. Old Bay seasoning
- 2 lb. cooked peel 'n' eat large shrimp
- 8 oz. fresh haricots verts (French green beans), trimmed and steamed
- 8 Persian cucumbers, quartered lengthwise
- 16 small carrots with tops, trimmed and halved lengthwise
- 16 radishes, halved if large

1. Using the flat side of a chef's knife, smash garlic on a cutting board. Run the flat side of knife over garlic until a paste forms, and place garlic paste in a medium bowl. Whisk in mayonnaise, ketchup, capers, mustard, Worcestershire, horseradish, and Old Bay until smooth. Transfer rémoulade to a serving bowl.
2. To serve, arrange bowl of rémoulade with shrimp and vegetables on a large platter. Store the rémoulade in an airtight container in the refrigerator up to 1 week.

SPIFFED-UP SPRITZER
Hot weather calls for a refreshing drink that's light and fizzy. Instead of the usual glass of wine topped with sparkling water, I love to mix **Bon & Viv Clementine Hibiscus Spiked Seltzer** with a splash of **fresh orange juice** and some **sparkling rosé**.

Crazy for Corn

Five delicious ways to make the most of summer's sweetest pick

GRILLED CHICKEN
AND CORN
WITH CHARRED
SCALLION-LIME
BUTTER

Grilled Chicken and Corn with Charred Scallion-Lime Butter

ACTIVE 20 MIN. - TOTAL 30 MIN.,
PLUS 30 MIN. SOAKING
SERVES 4

- 4   ears fresh corn, unshucked
- 1   bunch scallions, trimmed
- ½   cup unsalted butter, softened
- 2   Tbsp. chopped fresh chives
- 2   Tbsp. chopped fresh flat-leaf parsley
- 1   Tbsp. fresh lime juice (from 1 lime)
- 2¾ tsp. kosher salt, divided
- ¾   tsp. black pepper, divided
- 4   (6-oz.) bone-in, skin-on chicken thighs
     Lime wedges

1. Working with 1 corn ear at a time, peel husks back to the base of ear; do not break off husks. Remove silk from ear. Place husks back up around ear. Soak prepared ears in water 30 minutes. Drain.
2. Preheat grill to medium-high (400°F to 450°F). Place corn on unoiled grates. Grill, uncovered, turning occasionally, until husks are charred, 20 to 25 minutes. Remove from grill.
3. Meanwhile, coat scallions with cooking spray. Place on unoiled grates. Grill, uncovered, turning occasionally, until lightly charred and wilted, 5 to 6 minutes. Remove from grill; cool 5 minutes. Coarsely chop. Process charred scallions, butter, chives, parsley, lime juice, 1¼ teaspoons of the salt, and ¼ teaspoon of the pepper in a mini food processor until smooth, 30 seconds. Transfer to a serving bowl, reserving 1½ tablespoons in a separate bowl.
4. Sprinkle chicken evenly with remaining 1½ teaspoons salt and ½ teaspoon pepper. Place chicken, skin-side down, on oiled grates. Grill, covered, turning occasionally, until a thermometer inserted in thickest portion of thighs registers 170°F, 14 to 16 minutes.
5. Brush chicken with reserved 1½ tablespoons butter mixture. Serve chicken and corn with lime wedges and remaining butter mixture.

PICK THE RIGHT PAN

Keep the corn, pepper, and okra vibrant by preparing this recipe in a stainless steel or nonstick skillet. A cast-iron pan may cause the vegetables to take on a gray tone.

MAQUE CHOUX
WITH SAUSAGE

Maque Choux with Sausage

ACTIVE 25 MIN. - TOTAL 25 MIN.
SERVES 4

- 2   Tbsp. unsalted butter
- 8   oz. andouille sausage, diced
- 3   cups fresh corn kernels (from 6 ears)
- 7   oz. fresh okra, sliced (about 2 cups)
- 1   medium-size red bell pepper, chopped (about 1 cup)
- 1   medium onion, chopped (about 1 cup)
- 1   Tbsp. chopped fresh thyme
- 2½ tsp. kosher salt
- 3   medium garlic cloves, minced (2 tsp.)
- 1   cup heavy cream
- ½   tsp. cayenne pepper
- ½   tsp. black pepper

Melt butter in a large skillet over medium-high. Add andouille sausage. Cook, stirring occasionally, until lightly browned, 6 to 8 minutes. Add corn, okra, bell pepper, onion, thyme, salt, and garlic. Cook, stirring occasionally, until vegetables are softened, 6 to 8 minutes. Add cream and cayenne; bring mixture to a boil over medium-high. Reduce heat to medium. Simmer, stirring occasionally, until slightly thickened, 5 to 6 minutes. Stir in black pepper. Divide among 4 bowls.

Corn-and-Bacon Fettuccine

ACTIVE 30 MIN. - TOTAL 30 MIN.
SERVES 4

- 8 oz. uncooked fettuccine
- 4 ears fresh corn, shucked
- 4 thick-cut bacon slices, chopped
- ½ cup finely chopped shallots (from 2 shallots)
- 1 Tbsp. chopped fresh thyme
- ¼ cup thinly sliced fresh basil, divided
- 2½ tsp. kosher salt, divided
- 3 Tbsp. all-purpose flour
- 3 cups whole milk, divided
- ½ tsp. black pepper
- 1¼ oz. Parmesan cheese, shredded (about ½ cup)

1. Cook pasta according to package directions. Drain, and set aside.
2. Meanwhile, cut kernels from corn cobs; set aside. Using small holes of a box grater, scrape milky liquid from cobs into a small bowl; set aside.
3. Cook bacon in a large skillet over medium-high, stirring often, until crispy, 6 to 8 minutes. Stir in corn kernels, shallots, thyme, 2 tablespoons of the basil, and 1 teaspoon of the salt. Cook, stirring often, until mixture softens, 3 to 4 minutes. Remove from heat.
4. Whisk together flour and ½ cup of the milk in a small bowl until smooth. Stir together reserved corn cob liquid and remaining 2½ cups milk in a saucepan; bring to a simmer over high. Add flour mixture. Cook, whisking occasionally, until thickened and slightly reduced, 5 to 6 minutes. Stir in pepper and remaining 1½ teaspoons salt.
5. Return bacon mixture to medium-high. Add cooked pasta and thickened sauce; toss to coat. Cook, tossing occasionally, until mixture comes to a simmer, about 2 minutes. Divide pasta among 4 shallow bowls; sprinkle with Parmesan and remaining 2 tablespoons basil.

MAKE SOME MILK
Starchy, sweet corn "milk" (extra liquid from the cobs) thickens the sauce and adds flavor. To extract the liquid, run a de-kerneled cob over the small holes of a box grater.

Mexican Street Corn Pizza

ACTIVE 45 MIN. - TOTAL 45 MIN.
SERVES 4

- 3 ears fresh corn, shucked
- 1 small poblano chile
- 1 lb. fresh prepared pizza dough
  All-purpose flour, for work surface
- 1 Tbsp. cornmeal
- 2 Tbsp. olive oil
- 8 oz. low-moisture part-skim
  mozzarella cheese, shredded
  (2 cups)
- 2 tsp. kosher salt
- ½ tsp. black pepper
- 1 Tbsp. sour cream
- 1 Tbsp. fresh lime juice (from 1 lime)
- ⅓ cup crumbled Cotija cheese,
  (1½ oz.)
- ½ cup loosely packed fresh cilantro
  leaves
- ¼ tsp. smoked paprika
  Lime wedges

1. Place pizza stone in oven. Preheat oven to 500°F. Heat a grill pan over high; coat with cooking spray. Add corn and poblano to pan. Cook, turning occasionally, until charred, 8 to 10 minutes. Remove from heat; cool 5 minutes. Cut kernels from corn cobs; discard cobs. Chop poblano, discarding stem and seeds.

2. Roll dough out on a lightly floured surface into a 14-inch circle. Scatter cornmeal on preheated pizza stone. Transfer dough to stone. Prick dough liberally with a fork. Brush with oil. Top with mozzarella, leaving a 1-inch border. Top with corn and poblano; then sprinkle with salt and pepper. Bake in preheated oven until cheese is bubbly and crust is golden, 10 to 12 minutes.

3. Meanwhile, stir together sour cream and lime juice.

4. Remove pizza from oven. Drizzle evenly with sour cream mixture. Sprinkle with Cotija, cilantro, and paprika. Slice and serve with lime wedges.

NO STONE, NO PROBLEM

If you don't have a pizza stone, preheat a 13- x 9-inch sheet pan (not a cookie sheet). After it preheats, coat with cooking spray. Then sprinkle it with cornmeal before adding the pizza dough.

SUCCOTASH SWITCHEROO
Make it a meal by adding shrimp. Any summer vegetables and herbs you have on hand will taste great with corn. We like mixing it up with tomatoes, zucchini, basil, and field peas.

Shrimp-and-Corn Succotash

ACTIVE 25 MIN. · TOTAL 25 MIN.,
PLUS 30 MIN. CHILLING
SERVES 4

2 Tbsp. olive oil
1 lb. large peeled, deveined raw shrimp
2½ tsp. kosher salt, divided
4 oz. green beans, trimmed and cut into 1-inch pieces
¼ cup mayonnaise
2 Tbsp. apple cider vinegar
2 Tbsp. chopped fresh tarragon
2 Tbsp. chopped fresh flat-leaf parsley
½ tsp. black pepper

3 cups fresh corn kernels (from 6 ears)
1 lb. (2 cups) cooked fresh or frozen lima beans

1. Heat oil in a large skillet over medium-high. Add shrimp and ½ teaspoon of the salt. Cook, stirring occasionally, until shrimp turn pink and just opaque, 3 to 4 minutes. Transfer to a plate; chill in refrigerator 30 minutes.

2. Meanwhile, bring a large saucepan of salted water to a boil over high. Add green beans; cook until bright green and just tender, about 2 minutes. Drain; plunge into a bowl filled with ice water. Drain again.

3. Stir together mayonnaise, vinegar, herbs, pepper, and remaining 2 teaspoons salt in a large bowl. Add shrimp, green beans, corn, and lima beans; toss to combine. Divide among 4 plates.

Pancakes Squared

Whip up a light, fluffy batch in the oven

Sheet Pan Berry Pancakes with Honey–Butter Syrup

ACTIVE 20 MIN. · TOTAL 45 MIN.
SERVES 8

- 1¾ cups all-purpose flour
- 2 Tbsp. granulated sugar
- 1½ tsp. baking powder
- 1¼ tsp. kosher salt
- 1 tsp. baking soda
- 2 cups whole buttermilk
- 2 large eggs
- ¾ tsp. vanilla extract, divided
- 10 Tbsp. butter, melted, divided
- 1½ cups sliced fresh strawberries (from 1 qt.)
- ½ cup honey

1. Preheat oven to 350°F. Stir together flour, sugar, baking powder, salt, and baking soda in a large bowl. Whisk together buttermilk, eggs, and ½ teaspoon of the vanilla in a medium bowl. Gradually stir buttermilk mixture into flour mixture. Gently stir in ¼ cup of the melted butter. (Do not overmix; batter will be lumpy.)

2. Pour batter into a lightly greased (with cooking spray) 15- x 10-inch rimmed baking sheet. Bake in preheated oven 7 minutes; sprinkle evenly with strawberries. Continue baking until golden brown and a wooden pick inserted into thickest part comes out clean, 15 to 18 more minutes.

3. While pancakes bake, stir together honey and remaining 6 tablespoons melted butter and ¼ teaspoon vanilla in a small saucepan over medium-low; cook until warm, about 1 minute. Slice pancake into 16 squares, and serve with warm syrup.

FREEZE WITH EASE

Cool pancake squares completely. Wrap each one individually in plastic wrap; place in a large zip-top freezer bag. Freeze up to two months. To reheat, remove a pancake from bag, unwrap, place on a microwave-safe plate; microwave at HIGH until hot throughout, 30 to 45 seconds.

It's Taco Night!

One fast recipe and two tasty ways to change it up

Shrimp-Tomatillo Tacos

ACTIVE 20 MIN. - TOTAL 20 MIN.
SERVES 4

- 2 Tbsp. olive oil
- 1 medium white onion, finely chopped (about ½ cup)
- 5 fresh tomatillos, husks removed, rinsed, patted dry, and diced
- 1 serrano chile, seeded and chopped
- 2 small garlic cloves, minced
- 1 lb. medium peeled and deveined shrimp
- 1½ tsp. kosher salt
- 1 tsp. ground cumin
- ½ tsp. ancho chile powder
- 1 Tbsp. fresh lime juice (from 1 lime)
- 8 (6-inch) corn tortillas, lightly charred
  Shredded cabbage, sliced radishes and scallions, chopped cilantro

1. Heat oil in a large skillet over medium-high. Add onion, tomatillos, serrano, and garlic. Cook, stirring often, 7 to 8 minutes.
2. Stir in shrimp, salt, cumin, and chile powder. Cook, stirring often, until shrimp are cooked through, 3 to 4 minutes. Stir in lime juice. Serve in tortillas with toppings.

CALORIES: **312** – CARBS: **38G** – FAT: **10G**

Tasty Spin-Offs

Black Bean-Corn Tacos

Prepare recipe as directed in Step 1. In Step 2, substitute 1 (15-oz.) can drained and rinsed **black beans** and 1 cup **corn kernels** for shrimp; increase cook time to 5 minutes. Omit toppings from shrimp recipe; serve bean mixture in **corn tortillas** with diced **avocados**, sliced **scallions**, and **crema**.

CALORIES: **344** – CARBS: **61G** – FAT: **10G**

Chicken-Bell Pepper Tacos

Prepare recipe as directed in Step 1. In Step 2, substitute 2 cups chopped cooked **chicken** and 1 cup diced **red bell pepper** for shrimp; increase cook time to 5 minutes. Omit toppings from shrimp recipe; serve chicken mixture in **corn tortillas** with crumbled **queso fresco** and **cilantro leaves**.

CALORIES: **345** – CARBS: **40G** – FAT: **12G**

CHICKEN-BELL PEPPER TACOS

SHRIMP-TOMATILLO TACOS

BLACK BEAN-CORN TACOS

Snow Day

Enjoy these creamy, frosty treats in fresh and fruity flavors

Blueberry Snowballs

ACTIVE 20 MIN. - TOTAL 20 MIN.,
PLUS 12 HOURS FREEZING
SERVES 4

- 1 (6-oz.) container fresh blueberries
- 1 cup granulated sugar
- 2 Tbsp. fresh lemon juice (from 1 lemon)

1. Process berries in a food processor until completely smooth, about 20 seconds; set aside.
2. Bring 2 cups water and the sugar to a boil in a saucepan over medium-high, stirring occasionally. Stir in blueberry puree; reduce heat to medium. Simmer 2 minutes. Pour through a fine mesh strainer into a bowl, pressing lightly. Discard solids. Stir lemon juice into strained mixture. Cool completely, 30 minutes.
3. Pour mixture into an 8-inch square pan; cover tightly with aluminum foil. Freeze until completely frozen, 12 hours or up to 24 hours.
4. Break mixture into pieces using a spoon, and transfer about one-fourth of pieces to a food processor. Process until smooth but still frozen, about 1 minute; transfer to a container or serving bowl. Repeat until all pieces have been processed. Serve immediately, or cover and freeze until ready to serve.

Lime Snowballs
SERVES 4

Omit Steps 1 and 2 in the Blueberry Snowballs recipe. Bring 2¼ cups **water** and 1¼ cups **granulated sugar** to a simmer in a small saucepan over medium-high, stirring occasionally until sugar is dissolved. Remove from heat, and stir in 1 tsp. **fresh lime zest** and ¾ cup **fresh lime juice** (from 6 limes). Cool sugar-lime mixture completely, about 30 minutes. Proceed with Steps 3 and 4 as directed.

Watermelon Snowballs
SERVES 6

Omit Steps 1 and 2 in the Blueberry Snowballs recipe. Bring 1 cup **granulated sugar** and ½ cup **water** to a boil in a small saucepan over medium-high, stirring occasionally until sugar is dissolved. Chill sugar mixture 30 minutes. Process 5 cups **seedless watermelon** cubes and the chilled sugar mixture in a blender or food processor until completely smooth, about 1 minute. Pour mixture through a fine mesh strainer into a bowl, pressing lightly. Discard solids, and stir 3 tablespoons **fresh lime juice** (from 2 limes) into strained mixture. Proceed with Steps 3 and 4 as directed.

CHILL OUT

Unlike a granita, which is continually scraped with a fork for an icy texture, these snowballs are as soft and creamy as sorbet. And there's no scraping required—the frozen fruit mixture is blended in a food processor.

COOKING (SL) SCHOOL

MIX IT UP

Pancakes They'll Flip For

Start with our big-batch recipe (page 175), and add these creative combos

❶ Semisweet chocolate chips, cinnamon, and slivered almonds

❷ Blueberries and peach preserves

❸ Raspberries, lemon zest, and powdered sugar

❹ Thinly sliced apples, apple pie spice, and chopped pecans

"Always stir your pancake batter gently, and don't worry about lumps. This will ensure that they turn out delicate and tender, not rubbery and tough."

Pam Lolley
Test Kitchen Professional

TEST KITCHEN TECHNIQUE

The Right Way to Freeze Corn

We tried several methods, and this was the clear winner

SHUCK
Remove and discard the husks and the silks from corn cobs.

BLANCH
Cook corn on the cob in boiling water for 2 minutes. Remove and immediately plunge them into ice water for 2 minutes.

FREEZE
Cut kernels off the cobs; discard cobs. Place kernels in a zip-top plastic freezer bag, pressing out as much air as possible. Freeze up to 3 months.

KNOW-HOW

A Better Way to Butter

Buttering corn on the cob at the table can be a slippery task. Instead, melt 1 tablespoon of butter per ear on a sheet pan, and then roll the cooked ears of corn through the liquid until they're evenly coated. (You can also do this in a stockpot if you cut the ears in half first.)

August

STUFFED OKRA
POPPERS (PAGE 184)

The Wonders of Okra

Stuffed. Pickled. Fried. A vegetable with nostalgic roots shines in new and delicious ways

A three-acre garden doesn't offer any shade.

I learned this lesson all too well as a child when I'd spend time at my paternal grandparents' farm outside Grenada, Mississippi. They devoted the rest of their 10 acres to horses and an occasional cow, who had the luxury of shade trees along the fence line. But the tractor-plowed rows of garden took the brunt of the summer sun, helping it overflow with unruly field peas, green beans, tomatoes, peppers, watermelons, yellow squash, and okra–the last of which I developed a powerful love-hate relationship with.

Being allowed to harvest the produce was such fun for a kid like me who lived in town, a mere eight miles away, and who enjoyed playing the role of farm girl every now and then. At least it was fun for the first few minutes, before the heat and humidity fully registered. Thankfully, tomatoes were quick and easy to pick–squash, watermelons, peppers, peas, and beans, too. But the okra felt like punishment. I took my time with it, despite the heat, doing my best to avoid the prickly parts of the plant. Yet no matter how careful I was, those little spines on the stalks and leaves always got me. I wouldn't realize the damage until later, when a dip in the bathtub would make my tiny, invisible wounds painfully apparent. I imagine my grandparents laughing as they overheard me kid–cursing under my breath, mumbling "dadgum okra" as I rubbed the sore spots with a washcloth.

Even so, I cherished that okra. It was so fresh that it never saw the inside of the refrigerator. The pain was worth it; those tender pods with their asparagus-like flavor were a real treat. My grandmother would cut them into 1-inch slices, toss them in cornmeal and salt, and fry them. I loved her version of fried okra so much more than the heavily breaded kind at the cafeteria-style restaurants we'd sometimes visit. I'd painstakingly pick off most of the breading, trying to somehow re-create her ratio of okra to coating so more vegetable flavor would shine through. Sometimes, she'd toss a few slices into a pot of field peas to thicken the cooking liquid. And she would occasionally simmer okra with chopped tomatoes, creating that classic love-it-or-hate-it Southern side. The viscous texture didn't bother me; I speared several okra wheels on my fork so I could get a big mouthful in each bite.

As an adult, I still fry it the way my grandmother taught me, but I've expanded my repertoire over the years, stuffing the pods with cheese like you would jalapeño poppers, pickling them with a good splash of bourbon, or eating them–if they're small, tender, and very fresh–mostly raw in a salad.

I've even tried to grow okra with little success. I'm just a lousy gardener. Luckily, I have access to farmers' markets and produce stands where I can buy the fresh, young pods in the summertime. I'll still squeeze a few of them to make sure they're good, confirmed by the prick of those little spikes in my older fingers. Dadgum okra. –Ann Taylor Pittman

CRUNCHY OKRA-AND-CORN SALAD WITH RANCH DRESSING (PAGE 184)

CURRIED OKRA
SHOESTRING FRIES

Curried Okra Shoestring Fries

ACTIVE 40 MIN. - TOTAL 40 MIN.
SERVES 8

- ¼ cup Major Grey's chutney (such as Crosse & Blackwell)
- ¼ cup sour cream
- 1 lb. fresh okra pods, trimmed
- 4 cups canola oil
- ½ cup cornstarch
- 2 tsp. curry powder (preferably Madras)
- 1½ tsp. kosher salt

1. Stir together chutney and sour cream in a small bowl; set aside.
2. Cut each okra pod in half lengthwise. Place halves, cut-side down, on cutting board; cut each half lengthwise into 3 or 4 thin strips.
3. Heat oil in a large Dutch oven over high to 350°F to 375°F. Combine cornstarch, curry powder, and salt in a large zip-top plastic bag. Add okra strips to bag; seal and shake well to coat. Remove okra from bag, shaking off as much excess cornstarch as possible. Fry okra in 4 batches in hot oil until browned and crisp, about 4 minutes per batch. Drain on paper towels. Sprinkle with additional salt, if desired. Serve with sauce.

Fried Shrimp-and-Okra Po'Boys

ACTIVE 45 MIN. - TOTAL 45 MIN.
SERVES 4

- ½ cup mayonnaise (such as Duke's)
- 2 Tbsp. chopped fresh chives
- 2 Tbsp. Creole mustard
- 2 tsp. fresh lemon juice
- 2 tsp. chopped drained capers
- 1 tsp. Worcestershire sauce
- 8 oz. small fresh okra pods, trimmed
- 1 cup whole buttermilk
- 1½ cups fine yellow cornmeal
- 2 tsp. Creole seasoning (such as Tony Chachere's)
  Canola oil
- ¾ lb. large raw shrimp, peeled and deveined (about 20 shrimp)
- 2 (12-inch) po'boy rolls or French bread rolls, split, toasted, and cut in half crosswise
- 8 (⅛-inch-thick) tomato slices (from 1 medium tomato)
- 2 cups thinly sliced iceberg lettuce (from 1 head)

FRIED SHRIMP-AND-OKRA PO'BOYS

1. Stir together mayonnaise, chives, mustard, lemon juice, capers, and Worcestershire sauce in a small bowl; set aside.
2. Use a meat mallet or rolling pin to smash okra, starting at tip of pod and working toward stem end. Place buttermilk in a shallow dish. Stir together cornmeal and Creole seasoning in another shallow dish. Dip okra in buttermilk. Lift out with a slotted spoon; dredge in cornmeal mixture, shaking off excess. (Reserve remaining buttermilk and cornmeal mixture.)
3. Pour oil to a depth of 2 inches in a large cast-iron skillet. Heat oil over high to 350°F to 375°F. Fry okra in 2 batches in hot oil until crisp and browned, about 3 minutes per batch, turning once. Remove okra with a slotted spoon, and drain on paper towels.
4. Dip shrimp in buttermilk. Lift out with a slotted spoon, and dredge in cornmeal mixture, shaking off excess. Fry shrimp in 2 batches in hot oil until crisp and browned, about 3 minutes, turning once. Remove shrimp with a slotted spoon, and drain on paper towels.
5. Spread about half the sauce evenly over bottoms of toasted rolls. Layer evenly with tomato slices, shrimp, okra, lettuce, and remaining sauce. Cover with tops of rolls.

Okra Basics

Three tips for picking and prepping

SELECT SMALL Pods that are about 3 inches long are more likely to be tender, while those 6 inches or larger tend to be woody.

CHECK THE COLOR Pick pods that are vibrant green or purple. Even small ones can be surprisingly tough if they're pale.

BE QUICK Once you cut into fresh okra, it will start to release its mucilaginous goo. This sticky substance is great for thickening gumbo or field peas, but might not be what you want for your basket of fried okra. Work with speed to cut down on the slime, and don't chop okra into very small pieces, which will make it gooier.

Stuffed Okra Poppers

(Photo, page 180)

ACTIVE 30 MIN. - TOTAL 30 MIN.
SERVES 8

- 2 oz. extra-sharp cheddar cheese, shredded (about ½ cup)
- 2 oz. cream cheese
- ¼ tsp. cayenne pepper
- 1 small garlic clove, grated
- ¼ tsp. kosher salt
- 24 (4- to 5-inch) fresh okra pods, trimmed
- 12 bacon slices, cut in half crosswise

1. Preheat grill to medium-high (400°F to 450°F). Stir together cheddar, cream cheese, cayenne, garlic, and salt until well blended.
2. Cut a slit lengthwise in each okra pod to form a pocket, starting about ½ inch from top and stopping about ½ inch from bottom. Stuff about 1 teaspoon cheese mixture into each pod. (Use a ½ teaspoon measure to stuff ½ teaspoon of the filling in the top part of the slit and ½ teaspoon in the bottom part.) Wrap 1 bacon piece around each pod.
3. Place poppers, bacon-seam down, in a single layer on oiled grates. Grill, uncovered, turning occasionally, until bacon is browned and crisp, 8 to 10 minutes. Serve immediately.

Bourbon-Brined Pickled Peppered Okra

ACTIVE 15 MIN. - TOTAL 45 MIN., PLUS 24 HOURS CHILLING
MAKES 3 PINTS

- 1¼ lb. small okra pods, trimmed
- 3 medium red Fresno chiles, quartered lengthwise
- 3 small bay leaves
- 6 Tbsp. (3 oz.) bourbon
- 2 tsp. mustard seeds
- 2 tsp. coriander seeds
- 1 tsp. black peppercorns
- 1¼ cups white distilled vinegar
- ¼ cup granulated sugar
- ¼ cup kosher salt

1. Pack okra evenly into 3 (1-pint) jars, alternating tips and stem ends to get more in each jar. Stuff 4 chile quarters and 1 bay leaf in each jar. Pour 2 tablespoons bourbon into each jar.

BOURBON-BRINED PICKLED PEPPERED OKRA

2. Cook mustard seeds, coriander seeds, and peppercorns in a small saucepan over medium until toasted, lightly browned, and very fragrant, 3 to 4 minutes. Add vinegar, 1 cup water, sugar, and salt to saucepan. Increase heat to high; bring to a boil. Boil until sugar and salt completely dissolve, about 3 minutes. Pour mixture evenly into jars. Cool completely, about 30 minutes. Cover with lids; chill 24 hours before serving. Store in refrigerator up to 2 weeks.

Crunchy Okra-and-Corn Salad with Ranch Dressing

(Photo, page 181)

ACTIVE 15 MIN. - TOTAL 15 MIN.
SERVES 4

- ⅓ cup mayonnaise
- 3 Tbsp. whole buttermilk
- 1 Tbsp. chopped fresh chives
- 1 Tbsp. chopped fresh dill
- 1 tsp. chopped fresh thyme
- 1 tsp. apple cider vinegar
- 1 medium garlic clove, grated
- ¾ tsp. kosher salt, divided
- ½ tsp. black pepper, divided
- 1 Tbsp. canola oil, divided
- 8 oz. fresh purple okra pods, halved lengthwise
- 1 cup fresh corn kernels (from 1 ear)
- 8 cups torn iceberg lettuce (from 1 head)

1. Whisk together mayonnaise, buttermilk, chives, dill, thyme, vinegar, garlic, ¼ teaspoon of the salt, and ¼ teaspoon of the pepper in a medium bowl. Chill until ready to serve.
2. Heat a large cast-iron skillet over high. Add 1 teaspoon of the oil; swirl to coat. Add half of okra, cut-side down. Cook just until cut side is lightly seared and purple color is still vibrant, 30 to 45 seconds. Remove from skillet. Repeat procedure with 1 teaspoon of the oil and remaining okra. Sprinkle okra with ¼ teaspoon of the salt.
3. Add remaining 1 teaspoon oil to skillet; swirl to coat. Add corn and remaining ¼ teaspoon salt and ¼ teaspoon pepper. Cook until lightly charred, stirring constantly, about 1 minute.
4. Arrange 2 cups lettuce on each of 4 plates; drizzle dressing evenly over salads. Top evenly with corn and okra.

That's a Wrap!

Rise and shine with fix-and-freeze breakfast burritos

Freezer Breakfast Burritos

ACTIVE 30 MIN. · TOTAL 45 MIN.
MAKES 8

- 1 lb. frozen potato tots
- 1 lb. ground pork breakfast sausage
- ½ cup finely chopped bell pepper, (from 1 medium bell pepper)
- 2 scallions, thinly sliced (about ¼ cup)
- 10 large eggs, beaten
- ¼ tsp. kosher salt
- ¼ tsp. black pepper
- 8 (12-inch) flour tortillas
- 12 oz. pre-shredded Mexican blend cheese (about 3 cups)
- ⅓ cup finely chopped fresh cilantro Salsa

1. Cook tots according to package directions until crispy. Cool about 10 minutes.
2. Meanwhile, heat a large nonstick skillet over medium-high. Add sausage. Cook, stirring to crumble, until browned, 6 to 7 minutes. Transfer to a bowl using a slotted spoon, reserving drippings in skillet.
3. Reduce heat to medium. Add bell pepper and scallions to skillet. Cook, stirring occasionally, until softened, about 3 minutes. Add eggs; reduce heat to medium-low. Cook, stirring constantly, until eggs resemble small curds and are no longer wet, about 4 minutes. Remove from heat; stir in salt and pepper. Cool about 10 minutes.
4. Tear 8 (15- x 12-inch) sheets of aluminum foil. Place 1 tortilla on 1 foil sheet; sprinkle tortilla with about ⅓ cup cheese. Top with ⅓ cup scrambled egg mixture, ¼ cup crumbled sausage, 6 tots, and 1 teaspoon cilantro. Fold sides of tortilla over filling; roll up. Wrap burrito in foil. Repeat process using remaining tortillas, cheese, egg mixture, sausage, tots, and cilantro. Freeze burritos, or heat as desired and eat immediately. Serve with salsa.

FREEZE IT
Wrap burritos individually in foil. Freeze in a single layer until solid, about 2 hours. Place frozen burritos inside a zip-top plastic freezer bag, seal, and keep up to 3 weeks.

REHEAT IT
For thawed burrito: Remove foil; place thawed burrito on a paper towel-lined plate. Microwave on HIGH until heated through, about 2 minutes.
For frozen burrito: Remove foil, and place frozen burrito on a paper towel-lined plate. Microwave on HIGH until heated through, 3 to 4 minutes, turning halfway through cook time.

Cool Soups for Hot Days

Three refreshing recipes for chilling out when the weather feels like an oven

Cucumber-Buttermilk Soup

ACTIVE 15 MIN. - TOTAL 15 MIN.,
PLUS 1 HOUR CHILLING
SERVES 4

Peel, seed, and chop 2 **small cucumbers**. Dice 1 separate **small cucumber** to equal ¼ cup. (Reserve any remaining diced cucumber for another use.) Process chopped cucumbers, 2 cups **whole buttermilk**, 1 cup **plain whole-milk yogurt**, 3 Tbsp. each chopped **fresh mint** and chopped **fresh tarragon**, 1 Tbsp. **fresh lemon juice** plus 1 tsp. **lemon zest** (from 1 lemon), and 1 tsp. **kosher salt** in a blender until very smooth, about 2 minutes, stopping to scrape down sides as needed. Chill 1 hour. To serve, top with a swirl of **buttermilk**, and garnish with diced cucumber and **fresh tarragon leaves**.

SWEET CORN-
BELL PEPPER SOUP

SWEET PEA-
AVOCADO SOUP

Sweet Corn–
Bell Pepper Soup

ACTIVE 25 MIN. - TOTAL 25 MIN.,
PLUS 4 HOURS CHILLING
SERVES 4

Cut kernels from 4 ears **fresh yellow corn** (shucked) to equal about 3 cups. Reserve ¼ cup of the kernels in a small bowl for serving. Chop 2 **orange bell peppers** (about 2 cups); reserve ¼ cup peppers in another small bowl for serving. Melt 2 Tbsp. **unsalted butter** in a medium saucepan over medium-high. Combine remaining chopped peppers, ½ cup chopped **yellow onion** (from 1 medium onion), 2 minced **garlic cloves** (about 1 tsp.), 1 tsp. **kosher salt,**

½ tsp. **black pepper**, and remaining corn kernels. Cook, stirring occasionally, until onion is tender, about 8 minutes. Add 1½ cups **water**; bring to a boil. Cook until vegetables are tender, about 4 minutes. Transfer mixture to a blender; add 2 Tbsp. **extra-virgin olive oil.** Secure lid on blender, and remove center piece to allow steam to escape. Place a clean towel over opening. Process until smooth, about 2 minutes. Pour mixture through a fine mesh strainer into a bowl, and discard solids. Stir in 1 tsp. **white wine vinegar**. Cover; chill at least 4 hours or up to 8 hours. Drizzle servings evenly with **extra-virgin olive oil**; sprinkle with reserved ¼ cup corn kernels and chopped orange bell pepper.

Sweet Pea–Avocado Soup

ACTIVE 10 MIN. - TOTAL 10 MIN.,
PLUS 1 HOUR CHILLING
SERVES 4

Process 3 medium chopped **avocados,** 2½ cups cold **sparkling water** (such as LaCroix; from 3 [12-oz.] cans), 2 cups **water**, 2 cups chopped **baby spinach,** 1½ cups thawed **frozen sweet peas,** 3 Tbsp. **fresh lime juice** (from 3 limes), 2 Tbsp. **white wine vinegar,** 1½ tsp. **kosher salt,** and ¾ tsp. **black pepper** in a blender until smooth, about 2 minutes, stopping to scrape down sides as needed. Transfer to a bowl, and chill 1 hour. Stir together ¼ cup **sour cream,** 2 Tbsp. chopped **fresh cilantro,** 2 tsp. **lime zest,** and ¼ tsp. **kosher salt** in a bowl. Dollop servings with sour cream mixture, and garnish with additional peas and cilantro leaves.

So Fast, So Good

Toss these delicious foil-pack suppers on the grill, and dinner is done in minutes

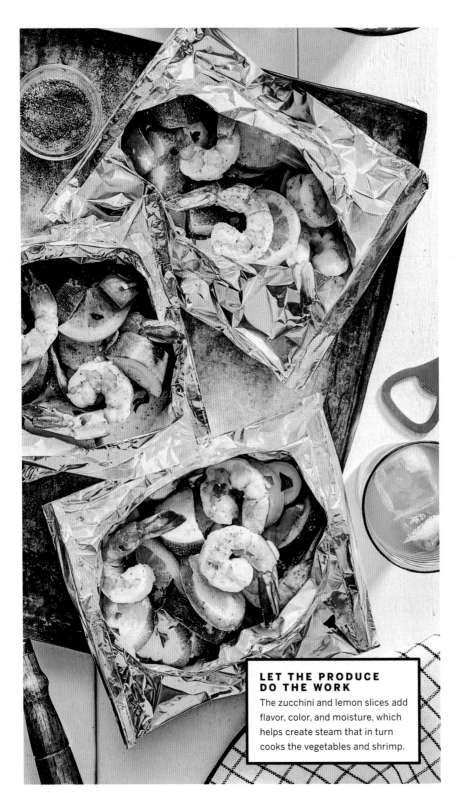

LET THE PRODUCE DO THE WORK

The zucchini and lemon slices add flavor, color, and moisture, which helps create steam that in turn cooks the vegetables and shrimp.

Cajun Shrimp with Red Potatoes and Zucchini

ACTIVE 10 MIN. · TOTAL 35 MIN.
SERVES 4

- 1½ lb. large peeled, deveined raw shrimp (tail on)
- 1 lb. baby red potatoes, cut into ¼-inch slices (about 3 cups)
- 3 zucchini, cut into 1-inch pieces (about 4 cups)
- 1 small red onion, cut into 1-inch pieces (about 1 cup)
- ¼ cup unsalted butter, melted
- 4 tsp. Cajun seasoning
- 1 tsp. kosher salt
- 1 lemon, halved lengthwise then cut crosswise into ¼-inch-thick slices
- 2 Tbsp. chopped fresh flat-leaf parsley (from 1 bunch)

1. Preheat a gas grill to medium (350°F to 400°F). Cut 4 (18- x 12-inch) sheets of heavy-duty aluminum foil; spray 1 side with cooking spray.
2. Toss together shrimp, potatoes, zucchini, onion, melted butter, Cajun seasoning, and kosher salt in a large bowl until mixture is evenly coated. Divide shrimp mixture evenly, and place in the center of the sprayed side of each foil sheet. Arrange shrimp so it is on top of the vegetable mixture; top evenly with lemon slices.
3. Bring up both long sides of foil until edges meet. Fold over ½ inch; close and seal edges. Fold over ½ inch again to further seal. Fold each short side over 1 inch to close and seal edges; fold over 2 more times to completely seal. Repeat with other packets.
4. Place packets on unoiled grates, folded-sides up. Grill, covered, until vegetables are tender and shrimp turn pink and are firm, about 10 minutes. Remove packets from grill; carefully unfold edges of long seam, allowing steam to escape. Sprinkle evenly with parsley; serve immediately.

Red Beans and Rice

ACTIVE 10 MIN. - TOTAL 45 MIN.

SERVES 4

- 1 (14.5-oz.) can fire-roasted diced tomatoes, undrained
- ¾ cup lower-sodium chicken broth
- ½ tsp. kosher salt
- 1 tsp. Cajun seasoning, divided
- 1 cup uncooked instant white rice
- 1 (16-oz.) can red kidney beans, drained and rinsed
- 2 cups chopped green bell pepper, (from 1 large bell pepper)
- 1 lb. andouille sausage, diagonally cut into 1½-inch-thick slices
- ¼ cup chopped scallions (from 1 bunch)

1. Preheat a gas grill to medium (350°F to 400°F). Cut 4 (18- x 12-inch) sheets of heavy-duty aluminum foil; spray 1 side with cooking spray.

2. Stir together tomatoes, broth, salt, and ½ teaspoon of the Cajun seasoning in a medium bowl. Stir in rice; let stand at room temperature until majority of liquid is absorbed, about 10 minutes. Stir in beans, bell pepper, and remaining ½ teaspoon Cajun seasoning. Divide rice mixture evenly, and place in the center of the sprayed side of each foil sheet. Top evenly with sausage.

3. Bring up both long sides of foil until edges meet. Fold over ½ inch; close and seal edges. Fold over ½ inch again to further seal. Fold each short side over 1 inch to close and seal edges; fold over 2 more times to completely seal. Repeat with other packets.

4. Place packets on unoiled grates, folded-side up. Grill, covered, 10 minutes. Rotate packets 90 degrees, cover, and continue cooking until rice is tender and sausage is cooked, 5 to 8 minutes. Remove packets from grill, and carefully unfold edges of long seam, allowing steam to escape. Garnish with chopped scallions.

ADD A TASTE OF LOUISIANA

Andouille, a coarsely ground smoked pork sausage, is used in Cajun and Creole cooking. Our Test Kitchen likes Savoie's brand, which is flavored with garlic and paprika.

Grilled Vegetables with Chickpeas, Feta, and Couscous

ACTIVE 10 MIN. - TOTAL 40 MIN.
SERVES 4

- 1½ cups uncooked couscous
- 1 cup vegetable broth
- 2 tsp. kosher salt, divided
- 1 (15-oz.) can chickpeas (garbanzo beans), drained and rinsed
- 2 large zucchini, halved lengthwise, diagonally cut into 1-inch pieces (about 4½ cups)
- 2 yellow squash, cut into ½-inch-thick slices (about 3 cups)
- 1 red bell pepper, cut into 1-inch pieces (about 2 cups)
- 2 Tbsp. olive oil
- 1 Tbsp. chopped fresh oregano, plus more for garnish
- ¼ cup crumbled feta cheese

1. Preheat a gas grill to medium (350°F to 400°F). Cut 4 (18- x 12-inch) sheets of heavy-duty aluminum foil; spray 1 side with cooking spray.
2. Stir together couscous, broth, and 1 teaspoon of the salt in a medium bowl; set aside. Stir together chickpeas, zucchini, squash, bell pepper, oil, oregano, and remaining 1 teaspoon salt. Divide chickpea mixture evenly, and place in the center of the sprayed side of each foil sheet. Top vegetables evenly with couscous mixture.
3. Bring up both long sides of foil until edges meet. Fold over ½ inch; close and seal edges. Fold over ½ inch again to further seal. Fold each short side over 1 inch to close and seal edges; fold over 2 more times to completely seal. Repeat with other packets.
4. Place packets on unoiled grates, folded-side up. Grill, covered, 10 minutes. Rotate packets 90 degrees. Cover and grill until vegetables and couscous are tender, about 5 minutes. Remove packets from grill; carefully unfold edges of long seam, allowing steam to escape. Gently fluff couscous, and stir into vegetables. Sprinkle servings with feta and oregano.

GRILLED VEGETABLES WITH CHICKPEAS, FETA, AND COUSCOUS

KNOW YOUR INGREDIENTS

Couscous steams right in the foil pack in this tasty meatless main. Be sure to buy the regular kind, not Israeli (pearled) couscous, which takes longer to cook.

Cheesy Green Chile Pork Chops

ACTIVE 15 MIN. - TOTAL 45 MIN.
SERVES 4

- 2 (16-oz.) cans pinto beans, drained and rinsed
- 1 (4.5-oz.) can chopped green chiles
- 2 small bell peppers, sliced (about 2 cups)
- 1 small red onion, sliced (about 1 cup)
- 1 Tbsp. olive oil
- 1½ tsp. kosher salt, divided
- ¾ tsp. chili powder
- ½ tsp. ground cumin
- 4 (8-oz.) boneless pork chops (1 to 1¼ inches thick)
- 4 oz. pepper Jack cheese, shredded (about 1 cup)
- Chopped fresh cilantro, for garnish
- Lime wedges, for serving

1. Preheat a gas grill to medium (350°F to 400°F). Cut 4 (18- x 12-inch) sheets of heavy-duty aluminum foil; spray 1 side with cooking spray.
2. Stir together beans, chiles, bell peppers, onion, oil, and ½ teaspoon of the salt in a bowl. Divide mixture evenly, and place in the center of the sprayed side of each foil sheet. Stir together chili powder, ground cumin, and remaining 1 teaspoon salt; season pork with spice mixture. Place 1 pork chop over vegetables in each packet.

3. Bring up both long sides of foil until edges meet. Fold over ½ inch; close and seal edges. Fold over ½ inch again to further seal. Fold each short side over 1 inch to close and seal edges; fold over 2 more times to completely seal. Repeat with other packets.

4. Place packets on unoiled grates, folded-side up. Grill, covered, 10 minutes. Rotate packets 90 degrees; cover. Continue grilling until a thermometer inserted in pork registers 140°F, about 8 minutes. Remove packets from grill; let stand 5 minutes. (Internal temperature will continue to rise to 145°F while pork stands.)

5. Cut a large X across top of packets. Carefully fold back edges, allowing steam to escape. Immediately sprinkle cheese evenly over pork chops; let stand until cheese is melted, about 1½ minutes. Garnish with cilantro, and serve with lime wedges.

Lemon–Basil Chicken Breasts

ACTIVE 15 MIN. · TOTAL 35 MIN.
SERVES 4

- 2 (8.5-oz.) pkg. fully cooked gemelli pasta, heated according to pkg. directions
- 2 pt. heirloom cherry tomatoes, halved (about 4 cups)
- 2 Tbsp. olive oil
- 2¼ tsp. kosher salt, divided
- 4 (6-oz.) boneless, skinless chicken breasts
- ½ tsp. black pepper
- ¼ cup unsalted butter, at room temperature
- 1 tsp. grated lemon zest (from 1 lemon)
- ¼ cup loosely packed small fresh basil leaves

1. Preheat a gas grill to medium (350°F to 400°F). Cut 4 (18- x 12-inch) sheets of heavy-duty aluminum foil; spray 1 side with cooking spray.

2. Stir together pasta, cherry tomatoes, oil, and 1 teaspoon of the kosher salt. Divide pasta mixture evenly, and place in the center of the sprayed side of each foil sheet.

3. Season chicken breasts with pepper and remaining 1¼ teaspoons salt. Place 1 breast on top of pasta mixture in each packet. Stir together butter and lemon zest. Spread about 1 tablespoon butter mixture over each chicken breast.

4. Bring up both long sides of foil until edges meet. Fold over ½ inch; close and seal edges. Fold over ½ inch again to further seal. Fold each short side over 1 inch to close and seal edges; fold over 2 more times to completely seal. Repeat with other packets.

5. Place packets on unoiled grates, folded-sides up. Grill, covered, 10 minutes. Rotate packets 90 degrees; cover. Continue grilling until a thermometer inserted in chicken registers 165°F, 8 to 10 minutes. Remove packets from grill, and carefully unfold edges of long seam, allowing steam to escape. Top with basil.

CHEESY GREEN CHILE PORK CHOPS

PICK THE RIGHT PORK

This recipe calls for thick boneless pork chops (rather than thin ones) because they won't overcook before the vegetables are tender.

LEMON-BASIL CHICKEN BREASTS

Summer on a Stick

Combine a marinade, your favorite spice blend, and fresh ingredients to make these quick kebabs

The Can't-Miss Kebab Marinade

ACTIVE 5 MIN. · TOTAL 5 MIN.
MAKES ABOUT 1¼ CUPS

Process ½ cup **olive oil**, ½ cup chopped **yellow onion** (from 1 small onion), ¼ cup **apple cider vinegar**, 2 medium **garlic cloves**, 1 Tbsp. **honey**, 2 tsp. **kosher salt**, and 1 tsp. **black pepper** in a blender until well blended, about 45 seconds.

Lemon Pepper-Salmon Kebabs

ACTIVE 20 MIN. · TOTAL 30 MIN., PLUS 2 HOURS MARINATING
SERVES 4

Stir together **marinade** and 2 tsp. **lemon pepper seasoning** in a medium bowl. Stir in 24 (1½-inch) pieces **skinless salmon** (about 1½ lb.), 24 **lemon** slices (from 2 large lemons), and 24 (¾-inch-thick) slices **zucchini** (from 1 lb. zucchini). Cover; chill at least 2 hours or up to 4 hours. Skewer onto 8 (10-inch) skewers. Discard marinade. Preheat grill to medium-high (400°F to 450°F). Place kebabs on oiled grate. Grill, covered, until salmon is cooked through, about 6 minutes, turning once halfway through cook time.

CALORIES: **433** – CARBS: **14G** – FAT: **26G**

Za'atar Chicken Kebabs

ACTIVE 25 MIN. - TOTAL 30 MIN., PLUS 4 HOURS MARINATING
SERVES 4

Combine **marinade** and 2 Tbsp. **za'atar seasoning** in a large bowl. Stir in 2 lb. **boneless, skinless chicken breasts** cut into 24 pieces, 1 lb. **yellow squash** cut into 16 slices, and 1 lb. **eggplant** cut into 16 cubes. Cover; chill at least 4 hours or up to 12 hours. Skewer onto 8 (10-inch) skewers. Discard marinade. Preheat grill to medium-high (400°F to 450°F). Place kebabs on oiled grates. Grill, covered, until chicken is cooked, about 8 minutes, turning halfway through cook time.

CALORIES: **496** – CARBS: **15G** – FAT: **24G**

Italian Shrimp Kebabs

ACTIVE 20 MIN. - TOTAL 30 MIN., PLUS 2 HOURS MARINATING
SERVES 4

Combine **marinade** and 1 Tbsp. **dried Italian seasoning** in a large bowl. Stir in 1½ lb. **large peeled, deveined raw shrimp**, 16 **cherry tomatoes**, and 16 pitted **Castelvetrano olives**. Cover; chill at least 2 hours or up to 4 hours. Skewer onto 8 (10-inch) skewers. Discard marinade. Preheat grill to medium-high (400°F to 450°F). Place kebabs on oiled grates. Grill, covered, until shrimp are cooked, about 6 minutes, turning halfway through cook time.

CALORIES: **321** – CARBS: **8G** – FAT: **21G**

Shrimp Boil Kebabs

ACTIVE 20 MIN. - TOTAL 30 MIN., PLUS 2 HOURS MARINATING
SERVES 4

Combine **marinade** and 2 tsp. **Old Bay seasoning** in a large bowl. Stir in 12 oz. **large peeled, deveined raw shrimp**, 16 pieces **andouille sausage**, 16 cooked **baby potatoes**, and 2 ears **corn** cut into 16 slices. Cover; chill at least 2 hours or up to 4 hours. Skewer onto 8 (10-inch) skewers. Discard marinade. Preheat grill to medium-high (400°F to 450°F). Place kebabs on oiled grates. Grill, covered, until shrimp are cooked, about 6 minutes, turning halfway through cook time. Sprinkle with chopped **parsley**.

CALORIES: **467** – CARBS: **26G** – FAT: **32G**

Chicken Fajita Kebabs

ACTIVE 25 MIN. - TOTAL 30 MIN., PLUS 4 HOURS MARINATING
SERVES 4

Combine **marinade** and 1 Tbsp. **fajita seasoning** in a large bowl. Stir in 2 lb. **boneless, skinless chicken thighs** cut into 24 pieces, 1 **onion** cut into 16 wedges, and 2 **bell peppers** cut into 16 pieces. Cover; chill at least 4 hours or up to 12 hours. Skewer onto 8 (10-inch) skewers. Discard marinade. Preheat grill to medium-high (400°F to 450°F). Place kebabs on oiled grates. Grill, covered, until chicken is cooked, 8 to 10 minutes, turning halfway through cook time. Sprinkle with chopped **cilantro**.

CALORIES: **474** – CARBS: **11G** – FAT: **29G**

Bake a Better Batch

It's hard to improve upon classic chocolate chip cookies, but these may rival your family's go-to recipe

COOKIES ON DEMAND
This dough freezes well, so you can bake (and eat) as many treats as you like at a time. Scoop the dough onto small cookie sheets, and place in the freezer until solid. Transfer dough to zip-top plastic freezer bags. Bake the frozen dough at 350˚F for 15 to 17 minutes per batch.

Browned Butter Chocolate Chip Cookies

ACTIVE 15 MIN. - TOTAL 50 MIN., PLUS 1 HOUR CHILLING
MAKES ABOUT 2½ DOZEN

- ¾ cup butter
- 1 cup packed light brown sugar
- ½ cup granulated sugar
- 2 large eggs
- 2 tsp. vanilla extract
- 2¼ cups plus 2 Tbsp. all-purpose flour
- 1 tsp. baking soda
- ¾ tsp. kosher salt
- 1 (12-oz.) pkg. semisweet chocolate chips
- 1 cup chopped toasted pecans (optional)

1. Melt butter in a small heavy saucepan over medium, stirring constantly, until butter begins to turn golden brown, 6 to 8 minutes. Immediately remove saucepan from heat, and pour butter into a small heatproof bowl. Cover and chill until butter is cool and begins to solidify, about 1 hour.

2. Preheat oven to 350°F. Line 3 baking sheets with parchment paper. Beat browned butter, brown sugar, and granulated sugar in a stand mixer fitted with a paddle attachment on medium speed until creamy, 1 minute. Add eggs and vanilla, beating until blended, 30 seconds.

3. Stir together flour, baking soda, and salt in a small bowl; gradually add to browned butter mixture, beating on low speed until just blended. Beat in chocolate chips and pecans until just combined.

4. Scoop and drop dough 2 inches apart on prepared baking sheets using a 2-tablespoon cookie scoop. Bake in preheated oven in batches, 1 sheet at a time, until cookies are golden and set around the edges, 11 to 13 minutes per batch. Transfer to wire racks; cool about 15 minutes.

Spiced-Up Slaw

This colorful and crunchy salad will be a star at the backyard cookout

Pineapple-Pepper Slaw

ACTIVE 15 MIN. - TOTAL 25 MIN.
SERVES 8

- 4 cups shredded green cabbage (from 1 head)
- 2 cups shredded red cabbage (from 1 small head)
- 2 cups small cubes fresh pineapple (about 6 oz.)
- 1 medium red bell pepper, thinly sliced
- ½ cup loosely packed fresh cilantro leaves
- ½ cup thinly sliced scallions (from 2 scallions)
- 2 Tbsp. minced seeded jalapeño chile (from 1 jalapeño)
- 1 tsp. lime zest plus 2 Tbsp. fresh juice (from 2 limes)
- 1 tsp. honey
- 1 tsp. kosher salt
- ¼ tsp. black pepper
- ⅓ cup extra-virgin olive oil

1. Toss together green cabbage, red cabbage, pineapple, bell pepper, cilantro, scallions, and jalapeño in a large bowl.
2. Whisk together lime zest and juice, honey, salt, and pepper in a small bowl. Add oil in a slow, steady stream, whisking constantly until smooth. Add vinaigrette to cabbage mixture; toss to coat. Let stand 10 minutes; toss again, and serve.

COOKING SL SCHOOL

HOW-TO

Make Your Own Marinade

Follow this simple formula to mix up tasty blends from pantry staples

START WITH (PICK ONE)	➡	ADD (PICK ONE)	➡	COMBINE WITH (PICK ANY TWO OR THREE)

3 PARTS OIL	**1 PART ACID**	**UP TO 5 TBSP. FLAVORING**

Olive Oil

Canola Oil

Sesame Oil

Apple Cider Vinegar

Red or White Wine Vinegar

Lemon or Lime Juice

Minced Fresh Ginger

Dried Spice Blends

Dried Herb Blends

Fresh Herbs

Minced Fresh Chile Pepper

Minced Garlic

To Make: In a bowl, combine 3 parts oil + 1 part acid + sweetener (such as sugar, honey, molasses) to taste + kosher salt to taste + 2 or 3 flavorings of your choice. (For example: 1 cup oil, 6 Tbsp. acid, 2 Tbsp. sweetener, 2 Tbsp. salt, and up to 5 Tbsp. flavorings)

TEST KITCHEN TIPS

Prepping Pointers

Before marinating or basting, brush up on these three rules

PICK THE BEST CONTAINER
Either a glass bowl or zip-top plastic bag is best. (Place the bag in a baking dish to catch any leaks.)

TIME IT RIGHT
Longer isn't better. Acids in a marinade help tenderize the protein, but if it soaks for too long, it can turn mushy.

PUT SAFETY FIRST
To avoid the spread of bacteria, it's important to never reuse a marinade that has been in contact with raw proteins. If you wish to baste as you grill, set aside a portion for that purpose beforehand.

KNOW-HOW

No-Fail Folds

Four steps to the neatest grilling packets

FOLD an 18- by 12-inch rectangle of heavy-duty aluminum foil in half crosswise to make a double layer.

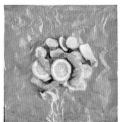

PLACE ingredients in the middle of the foil.

CRIMP and fold the long edges together over the ingredients.

SEAL the packet by folding and crimping both ends. Don't secure too tightly; you want a bit of space at the top so the steam can expand.

September

APPLE BUTTER DOUGHNUTS
WITH SALTED CARAMEL GLAZE
(PAGE 200)

Falling for Apple Butter

The fruit of Appalachian traditions, this sweet ingredient is a baker's best friend

Making apple butter is a hallmark of Appalachian cooking. With so many varieties of apples available in the mountainous region during the fall, farmers and other locals always looked for different ways to preserve the abundance nature provided. Aside from eating them fresh picked, home cooks dried and fried them, pressed them into cider, and stored them in cellars. For a real treat, they canned jars of apple butter, a sweet, smooth spread that's similar to applesauce but cooked much longer for a thick, jamlike consistency.

Like syrup making, preparing apple butter was a seasonal community event. For generations, families and friends gathered around large copper kettles set over open fires and shared in the laborious, daylong work of peeling, coring, chopping, seasoning, and boiling apples. After many hours of tending the pots, they were rewarded with delicious caramel-color apple butter.

Walter Harrill of Imladris Farm in Spring Mountain, North Carolina, is well acquainted with this tradition. He lives and works on land settled by his great-grandparents and grew up watching his grandmother make apple butter in her own kettle on the stove. Today, he continues the custom with a few modern adaptations. "While we've changed the copper kettle over the fire to a stainless steel steam kettle, the process is still the same," he says. "I use mixed varieties of apples cooked for 16 hours or so with spices."

Even though there is no longer a crowd gathered around the fire, he has found a way to make the community a part of his process by purchasing apples from neighboring farms. "The methods have changed over the years," Harrill says, "but it still takes hard work, time, and patience to turn out a good batch of apple butter—and it's worth every minute of it."

SLOW-COOKER APPLE BUTTER

Slow-Cooker Apple Butter

North Carolina farmer Walter Harrill follows his grandmother's method for making apple butter (available at imladrisfarm.com). The recipe, adapted here, is best made using a mix of sweet and tart apples.

ACTIVE 25 MIN. - TOTAL 25 MIN., PLUS 10 HOURS SLOW-COOKING

MAKES ABOUT 5 CUPS

- 5 lb. mixed apples, peeled and cored (such as Gala, Granny Smith, Honey Crisp, or Golden Delicious)
- 3 cups granulated sugar, divided
- 1½ tsp. ground cinnamon
- ½ tsp. ground nutmeg
- ½ tsp. ground cloves

1. Cut apples into 1-inch cubes; place apple cubes and 1½ cups of the sugar in a 6-quart slow cooker. Cover and cook on HIGH 6 hours.
2. Stir in cinnamon, nutmeg, cloves, and remaining 1½ cups sugar. Cover; cook on LOW until apples are very soft, 4 hours.
3. Place half of apple mixture in a blender. Secure lid on blender, and remove center piece to allow steam to escape. Place a clean towel over opening. Pulse until smooth or to desired texture; repeat with remaining apple mixture. Cool completely. Store in an airtight container in the refrigerator up to 1 month.

Apple Butter Doughnuts with Salted Caramel Glaze

(Photo, page 198)

ACTIVE 45 MIN. - TOTAL 45 MIN.,
PLUS 2 HOURS CHILLING
MAKES 30

DOUGHNUTS
- ½ cup packed light brown sugar
- ½ cup granulated sugar
- 2 Tbsp. butter, softened
- 2 large eggs
- 1 Tbsp. vanilla extract
- 4½ cups all-purpose flour, plus more for work surface
- 2 tsp. baking powder
- 1 tsp. baking soda
- 1 tsp. kosher salt
- 1 cup Slow-Cooker Apple Butter (recipe, page 199)
- ½ cup whole buttermilk
   Canola oil

GLAZE
- ¾ cup packed light brown sugar
- 6 Tbsp. butter
- 3 Tbsp. whole milk
- 1 tsp. vanilla extract
- ¼ tsp. kosher salt
   Flaky sea salt

1. Prepare the Doughnuts: Beat brown sugar, granulated sugar, and butter in bowl of a heavy-duty stand mixer fitted with paddle attachment on medium speed until crumbly, about 2 minutes. Add eggs, 1 at a time, beating just until combined after each addition. Beat in vanilla.

2. Stir together flour, baking powder, baking soda, and salt in a large bowl. Stir together Slow-Cooker Apple Butter and buttermilk in a 2-cup glass measuring cup. Beating on low speed, gradually add flour mixture to brown sugar mixture alternately with apple butter mixture, beginning and ending with flour mixture until fully incorporated. Cover and chill at least 2 hours or up to 24 hours.

3. Turn dough out onto a lightly floured work surface, and knead 5 or 6 times. Roll dough to ¼-inch thickness, and cut with a 2½-inch round cutter. Cut holes out of center using a 1-inch round cutter. Reroll all scraps once; repeat cutting process.

4. Heat 2 inches of oil in a large Dutch oven to 375°F; fry 4 or 5 Doughnuts at a time (do not overcrowd) until browned and done, 1 to 2 minutes per side. Transfer to a baking sheet lined with paper towels.

5. Prepare the Glaze: Bring brown sugar, butter, and milk to a boil in a small saucepan over medium, stirring constantly. Boil, stirring constantly, 1 minute. Remove from heat, and stir in vanilla and kosher salt. Stir constantly 2 minutes; use immediately. Dip top half of Doughnuts in Glaze, and sprinkle with flaky sea salt. Let stand 10 minutes; serve warm.

Apple Butter Cinnamon Rolls with Apple Cider Glaze

ACTIVE 45 MIN. - TOTAL 3 HOURS, 30 MIN.
MAKES 12

- 1 cup plus 2 Tbsp. whole milk, divided
- 1½ Tbsp. active dry yeast (from 3 [¼-oz.] envelopes)
- ⅔ cup, plus 1 tsp. granulated sugar, divided
- ½ cup butter, cut into 4 pieces and softened, plus more for skillet
- 2 large eggs, lightly beaten
- 1 Tbsp. fresh lemon juice (from 1 lemon)
- ¼ tsp. ground nutmeg
- ½ tsp., plus ⅛ tsp. kosher salt, divided
- 4⅓ cups bread flour, plus more for work surface
- 1 cup Slow-Cooker Apple Butter (recipe, page 199)
- ½ cup packed light brown sugar
- 2 Tbsp. all-purpose flour
- ½ tsp. ground cinnamon
- 2½ cups powdered sugar
- 2 Tbsp. apple cider
- 1 tsp. vanilla extract

1. Heat 1 cup of the milk in a small saucepan over low until it reaches 95°F to 100°F. Pour warm milk into bowl of a heavy-duty stand mixer fitted with dough hook. Sprinkle yeast and 1 teaspoon of the granulated sugar over milk, and stir to combine. Let stand until foamy, about 5 minutes. Add softened butter, eggs, lemon juice, nutmeg, ½ teaspoon of the salt, and remaining ⅔ cup granulated sugar; beat on low speed just until combined.

2. Continue beating on low speed, and gradually add bread flour until well combined. Increase speed to medium, and beat until a soft dough begins to form, about 3 minutes. Increase speed to

medium-high, and beat until dough is soft and supple and begins to pull away from bowl, 7 to 9 minutes.

3. Scrape dough onto a lightly floured work surface; knead 3 or 4 times. Shape dough into a ball, and transfer to a lightly greased (with cooking spray) large bowl. Cover with plastic wrap. Let rise in a warm place, free from drafts, until doubled in bulk, 1 to 2 hours.

4. Punch dough down, and place on a heavily floured work surface; roll dough into an 18- x 14-inch rectangle. Spread Slow-Cooker Apple Butter over dough, leaving a 1-inch border around edges. Stir together brown sugar, all-purpose flour, and cinnamon in a small bowl. Sprinkle brown sugar mixture over apple butter.

5. Starting at 1 long side, roll up dough, jelly roll style, gently pushing and pressing ends to maintain an 18-inch length. Cut into 12 (1½-inch-thick) slices. Place rolls, cut-side down, in a buttered 12-inch cast-iron skillet; cover with plastic wrap.

6. Let rolls rise in a warm place, free from drafts, until doubled in bulk, 1½ to 2 hours. (Rolls can also be placed in a buttered 13- x 9-inch baking pan, covered with plastic wrap, and chilled 8 hours or overnight. Let come to room temperature before baking.)

7. Preheat oven to 350°F. Bake until golden brown and dough in center is cooked through, 25 to 30 minutes, covering with aluminum foil for the last 10 minutes, if needed, to prevent excessive browning. Cool in pan on a wire rack 15 minutes.

8. Meanwhile, as rolls cool, whisk together powdered sugar, apple cider, vanilla, 1 tablespoon of the milk, and remaining ⅛ teaspoon kosher salt in a small bowl, stirring in remaining 1 tablespoon milk, 1 teaspoon at a time, until desired consistency is reached. Brush glaze over warm cinnamon rolls, and serve warm.

Apple Butter Cobbler with Drop Biscuits

ACTIVE 25 MIN. - TOTAL 1 HOUR, 10 MIN.
SERVES 8

FILLING
- 2 lb. Granny Smith apples (about 4 medium apples), peeled and cut into ½-inch wedges
- 2 lb. Honey Crisp or Gala apples (about 4 medium apples), peeled and cut into ½-inch wedges

1¼ cups packed light brown sugar
5 Tbsp. all-purpose flour
4 Tbsp. butter
1 cup Slow-Cooker Apple Butter
(recipe, page 199)
1 tsp. lemon zest plus 2 Tbsp. fresh
juice (from 1 large lemon)
½ tsp. salt

BISCUITS
2 cups all-purpose flour
1 Tbsp. baking powder
1 tsp. kosher salt
¼ cup granulated sugar, divided
10 Tbsp. cold butter, cut into small
cubes
1 cup whole milk
2 Tbsp. butter, melted

1. Prepare the Filling: Preheat oven to
425°F. Toss together apples, brown sugar,
and flour in a large bowl. Melt butter in
a 12-inch cast-iron skillet over medium-
high. Add apple mixture (skillet will be
very full), and cook, stirring often, until
apples are almost tender and syrup
thickens, about 10 minutes.
2. Remove apple mixture from heat; stir
in Slow-Cooker Apple Butter, lemon zest,
lemon juice, and salt. Bake in preheated
oven 15 minutes, placing a baking sheet
on oven rack directly below skillet to catch
any drips.
3. Prepare the Biscuits: While the Filling
bakes, whisk together flour, baking
powder, salt, and 3 tablespoons of the
sugar in a large bowl. Using a pastry
blender or fork, cut butter into flour
mixture until texture resembles coarse
meal with some pea-size pieces.
4. Stir in milk with a fork just until mixture
is evenly moistened. Remove Filling from
oven, and scoop dough into 8 (about
⅓ cup) mounds on top, spacing about
2 inches apart. Brush dough mounds with
melted butter; sprinkle with remaining
1 tablespoon sugar. Return to oven;
bake until Biscuits are golden brown
and Cobbler is bubbly, 18 to 20 minutes.
Remove to a wire rack, and let stand
20 minutes. Serve warm.

APPLE BUTTER CINNAMON ROLLS
WITH APPLE CIDER GLAZE

APPLE BUTTER COBBLER
WITH DROP BISCUITS

APPLE BUTTER
POUND CAKE WITH
CARAMEL FROSTING

Apple Butter Pound Cake with Caramel Frosting

ACTIVE 20 MIN. - TOTAL 1 HOUR, 45 MIN., PLUS 2 HOURS COOLING
SERVES 12

- 1 cup Slow-Cooker Apple Butter (recipe, page 199)
- ¼ cup finely chopped toasted pecans
  Vegetable shortening
- 3 cups all-purpose flour, plus more for pan
- 1½ cups butter, softened
- 1 (8-oz.) pkg. cream cheese, softened
- 3 cups granulated sugar
- 6 large eggs
- 3 tsp. vanilla extract, divided
- ½ cup packed light brown sugar
- ¼ cup butter
- 3 Tbsp. whole milk
- 1 cup powdered sugar
- ½ cup dried apple chips (optional)

1. Stir together Slow-Cooker Apple Butter and pecans in a small bowl; set aside. Grease (with vegetable shortening) and flour a 14-cup Bundt pan; set aside.
2. Preheat oven to 325°F. Beat softened butter and cream cheese in bowl of a heavy-duty stand mixer fitted with paddle attachment on medium speed until creamy, about 2 minutes. Gradually add granulated sugar, beating on medium speed until light and fluffy, about 3 minutes. Add eggs, 1 at a time, beating just until blended after each addition.
3. Reduce speed to low, and gradually add the remaining 3 cups of flour to butter mixture, beating just until blended after each addition, stopping to scrape down bowl as needed. Stir in 2 teaspoons of the vanilla.
4. Stir ¼ cup batter into apple butter mixture. Pour half of the remaining batter into prepared Bundt pan. Using a small offset spatula or knife, make about a ¾-inch-wide x ¾-inch-deep trench (or channel) in center of batter around pan. Spoon apple butter mixture into trench. Top with remaining cake batter.
5. Bake in preheated oven until a long wooden pick inserted in center comes out clean (1 hour, 20 minutes to 1 hour, 35 minutes). Cool cake in pan on a wire rack 10 minutes, and remove from pan to wire rack. Cool completely, about 2 hours.
6. Meanwhile, as cake cools, bring brown sugar, ¼ cup butter, and milk to a boil in a small saucepan over medium, whisking constantly. Boil, whisking constantly,

1 minute. Remove from heat; stir in remaining 1 teaspoon vanilla. Gradually whisk in powdered sugar until smooth, and whisk gently until mixture begins to cool and thickens slightly, 3 to 5 minutes. Immediately spoon over cooled cake; top with apple chips, if desired.

Blackberry–Apple Butter Pie Bars

ACTIVE 30 MIN. - TOTAL 1 HOUR, 45 MIN.
SERVES 12

- 2 (14.1-oz.) pkg. refrigerated piecrusts, divided
  All-purpose flour, for work surface
- 1 Tbsp. butter
- 2 cups diced Honey Crisp, Braeburn, or Gala apples (from 2 [8-oz.]) apples)
- 3 (6-oz.) pkg. fresh blackberries (about 4 cups)
- 2 cups Slow-Cooker Apple Butter (recipe, page 199)
- 1 large egg
- 1 Tbsp. Demerara sugar
  Vanilla ice cream (optional)

1. Preheat oven to 375°F. Unroll 1 package piecrusts (2 piecrusts) on a lightly floured work surface. Place crusts side by side, and then overlap 1 on top of the other by about 3 inches. Roll together into about an 18- x 13-inch rectangle. Wrap dough around a lightly floured rolling pin; gently unroll over a lightly greased (with cooking spray) 15- x 10-inch rimmed baking sheet. Fit dough into rimmed baking sheet. Turn edges under, and crimp. Prick bottom and sides with a fork. Line pastry with parchment paper; fill with pie weights or dried beans.
2. Bake in preheated oven 10 minutes. Remove weights and parchment paper; bake 5 more minutes. Transfer to a wire rack; cool completely, about 30 minutes.
3. Reduce oven temperature to 350°F. Melt butter in a medium skillet over medium-high. Add diced apples; cook, stirring often, until apples are tender-crisp, 7 to 8 minutes. Cool 15 minutes.
4. Stir together apples, blackberries, and Slow-Cooker Apple Butter in a bowl. Spread mixture in prepared crust.
5. Unroll remaining piecrusts on a lightly floured surface. Place crusts side by side, and then overlap 1 on top of the other by about 3 inches. Roll together into about an 18- x 13-inch rectangle. Wrap dough around lightly floured rolling pin; gently unroll on top of filling. Turn edges under, and crimp, attaching to edges of baked piecrust. Cut random slits in top dough with a sharp knife. Whisk together egg and 1 tablespoon water in a small bowl. Brush top and edges of pie with egg wash, and sprinkle with Demerara sugar.
6. Bake in preheated oven until crust is golden brown and filling is bubbly, 35 to 40 minutes. Cool in pan on a wire rack 30 minutes. Cut into 12 (3⅓- x 3¾-inch) bars. Serve warm, or cool completely, about 1 hour, with ice cream, if desired.

BLACKBERRY-APPLE BUTTER PIE BARS

Apple Butter-Pecan Quick Bread

ACTIVE 20 MIN. - TOTAL 2 HOURS, 40 MIN.
MAKES TWO (8- X 4-INCH) LOAVES

STREUSEL TOPPING
- ½ cup coarsely chopped pecans
- ¼ cup plus 1 Tbsp. all-purpose flour
- ⅓ cup packed light brown sugar
- 3 Tbsp. butter, melted
- ½ tsp. ground cinnamon
- ¼ tsp. kosher salt

BREAD
- ¾ cup butter, softened
- 1 (8-oz.) pkg. cream cheese, softened
- 1½ cups packed light brown sugar
- 2 large eggs
- 3 cups all-purpose flour, plus more for pans
- ½ tsp. baking powder
- ½ tsp. baking soda
- ½ tsp. kosher salt
- 1 cup Slow-Cooker Apple Butter (recipe, page 199)
- 1 cup chopped toasted pecans
- 1 tsp. vanilla extract
- Vegetable shortening

1. Prepare the Streusel Topping: Stir together coarsely chopped pecans, flour, brown sugar, melted butter, cinnamon, and salt. Let stand 30 minutes. Crumble into small pieces.

2. Prepare the Bread: Meanwhile, preheat oven to 350°F. Beat butter and cream cheese in bowl of a heavy-duty stand mixer on medium speed until creamy, about 2 minutes. Gradually add brown sugar, beating until light and fluffy, about 3 minutes. Add eggs, 1 at a time, beating just until blended after each addition.

3. Stir together flour, baking powder, baking soda, and salt in a medium bowl; gradually add to butter mixture, beating on low speed just until blended. Stir in Slow-Cooker Apple Butter, chopped toasted pecans, and vanilla. Spoon batter into 2 greased (with vegetable shortening) and floured 8- x 4-inch loaf pans. Sprinkle top of batter evenly with Streusel Topping.

4. Bake in preheated oven until a long wooden pick inserted in center of each loaf comes out clean and sides pull away from pans, 50 minutes to 1 hour, shielding tops of pans with aluminum foil during last 10 minutes to prevent excessive browning, if necessary. Cool loaves in pans on wire racks 10 minutes. Remove from pans; cool completely, about 1 hour.

APPLE BUTTER-PECAN QUICK BREAD

Apple Butter-Pecan Muffins

Make some muffins—you can adapt the quick-bread recipe (above) to bake individual treats.

ACTIVE 20 MIN. - TOTAL 1 HOUR, 40 MIN.
MAKES 2 DOZEN

Preheat oven to 350°F. Double Streusel Topping recipe, and prepare as directed. Prepare batter for Bread as directed. Spoon batter into 24 paper muffin cups in muffin pans, filling about two-thirds full. Top evenly with Streusel Topping. Bake until a wooden pick inserted in center comes out clean, 20 to 30 minutes. Cool in pans 10 minutes. Remove from pans, and cool completely on wire racks, about 1 hour.

All Fired Up

This vegetarian dip is just the thing to enjoy while watching sports (or your Netflix queue)

Spicy Black Bean-and-Corn Dip

ACTIVE 20 MIN. - TOTAL 30 MIN.
SERVES 12

2½ cups fresh corn kernels
  (from 5 ears)
1 Tbsp. olive oil
2 tsp. ground cumin
1 cup chopped red bell pepper
  (from 1 medium pepper)
2 (15-oz.) cans black beans, drained
  and rinsed

1 cup chopped plum tomatoes
  (from about 2 medium
  tomatoes)
1 cup chopped red onion
  (from 1 small onion)
½ cup chopped fresh cilantro
  (from 1 bunch cilantro)
3 Tbsp. fresh lime juice
  (from 2 limes)
1 Tbsp. finely chopped jalapeño
  chile (from 1 small chile)
¾ tsp. kosher salt
  Tortilla chip, for serving

1. Heat a medium cast-iron skillet over medium-high until hot. Add corn and oil. Cook, stirring occasionally, until corn is browned, 5 to 7 minutes. Add cumin. Cook, stirring occasionally, until fragrant, about 1 minute. Remove from heat; stir in bell pepper until combined. Transfer mixture to a large bowl.
2. Add beans, tomatoes, onion, cilantro, lime juice, jalapeño, and salt to corn mixture; toss gently to combine. Let stand 10 minutes before serving with tortilla chips.

Cooks of the Year

Inspiring women who are taking Southern food from their past into the future

Southern food is often thought of as fixed in time—as if there were only one correct way to bake biscuits or cook grits. We can find these long-held cooking tenets in weathered recipe cards, in the margins of spiral-bound cookbooks, and in our treasured memories of family members long gone. But as the following talented cooks from across the South show, there is a way to marry the past and the present. And it's delicious. In Tennessee, Mee McCormick makes gluten-free fried chicken that rivals any traditional recipe. In Kentucky, Samantha Fore has earned a following for her vibrant Sri Lankan–meets–Southern dishes. And in Texas, Vianney Rodriguez gives Tex-Mex food the respect and recognition it deserves. Through cookbooks, food blogs, pop-up restaurants, and more, all seven of our 2020 Cooks of the Year are expanding the way we define Southern food and making sure there's a seat at the table for everyone.

SALTED IRISH CREAM-APPLE CROSTATA

POACHED-SHRIMP CURRY WITH COCONUT RICE MIDDLINS (PAGE 208)

Jerrelle Guy

Jerrelle Guy doesn't like measuring cups. "That's never been how anyone in my family has cooked," Guy says. "Everything gets eyeballed. You phone a relative to see what secret thing they added to make it so good, and usually it's whatever they had on hand and thought to throw into the mix."

In *Black Girl Baking,* her 2018 debut cookbook, Guy weaves recipes for Baked Buttermilk Beignets and Orange Peel Pound Cake with stories of her childhood in Lantana, Florida. Her recipes may be nostalgic, but they are modern, too, offering gluten-free or vegan options.

Like her inclusive approach to baking, she views the kitchen as a safe space to grapple with complicated questions of race, politics, and identity. Guy, also a food stylist and photographer, worked with author Toni Tipton-Martin on her cookbook, *Jubilee,* which celebrates two centuries of African American cuisine and won a 2019 James Beard Award.

"The food I ate growing up makes me who I am, and while I shift and adjust to fit the current culture I'm a part of, I'm still bringing my past, my cravings, my memories, and what I find comforting and fulfilling along with me," Guy says. "Everything gets measured against and filtered through that."

Salted Irish Cream–Apple Crostata

ACTIVE 40 MIN. · TOTAL 2 HOURS, PLUS 1 HOUR CHILLING
SERVES 10

- 2 Tbsp. granulated sugar
- 2 cups plus 2 Tbsp. unbleached all-purpose flour, divided
- 1¼ tsp. fine sea salt, divided
- 10 Tbsp. plus 6 Tbsp. cold unsalted butter, divided
- 3 to 4 Tbsp. ice water, as needed
- 2 Tbsp. plus ⅓ cup Irish cream liqueur (such as Baileys), divided, plus more for brushing
- 4 small (about 1¼ lb. total) Gala apples
- ⅔ cup packed light brown sugar
- ¼ tsp. ground cinnamon
      Vanilla ice cream

1. Process granulated sugar, 2 cups of the flour, and ¼ teaspoon of the salt in a food processor until combined, about 5 seconds. Cube 10 tablespoons of the butter, and add to mixture. Pulse mixture, gradually adding 3 tablespoons of the ice water and 2 tablespoons of the Irish cream, until mixture is combined and butter is about the size of peas or slightly larger, 4 to 5 pulses. If needed, pulse in remaining water 1 teaspoon at a time until mixture just comes together. Transfer dough to a clean work surface. Knead until dough just gathers into a ball, 1 to 2 minutes (do not overknead or overhandle). Shape into a 1-inch-thick disk. Wrap disk in plastic wrap; chill at least 1 hour or up to 12 hours.
2. Remove dough from refrigerator, and place between 2 sheets of parchment paper. Roll dough into a ⅛-inch-thick 14-inch round (discard any scraps). Transfer rolled crust, still sandwiched between parchment paper, to a large baking sheet. Chill until ready to use.
3. Peel and core apples; thinly slice about ¼ inch thick. Toss together apples and remaining 2 tablespoons flour in a large bowl until evenly coated.
4. Remove crust from refrigerator; remove and discard top parchment sheet. Arrange apple mixture over crust, leaving a 2- to 2½-inch border. Fold exposed edges of crust up and over apples toward center. Transfer pastry on baking sheet to freezer; freeze at least 15 minutes or up to 12 hours.
5. Meanwhile, preheat oven to 400°F. Melt remaining 6 tablespoons butter in a small saucepan over medium. Whisk in brown sugar. Cook, whisking constantly, until mixture thickens and begins to pull away from sides of pan, about 5 minutes. Remove from heat. Whisk in remaining 1 teaspoon salt and ⅓ cup Irish cream (mixture will begin to bubble). Return to heat over medium. Cook, whisking constantly, until sugar crystals completely dissolve, about 1 minute. Remove from heat; set aside.
6. Remove pastry from freezer. Brush crust edges with additional Irish cream; sprinkle crust with cinnamon. Drizzle warm butter-Irish cream sauce over apples in pastry. Bake in preheated oven until crust is cooked through and flaky, 35 to 40 minutes. Remove from oven; cool 10 to 15 minutes. Slice and serve warm with vanilla ice cream.

Samantha Fore

Like many Southern chefs, Samantha Fore has devoted fans who adore her fried chicken and shrimp and grits. But for Fore, those familiar dishes are gateways to expand people's palates and minds. At Tuk Tuk Sri Lankan Bites, her traveling pop-up based in Lexington, Kentucky, the chicken is brined in a buttermilk–curry mixture and the shrimp is flavored with lemongrass, ginger, and lime and served over coconut rice grits.

Since Tuk Tuk opened in 2016, Fore has hooked Lexington and other cities across the country with her original takes on Sri Lankan food. She was born in Kentucky to Sri Lankan parents, so dishes that blend Southern and South Asian ingredients and cooking techniques come naturally to her.

Tuk Tuk does more than serve delicious food. Fore says it also translates her experience as a first-generation American and helps break down barriers people put up around things that seem different or "other." "When you're a kid and your parents are from another country, by the time you're cognizant of it, there is a feeling of othering: 'Your backpack smells weird,' or 'Your food looks strange,' " she says. "If I can keep kids from feeling the way I did when I was in elementary school, that's enough of a mission for me."

Through the pop-up, a cookbook in development, and other projects on the horizon, Fore aims to introduce people to new flavors and cultures while showing them that we all have more in common than we might think. "If I can push those borders just a little bit, then it's all worth it."

Poached-Shrimp Curry with Coconut Rice Middlins

(Photo, page 206)

ACTIVE 25 MIN. - TOTAL 45 MIN.
SERVES 4

- 1 (13.2-oz.) can coconut milk, well shaken and stirred
- 1 cup rice grits (rice middlins)
- 1 Tbsp. coconut oil
- 3 tsp. kosher salt, divided
- 1 small red onion, thinly sliced (about ¾ cup)
- 1 plum tomato, cored and sliced
- 1 banana pepper, seeded and sliced
- 1 (6-inch) lemongrass stalk, split lengthwise
- 2 garlic cloves, thinly sliced
- 1 Tbsp. thinly sliced fresh ginger (from 1 [1-inch] piece)
- 1 Tbsp. Madras curry powder
- ½ tsp. fenugreek seeds
- ½ tsp. ground turmeric
- ½ tsp. tamarind concentrate
- 1 (1-inch) cinnamon stick
- 1 (4-inch) curry leaf sprig (optional)
- ½ serrano chile, seeded and sliced
  Fresh cracked pepper
- 1 lb. extra-large raw shrimp, peeled and deveined
- 1 Tbsp. fresh lime juice (from 1 lime)
  Sliced scallions or chile threads

1. Heat coconut milk in a large saucepan over medium-high, stirring occasionally, until blended and warm, 2 to 3 minutes. Transfer ½ cup to a medium saucepan; set aside remaining coconut milk.
2. Stir 2½ cups water, grits, coconut oil, and 1 teaspoon of the salt into warm coconut milk in medium saucepan. Bring to a boil over medium-high, and reduce heat to low. Simmer, stirring often, until grits are tender and liquid is absorbed, 10 to 15 minutes. Remove from heat, and set aside.
3. Meanwhile, as rice grits cook, add onion, tomato, banana pepper, lemongrass, garlic, ginger, curry powder,

fenugreek, turmeric, tamarind, cinnamon stick, curry leaf sprig (if desired), remaining 2 teaspoons salt, and serrano chile to remaining warmed coconut milk in large saucepan. Sprinkle with several grinds of pepper. Simmer over medium-low, stirring occasionally, 20 minutes.
4. Add shrimp; poach until just cooked through, about 8 minutes. Remove from heat; discard lemongrass, cinnamon, and curry leaf sprig. Stir in lime juice; add salt and pepper to taste. Serve shrimp curry over rice grits, and garnish with scallions or chile threads.

Mee McCormick

At Mee McCormick's restaurant, Pinewood Kitchen & Mercantile, a sign out front illustrates the establishment's philosophy: real food for everyone, regardless of your ability to pay. Since it opened in 2015 in the town of Nunnelly, Tennessee, dishes like fried fish and grass-fed beef burgers have won over locals and attracted people to Pinewood just to eat. It's not easy to find comfort food that can be made gluten free, dairy free, or vegan.

Years of chronic health issues led McCormick on a path to learn about the role that food plays in our well being. She and her husband, Lee, opened Pinewood to accommodate special diets and expand the definition of "healthy eating." "Chefs should not look at food allergies as a burden, but as an opportunity to try new things and create good food that will nourish people," she says.

And as the sign says, a lack of money isn't an issue either. "If a guest can't pay, the staff will offer a friendly, 'We got this today!'" she says.

In addition to running the restaurant and a biodynamic farm, McCormick published her first cookbook, *My Pinewood Kitchen*. She says, "I am

fueled by gratitude for my own good health and inspired to help people discover their own paths to wellness through supportive food."

Pinewood Fried Chicken

(Photo, page 211)

ACTIVE 1 HOUR, 20 MIN. - TOTAL 2 HOURS, 50 MIN.
SERVES 6

- ¼ cup granulated sugar
- ¼ cup, plus 1 tsp. kosher salt, divided
- 3½ lb. bone-in, skin-on chicken pieces (with breasts cut in half crosswise and trimmed)
- 1 cup cornstarch, divided
- 1 large egg
- 1 cup whole buttermilk
- 1 tsp. baking powder
- ½ tsp. baking soda
- 1 cup yellow cornmeal
- 1½ tsp. garlic powder
- 1½ tsp. paprika
- ¼ tsp. cayenne pepper
- 3 to 4 qt. grapeseed oil or canola oil
  Coarse sea salt, for sprinkling

1. Whisk together 1 quart water, sugar, and ¼ cup of the kosher salt in a large bowl until dissolved. Add chicken pieces to brine mixture; cover and refrigerate at least 1 hour or up to 12 hours.
2. Remove chicken from brine mixture; pat dry with paper towels. Set aside.
3. Place ½ cup of the cornstarch in a large zip-top plastic bag. Whisk together egg, buttermilk, baking powder, and baking soda in a medium bowl. Whisk together cornmeal, garlic powder, paprika, cayenne, and remaining 1 teaspoon kosher salt and ½ cup cornstarch in a shallow dish.
4. Working in batches, place a few chicken pieces in plastic bag with cornstarch; seal and shake well to coat. Using tongs, remove chicken from bag, shaking off excess. Dip chicken in egg mixture. Let excess drip off, and dredge in cornmeal mixture, pressing gently to adhere. Place dredged chicken, skin-side up, on a wire rack. Cover with aluminum foil or a clean kitchen towel, and let stand 30 minutes.
5. Pour oil into a large Dutch oven; heat over medium-high until oil reaches 350°F. Meanwhile, preheat oven to 200°F. Working in batches, carefully add a couple of the larger chicken pieces, skin-side down, to hot oil in Dutch oven. Cover

and fry, moving chicken occasionally to prevent it from sticking together, until it turns golden brown, about 12 minutes. (Adjust heat under Dutch oven as needed to maintain oil temperature between 300°F and 325°F.) Flip chicken; cook until a thermometer inserted in thickest portion of breasts registers 165°F and drumsticks and/or thighs register 175°F, about 8 minutes. Transfer cooked chicken to a clean wire rack, and sprinkle with sea salt. Transfer to a rimmed baking sheet, and place in oven to keep warm.

6. Repeat Step 5 with smaller chicken pieces, cooking until meat reaches temperatures as specified, about 8 minutes per side. Remove all cooked chicken from oven, and serve.

Melissa Martin

"Everything happens in the kitchen," says Melissa Martin. White beans stewing, fish frying, a cast of aunts and uncles rotating in and out to pick up fish or drop off a bucket of crabs. For Martin, these are the daily rituals that measure a life on the bayou.

The Cajun cooking of Martin's childhood in Chauvin, Louisiana, was simply seasoned and heavily rooted in seafood. After gaining a culinary education in restaurant kitchens in California's Napa Valley, she turned to a source closer to home. "I wanted to let people in on all the food I grew up eating," says Martin.

The tasting menu at Mosquito Supper Club (Martin's New Orleans restaurant) promises home-style Cajun cooking with a touch of sophistication. "At some point, you've got to get rid of the Mason jars and give people wineglasses," she says, laughing. At each nightly seating, diners enjoy long, leisurely meals of dishes like oyster soup and crab cakes.

Above all, Martin views her restaurant and her cookbook—*Mosquito Supper*

Club—as avenues to tell the story of Louisiana's bayous. "Let's talk about this little town in South Louisiana. Let's talk about coastal erosion and the environment and running a zero-waste, sustainable restaurant," she says. "Really, the story is the most important part."

Lagniappe Bread Rolls

(Photo, page 211)

ACTIVE 35 MIN. · TOTAL 1 HOUR, 25 MIN., PLUS 1 HOUR, 20 MIN. RISING

MAKES ABOUT 2 DOZEN

>   3 cups warm water (105°F to 110°F)
> ¼ cup honey
>   3 Tbsp. active dry yeast
> ¼ cup leaf lard or 5 Tbsp. shortening, melted, plus more for greasing
>   4 tsp. coarse sea salt, divided
> 5½ cups all-purpose flour
>   1 cup whole-wheat flour, plus more for work surface
>   1 large egg yolk
>   1 tsp. heavy whipping cream

1. Place warm water in a large bowl; whisk in honey and yeast. Let stand 5 minutes.
2. Add melted lard and 1 tablespoon of the sea salt to yeast mixture, and stir to combine. Add all-purpose flour and whole-wheat flour. Using a rubber spatula, stir until dough comes together and forms a manageable ball.
3. Turn dough out onto a surface heavily floured with whole-wheat flour. Knead 10 minutes, adding flour a little at a time as needed so the dough doesn't stick to the surface, about every 5 turns. Incorporate the least amount of flour that you need to manage the dough.
4. Place dough in a large bowl greased with lard, and cover with plastic wrap or a clean dish towel. Set aside in a warm, draft-free spot until doubled in size, about 1 hour. Watch that the dough does not rise too much and fall in on itself.
5. Turn dough out onto a lightly floured surface. Don't overflour the surface, or you won't have any resistance when rolling the dough. You need resistance in order to give the dough shape. Divide dough into 20 to 24 balls, about 1½ ounces per ball. Use the sides of your hands flat on the surface with thumbs up, moving in a circular motion, to guide the dough ball toward your body. Don't use the palms of your hands, which will flatten the dough. Place dough balls, touching,

in 2 greased (with lard) 9- to 10-inch cast-iron skillets or 9-inch square pans or baking dishes. Set aside in a warm, draft-free spot until doubled in size, 20 minutes to 1 hour.
6. Meanwhile, preheat oven to 375°F. Stir together egg yolk, heavy cream, and remaining 1 teaspoon salt in a bowl.
7. Brush egg yolk mixture over rolls. Bake immediately in preheated oven until tops are golden brown, 40 to 50 minutes. Remove from oven, cover with a clean dish towel, and let rest 5 minutes before serving.

Coby Ming & Damaris Phillips

If one word defines the creative team of Damaris Phillips and Coby Ming, it is "connection." There is the connection between the two chefs who are friends and business partners, the connection to the farmers they work with, and the connection with their guests.

The two met more than 20 years ago while working at Lynn's Paradise Café in Louisville, Kentucky. Although their careers took them in different directions (Ming worked as a chef in several local restaurants; Phillips was a winner on the television series *Food Network Star* and got her own show, *Southern at Heart*), they kept in touch and shared the same desire to take their culinary and hospitality experience on a different route. "After years of talking about what we could do together, we decided to quit talking and start walking," says Ming.

In 2019, Phillips and Ming launched the Bluegrass Supper Club—monthly ticketed events that celebrate community, regional history, and locally sourced food. Built on the concept that eating together should be fun, each supper club has a different theme and location around Louisville, that are both kept secret until two days before the event. Ticket holders may find themselves at a swanky 1950s cocktail hour eating Swedish meatballs and deviled eggs or at a casual Sunday supper with fried chicken and bourbon coleslaw. Since COVID-19 put a temporary halt on large gatherings, they have offered to-go picnic baskets for Mother's Day, Memorial Day, date nights, and more.

Menus vary depending on the theme and what's in season. Instead of telling the farmers what they want to prepare, Phillips and Ming rely on the growers to let them know what's in season and build their menu from there. "Dining experiences used to be fun," says Phillips, "People would spend hours dancing and talking–today it's just eat and run." To get people mingling, they set up diversions like an activity that included mystery gifts that could be unlocked only if the participants followed clues.

"Creating a relationship where none existed is so important to fostering understanding and empathy," says Phillips. "If you can get people to share a meal and have fun together, you've got a good start," adds Ming.

Sumac Carrots with Feta Mousse and Crispy Panko

ACTIVE 30 MIN. - TOTAL 1 HOUR
SERVES 2

- ½ cup panko breadcrumbs
- 3 medium carrots (6 to 8 oz. total), peeled
- 2 Tbsp. vegetable oil
- 2 tsp. honey
- ½ to 1 tsp. ground sumac
- 1 tsp. kosher salt, divided
- ½ tsp. black pepper, divided
- 6 oz. feta cheese, crumbled (about 1½ cups), at room temperature
- 2 oz. cream cheese, at room temperature
- 2 Tbsp. heavy whipping cream
- 2 Tbsp. fresh lemon juice (from 1 lemon)
  Torn fresh mint leaves

1. Toast panko in a 12-inch skillet over medium-high, stirring constantly, until golden, 4 to 5 minutes. Set aside.

2. Cut carrots into thirds, and then cut each third in half lengthwise (or into fourths, depending on width of carrots).
3. Heat oil in a cast-iron skillet over medium until hot. Cook carrots, flat-side down, in hot oil, without turning, until tender, 10 to 12 minutes. (The cut sides will be very dark.)
4. Remove skillet from heat; stir in ¼ cup water, honey, and sumac. Return to heat. Cook, stirring constantly, until most of the water has cooked off and carrots are coated, 4 to 5 minutes. Season with ½ teaspoon of the salt and ¼ teaspoon of the pepper, and transfer to an airtight container. Chill carrots about 30 minutes.
5. Meanwhile, pulse feta and cream cheese in a food processor until blended, about 5 pulses. Add whipping cream, lemon juice, and remaining ½ teaspoon salt and ¼ teaspoon pepper. Process mixture until smooth, 2 to 3 minutes. Set aside until ready to use.
6. Spread feta mousse onto bottom of serving plate, and top with carrots. Sprinkle carrots with toasted panko and mint before serving.

Vianney Rodriguez

Vianney Rodriguez's earliest culinary memory is watching her mother and abuelita (grandmother) roll out empanada dough. "They had a perfect rhythm going," she says. "It was their little magic, and I always wanted to be a part of that."

Rodriguez says she is a Texan through and through–"thank God for brisket and queso," she says, laughing–but she's also a proud first-generation Mexican American. "I would go to school and speak English, but as soon as I walked in the door at home, we would speak only Spanish," she says. "It gave me the best of both worlds."

Through her blog, Sweet Life, and her cookbooks, *Latin Twist* and *The Tex-Mex Slow Cooker*, she embraces all

facets of her identity and celebrates the resourcefulness and cultural fusion of Tex-Mex food.

For Rodriguez, it all goes back to her grandmother's kitchen. "Now that I have kids, I want those memories with them. It's about the moments that lead up to the recipe."

Concha Tres Leches Cake

ACTIVE 15 MIN. - TOTAL 1 HOUR, 55 MIN.
SERVES 10 TO 12

- 3 to 4 conchas (from a Mexican bakery)
- 1 (15.25-oz.) pkg. white cake mix
- 1 Tbsp. vegetable oil
- 2 tsp. vanilla extract
- 4 large eggs
- 1 (14-oz.) can sweetened condensed milk
- 1 (12-oz.) can evaporated milk
- 1½ cups heavy whipping cream
  Thawed frozen whipped topping

1. Preheat oven to 350°F. Coat a 13- x 9-inch baking dish with cooking spray. Slice tops off conchas. Crumble; set aside. Cut conchas into 1-inch cubes (4 cups); set aside.
2. Place cake mix, 1¼ cups water, oil, vanilla, and eggs in a large bowl. Beat with an electric mixer on medium speed until well blended, 2 minutes, stopping to scrape down sides as needed. Pour into prepared pan. Sprinkle with concha cubes; pat them partially into batter.
3. Bake in preheated oven until a wooden pick inserted in center comes out clean, 34 to 38 minutes. (The conchas will turn dark brown, and the cake will be golden.)
4. Stir together condensed and evaporated milks and cream. Set aside.
5. Remove cake from oven, and cool in pan 5 minutes. Using a knife, pierce every ½ inch. Pour milk mixture evenly over top. Cover; chill until mixture is absorbed into cake, 1 hour. Top with whipped topping and crumbled conchas.

PINEWOOD
FRIED CHICKEN
(PAGE 208)

LAGNIAPPE BREAD
ROLLS (PAGE 209)

SUMAC CARROTS
WITH FETA
MOUSSE AND
CRISPY PANKO

CONCHA
TRES LECHES
CAKE

Queen of Kolaches

Lydia Faust uses her baking skills to pass on the traditions of her Czech ancestors

On a Saturday morning, the aromas of melted butter and developing yeast wafted through the cafeteria of Snook Elementary School in Snook, Texas. In the kitchen, convection ovens hummed while baking carts rolled here and there like props in a theatrical performance. Near the entrance, organizers of the local youth club cranked out long sheets of fresh egg noodles.

Around tables near the back, over an assembly line of mixing bowls and measuring cups, a group of enthusiastic bakers were holding wooden spoons and bowls of their own and listening apron-clad woman in wire-frame glasses. All of today's attendees had gathered to learn the art of kolache making from the master herself—Lydia Faust, Snook's resident queen of kolaches.

Laura Sebesta and her three kids have been coming to the workshop for over a decade. "Kolaches are all about the dough, and coming from Lydia, it's going to be the best," she said.

Like smoked sausage and brisket, the kolache (pronounced ko-LAH-tch, with no "-ee," in local parlance) is among the iconic foods of Central Texas, where German and Czech immigrants settled in the early 1900s. According to Lydia, the workshops serve two purposes: They help carry on the culinary traditions of her mother and grandmother and also raise funds for a local youth group.

If Lydia moves a bit slower at 87 years old, she reveals a timeless vivacity whenever a wooden spoon and mixing bowl are in her hands. "Make sure your cups are even," she gently instructed a handful of kids scooping sugar and flour. Then, peering into another student's bowl, she said, "You've got to get the lumps out," and proceeded to beat the batter smooth in vigorous, rhythmic strokes. Lydia circulated among the

students, assisting when needed. "You're just shaking the dough," she said to a girl who wasn't mixing assertively enough. "You want the spoon to go underneath the dough."

Lydia was born in Rogers, Texas, in 1933 and then moved to Snook, her father's birthplace, in 1945. Growing up on her family's farm meant hard work from as early as she can remember. As a young girl, she milked cows in the morning and worked in the cotton fields after school. Baking, by contrast, was a respite and privilege—something she could do on Sundays or when weather allowed her to skip chores.

Like other members of the community, her mother prepared

kolaches with whatever was on hand—cottage cheese made from their cow's milk, poppy seeds grown in the garden and ground by hand, and jams made from the fruit of a backyard tree.

Lydia eventually married Moody Faust in 1953. Together, they raised four children and continued to farm for the next decade. But her path as a farmwife took an unexpected detour when a man named Charlie Sebesta hired Moody to work in his furniture store. Charlie, it turns out, had a sweet tooth and figured the town of Snook (and his store) could use a gathering place next door. When Charlie asked Lydia if she'd like to open a bakery, she was game. Snook Baking Co. started in 1968.

Known for coffee that started brewing at the crack of dawn and exquisitely tender, buttery pastries, the bakery found an adoring audience. Fifteen years later, Lydia and Moody had saved enough to purchase the business and call it their own.

In the mid-nineties, Lydia sold it and gave up 14-hour workdays. But her kolache baking was far from over. Occasionally, she sells orders to local organizations, mixing each batch by hand in her small kitchen, but mostly she bakes them for and with family and friends. "I'm comfortable making 20 dozen in my kitchen," she said, "but after that, it's too much."

A stand mixer might make those orders easier, but she shook her head at the notion. Because Lydia, like her children, grandchildren, and workshop attendees, knows the secret to a great kolache: "The feel of the dough isn't something I was taught," she explained. "It's something you have to experience on your own."

Lydia's Kolaches

ACTIVE 1 HOUR · TOTAL 2 HOURS, PLUS 2 HOURS, 5 MIN. RESTING
MAKES ABOUT 3 DOZEN

- 1½ Tbsp. active dry yeast (from 2 [¼-oz.] envelopes)
- ½ cup warm water (105°F to 115°F)
- ¼ cup unsalted butter
- ¼ cup vegetable shortening
- 1½ cups lukewarm whole milk (100°F to 105°F)
- 6 cups all-purpose flour, divided, plus more for work surface
- ¾ cup evaporated milk
- ⅓ cup granulated sugar
- 1 Tbsp. kosher salt
- 2 large eggs
- 1 large egg yolk
- 5 Tbsp. unsalted butter, melted, divided
- Fillings (recipes at right)
- Posypka (Streusel Topping, recipe at right)

1. Sprinkle yeast over warm water; stir to combine. Set aside. Place butter and shortening in a large microwavable bowl, and microwave on HIGH until melted, about 1 minute. Stir to combine. Whisk in lukewarm whole milk and yeast mixture.
2. Transfer mixture to bowl of a stand mixer fitted with whisk attachment. Sift 3 cups of the flour over mixture. Add evaporated milk, sugar, salt, eggs, and egg yolk. Beat on medium speed until smooth, about 1 minute. Remove whisk attachment; replace with dough hook. Sift remaining 3 cups flour; gradually add to flour mixture. Beat on medium speed until dough is smooth, about 2 minutes. Let sit at room temperature 5 minutes; beat on medium-high speed until elastic and very smooth, 10 minutes.
3. Brush top of dough with 1 tablespoon of the melted butter. Cover bowl with plastic wrap; let rise until doubled in size, about 1 hour. Punch dough down, and re-cover. Let rise until doubled, about 30 more minutes. While dough rises, prepare desired Filling.
4. Flour a work surface generously. Gently roll dough out to a 1-inch-thick rectangle (about 18 x 14 inches). Using a 2-inch round cutter, cut out circles, and place 1 inch apart on parchment paper-lined baking sheets. Brush tops with 2 tablespoons of the melted butter. Let rise in a warm place until almost doubled in bulk, about 20 minutes.
5. Use your fingers to make 1 small indentation in center of each dough circle, and fill each with about 1 tablespoon Filling. Sprinkle each kolache with 1 to 2 teaspoons Posypka. Let rise until doubled in size, 20 to 30 minutes.
6. Preheat oven to 350°F. Position racks in top third and lower third of oven. Bake until golden brown, about 20 minutes, rotating baking sheets between top and bottom racks halfway through the baking time. Remove from oven. Brush with remaining 2 tablespoons melted butter. Transfer kolaches to wire racks. Cool completely, about 30 minutes.

Plum/Apricot Filling

ACTIVE 5 MIN. · TOTAL 35 MIN.
MAKES ABOUT 2½ CUPS

Place 12 oz. **dried apricots** or **dried pitted plums** (about 2¼ cups) in a heavy saucepan. Cover with water, and bring to a boil over medium-high. Reduce heat to medium-low, and simmer until the fruit is soft and tender, about 15 minutes. Remove from heat, and let fruit cool completely in liquid, around 15 minutes. Drain and discard liquid; place solids in a food processor. Add 1 cup **granulated sugar**, 2 Tbsp. **melted unsalted butter**, 1 tsp. **vanilla extract**, and ½ tsp. **ground cinnamon**. Process until smooth, about 30 seconds.

Poppy Seed Filling

ACTIVE 10 MIN. · TOTAL 25 MIN.
MAKES ABOUT 2 CUPS

Stir together 1¼ cups **ground whole poppy seeds**, 1 cup **granulated sugar**, and 2 Tbsp. **all-purpose flour** in a medium bowl. Heat 1 cup **whole milk** in a heavy saucepan over medium-high until milk just comes to a boil, 5 minutes. Reduce heat to medium-low; add poppy seed mixture to milk. Cook, stirring constantly, until thick, about 1 minute. Remove from heat, and stir in 2 Tbsp. **unsalted butter** and 1 tsp. **vanilla extract**. Cool completely, about 15 minutes.

Cream Cheese Filling

ACTIVE 5 MIN. · TOTAL 5 MIN.
MAKES ABOUT 2½ CUPS

Combine 2 (8-oz.) pkg. softened **cream cheese**, ½ cup **granulated sugar**, 1 large **egg yolk**, and ¼ tsp. **vanilla or almond extract** in bowl of an electric mixer. Beat on medium speed until completely smooth and combined, about 1 minute, stopping to scrape the sides and bottom of bowl as necessary.

Posypka (Streusel Topping)

ACTIVE 5 MIN. · TOTAL 5 MIN.
MAKES ABOUT 2½ CUPS

Use a pastry cutter or your fingers to combine 1 ½ cups **granulated sugar**, 1 cup **all-purpose flour**, ½ cup cold **unsalted butter**, and ¼ tsp. **vanilla extract** or **ground cinnamon** to form a crumbly texture.

A Storied Meal

Asheville chef Ashleigh Shanti brings history, memory, and the art of gathering to the table

Inez Miller was a woman of few words, but the way she brought people into her kitchen was something worth talking about. This lady with impeccable curls and honey-colored eyes was a maker in every sense of the word. She gardened. She quilted. She collected blue ribbons for her prizewinning pickles.

"The kitchen was her happy place," remembers Ashleigh Shanti, Miller's great-granddaughter and also the chef de cuisine at Benne on Eagle in Asheville, North Carolina. "She naturally drew people to her."

Shanti recalls how her family would choose to sit on the stools in her great-grandmother's South Carolina kitchen instead of on the nearby living room furniture, just to be close to the heart of her home. Amid jars of fat that lined the stove, rolling pots of butter beans, and towering walls of pickled peaches, the importance of gathering settled deep into the fabric of Shanti's memory.

After working in professional kitchens for more than a decade, the chef moved to the mountains of western North Carolina to helm the kitchen at Benne on Eagle alongside Executive Chef/Owner John Fleer. The restaurant, located inside Asheville's The Foundry Hotel, opened in December 2018 in a historically Black neighborhood known as "The Block." In its heyday, The Block was a bustling hub of entrepreneurship.

From the start, Shanti envisioned her work at Benne as more than another cooking gig. In 2017, while hiking the Appalachian Trail, she had a revelatory experience when she discovered a small placard in the Shenandoah National Park that spoke of the history of Black Appalachians, which has received little documentation. She was determined to lift them up along with other Black culinarians throughout history.

"One of the reasons for coming here [to Asheville] was to pay homage to the women who have been here," says Shanti. She brought a commitment to honor her own lived experience, the matriarchs of her family, and the women—cooks, bakers, business owners—who shaped The Block. Portraits of locals such as Erline McQueen, Mary Frances Hutchinson, Mary Jo Johnson, and Hanan Shabazz hang on the restaurant's walls.

The menu at Benne is a rich tapestry of stories intricately woven together. In dishes such as mountain trout cooked inside a plantain leaf with a fiery shito sauce, Shanti celebrates the West African roots that bind the Geechee culture of coastal Carolina, the place from which Inez Miller hailed. Appalachian influences gleaned from summers hanging creasy beans with her maternal great-grandmother Hattie Mae Womack in Dan River, Virginia, become buttermilk britches or (as

Shanti refers to it) "Appalachian green bean casserole." A plate of oxtails is a remembrance of Sunday suppers back home in Virginia Beach, updated with Shanti's distinct touches—locally foraged sumac, a tart, lemony spice made from the red berries of the sumac bush, and her signature showering of black pepper and citrus juice. "When I'm stumped or lacking inspiration, I think about what my grandmothers would make and how they cooked," says Shanti.

"Ashleigh is a culinary storyteller, devoted to telling an authentic tale of place on a plate," says Ronni Lundy, an author and seminal writer on Appalachian foodways. Lundy acknowledges that Black women cooks are an elemental part of the Appalachian narrative, though they are hardly ever recognized. Even Malinda Russell, who wrote *A Domestic Cook Book*, the first known cookbook by an African American woman (and the first Appalachian cookbook, according to Lundy), is often painted as an obscure figure, when in reality she was highly skilled, well known, and well traveled. "She [Ashleigh] immerses herself deeply into place and brings together this narrative and so many stories," says Lundy. "It's not just Appalachian food. It's not just soul food. That's what's incredible about her cuisine—it has so many dimensions."

For Shanti, creating a meal that taps into memory and history is just part of the equation. Providing an experience that invites togetherness is just as important. It's a point made all too clear this year. Benne on Eagle decided to temporarily close its doors to the public in response to the COVID-19 pandemic. Across the nation, restaurants responded to the sweeping new developments, many of them shutting their doors indefinitely. Shanti says, "I think that this has shown me how much more my job means to me than just cooking. It has so much more to do with people gathering together and breaking bread."

A giant window runs the length of the restaurant's street-side facade on Eagle Street. During normal times, Shanti says, the activity inside the restaurant

would draw in passersby all day long. Farmers would arrive with the season's picks, and foragers would drop by with their wild hauls. Congregants from Mt. Zion Baptist Church, Benne's next-door neighbor, would stop in to "see what was going on," and folks who have been fed by the hands of Hanan Shabazz, Benne's culinary advisor and a lifelong resident of The Block, would often peek their heads in, looking for a plate.

Shabazz, whom many call "Grandmother," is a living legacy of the neighborhood itself. Her soulful cornbread and fish burgers (known as Hanan's Fish Cake on Benne's menu) draw folks in for a comforting taste of down-home cooking. Shabazz comes

from a long line of women compelled to feed everyone, no matter the circumstance. Her grandmother had 16 children, and Shabazz was one of 10. "We always had a thousand people around the house," Shabazz says. If you were hungry, you got fed–a mantra instilled deep in her bones.

In Shabazz, Shanti has found an elder who conjures the women who line the halls of her memory, but with living wisdom on offer. "You have to cook with love," Shanti says of what she's internalized from Shabazz. "You have to believe in the food that you're making."

Even with a James Beard Award nomination and heaps of national praise under her belt, Shanti holds fast to the lessons she's learned from the women who came before–a specific way of drawing folks in with a generosity of spirit, inviting them without a word to the heart of your kitchen. That same magnetism attracts passersby on Eagle Street. It's a presence that says, "Come in. Stay awhile. You are welcome."

Cracked-Corn Spoon Bread

ACTIVE 35 MIN. · TOTAL 1 HOUR, 40 MIN.
SERVES 12

- 8 cups whole milk
- 2 cups coarse-ground yellow cornmeal
- 1 cup unsalted butter, cubed
- 6 large eggs, separated
- 1 cup chopped scallions (from 1 bunch)
- 2 Tbsp. kosher salt
- 1 Tbsp. black pepper

1. Preheat oven to 350°F. Coat a 13- x 9-inch baking dish with cooking spray. Bring milk to a boil in a large saucepan over medium-high, stirring occasionally. Whisk in cornmeal and butter. Reduce heat to low. Cover; cook, stirring occasionally, until tender, 25 to 30 minutes. Remove from heat; cool 15 minutes. Stir in egg yolks, scallions, salt, and pepper until combined.
2. Whisk egg whites in a medium bowl until foamy, about 30 seconds; gently stir into cornmeal mixture. Spoon mixture into prepared dish. Bake in preheated oven until puffed and golden brown, 45 to 50 minutes. Remove from oven; cool 5 minutes.

Roasted Cauliflower with Seed Salsa

ACTIVE 30 MIN. · TOTAL 1 HOUR
SERVES 8

- 2 small heads cauliflower or Romanesca cauliflower, quartered
- 2 Tbsp. red palm oil
- 1½ tsp. kosher salt
- 1 chile de árbol
- ¼ cup grapeseed oil
- 2 Tbsp. sunflower seeds
- 2 Tbsp. benne (sesame) seeds
- 1½ tsp. yellow mustard seeds
- 1 tsp. cumin seeds
- 1 tsp. coriander seeds

1. Preheat oven to 425°F. Gently stir together cauliflower, palm oil, and salt in a large bowl until coated. Arrange in an even layer on a large rimmed baking sheet. Roast until golden brown, 30 to 35 minutes.
2. Meanwhile, place chile, grapeseed oil, sunflower seeds, sesame seeds, mustard seeds, cumin seeds, and coriander seeds in a medium saucepan; bring to a simmer over medium. Reduce heat to medium-low. Cook, stirring occasionally, until seeds are toasted, about 20 minutes.
3. Serve roasted cauliflower alongside seed salsa.

Red Rice–Smoked Chicken Perloo

ACTIVE 1 HOUR, 35 MIN. · TOTAL 1 HOUR, 45 MIN.
SERVES 8

- 8 cups unsalted chicken stock
- ½ cup bacon, diced (1 to 2 bacon slices)
- 4 large celery stalks, diced (about 2 cups)
- 3 medium (10- to 12-oz.) red bell peppers, diced (about 4 cups)
- 2 large (12- to 14-oz.) yellow onions, diced (about 8 cups)
- 2 cups uncooked red rice (or other heritage variety)
- 3 garlic cloves, minced (1 Tbsp.)
- ½ cup white wine
- 1 tsp. smoked paprika
- 3½ tsp. kosher salt, divided
- 3 cups shredded smoked chicken or shredded rotisserie chicken
- 1 cup chopped fresh flat-leaf parsley (from 1 bunch)
- 1 Tbsp. unsalted butter
- 1 tsp. black pepper
  Chopped scallions

1. Bring chicken stock to a simmer in a saucepan over medium; cover and remove from heat. Meanwhile, heat a 12-inch cast-iron skillet over medium; add bacon. Cook, stirring occasionally, until crisp, about 8 minutes. Transfer bacon to a plate lined with paper towels to drain, reserving drippings in skillet. Add celery, bell peppers, and onions to skillet. Cook, stirring occasionally, until tender, about 20 minutes. Add rice and garlic. Cook, stirring often, 3 minutes. Stir in wine, paprika, and 2 teaspoons of the salt. Cook, stirring constantly, until liquid is completely absorbed, about 1 minute.
2. Add 2 cups stock to mixture in skillet. Cook over medium, stirring occasionally, until liquid is almost completely absorbed, about 15 minutes. Repeat process using remaining 6 cups stock, adding 2 cups at a time and stirring until absorbed between additions.
3. Stir chicken into mixture in skillet; cover and reduce heat to low. Cook until rice is tender, about 10 minutes. Remove from heat. Stir in parsley, butter, pepper, reserved bacon, and remaining 1½ teaspoons salt. Garnish with scallions.

CRACKED-CORN SPOON BREAD

ROASTED CAULIFLOWER WITH SEED SALSA

RED RICE-SMOKED CHICKEN PERLOO

PEANUT-PUMPKIN
STEW WITH HOMINY

Peanut-Pumpkin Stew with Hominy

ACTIVE 35 MIN. - TOTAL 1 HOUR, 25 MIN.
SERVES 6

- 3 cups diced peeled pumpkin (from 1 medium pumpkin)
- ½ cup chopped blanched raw peanuts, plus more for garnish
- 4 garlic cloves, unpeeled
- 2 Tbsp. grapeseed oil, divided
- 1 Tbsp. coconut oil
- ¾ cup diced yellow onion (from 1 small onion)
- 1 tsp. grated fresh ginger
- 4 cups unsalted vegetable broth, divided
- 1½ cups cooked hominy (from 1 [15-oz.] can)
- 1½ cups baby spinach
- ½ tsp. kosher salt
- ½ tsp. paprika
- ¼ tsp. cayenne pepper

1. Preheat oven to 400°F. Toss together pumpkin, peanuts, garlic cloves, and 1 tablespoon of the grapeseed oil in a large bowl. Spread in an even layer on a large rimmed baking sheet. Bake until pumpkin is tender, about 40 minutes, stirring halfway through cook time.
2. Meanwhile, heat coconut oil and remaining 1 tablespoon grapeseed oil in a medium-size Dutch oven over medium-high. Add onion. Cook, stirring occasionally, until tender, about 5 minutes. Add ginger. Cook, stirring constantly, until tender, about 1 minute. Remove from heat. Set aside until ready to use.
3. Remove pumpkin mixture from oven; let cool 5 minutes. Carefully remove and discard skins from garlic cloves. Place pumpkin mixture, peeled garlic, and 1 cup of the broth in a blender. Secure lid on blender, and remove center piece to allow steam to escape. Place a clean towel over opening. Process until smooth, about 1 minute.
4. Add pumpkin puree, hominy, spinach leaves, salt, paprika, cayenne, and remaining 3 cups broth to onion mixture in Dutch oven. Bring to a simmer over medium-low. Simmer, stirring occasionally, 25 minutes. Ladle into 6 bowls; garnish with peanuts.

Oxtails with Sumac-Apple Relish

ACTIVE 35 MIN. - TOTAL 35 MIN., PLUS 4 HOURS CHILLING AND 5 HOURS BAKING
SERVES 8

- 5 lb. oxtails, cut at joints
- 1 Tbsp. kosher salt
- 2 tsp. black pepper
- ¼ cup olive oil
- 3 dried bay leaves
- ½ oz. thyme sprigs
- 2 Tbsp. black peppercorns
- 1 Tbsp. juniper berries (optional, found in the spice aisle)
- 1 (750-ml) bottle dry red wine
- 3 qt. unsalted beef stock
- 1½ lb. yellow onions, roughly chopped (4½ cups)
- ½ lb. celery stalks, roughly chopped (2 cups)
- ½ lb. carrots, roughly chopped (2 cups)
- 1 garlic head, halved crosswise
  Sumac-Apple Relish (recipe follows)

1. Sprinkle oxtails all over with salt and black pepper. Cover and refrigerate at least 4 hours or up to 12 hours.
2. Preheat oven to 275°F. Heat oil in a large skillet over medium-high. Working in about 2 batches, add oxtails. Cook, turning occasionally, until evenly browned on all sides, about 12 minutes. Transfer browned oxtails to a large roasting pan.
3. Place bay leaves, thyme, peppercorns, and juniper berries (if desired) on a piece of cheesecloth; bundle and secure sachet using kitchen twine. Add herb sachet, wine, stock, onions, celery, carrots, and garlic to oxtails in roasting pan. Cover with a layer of parchment paper and then a layer of aluminum foil. Bake in preheated oven until oxtails are tender, about 5 hours. Remove and discard sachet. Strain; discard juices, or reserve for another use. Serve oxtails alongside Sumac-Apple Relish.

Sumac-Apple Relish

ACTIVE 10 MIN. - TOTAL 10 MIN.
SERVES 8

Gently stir together 2 medium **Gala apples**, peeled and finely diced (about 2½ cups); 2 Tbsp. finely chopped **fresh chives**; 1½ Tbsp. **extra-virgin olive oil**; 1 tsp. **lime zest** plus 2 tsp. **fresh juice (from 1 lime)**; ¾ tsp. **ground sumac**; ½ tsp. **flaky sea salt**; and ½ tsp. **black pepper** in a medium bowl.

OXTAILS WITH SUMAC-APPLE RELISH

"I think that this has shown me how much more my job means to me than just cooking. It has so much more to do with people gathering together and breaking bread."

Parsnip-Buttermilk Tart

ACTIVE 45 MIN. - TOTAL 2 HOURS, 20 MIN.
SERVES 10

CRUST
- ¾ cup graham cracker crumbs (from 1 [13½-oz.] pkg.)
- ½ cup finely chopped pecans
- ¼ cup cacao nibs
- 2 Tbsp. light brown sugar
- ⅛ tsp. kosher salt
- 1 large egg white, beaten
- 2 Tbsp. unsalted butter, melted

FILLING
- 8 oz. fresh parsnips, chopped (1½ cups)
- 1 cup whole milk
- 1 large egg
- ¾ cup whole buttermilk
- ¼ cup plus 2 Tbsp. packed light brown sugar
- ¼ tsp. kosher salt
- ⅛ tsp. ground cinnamon
- ⅛ tsp. ground nutmeg

PAN-ROASTED APPLES
- 1 Tbsp. unsalted butter
- 2 medium Honey Crisp apples, unpeeled, cored, and sliced (about 3 cups)
- 2 Tbsp. light brown sugar
- 1 rosemary sprig
- 1 (3- x 1-inch) lemon peel strip (from 1 lemon)

ADDITIONAL INGREDIENT
- ½ cup Spiced Apple Butter, or to taste (recipe follows)

1. Prepare the Crust: Preheat oven to 325°F. Coat a 10-inch tart pan with a removable bottom with cooking spray. Stir together cracker crumbs, pecans, cacao nibs, brown sugar, and salt in a medium bowl. Stir in egg white and melted butter until combined. Spread mixture evenly in prepared tart pan, pushing into bottom and up sides of pan. Bake until set, about 15 minutes. Remove from oven; cool at least 15 minutes or up to 2 hours.

2. Meanwhile, prepare the Filling: Bring parsnips and milk to a boil in a medium saucepan over medium. Boil, stirring occasionally, until tender, 10 to 12 minutes. Pour mixture through a fine mesh strainer into a heatproof bowl; reserve strained milk. Place parsnips in a blender. Secure lid on blender, and remove center piece to allow steam to escape. Place a clean towel over opening. Process until smooth, about 1 minute, adding ½ cup to 1 cup strained milk until mixture is smooth. Measure parsnip puree to 1 cup. Discard remaining puree and strained milk, or reserve for another use. Whisk together parsnip puree, egg, buttermilk, brown sugar, salt, cinnamon, and nutmeg in a large bowl until smooth.

3. Pour Filling into cooled Crust. Place tart on a large rimmed baking sheet, and bake in preheated oven until set, about 20 minutes. Transfer to a wire rack; let cool completely, about 1 hour. Remove tart from pan.

4. Meanwhile, as the tart cools, prepare the Pan-Roasted Apples: Melt butter in a 10-inch cast-iron skillet over medium-high. Continue cooking, undisturbed, until light brown, about 2 minutes. Add apples, brown sugar, rosemary sprig, and lemon peel strip. Stir together, and spread mixture in an even layer. Transfer to preheated oven and bake until tender, about 20 minutes. Remove and discard rosemary and lemon peel.

5. Dollop Spiced Apple Butter onto tart, and top with Pan-Roasted Apples.

Spiced Apple Butter

ACTIVE 2 HOURS, 15 MIN. - TOTAL 2 HOURS, 15 MIN.
MAKES 4 CUPS

- 6 medium (about 3 lb. total) Honey Crisp apples, unpeeled, cored, and diced (about 10 cups)
- 1½ cups packed light brown sugar
- ¼ cup bourbon
- 1 Tbsp. ground cinnamon
- 1 tsp. kosher salt

1. Stir together all ingredients and 1½ cups water in a large saucepan or Dutch oven. Bring to a simmer over medium-high, stirring occasionally. Reduce heat to low. Cook, stirring occasionally, until apples break down and become very soft, 1 hour, 45 minutes to 2 hours. Remove from heat; cool 10 minutes.

2. Transfer mixture to a blender. Secure lid on blender, and remove center piece to allow steam to escape. Place a clean towel over opening. Process until smooth, 1 minute. Store in an airtight container in refrigerator up to 1 month.

PARSNIP-BUTTERMILK TART

Bake a Better Breakfast

Wake up your morning with something savory or sweet

SLOW-COOKER
CINNAMON
MONKEY BREAD
CASSEROLE

Slow-Cooker Cinnamon Monkey Bread Casserole

ACTIVE 20 MIN. · TOTAL 4 HOURS
SERVES 12

- ½ cup granulated sugar
- ½ cup packed light brown sugar
- 1 tsp. ground cinnamon
- 2 (16.3-oz.) cans refrigerated Southern home-style biscuits, separated and cut into fourths (about 64 pieces total)
- ½ cup butter, melted, plus 2 Tbsp. butter, softened, divided
- 4 large eggs
- ¼ tsp. kosher salt
- ⅔ cup, plus 2 to 3 Tbsp. half-and-half, divided
- 2 tsp. vanilla extract, divided
- ½ cup chopped toasted pecans
- 1 (3-oz.) pkg. cream cheese, softened
- 2¼ cups powdered sugar, divided

1. Line bottom and sides of a 6-quart slow cooker with aluminum foil; lightly coat foil with cooking spray. Stir together granulated sugar, brown sugar, and ground cinnamon in a small bowl. Toss together biscuit pieces and ½ cup melted butter in a large bowl until biscuits are coated.

2. Working in batches, add biscuits to the sugar mixture, and toss to coat; transfer biscuits to prepared slow cooker. Sprinkle any remaining sugar mixture over biscuits in slow cooker.

3. Whisk together eggs, salt, ⅔ cup of the half-and-half, and 1 teaspoon of the vanilla in a bowl until well combined, and pour over biscuits in slow cooker. Sprinkle with toasted pecans.

4. Beat cream cheese and 2 tablespoons softened butter in a large bowl with an electric mixer on medium speed until thoroughly combined, about 30 seconds. Add 1 cup of the powdered sugar and remaining 1 teaspoon vanilla; beat until smooth, about 1 minute.

5. Add the remaining 1¼ cups powdered sugar gradually to cream cheese mixture alternately with 2 tablespoons of the half-and-half, beating on high speed until frosting is smooth, creamy, and a little loose, about 1 minute. Add remaining 1 tablespoon half-and-half, 1 teaspoon at a time, if needed to reach desired consistency.

CRUSTLESS HAM-AND-SPINACH QUICHE

6. Drizzle half of the frosting over biscuit mixture in slow cooker. (Cover remaining frosting; set aside until ready to serve.) Cover slow cooker, and cook on LOW until center of casserole is set and biscuit bottoms are browned, about 3½ to 4 hours. Drizzle with remaining frosting; serve warm.

Crustless Ham-and-Spinach Quiche

ACTIVE 20 MIN. · TOTAL 1 HOUR
SERVES 6 TO 8

- 1½ tsp. olive oil
- 1 cup chopped baked ham
- ½ (16-oz.) pkg. frozen chopped spinach, thawed and drained
- ½ cup diced sweet onion
- 6 oz. Monterey Jack cheese, shredded (1½ cups)
- 1 cup milk
- 2 large eggs
- ½ cup all-purpose baking mix
- ¼ tsp. kosher salt

1. Preheat oven to 400°F. Heat oil in a large skillet over medium-high heat. Then add ham, and sauté 5 minutes or until browned. Stir in spinach and onion; sauté 5 minutes or until onion is tender and liquid evaporates. Layer half of spinach mixture in a lightly greased (with cooking spray) 9-inch pie plate; top with ¾ cup cheese. Repeat layers once.

2. Whisk together milk and the remaining ingredients until smooth; pour over spinach-and-cheese mixture in pie plate.

3. Bake in preheated oven 25 to 35 minutes or until a knife inserted in center comes out clean. Let stand 10 minutes before serving.

School Night Suppers

Five kid-approved dinners you can pull off on the busiest weeknight

MACARONI PIE

JUMP-START SUPPER
Cut prep time by using a store-bought frozen crust that comes in a pan. Or press a refrigerated crust into a metal pie plate, wrap tightly with aluminum foil, and freeze up to a week in advance.

Macaroni Pie

ACTIVE 30 MIN. - TOTAL 1 HOUR, 45 MIN.
SERVES 6

- ½ (14.1-oz.) pkg. refrigerated piecrusts
- 8 oz. uncooked large elbow macaroni
- 3 Tbsp. unsalted butter
- ⅓ cup all-purpose flour
- 1½ cups whole milk
- 2 tsp. Dijon mustard
- ½ tsp. black pepper
- ¼ tsp. kosher salt
- 4 oz. Gruyère cheese, shredded (1 cup)
- 2 oz. extra-sharp white cheddar cheese, shredded (½ cup)
- 2 oz. fontina cheese, shredded (½ cup)
- Fresh thyme leaves, for garnish

1. Preheat oven to 350°F. Press crust into a 9-inch metal pie plate; crimp edges. Freeze 15 minutes. Line crust with aluminum foil; fill with pie weights or dried beans. Bake until golden brown, about 20 minutes. Remove foil and weights. Return crust to oven, and bake until bottom is dry, 5 minutes. Cool 10 minutes.
2. Prepare pasta according to package directions. Drain, rinse, and set aside.
3. Melt butter in a medium saucepan over medium. Add flour; cook, stirring constantly, until a light golden paste forms, about 1 minute. Gradually add milk in a steady stream, whisking constantly, until fully combined. Add mustard, pepper, and salt, whisking constantly, until thick, about 2 minutes. Gradually add cheeses, whisking between each addition until smooth. Remove from heat; gently fold in pasta.
4. Spoon mixture into prepared piecrust. Bake in preheated oven until golden brown, 25 to 30 minutes. Sprinkle with thyme. Cool 10 minutes.

LOADED PULLED-PORK NACHOS

Loaded Pulled-Pork Nachos

This meal is fun, fully customizable, and comes together quickly

ACTIVE 15 MIN. - TOTAL 15 MIN.
SERVES 6

- 1 (9-oz.) pkg. tortilla chips
- 2 (15-oz.) cans refried black beans, warmed
- 8 oz. shredded smoked pork
- 1 lb. pepper Jack cheese, shredded (about 4 cups)
- ¼ cup sour cream
- 2 Tbsp. fresh lime juice (from 1 large lime)
- 1 medium ripe avocado, chopped
- ¾ cup chopped plum tomato (from 1 large tomato)
- ½ cup fresh corn kernels (from 1 ear)
- ¼ cup sliced pickled jalapeño chile
- ¼ cup packed fresh cilantro leaves (from 1 bunch cilantro)

1. Preheat oven to 500°F. Line a large rimmed baking sheet with aluminum foil. Arrange layers of chips, beans, pork, and cheese on prepared baking sheet. Bake until cheese is melted and chips are lightly browned, about 5 minutes.
2. Meanwhile, stir together sour cream and lime juice in a small bowl. Set aside.
3. Remove nachos from oven; sprinkle with avocado, tomato, corn, jalapeño, and cilantro. Drizzle with sour cream mixture. Serve immediately.

SUPREME
PIZZA

Supreme Pizza

Make dinner together. Older kids can shape the dough, and little ones can add toppings.

ACTIVE 20 MIN. - TOTAL 30 MIN.

SERVES 4

- 1 lb. fresh prepared pizza dough
    All-purpose flour, for work surface
- 1 cup marinara sauce
- 2 oz. Canadian bacon slices
    (about 3 slices), quartered
- 1 oz. pepperoni slices
    (about 15 slices)
- 2 small bell peppers, cut into
    ¼-inch-thick rounds (½ cup)
- 1 small red onion, cut into ¼-inch-
    thick rounds (½ cup)
- 1 (2¼-oz.) can sliced black olives,
    drained
- 6 oz. low-moisture part-skim
    mozzarella cheese, shredded
    (1½ cups)
- ¼ cup grated Parmesan cheese
- ¼ cup torn fresh basil leaves

Place a pizza stone or baking sheet on middle rack in oven. Preheat oven to 500°F (do not remove pizza stone while oven preheats). Roll dough out into a 14-inch circle on a lightly floured work surface. Transfer dough circle to a piece of parchment paper. Spread marinara over dough, leaving a 1-inch border. Top with Canadian bacon, pepperoni, bell peppers, red onion, black olives, and mozzarella. Transfer parchment with pizza to hot pizza stone. Bake until cheese is bubbly and lightly browned, 9 to 10 minutes. Remove pizza, and let stand 5 minutes; sprinkle with Parmesan and basil.

Baked Pasta with Chicken and Creamy Ranch Sauce

Ranch dressing mix gives this rich and cheesy pasta casserole a tangy kick

ACTIVE 30 MIN. - TOTAL 50 MIN.

SERVES 6

- 8 oz. uncooked mini penne
- 4 bacon slices, chopped
- 3 garlic cloves, minced (about
    1 Tbsp.)
- ¾ cup heavy whipping cream
- 1 (8-oz.) pkg. cream cheese, cubed
    and softened
- 2 oz. Parmesan cheese, grated
    (about ½ cup)
- 2 Tbsp. ranch dressing mix
    (from 1 [1-oz.] pkg.)
- ¼ tsp. black pepper
- 3 cups shredded, cooked chicken
    (from 1 rotisserie chicken)
- 8 oz. low-moisture part skim
    mozzarella cheese, shredded
    (about 2 cups), divided
- 2 Tbsp. chopped fresh flat-leaf
    parsley

1. Preheat oven to 375°F. Cook penne according to package directions; drain, reserving 1 cup cooking water. Place pasta in a large bowl, and set aside.
2. Heat a large skillet over medium. Add bacon, and cook, stirring often, until crisp, about 5 minutes. Using a slotted spoon, transfer bacon to a plate lined with paper towels. Reserve drippings in skillet.
3. Add garlic to hot drippings in skillet over medium. Cook, stirring constantly, until fragrant, about 1 minute. Whisk in whipping cream and cream cheese. Cook, whisking often, until cream cheese is melted and mixture is smooth, about

BAKED PASTA WITH
CHICKEN AND CREAMY
RANCH SAUCE

HAMBURGER STEW
WITH CROUTONS

2 minutes. Remove from heat, and stir in Parmesan, ranch dressing mix, pepper, and reserved 1 cup cooking water. Pour over pasta. Fold in chicken and 1 cup of the mozzarella cheese. Pour mixture into a lightly greased (with cooking spray) 13- x 9-inch baking dish. Top with bacon and remaining 1 cup cheese.

4. Bake in preheated oven until golden and bubbly, about 20 minutes. Sprinkle with parsley, and serve hot.

Hamburger Stew with Croutons

Enjoy burger night in a bowl, topped off with crunchy hamburger-bun croutons

ACTIVE 30 MIN. - TOTAL 50 MIN.
SERVES 6

1¼	lb. ground chuck
1½	tsp. dry mustard
½	tsp. dried oregano
1¾	tsp. kosher salt, divided
1	cup chopped yellow onion (from 1 medium onion)
4	medium garlic cloves, finely chopped (about 1½ Tbsp.)
1	Tbsp. tomato paste
2	Tbsp. all-purpose flour
4	cups beef broth
1	(14.5-oz.) can diced tomatoes, undrained
2	Tbsp. ketchup
12	oz. baby red potatoes, quartered
2	cups frozen mixed vegetables (carrots, corn, lima beans, peas, and green beans)
2	(1½-oz.) hamburger buns, cut into ¾-inch pieces
1	Tbsp. olive oil

1. Preheat oven to 350°F. Heat a large Dutch oven over medium-high. Add ground chuck, mustard, oregano, and 1 teaspoon of the salt. Cook, stirring occasionally, until crumbled and browned, about 8 minutes. Using a slotted spoon, transfer beef mixture to a bowl lined with paper towels, reserving 1 tablespoon drippings in Dutch oven.

2. Return Dutch oven to medium heat; add onion. Cook, stirring often, until softened, about 4 minutes. Add garlic and tomato paste. Cook, stirring constantly, until fragrant and warmed through, about 1 minute. Add flour; cook, stirring often, 1 minute. Add broth, tomatoes, and ketchup, scraping bottom of pan to loosen browned bits. Stir in cooked beef. Increase heat to medium-high, and bring to a boil. Add potatoes and ½ teaspoon salt; reduce heat to medium. Simmer until potatoes are tender, about 20 minutes. Stir in mixed vegetables, and cook until warmed through, 2 to 3 minutes.

3. Meanwhile, as potatoes cook, toss together bun pieces, olive oil, and remaining ¼ teaspoon salt on a parchment paper-lined baking sheet; spread into a single layer. Bake in preheated oven until golden and crisp, about 10 minutes. Serve with stew.

Spice Up Your Slow Cooker

It takes only six ingredients to make this tender, tangy chicken you'll want to eat all week long

Slow-Cooker Salsa Chicken

This recipe makes a lot of chicken, which is great because you can eat it in different ways. Instead of serving with rice, spoon it atop baked potatoes, tuck it into warm tortillas or taco shells, or stir it into hot cooked pasta.

ACTIVE 15 MIN. · TOTAL 2 HOURS, 20 MIN.
SERVES 8

2 lb. boneless, skinless chicken thighs
1 tsp. kosher salt
½ tsp. black pepper
2 (16-oz.) containers refrigerated medium salsa
¼ cup chopped fresh oregano
8 cups hot cooked yellow rice (from 2 [5-oz.] pkg., such as Mahatma Yellow Seasoned Rice)
   Chopped fresh cilantro and lime wedges, for serving

Place chicken in a 6-quart slow cooker, and sprinkle evenly with salt and pepper. Add salsa and oregano. Cover and cook on HIGH until a thermometer inserted in thickest portion of thighs registers 165°F, about 2 hours. Turn off slow cooker. Transfer chicken to a large heatproof bowl, and cool 10 minutes. Shred meat into bite-size pieces. Add liquid in slow cooker to chicken, and toss to coat. Serve over hot rice. Garnish with fresh cilantro, and serve with lime wedges.

CALORIES: **294** – CARBS: **34G** – FAT: **5G**

The Skinny on Baked Fries

Satisfy after-school cravings with tender-on-the-inside, crisp-on-the-outside sweet potatoes

HOW TO KEEP THEM CRISPY
The key to perfect oven-baked fries is a light coating of cornstarch, which helps the exteriors crisp up. Also be careful to avoid overcrowding the sweet potatoes on the sheet pan, which will cause them to steam and become soggy.

Baked Sweet Potato Fries

ACTIVE 15 MIN. · TOTAL 40 MIN.
SERVES 4

- 1 lb. unpeeled sweet potatoes, cut into ¼-inch matchsticks
- 1 Tbsp. cornstarch or potato starch
- 2 Tbsp. peanut oil or canola oil
- ½ tsp. kosher salt

1. Preheat oven to 425°F with racks in upper third and lower third positions. Toss together sweet potatoes and cornstarch in a large bowl until evenly coated. Drizzle with oil, and toss until evenly coated. Arrange in a single layer, evenly spaced on 2 baking sheets lined with parchment paper. Bake until bottoms start to brown, about 15 minutes.

2. Remove from oven. Flip fries using tongs, moving smaller fries toward center of baking sheet if browning too quickly. Return to oven, rotating sheets between top and bottom racks. Bake until browned and crisp, about 10 to 15 minutes. Remove from oven. Sprinkle fries evenly with salt. Serve immediately.

COOKING ⒮ SCHOOL

Flavor Boosters

Add depth and richness to vegetarian dishes

DOUBLE-CONCENTRATED TOMATO PASTE

Tomatoes are naturally full of umami (the savory fifth taste), and this extra-strength paste makes sauces, stews, and soups more robust.

SMOKED PAPRIKA

This aromatic spice is a surprisingly good stand-in for bacon and smoked meats. Add it to chili, or sprinkle on grilled vegetables.

BETTER THAN BOUILLON SEASONED VEGETABLE BASE

Mix this intense paste of pureed roasted vegetables and spices with water to make an instant broth that's more flavorful than the boxed kind.

IN SEASON

An Apple for Everything

Our handy guide for making the right choice

1	**2**	**3**	**4**
BEST FOR APPLESAUCE **McINTOSH**	**BEST FOR SAVORY DISHES** **GOLDEN DELICIOUS**	**BEST FOR PIES** **GRANNY SMITH**	**BEST FOR BAKING WHOLE** **HONEY CRISP**
A juicy pick, it has a slight tang and a soft texture that breaks down easily and turns creamy and smooth when cooked.	The mild flavor complements grilled cheese sandwiches, roasted proteins like pork and chicken, and green salads.	This tart fruit pairs well with brown sugar and warm spices, and its firm texture won't break down during longer cook times.	True to its name, this type is crunchy and sweet and will also hold its shape when cored and baked.

"When making a streusel topping, combine the ingredients and let it sit for 30 minutes. The flour will absorb the fat, making the mixture solid and easier to crumble."

Pam Lolley,
Test Kitchen Professional

October

CORNMEAL CRÊPES
WITH BLACKBERRIES AND
BUTTERMILK CREAM

The Sweet Side of Cornmeal

An Alabama family takes an heirloom ingredient from the past to the future

When James Lipscomb first planted corn in the fertile soil of Baldwin County, Alabama, in 1875, he had no way of knowing he was sowing his family's legacy as well. Generations of Lipscombs planted this colorful heirloom Indian corn (which was mostly dried and used for cattle feed) until 1987. By that time, the agricultural industry had slowed, and many farmers were forced to either downsize or sell their operations.

The six Lipscomb brothers, all great-grandsons of James, made the decision to stop planting the family corn. Not willing to completely lose their great-grandfather's legacy, one of the brothers, Claude, put about a pound of the seed in an old barn freezer where it remained, untouched but not forgotten, for 24 years.

In 2011, three of the brothers, Edward, Claude, and Sheldon, wondered if that old corn seed was still any good after being frozen for so long, so each of them took a handful as an experiment. Sheldon planted 98 kernels, and the family estimates that 96 germinated. For each of the next three years, they grew a little more. In the spring of 2015, Sheldon planted a total of 5 acres of his great-grandfather's corn.

The Lipscomb brothers had always thought about milling it. The same year that Sheldon planted 5 acres, his grandsons, Josh and Jarred Higginbotham, coarsely ground some into speckled meal and used it to make cornbread. "We knew the grinding needed to be perfected more, but we could tell the aroma was different, the taste was different," says Jarred. "We knew we had something unique."

That summer, Josh and Jarred decided to take their cornmeal to the Coastal Alabama Farmers and Fishermens Market in Foley. They sold out the first day. Soon after, they opened Bayou Cora Farms, which also sells grits, corn flour, and fish fry breading.

While Jarred and his twin brother have always had an interest in agriculture and keeping up the family tradition, he says, "We didn't always have this project on the radar." This type of farming–creating a specialty product–is different from their traditional approach, but Jarred says, "It helps support local businesses, keeps heirloom plants going, and shares the stories of the people behind them."

Our Test Kitchen used Bayou Cora Farms products for these four recipes– from crêpes to tarts. Order a bag for yourself, and taste the difference. Or simply use your favorite cornmeal to make these seasonal desserts.

Cornmeal Crêpes with Blackberries and Buttermilk Cream

When the crêpe is almost set, loosen the edges with a small offset spatula and then flip with a fish spatula or your fingers.

ACTIVE 1 HOUR - TOTAL 1 HOUR, 30 MIN., PLUS 2 HOURS CHILLING
SERVES 6

- 2 large eggs
- 1/2 cup all-purpose flour
- 1/2 cup fine yellow cornmeal or Bayou Cora Farms Heirloom Corn Flour
- 1 tsp. vanilla extract
- 1 1/2 cups whole buttermilk, divided
- 2/3 cup, plus 1 1/2 Tbsp. granulated sugar, divided
- 3/4 tsp. kosher salt, divided
- 4 cups fresh blackberries (about 1 1/4 lb.)
- 1 Tbsp. fresh lemon juice (from 1 lemon)
- 1 1/2 cups heavy cream
- 1 1/2 tsp. canola oil, divided
  Powdered sugar

1. Process eggs, flour, cornmeal, vanilla, 1 cup of the buttermilk, 1/3 cup of the sugar, and 1/4 teaspoon of the salt in a blender until smooth, about 15 seconds. Cover; chill batter at least 2 hours or up to 8 hours (or overnight).

2. Meanwhile, stir together blackberries, lemon juice, 1/3 cup of the sugar, and 1/4 teaspoon of the salt in a small saucepan. Cook over medium, stirring occasionally, until berries begin to break down and mixture thickens slightly, 30 to 35 minutes. Remove from heat; cool at room temperature until ready to serve (at least 30 minutes or up to 4 hours).

3. Beat heavy cream, remaining 1 1/2 tablespoons sugar and 1/4 teaspoon salt with a stand mixer fitted with a whisk attachment on medium speed until soft peaks form, about 2 minutes. Gradually add remaining 1/2 cup buttermilk, beating until medium peaks form, about 30 seconds. Cover and chill until ready to assemble crêpes (up to 4 hours).

4. Heat an 8-inch nonstick skillet over medium-low. Brush skillet lightly with 1/8 teaspoon of the oil; pour about 2 1/2 tablespoons batter into skillet. Quickly tilt skillet so batter covers bottom of skillet. Cook until crêpe is almost set and can be shaken loose from skillet, about 1 1/2 minutes. Flip crêpe, and cook 30 seconds. Remove from skillet. Repeat with remaining oil and batter to yield 12 crêpes.

5. Spread about 3 tablespoons of the buttermilk cream over half of each crêpe. Fold crêpes into quarters, and arrange on 6 plates. Top each serving with about 1/4 cup blackberry compote. Garnish with powdered sugar. Serve immediately.

Thyme–Cornmeal Pound Cake

ACTIVE 20 MIN. - TOTAL 1 HOUR, 50 MIN.,
PLUS 1 HOUR COOLING
SERVES 10

½   cup unsalted butter, softened,
      plus more for pan

1   cup all-purpose flour, plus more
      for pan

1¼   cups granulated sugar

3   large eggs

½   cup fine yellow cornmeal or Bayou
      Cora Farms Heirloom Cornmeal

½   tsp. kosher salt

⅛   tsp. baking soda

½   cup sour cream

1   tsp. lemon zest, plus 2 Tbsp. fresh
      juice (from 1 lemon), divided

1   tsp. finely chopped fresh thyme,
      plus thyme sprigs for garnish

2   cups unsifted powdered sugar

2   to 3 Tbsp. whole milk, as needed

1. Preheat oven to 325°F. Grease a
9- x 5-inch loaf pan with butter, and dust with flour; set aside. Beat granulated sugar and butter with a stand mixer fitted with a paddle attachment on medium speed until light and creamy, 5 to 6 minutes. Add eggs 1 at a time, beating until just incorporated after each addition.
2. Stir together flour, cornmeal, salt, and baking soda in a small bowl. Add flour mixture to butter mixture in 3 additions alternating with sour cream, beginning and ending with flour mixture, beating on low speed just until combined after each addition. Stir in lemon zest, chopped thyme, and 1 tablespoon of the lemon juice. Pour batter into prepared pan, spreading evenly.
3. Bake in preheated oven until cake is golden brown and a wooden pick inserted in center comes out clean, 1 hour to 1 hour and 10 minutes. Let cool in pan on a wire rack 10 minutes. Remove cake from pan; cool completely on a wire rack, about 1 hour.
4. Whisk together powdered sugar, 2 tablespoons of the milk, and remaining 1 tablespoon lemon juice in a small bowl, whisking in an additional 1 tablespoon milk, 1 teaspoon at a time, until glaze reaches desired consistency. Spoon glaze over cooled cake. Let stand 20 minutes. Garnish with thyme sprigs.

THYME-CORNMEAL
POUND CAKE

Apple–and–Pear Cornmeal Galette

ACTIVE 30 MIN. - TOTAL 1 HOUR, 35 MIN.,
PLUS 2 HOURS CHILLING
SERVES 8

1½   cups all-purpose flour

1   cup, plus 1 Tbsp. fine yellow
      cornmeal or Bayou Cora Farms
      Heirloom Corn Flour, divided

¼   cup, plus 2 Tbsp. granulated sugar,
      divided

1¼   tsp. kosher salt, divided

1   cup cold unsalted butter, cut into
      ½-inch pieces

4   to 6 Tbsp. ice water, as needed

2   medium (about 1 lb. total) Fuji
      apples, peeled, cored, and cut
      into ¼-inch-thick slices

2   large (about 1 lb. total) green
      Anjou pears, peeled, cored, and
      cut into ¼-inch-thick slices

½   tsp. ground cinnamon

1   large egg, beaten

1   Tbsp. turbinado sugar

2   Tbsp. apple jelly
      Vanilla ice cream

1. Pulse flour, 1 cup of the cornmeal, 2 tablespoons of the granulated sugar, and 1 teaspoon of the salt in a food processor until combined, about 5 pulses. Add butter, and pulse until mixture resembles small peas, 10 to 12 pulses. With food processor running, gradually add 4 tablespoons ice water, processing until mixture is evenly moistened and just starts to clump together, about 15 seconds. If needed, add remaining 2 tablespoons ice water, 1 tablespoon at a time, pulsing 3 to 5 times to combine after each addition. Turn out dough onto a clean work surface, and knead gently to just bring dough together, 3 to 4 times. Shape into a disk, and wrap tightly in plastic wrap. Chill dough at least 2 hours or up to 2 days.
2. Preheat oven to 425°F with oven rack in lower third position. Let dough stand at room temperature until slightly softened, about 10 minutes. Unwrap dough, and place between 2 sheets of parchment paper. Roll into a 12- x 14-inch oval (about ¼ inch thick). If desired, trim edges for smooth sides. Transfer dough (still between parchment paper) to a large baking sheet.
3. Remove top sheet of parchment paper from dough. Sprinkle dough evenly with remaining 1 tablespoon cornmeal or corn flour. Arrange sliced apples and pears, overlapping slightly, on top of dough, leaving a 1½-inch border.
4. Stir together cinnamon and remaining ¼ cup granulated sugar and ¼ teaspoon salt in a small bowl. Sprinkle cinnamon-sugar mixture over apple-pear filling. Fold edges of dough up and over filling, pleating or overlapping dough as needed. Lightly brush crust edges with beaten egg, then sprinkle evenly with turbinado sugar. Chill 15 minutes.
5. Bake in preheated oven until crust is golden brown and fruit is tender, 28 to 32 minutes. Transfer galette (still on parchment paper) to a wire rack. Cool slightly, about 10 minutes.
6. Microwave apple jelly in a small microwaveable bowl on HIGH until melted and smooth, about 25 seconds. Brush melted apple jelly over galette filling. Slice galette with a serrated knife while it is still warm. Serve slices topped with ice cream.

APPLE-AND-PEAR
CORNMEAL GALETTE

Ginger–Fig Tart with Cornmeal Crust

The creamy, slightly spicy tart filling pairs well with fresh figs or other juicy fruits such as sliced pears and persimmons.

ACTIVE 20 MIN. - TOTAL 20 MIN.,
PLUS 3 HOURS CHILLING

SERVES 10

- 4 large egg yolks
- 2 Tbsp. cornstarch
- 1½ cups whole milk, divided
- ¾ cup granulated sugar
- 1 tsp. grated fresh ginger (from 1 [2-inch] piece)
- ¼ tsp. kosher salt
- ¼ cup unsalted butter
  Cornmeal Crust (recipe follows)
- 8 oz. fresh figs, quartered (about 2 cups)

1. Whisk together egg yolks, cornstarch, and ¼ cup of the milk in a medium bowl until smooth.
2. Stir together sugar, ginger, salt, and remaining 1¼ cups milk in a small saucepan. Cook over medium, stirring occasionally, until sugar is dissolved and mixture is hot but not boiling, about 4 minutes. Slowly and gradually add milk mixture to egg mixture, whisking constantly; return mixture to pan. Cook over medium, whisking constantly, until custard thickens and bubbles, 3 to 4 minutes. Remove from heat, and whisk in butter.
3. Pour custard mixture through a fine mesh strainer into cooled Cornmeal Crust; discard solids. Smooth custard top with a small offset spatula, and press plastic wrap directly onto surface to cover. Chill until set, at least 3 hours or up to 2 days. When ready to serve, arrange figs on top of tart.

Cornmeal Crust

ACTIVE 10 MIN. - TOTAL 1 HOUR,
PLUS 1 HOUR COOLING

MAKES 1 (9-INCH) ROUND TART SHELL

- ⅔ cup all-purpose flour
- ⅓ cup unsifted powdered sugar
- ⅓ cup fine yellow cornmeal or Bayou Cora Farms Heirloom Cornmeal
- ¼ tsp. kosher salt
- 6 Tbsp. cold unsalted butter, cut into ½-inch pieces
- 2 large egg yolks

1. Preheat oven to 350°F. Lightly coat a 9-inch round fluted tart pan with removable bottom with cooking spray. Pulse flour, powdered sugar, cornmeal, and salt in a food processor until well combined, about 5 pulses. Add butter; pulse until mixture resembles small peas, about 10 pulses. Add egg yolks; process until mixture is evenly moistened and crumbly, about 10 seconds.
2. Transfer mixture to prepared tart pan; firmly press mixture into bottom and up sides of pan. Chill until firm, about 30 minutes.
3. Bake in preheated oven until golden brown, 20 to 22 minutes. Transfer tart shell to a wire rack (still in pan); cool completely, about 1 hour.

GINGER-FIG TART WITH
CORNMEAL CRUST

Eat Your Greens (and Beans)

Try these ways to make a hearty fall soup

WHITE BEAN-
AND-CHARD
SOUP

White Bean-and-Chard Soup

ACTIVE 40 MIN. - TOTAL 40 MIN.
SERVES 6

- 2 Tbsp. olive oil
- 1 small yellow onion, chopped (1½ cups)
- 2 garlic cloves, finely chopped (1 Tbsp.)
- 1 tsp. finely chopped fresh rosemary
- ¾ tsp. kosher salt
- ½ tsp. black pepper
- 3 (15-oz.) cans lower-sodium cannellini beans, drained and rinsed
- 4 cups lower-sodium chicken broth
- 1 dried bay leaf
- 3 cups packed roughly chopped Swiss chard (stems and ribs removed; from 1 [8-oz.] bunch)
   Shaved Parmesan cheese

1. Heat oil in a Dutch oven over medium-high. Add onion. Cook, stirring occasionally, until softened and translucent, 5 to 7 minutes. Add garlic, rosemary, salt, and pepper. Cook, stirring constantly, 1 minute. Add beans, broth, and bay leaf.

2. Bring mixture to a boil over high. Reduce heat to low; simmer, stirring occasionally, 15 minutes. Remove and discard bay leaf.

3. Ladle 2 cups soup into a blender. Secure lid on blender, and remove center piece to allow steam to escape. Place a clean towel over opening. Process until completely smooth, 1 minute. Return pureed soup to remaining soup in saucepan, and bring to a simmer over medium-high.

4. Stir in chard. Cook, stirring often, until wilted and slightly softened, 2 to 3 minutes. Garnish with Parmesan.

CALORIES: **256** – CARBS: **37G** – FAT: **6G**

WHITE BEAN SOUP WITH PASTA AND SAUSAGE

CREAMY WHITE BEAN-AND-CHARD SOUP

Tasty Spin-Offs

White Bean Soup with Pasta and Sausage

Proceed with Step 1 as directed, adding 1 (13-oz.) pkg. **smoked turkey kielbasa** (Polish sausage), cut into half-moons, to Dutch oven with onion; add 2 cans beans with broth, and the bay leaf. Proceed with Step 2 as directed, adding ½ cup uncooked **ditalini pasta** to simmering soup after about 8 minutes. Skip Step 3. Proceed with Step 4 as directed.

CALORIES: **284** – CARBS: **38G** – FAT: **8G**

Creamy White Bean-and-Chard Soup

Proceed with Steps 1 and 2 as directed above. Add chard to Dutch oven. Cook over low, stirring occasionally, until chard is very tender and wilted, about 6 minutes. Working in 2 batches, ladle soup into a blender as directed in Step 3; process until smooth, 2 to 3 minutes per batch. Return pureed soup to Dutch oven, and bring to a simmer over medium-high. Stir together ⅓ cup **sour cream** and 1 Tbsp. **whole milk** in a bowl. Top servings with sour cream mixture; garnish with chopped **fresh chives** and **crushed red pepper.**

CALORIES: **391** – CARBS: **49G** – FAT: **10G**

Pasta Pronto!

Enjoy gooey cheese, bubbling sauce, and tender noodles in 30 minutes or less

Baked Ziti and Meatballs

ACTIVE 10 MIN. - TOTAL 30 MIN.
SERVES 8

- 1 (16-oz.) pkg. ziti, cooked according to pkg. directions for al dente
- 2 (24-oz.) jars marinara sauce
- 2 (14-oz.) pkg. frozen home-style beef meatballs, thawed
- 1 (8-oz.) pkg. cremini mushrooms, sliced (about 4 cups)
- 2 cups baby spinach
- 1 cup chopped pepperoni
- ½ cup fresh orange juice (about 1 large orange)
- 4 oz. mozzarella cheese, shredded (about 1 cup)
  Fresh basil leaves, for garnish

1. Preheat oven to 450°F. Coat a 13- x 9-inch baking dish with cooking spray. Line a large rimmed baking sheet with aluminum foil, and place baking dish on prepared baking sheet. Stir together pasta, marinara sauce, meatballs, mushrooms, spinach, pepperoni, and orange juice in baking dish.

2. Bake in preheated oven 10 minutes. Sprinkle with cheese, and continue baking until cheese is melted and pasta is thoroughly heated, about 10 minutes. Garnish with basil.

SECRET INGREDIENT
Sugar is often added to tomato sauce to help balance acidity. This recipe uses fresh orange juice instead for sweet citrus notes that boost the flavor of the marinara.

BAKED ZITI AND MEATBALLS

Sheet Pan Butternut Squash Mac and Cheese

ACTIVE 20 MIN. · TOTAL 30 MIN.
SERVES 6

- 2 Tbsp. unsalted butter
- 2 Tbsp. all-purpose flour
- 2 cups whole milk, warmed
- 12 oz. extra-sharp cheddar cheese, shredded (about 3 cups)
- 1 cup canned butternut squash or pumpkin (from 1 [15-oz.] can)
- ¼ tsp. black pepper
- ¾ tsp. kosher salt, divided
- 3 (8.5-oz.) pkg. precooked microwaveable pasta (such as Barilla Ready Pasta)
- ½ cup panko breadcrumbs
- 1½ Tbsp. extra-virgin olive oil
- 1 tsp. minced fresh rosemary, plus more for garnish

1. Preheat oven to 400°F. Coat a 15- x 10-inch rimmed baking sheet with cooking spray and set aside. Melt butter in a large saucepan over medium; whisk in flour until smooth, and cook, whisking constantly, 1 minute. Gradually whisk in warm milk until smooth, and bring to a simmer, whisking occasionally. Cook, whisking often, until slightly thickened, about 5 minutes. Gradually whisk in cheese, squash, pepper, and ½ teaspoon of the salt until smooth.
2. Remove pan from heat, and stir in pasta until fully coated. Spoon pasta mixture into prepared baking sheet in even layer. Bake in preheated oven until bubbly, about 8 minutes.
3. Meanwhile, stir together breadcrumbs, olive oil, rosemary, and remaining ¼ teaspoon salt in a small bowl. Remove pasta mixture from oven, and increase oven temperature to broil. Sprinkle breadcrumb mixture evenly over pasta mixture, and broil on center oven rack in preheated oven until bubbly and golden brown, 1 to 2 minutes. Garnish with rosemary.

SIMPLE SWAP
If you can't find canned butternut squash puree at the supermarket, use canned pumpkin puree instead. Make sure that it's pure pumpkin, not pumpkin pie filling, which contains sugar and spices.

Chicken-and-Broccoli Skillet Pasta

ACTIVE 30 MIN. - TOTAL 30 MIN.
SERVES 8

- 6 thick-cut bacon slices, chopped (about 1 cup)
- 2 Tbsp. unsalted butter
- 2 garlic cloves, minced (about 2 tsp.)
- 6 Tbsp. all-purpose flour
- 3 cups chicken broth
- 1 cup heavy whipping cream
- ½ tsp. kosher salt
- ½ tsp. black pepper
- 1 (15-oz.) pkg. frozen broccoli florets, thawed
- 8 oz. Parmesan cheese, shredded (about 2 cups)
- 2 oz. Monterey Jack cheese, shredded (about ½ cup)
- 1 (12-oz.) pkg. wide egg noodles, cooked according to pkg. directions
- 3 cups shredded cooked chicken (from 1 rotisserie chicken)
- ½ cup chopped Peppadew or sweet cherry peppers (from a [16-oz.] jar)
- ½ cup panko (Japanese breadcrumbs)

1. Preheat oven to broil with oven rack 6 inches from heat. Heat a 12-inch ovenproof skillet over medium. Add bacon, and cook, stirring often, until crisp, about 10 minutes. Using a slotted spoon, transfer bacon to a plate lined with paper towels, reserving 2 tablespoons bacon drippings in skillet.

2. Add butter and garlic to hot drippings in skillet. Cook, stirring constantly, until fragrant, about 1 minute. Whisk in flour, and cook, whisking constantly, 2 minutes. Gradually whisk in chicken broth, cream, salt, and pepper until smooth. Bring to a simmer over medium-high, whisking occasionally. Stir in broccoli. Cook, stirring occasionally, until sauce is slightly thickened, about 7 minutes.

3. Remove from heat; stir in cheeses until smooth. Stir in cooked pasta, chicken, peppers, and half the reserved bacon. Sprinkle with breadcrumbs. Broil in preheated oven until lightly toasted, 1 to 2 minutes. Sprinkle with remaining bacon.

PICK THIS PEPPER

Peppadew is the brand name of the piquanté pepper, which is small, round, and pickled in a sweet-and-spicy brine. Look for this type in the olive bar in your grocery store's deli section, or use jarred sweet cherry peppers.

THE QUICKEST NOODLES
Fresh refrigerated linguine has a shorter cook time than dry pasta, which allows this dish to come together quickly. Don't worry about the large amount of liquid in the pan. As the pasta cooks, starch will be drawn out to thicken the sauce.

Baked Linguine with Spicy Tomato-Cream Sauce

ACTIVE 20 MIN. · TOTAL 20 MIN.
SERVES 6

- 3 Tbsp. unsalted butter
- 2 garlic cloves, finely chopped (about 2 tsp.)
- ¼ tsp. crushed red pepper
- 1 (14.5-oz.) can diced fire-roasted tomatoes, undrained
- 1 cup heavy whipping cream
- ½ tsp. black pepper
- 1¼ tsp., plus ⅛ tsp. kosher salt, divided

- 2 (9-oz.) pkg. refrigerated linguine (such as Buitoni)
- 6 oz. pre-shredded Italian 6-cheese blend, (about 1½ cups), divided
- 1 pt. cherry tomatoes, halved (about 2 cups)
- 1 tsp. extra-virgin olive oil
  Torn fresh basil leaves, for garnish

1. Preheat oven to broil with oven rack about 4 inches from heat. Melt butter in a 12-inch ovenproof skillet over medium. Add garlic and red pepper, and cook, stirring constantly, until fragrant, about 1 minute. Add diced tomatoes, and cook, stirring occasionally, 5 minutes. Stir in 1¾ cups water, heavy cream, black pepper, and 1¼ teaspoons of the salt; bring to a simmer. Stir in pasta. Cook, stirring constantly, until pasta is tender, about 2 minutes. Reduce heat to low; stir in ¾ cup of the cheese until melted and pasta is fully coated. Sprinkle with remaining ¾ cup cheese.

2. Broil in preheated oven until sauce is bubbly and cheese is golden brown, about 2 minutes. Meanwhile, stir together cherry tomatoes, olive oil, and remaining ⅛ teaspoon salt in a small bowl. Spoon tomato mixture over pasta; garnish with basil.

Baked Tortellini Alfredo with Mushrooms

ACTIVE 15 MIN. - TOTAL 25 MIN.
SERVES 4

¼ cup unsalted butter
1 (8-oz.) pkg. cremini mushrooms, sliced (4 cups sliced)
2 garlic cloves, minced (about 2 tsp.)
1 cup heavy whipping cream
½ cup whole milk
½ tsp. kosher salt
¼ tsp. black pepper
¼ tsp. ground nutmeg
8 oz. Parmesan cheese, finely shredded (about 2 cups), divided
2 (8-oz.) pkg. refrigerated three-cheese tortellini (such as Buitoni), cooked according to pkg. directions
2 Tbsp. chopped fresh flat-leaf parsley

1. Preheat oven to broil with rack 8 inches from heat. Melt butter in a 10-inch ovenproof skillet over medium. Add mushrooms in even layer, and cook, undisturbed, 4 minutes. Stir and continue cooking, stirring occasionally, until golden brown, about 4 minutes. Stir in garlic. Cook, stirring constantly, until fragrant, about 1 minute.

2. Stir in cream and milk; bring to a simmer over medium, stirring occasionally. Cook, stirring often, until slightly thickened, about 8 minutes. Stir in salt, pepper, nutmeg, and 1¾ cups of the Parmesan until smooth.

3. Stir in cooked tortellini until coated. Sprinkle with remaining ¼ cup Parmesan. Broil in preheated oven until sauce is bubbly and cheese is light golden brown, 3 to 5 minutes. Sprinkle with parsley.

THICK-SAUCE POINTERS
Let the mushrooms cook all the way to allow excess moisture to evaporate. Use a mixture of heavy cream and whole milk for added richness.

Smart Cookies

Start your day with a good-for-you treat that will keep you going all morning long

Breakfast Cookies

ACTIVE 20 MIN. - TOTAL 1 HOUR,
PLUS 1 HOUR COOLING

MAKES 20

2 cups uncooked old-fashioned
   regular rolled oats
2 cups toasted pecan halves,
   chopped
1 cup dried cranberries
⅔ cup whole wheat pastry flour
2 tsp. ground cinnamon
1 tsp. baking powder
1 tsp. kosher salt
½ tsp. baking soda
2 large eggs, beaten
1 cup creamy almond butter
1 cup unsweetened applesauce
1 cup packed dark brown sugar
1 tsp. vanilla extract

1. Preheat oven to 350°F. Line 2 baking
sheets with parchment paper. Stir
together oats, pecans, cranberries,
flour, cinnamon, baking powder, salt,
and baking soda in a medium bowl until
well combined.
2. Whisk together eggs, almond butter,
applesauce, sugar, and vanilla in a large
bowl until smooth. Add oat mixture; stir
just until combined.
3. Scoop cookie dough by ¼ cupfuls,
spaced 2 inches apart, onto prepared
baking sheets. Bake in preheated oven
in 2 batches until edges are light brown
(cookies will still be soft), 16 to 18 minutes
per batch. Remove from oven, and cool
10 minutes on baking sheet. Transfer to
a wire rack, and cool completely, 1 hour.
Store cookies in an airtight container up
to 1 week.

HAVE IT YOUR WAY
Swap out the almond butter for another
nut butter, replace some or all of the
cranberries with other dried fruits, or
substitute walnuts for the pecans.

COOKING ⟨SL⟩ SCHOOL

TEST KITCHEN TIPS

Better Baked Pasta

Easy ways to improve lasagna, mac and cheese, ziti, and more

① UNDERCOOK THE NOODLES

Boil pasta 3 minutes less than the package directions; it will finish cooking in the oven.

② SAUCE GENEROUSLY

Make sure all of the pasta is well coated in sauce so the noodles won't dry out as they bake.

③ MAKE THE BREADCRUMBS

Homemade crumbs vary in size, which creates a crunchier topping.

④ LET IT SIT

Freshly baked pasta should rest for about 5 minutes so it can firm up and become easier to serve.

"When making a baked pasta, grate hard cheeses like Parmesan yourself. It takes a little more time but will melt much better than the pregrated kind."

—Pam Lolley
Test Kitchen Professional

Know Your Mozzarellas

Learn the difference between these two common types

FRESH: Tender balls of fresh mozzarella are sold in containers filled with water. Enjoy this kind cold or at room temperature, but keep in mind that it's not the best for baking.

LOW MOISTURE: This cheese can be bought in plastic-wrapped blocks or shredded in bags. It contains less water and melts really well, making it an excellent choice for pizzas and oven-baked pastas.

EDITORS' PICK

The Best Marinara

Containing just eight ingredients, Rao's Homemade Marinara sauce has a bright, tangy flavor that's not too sweet.

November

Memories of a Texas-Size Thanksgiving

We photographed Tom Perini's annual family gathering in 2019, long before social distancing was a thing. Think of this story as a reason to be grateful for the past and hopeful for the future

The potluck meal includes favorite dishes such as cranberry sauce and bourbon-pecan carrots.

As a young man, Tom Perini spent holidays with a ragtag group around his family's table. After his father passed away in 1965, his mother, Maxine, invited their neighbors (the Wagstaffs), as well as friends who would otherwise spend Thanksgiving or Christmas by themselves, to join her for celebratory meals. "Mother would not let anyone be alone on these holidays," says Tom. "For all those years, this is what we had. We had family, friends of family, and family that had lost family." Before Maxine died in 2001, she asked Tom to continue celebrating Thanksgiving with

the Wagstaffs and to mark each annual gathering with a prayer of gratitude and a toast to those who had passed away.

Nineteen years later, Tom and his wife, Lisa, are still making good on that promise.

"It's sort of a standing invitation," says Lisa. "Tom and I have now been hosting it so long that there's just an assumption that Thanksgiving is here. People know to come."

Every year, around 60 to 70 people make the trip from as far as California to Buffalo Gap, Texas, a tiny town about 15 miles southwest of Abilene,

for Thanksgiving at the Perini Ranch Steakhouse. Tom first opened the restaurant in 1983 as a way to support the family's cattle-raising business. In the 37 years since, it's become a much-loved and -lauded destination in and of itself, inspiring two cookbooks and welcoming folks from around the world to enjoy a Texas chuckwagon-style cooking experience.

But on Thanksgiving, the employees—and the beef—take the day off.

Tom starts early in the morning, cooking four 15-pound turkeys for the crowd. Lisa sets the tables with blue

Gracious hosts Tom and Lisa Perini at the steakhouse

SOUTHERN SWEET POTATOES WITH BROWN SUGAR PECANS

Spode china and hand–me–down silver, ensuring that not even a couple of guests are seated apart from the rest. Everybody else brings the sides.

"Tom's daughter, Jessica, makes the best gravy on the planet, so she brings that, no matter what," says Lisa. "I make cranberry sauce."

There are other signature recipes that make an appearance each year too: Tom's daughter Caroline's bourbon milk punch is a must-have, along with roasted corn–and–poblano pudding and a "secret" family dessert.

"At Thanksgiving, my mother would make Grandmother's pound cake," says Tom. "When we were doing our first cookbook, I told her, 'I need to have that recipe.' And she thought for a minute and said, 'If you'll turn to page 520 in *The Boston Cooking–School Cook Book*, it's there.'"

And that's when Tom realized his own grandmother was not the originator of the beloved dessert.

"All these years, I could see my little grandmother adding a pound of butter," he says with a hearty laugh. "And that's not the way it was, but I don't care if it came out of the *Boston* cookbook. Those things make traditions. That's what it's about."

There are other traditions even more treasured than the pound cake: Each year, the youngest guests read from the family prayer book and there's a toast to loved ones who have passed away, just like Tom promised his mother 19 years ago.

"I think she was looking ahead," he says. "You know, this old life goes real fast, and you don't realize it until you get a little older. But it does, and she knew it. And now I know it. So it makes me feel good that we can do this."

Southern Sweet Potatoes with Brown Sugar Pecans

ACTIVE 20 MIN. · TOTAL 2 HOURS
SERVES 6

SWEET POTATO FILLING
- 3 lb. medium sweet potatoes (about 6 sweet potatoes), preferably Garnet or another deeply colored type
- 3 large eggs, lightly beaten
- 1 cup granulated sugar
- ½ cup whole milk
- 6 Tbsp. butter
- 1½ tsp. vanilla extract
- 1 tsp. kosher salt

TOPPING
- 1 cup chopped pecans
- 1 cup packed brown sugar
- ½ cup all-purpose flour
- ¼ tsp. kosher salt
- ¼ cup butter, melted

1. Prepare the Sweet Potato Filling: Preheat oven to 400°F. Coat a 13- x 9-inch glass baking dish with cooking spray, or lightly butter a 12-inch cast-iron skillet. Using a fork, poke several sets of holes in each sweet potato. Arrange sweet potatoes in prepared baking dish. Bake until very tender when pierced with a fork, 50 minutes to 1 hour. Remove from oven; cool in baking dish until cool enough to handle, 15 to 20 minutes (do not turn the oven off).

2. Remove sweet potatoes from baking dish; set dish aside. Cut sweet potatoes in half lengthwise, and scoop flesh into a large bowl. Discard skins.

3. Mash sweet potato flesh well using a potato masher. Add eggs, granulated sugar, milk, butter, vanilla extract, and salt. Beat mixture with an electric mixer on medium speed until smooth, about 1 minute. Spoon mixture into baking dish.

4. Prepare the Topping: Stir together pecans, brown sugar, flour, and salt in a medium bowl. Add melted butter, and stir until well combined. Sprinkle evenly over Sweet Potato Filling in baking dish.

5. Bake in preheated oven until Topping is browned and Sweet Potato Filling is hot and bubbly throughout, 35 to 45 minutes, covering with aluminum foil during final 10 minutes of bake time if needed to prevent overbrowning. Serve hot.

The First Bites

Delicious appetizers kick off the big meal without filling everyone up

BACON-WRAPPED
SHRIMP SKEWERS
WITH CHIPOTLE
COMEBACK SAUCE

Bacon-Wrapped Shrimp Skewers with Chipotle Comeback Sauce

ACTIVE 35 MIN. · TOTAL 35 MIN.
SERVES 8

- 1 cup mayonnaise
- 2 Tbsp. adobo sauce (from 1 can chipotle chiles in adobo)
- 1 Tbsp. ketchup
- 2 tsp. Worcestershire sauce
- 1 tsp. yellow mustard
- 36 medium peeled, deveined raw shrimp
- 2 medium garlic cloves, minced (2 tsp.)
- 1 tsp. kosher salt
- ½ tsp. black pepper
- 10 bacon slices, cut into 2½-inch pieces
- 1 Tbsp. thinly sliced chives

1. Preheat a grill to medium-high (400°F to 450°F). Meanwhile, stir together first 5 ingredients in a small bowl. Cover; chill until ready to use.
2. Place shrimp in a bowl. Add garlic, salt, and black pepper; toss to coat. Wrap 1 bacon piece around middle of each shrimp, with ends of bacon overlapping. Thread 5 wrapped shrimp onto 1 (12-inch) skewer, using skewer to hold bacon in place and leaving at least ¼ inch between shrimp. Repeat with 7 additional skewers.
3. Grill, uncovered, on oiled grates, turning once, until bacon and shrimp are cooked through and bacon is crisp, about 3 minutes per side. Transfer to a serving platter; sprinkle with chives. Serve with sauce.

Spicy Sweet Potato Crostini

ACTIVE 20 MIN. · TOTAL 35 MIN.
SERVES 8

- 1 lb. medium sweet potatoes (about 2 potatoes), peeled and cut into ⅓-inch-thick slices
- 1 Tbsp. plus ½ tsp. kosher salt, divided
- ¼ cup honey
- ⅛ tsp. cayenne pepper
- ⅛ tsp. paprika
- ¼ cup unsalted butter, melted
- 1 (4-oz.) goat cheese log, at room temperature
- ¼ cup chopped toasted pecans

1. Place sweet potatoes and 1 tablespoon of the salt in a large saucepan; add water to cover by 1 inch. Bring to a boil over high. Reduce heat to medium-low; cook until potatoes just begin to soften, about 5 minutes. Drain potatoes very well; pat dry.
2. While potatoes cook, whisk together honey, cayenne, and paprika in a small microwavable bowl. Microwave on HIGH for 30 seconds; set aside.
3. Preheat oven to broil with rack 6 inches from heat. Place potatoes in 1 layer on a lightly greased (with cooking spray) aluminum foil-lined baking sheet. Brush with melted butter; sprinkle with remaining ½ teaspoon salt. Broil until golden, about 8 minutes. Cool 5 minutes. Using an offset spatula, spread cheese over rounds (½ heaping teaspoon per round). Transfer to a serving plate. Sprinkle with pecans; drizzle with honey mixture. Serve warm.

Mushroom-Stuffed Phyllo Cups

ACTIVE 20 MIN. · TOTAL 25 MIN.
SERVES 8

- 1 (8-oz.) pkg. gourmet fresh mushroom blend
- 1 shallot, chopped (about ½ cup)
- 2 medium garlic cloves (2 tsp.)
- 3 Tbsp. olive oil
- 1 tsp. kosher salt
- ¾ tsp. black pepper
- 2 Tbsp. sherry

SPICY SWEET
POTATO CROSTINI

MUSHROOM-
STUFFED
PHYLLO CUPS

- 2 tsp. chopped fresh thyme, plus more for garnish
- ½ cup heavy whipping cream
- 3 oz. Gruyère cheese, shredded (about ¾ cup), divided
- 2 (1.9-oz.) pkg. frozen mini phyllo pastry shells
- 2 Tbsp. minced fresh chives

1. Preheat oven to 350°F. Combine mushrooms, shallot, and garlic in a food processor; pulse until coarsely chopped, about 15 times.
2. Heat oil in a large skillet over medium-high. Add mushroom mixture, salt, and pepper. Cook, stirring occasionally, until mushrooms are golden and fragrant, about 5 minutes. Add sherry and chopped thyme. Cook, stirring constantly, until most sherry evaporates, about 30 seconds. Add cream; bring to a boil. Boil, stirring constantly, until thickened slightly, about 2 minutes. Remove from heat; add ½ cup of the cheese, stirring until melted.
3. Place phyllo shells on a rimmed baking sheet. Spoon 1 heaping teaspoon of mushroom mixture into each cup, and sprinkle remaining ¼ cup of cheese over shells (about ½ teaspoon per shell). Bake in preheated oven until tops are golden and cheese is melted, about 5 minutes. Sprinkle with chives and additional thyme. Serve warm or at room temperature.

PEAR-AND-BRIE
PUFF PASTRY TART

Pear-and-Brie
Puff Pastry Tart

ACTIVE 10 MIN. - TOTAL 40 MIN.,
PLUS 30 MIN. FREEZING
SERVES 8

1 (8-oz.) Brie round
1 (17.3-oz.) pkg. frozen puff pastry
   sheets, thawed
2 firm medium red Anjou pears,
   cored and thinly sliced
   lengthwise (about 3½ cups)
1 tsp. chopped fresh rosemary, plus
   more for garnish
⅛ tsp. black pepper
2 Tbsp. olive oil
½ tsp. flaky sea salt

1. Place Brie in freezer until firm but not
frozen, about 30 minutes. Line 2 baking
sheets with parchment paper.

2. Preheat oven to 400°F with racks in top
third and middle positions. Cut rind from
Brie; discard rind. Cut Brie into ¼-inch-
thick pieces. Place 1 puff pastry sheet on
each prepared baking sheet. Using a small
knife, create a border on each pastry
sheet by scoring ½ inch from edges.
Fold edges in on score line. (If needed,
brush edges with water to help secure
edges.) Prick inside of pastry all over
with a fork. Evenly distribute Brie pieces
between pastry. Arrange pear slices over
Brie. Sprinkle with rosemary and pepper.
Drizzle with olive oil.

3. Place 1 baking sheet on each rack
in preheated oven; bake until pastry
is golden and cheese is bubbly, about
20 minutes, rotating sheets between
top and bottom racks halfway through
baking time. Remove from oven; sprinkle
with sea salt. Cool 10 minutes. Sprinkle
with additional rosemary; cut each pastry
sheet into 8 pieces.

Broiled Oysters with
Tasso Breadcrumbs

ACTIVE 30 MIN. - TOTAL 30 MIN.
SERVES 6

4 to 5 thick slices day-old
   sourdough bread, crusts
   removed, bread torn into
   1-inch pieces
3 Tbsp. unsalted butter
4 oz. finely chopped pork tasso
   (about 1 cup)
1 bunch scallions, white parts finely
   chopped (about ¼ cup) and
   green parts reserved
1 Tbsp. chopped garlic (3 medium
   garlic cloves)
¾ tsp. kosher salt
½ tsp. black pepper
¼ cup lager beer (such as Miller Lite)
1 (4-lb.) pkg. rock salt
36 oysters on the half shell
   Lemon wedges and hot sauce, for
   serving

1. Preheat oven to broil with rack 6 inches
from heat. Place bread pieces in a food
processor, and pulse until biggest pieces
are pea-size, 10 to 15 pulses. (You will
need 3 cups of breadcrumbs.) Melt
butter in a large skillet over medium-high.
Add breadcrumbs, tasso, white parts of
scallions, garlic, kosher salt, and pepper.
Cook, stirring often, until breadcrumbs
begin to toast and tasso begins to brown,
about 7 minutes. Add beer. Cook, stirring
constantly, until beer has been absorbed
by bread and mixture is moist but not wet,
about 15 more seconds.

2. Spread rock salt evenly on 2 rimmed
baking sheets, and arrange oysters evenly
on salt. Spoon about 1 tablespoon of
breadcrumb mixture onto each oyster.
Broil 1 pan at a time in preheated oven
until breadcrumb mixture is golden
brown, about 4 minutes. Thinly slice
green parts of scallions, and sprinkle over
broiled oysters. Serve oysters hot with
lemon wedges and hot sauce.

BROILED OYSTERS
WITH TASSO
BREADCRUMBS

Holiday Classics–With a Twist

It's not Thanksgiving without the big three: turkey, dressing, and gravy. Brush up on the basics, or give your tried-and-true recipes a new spin with simple upgrades from our Test Kitchen

SIMPLE ROASTED TURKEY

OLD-FASHIONED TURKEY GRAVY (PAGE 258)

BEST CORNBREAD DRESSING (PAGE 256)

MASTER THE CLASSIC

Simple Roasted Turkey

ACTIVE 15 MIN. · TOTAL 3 HOURS
SERVES 10 TO 12

- 1 (14- to 16-lb.) fresh or frozen, thawed whole turkey, with giblets and neck reserved for Homemade Turkey Stock (recipe, page 258)
- 2 Tbsp. kosher salt
- 1 Tbsp. black pepper
- 1 large (12 oz.) yellow onion, quartered
- 3 bay leaves
- 1 head garlic, halved crosswise
- 2 Tbsp. olive oil

1. Preheat oven to 450°F with oven rack in lower third of oven. Place a roasting rack in a large roasting pan lined with aluminum foil. Pat turkey dry with paper towels. Season on all sides with salt and pepper; place onion, bay leaves, and garlic in cavity. Tie ends of legs together with kitchen twine; tuck wingtips under. Place on rack in prepared pan, breast-side up, and brush with oil.

2. Bake in lower third of preheated oven 45 minutes. Loosely cover turkey with aluminum foil, and reduce oven temperature to 350°F. Continue baking until golden brown and a meat thermometer inserted in thickest portion of thigh registers 165°F, 1½ to 2 hours. Transfer to a cutting board, and rest 30 minutes before carving. Pour pan drippings through a fine mesh strainer into a bowl; discard solids. Reserve 1½ cups strained drippings for Old-Fashioned Turkey Gravy or Mushroom Gravy (recipes, page 258).

Herb-Brined Turkey

ACTIVE 20 MIN. · TOTAL 3 HOURS,
PLUS 8 HOURS BRINING

Omit Step 1. Stir together 2 cups **hot water**, 1 cup **kosher salt**, and 1 cup packed **light brown sugar** in a large stockpot or plastic container until dissolved. Stir in 1 quartered **large yellow onion**; 1 halved **garlic head**; 3 halved **lemons**; 3 **bay leaves**; 1 (½-oz.) pkg. each of **fresh sage** and **rosemary**, torn; 10 **thyme sprigs**; and 3 Tbsp. **black peppercorns** until combined. Add 1 (14- to 16-lb.) **fresh or frozen, thawed whole turkey** (giblets and neck removed and reserved for Homemade Turkey Stock, recipe, page 258) to brine mixture. Add enough **cool water** to cover by 2 inches. Cover and chill at least 8 hours or up to 24 hours. Preheat oven to 450°F with oven rack in lower third of oven. Place a roasting rack in a large roasting pan lined with aluminum foil. Drain brined mixture, discarding brining liquid. Place brined vegetable mixture in cavity of turkey. Pat turkey dry with paper towels. Tie ends of legs together with kitchen twine, and tuck wing tips under. Place turkey on rack in prepared pan, breast-side up, and brush with 2 Tbsp. **olive oil**. Proceed with recipe as directed in Step 2.

Spice-Rubbed Turkey

ACTIVE 15 MIN. · TOTAL 2 HOURS, 50 MIN.,
PLUS 8 HOURS BRINING

Omit Step 1. Stir together 1 Tbsp. **smoked paprika**, 1 Tbsp. **chili powder**, 2 Tbsp. **kosher salt**, and 1 Tbsp. **black pepper** in a small bowl; set aside 1 tsp. spice-rub mixture. Rub remaining spice-rub mixture over 1 (14- to 16-lb.) **fresh or frozen, thawed whole turkey**, patted dry with paper towels (giblets and neck removed and reserved for Homemade Turkey Stock, recipe, page 258). Place turkey, breast-side up, on a roasting rack in a large roasting pan lined with aluminum foil. Chill, uncovered, 8 hours or up to 24 hours. Preheat oven to 450°F with oven rack in lower third of oven. Place 1 quartered **medium-size yellow onion**, 3 **bay leaves**, 1 halved **garlic head**, and 5 each of **thyme** and **oregano sprigs** in cavity. Tie legs together with kitchen twine, and tuck wing tips under. Lightly brush turkey with 2 Tbsp. **olive oil**, being careful not to remove too much of the spice-rub mixture from skin. Sprinkle evenly with reserved 1 tsp. spice-rub mixture. Proceed with recipe as directed in Step 2.

SPICE-RUBBED TURKEY

Best Cornbread Dressing

(Photo, page 254)

ACTIVE 15 MIN. · TOTAL 1 HOUR, 45 MIN.
SERVES 10 TO 12

- 1 Tbsp. canola oil
- 1 medium yellow onion, chopped (about 1½ cups)
- 2 garlic cloves, minced (about 2 tsp.)
- 1 Tbsp. chopped fresh thyme, plus more for garnish
- 12 cups ½-inch cornbread cubes (from 3 (6-oz.) pkg. Martha White Buttermilk Cornbread & Muffin Mix, baked according to pkg. directions)
- 4 cups lower-sodium chicken broth
- 4 large eggs, beaten
- 1 tsp. kosher salt
- ½ tsp. black pepper

1. Preheat oven to 350°F. Coat a 13- x 9-inch baking dish with cooking spray. Heat oil in a large skillet over medium-high. Add onion. Cook, stirring occasionally, until tender, 5 minutes. Add garlic and thyme. Cook, stirring constantly, until fragrant, 1 minute. Remove from heat.

2. Stir together cornbread cubes, broth, eggs, salt, pepper, and onion mixture in a large bowl until well combined. Spoon cornbread mixture into prepared dish; let stand 30 minutes at room temperature to allow liquid to absorb into dry ingredients. Cover with aluminum foil.

3. Bake in preheated oven 45 minutes. Uncover; continue baking until golden brown and set, about 15 minutes. Garnish with chopped thyme.

EASY UPGRADE: MAKE CORNBREAD FROM SCRATCH

Brown Butter Cornbread

ACTIVE 15 MIN. · TOTAL 50 MIN.
SERVES 8

Preheat oven to 425°F. Place ½ cup **unsalted butter** in a 10-inch cast-iron skillet, and place in oven until butter is browned, about 8 minutes. Meanwhile, whisk together 2 cups **plain yellow cornmeal**, 1 cup **all-purpose flour**, 1 Tbsp. **baking powder**, 1½ tsp. **kosher salt**, and 1 tsp. **granulated sugar** in large bowl. Remove skillet from oven. (Do not turn oven off.) Carefully pour 6 Tbsp. of the melted brown butter into a small heatproof bowl; reserve remaining brown butter in skillet. Whisk together 2½ cups **whole buttermilk**, 2 **large eggs**, and the 6 Tbsp. brown butter in a separate large bowl. Make a well in center of cornmeal mixture, and add buttermilk mixture, stirring until just combined. Pour batter into remaining browned butter in hot skillet. Bake until cornbread is golden brown and a wooden pick inserted in center comes out clean, 25 to 28 minutes. Cool completely, 35 to 40 minutes, and cut into ½-inch cubes to equal 12 cups.

EASY UPGRADE: THREE DELICIOUS TWISTS WITH CORNBREAD DRESSING STIR-INS

Cheesy Bacon and Sage

ACTIVE 15 MIN. · TOTAL 1 HOUR, 45 MIN.

Prepare Best Cornbread Dressing recipe, stirring 6 cooked, crumbled **bacon** slices (¾ cup), 1½ cups shredded **Gruyère cheese**, and 1½ tsp. chopped **fresh sage** into cornbread mixture in Step 2. Sprinkle with ½ cup shredded **Gruyère**; cover with aluminum foil.

Spicy Mushroom, Sausage, and Walnut

ACTIVE 25 MIN. · TOTAL 2 HOURS, 10 MIN.

Cook 1 lb. **hot Italian sausage** in a skillet over medium-high until crumbled and browned, 8 minutes. Transfer to paper towels; reserve drippings in pan. Add 1 (8-oz.) pkg. sliced **baby portobello mushrooms** to pan; cook until golden. Prepare Best Cornbread Dressing recipe, stirring sausage, mushrooms, and 1 cup toasted **walnuts** into cornbread mixture in Step 2.

Cranberry-Apple-Pecan

ACTIVE 15 MIN. · TOTAL 1 HOUR, 45 MIN.

Prepare Best Cornbread Dressing recipe, stirring 1 cup **dried cranberries**, 2 cups chopped **apple**, 1 cup chopped **pecans**, and 1½ tsp. chopped **fresh rosemary** into cornbread mixture in Step 2.

BROWN BUTTER CORNBREAD

CRANBERRY-APPLE-
PECAN CORNBREAD
DRESSING

SPICY MUSHROOM,
SAUSAGE, AND WALNUT
CORNBREAD DRESSING

CHEESY BACON AND
SAGE CORNBREAD
DRESSING

MUSHROOM
GRAVY

HOMEMADE
TURKEY STOCK

EASY UPGRADE: MAKE YOUR OWN STOCK

Homemade Turkey Stock

ACTIVE 15 MIN. · TOTAL 1 HOUR, 45 MIN.
MAKES ABOUT 4 CUPS

Bring reserved **turkey giblets and neck** (from Simple Roasted Turkey, Herb-Brined Turkey, or Spiced-Rubbed Turkey); 6 cups **water**; 1 quartered **medium-size yellow onion**; 2 **large celery stalks**, cut into 2-inch pieces; 1 **large carrot**, cut into 2-inch pieces; 1 **bay leaf**; and 1 tsp. **black peppercorns** to a boil in a large saucepan over medium-high. Reduce heat to medium-low, and cook, occasionally skimming off and discarding foam, 1½ hours. Pour mixture through a fine mesh strainer into a large bowl; discarding vegetable mixture. Cool 30 minutes. Cover; chill until ready to use.

EASY UPGRADE: MAKE MUSHROOM GRAVY

Mushroom Gravy

ACTIVE 20 MIN. · TOTAL 20 MIN.
MAKES 5 CUPS

Melt ¼ cup **unsalted butter** in a medium saucepan over medium-high. Stir in 6 cups **sliced mushrooms** (from 2 [8-oz.] pkg.), and cook, stirring often, until golden brown, 16 to 18 minutes. Reduce heat to medium; sprinkle with ¼ cup **all-purpose flour**. Cook, stirring constantly, until well incorporated, about 1 minute. Gradually stir in 2½ cups **unsalted chicken stock** or **Homemade Turkey Stock** and 1½ cups reserved **strained drippings** from Simple Roasted Turkey, Herb-Brined Turkey, or Spiced-Rubbed Turkey; bring to a simmer. Cook, stirring occasionally, until thickened, about 5 minutes. Stir in 2 tsp. **sherry vinegar**, 1 tsp. chopped **fresh thyme**, ½ tsp. **kosher salt**, and ¼ tsp. **black pepper**.

Secrets to Great Gravy

SCRAPE THE PAN When collecting the turkey drippings, scrape the bottom of the roasting pan to get any flavorful browned bits.

TASTE THE DRIPPINGS Prevent over- or under-salted gravy by tasting the pan drippings before you use them.

STIR IT UP For the smoothest texture, add stock to the roux gradually, and whisk out any lumps before each new addition.

GET FANCY Make basic gravy even more flavorful by whisking in a splash of white wine or sherry, a tablespoon of finely chopped fresh herbs (parsley, rosemary, thyme, sage, tarragon), a teaspoon of roasted garlic, or a teaspoon of soy sauce.

MASTER THE CLASSIC

Old-Fashioned Turkey Gravy

(Photo, page 254)

ACTIVE 15 MIN. · TOTAL 15 MIN.
SERVES 10 TO 12

Heat 1½ cups reserved **strained turkey dripping**s in a medium saucepan over medium-high. Whisk in ¼ cup **all-purpose flour**. Cook, whisking constantly, 2 minutes. Gradually whisk in 2½ cups **unsalted chicken stock** or **Homemade Turkey Stock** (recipe right) until smooth. Bring to a simmer, and cook, whisking often, until slightly thickened, 5 to 8 minutes. Stir in ¼ tsp. **kosher salt**.

It's All Gravy

We turned a hearty classic into a freezer-friendly breakfast casserole

Sausage Gravy Casserole with Cheddar-Cornmeal Biscuits

ACTIVE 50 MIN. · TOTAL 1 HOUR, 30 MIN., PLUS 45 MIN. COOLING
SERVES 12

SAUSAGE GRAVY

- 1 lb. hot ground pork sausage (such as Odom's Tennessee Pride Hot Country Sausage)
- ½ cup chopped sweet onion (from 1 small onion)
- ¼ cup chopped red bell pepper (from 1 small bell pepper)
- ¼ cup butter
- ⅓ cup all-purpose flour
- 3 cups whole milk
- ¾ tsp. kosher salt

CHEDDAR-CORNMEAL BISCUITS

- 1¾ cups self-rising soft-wheat flour (such as White Lily Enriched Bleached Self-Rising Flour), plus more for work surface
- ¼ cup plain yellow cornmeal
- ½ cup cold butter, cut into ½-inch cubes
- 3 oz. sharp cheddar cheese, shredded (about ¾ cup)
- 4 Tbsp. chopped fresh chives, divided
- 1 cup heavy whipping cream
- 1 Tbsp. butter, melted

1. Prepare the Gravy: Coat a 13- x 9-inch baking dish with cooking spray; set aside. Cook sausage, onion, and bell pepper in a large skillet over medium, stirring often, until sausage is crumbled and browned and vegetables are tender, 10 to 12 minutes. Transfer mixture to a plate lined with paper towels to drain. Wipe skillet clean.

2. Add butter to cleaned skillet; cook over low, whisking often, until melted. Whisk in all-purpose flour until smooth. Cook, whisking constantly, 1 minute. Gradually whisk in milk. Increase heat to medium. Cook, whisking occasionally, until thick and bubbly, 8 to 10 minutes. Stir in sausage mixture and salt; remove from heat. Spoon into prepared baking dish. Cool completely, about 45 minutes.

3. Prepare the Biscuits: Whisk together self-rising flour and cornmeal in a large bowl. Add butter cubes; cut into flour mixture using a pastry blender or 2 forks until mixture is crumbly and resembles small peas. Stir in cheese and 2 tablespoons of the chives. Stir in cream until ingredients are just moistened. Turn dough out onto a floured work surface, and lightly knead until dough comes together, 3 or 4 times. Pat dough into an 8- x 6-inch rectangle. Cut into 12 (2-inch) squares, and cut each square in half diagonally. Cover; chill until ready to use. Arrange Biscuits spaced ¼ to ½ inch apart on top of cooled Gravy.

4. Preheat oven to 350°F. Bake until casserole is bubbly and Biscuits are golden brown, about 40 to 45 minutes. Remove from oven. Brush tops of Biscuits with melted butter; sprinkle with remaining 2 tablespoons chopped chives. Serve hot.

To freeze: After Step 3, wrap freezer-safe baking dish tightly with 2 layers of aluminum foil. Freeze at least 4 hours or up to 2 months. When ready to serve, transfer casserole to refrigerator; thaw completely, about 24 hours. Unwrap dish; bake as directed in Step 4.

Shortcut Biscuits

Follow Steps 1 and 2 as directed. Arrange 12 **frozen (unthawed) buttermilk home-style biscuits** (from 1 [25-oz.] pkg.) spaced ¼ to ½ inch apart on top of cooled sausage gravy. Brush tops of biscuits with 1 Tbsp. melted **butter**; sprinkle with 3 oz. **shredded sharp cheddar cheese** (about ¾ cup) and 2 Tbsp. chopped **fresh chives**. Bake as directed in Step 4. To freeze, follow freezing and thawing instructions above, and then bake as directed.

HARVEST SALAD
(PAGE 262)

The Harvest Table

Celebrate the season with side dishes made using a cornucopia of fall ingredients

GREEN BEANS
WITH BACON
BREADCRUMBS
(PAGE 262)

Harvest Salad

(Photo, page 260)

ACTIVE 15 MIN. - TOTAL 35 MIN.
SERVES 8

¼ cup fresh orange juice
1 small shallot, minced
(about 2 Tbsp.)
1 Tbsp. distilled white vinegar
1 Tbsp. pure maple syrup
1 Tbsp. Dijon mustard
2½ tsp. kosher salt, divided
½ tsp. black pepper, divided
⅓ cup, plus 2 Tbsp. extra-virgin olive
oil, divided
1 (1½-lb.) kabocha squash, seeded
and cut into 2- x ¾-inch wedges
1 lb. fresh Brussels sprouts,
trimmed and halved lengthwise
2 bunches Lacinato kale, stemmed
and chopped (about 12 cups)
1 medium Honey Crisp apple, thinly
sliced (about 1½ cups)
½ cup toasted pecans, chopped
1 oz. Parmesan cheese, shaved
(about ½ cup)

1. Preheat oven to 450°F. Whisk together orange juice, shallot, vinegar, maple syrup, mustard, 1½ teaspoons of the salt, and ¼ teaspoon of the pepper in a small bowl. Gradually whisk in ⅓ cup of the olive oil until well combined. Set aside.
2. Toss together squash, Brussels sprouts, and remaining 1 teaspoon salt, ¼ teaspoon pepper, and 2 tablespoons olive oil on a large rimmed baking sheet until combined. Roast in the preheated oven until tender and browned, about 20 minutes, rotating baking sheet halfway through cook time.
3. Using your hands, massage kale and ¼ cup vinaigrette in a large bowl until kale softens, 1 minute. Add apple and roasted vegetables; toss to combine. Transfer to a platter. Sprinkle with pecans and Parmesan. Drizzle with remaining vinaigrette.

Green Beans with Bacon Breadcrumbs

(Photo, page 261)

ACTIVE 55 MIN. - TOTAL 55 MIN.
SERVES 6

1 lb. haricots verts (French green
beans), trimmed
6 thick-cut bacon slices

1½ cups torn sourdough bread (from
1 [1-lb.] loaf)
1 medium yellow onion, thinly sliced
(about 2 cups)
1 Tbsp. canola oil
1 cup heavy cream
1 tsp. kosher salt
⅛ tsp. black pepper

1. Bring a large pot of salted water to a boil over high. Add green beans; cook until tender-crisp, 3 to 5 minutes. Drain; rinse with cold water. Drain; set aside.
2. Cook bacon in a 10-inch skillet over medium-high, stirring occasionally, until crisp, about 10 minutes. Remove from heat. Transfer bacon to a plate lined with paper towels, reserving drippings in skillet. Pulse bread pieces in a food processor until breadcrumbs form, about 20 pulses. (You'll have about 1 cup.) Add breadcrumbs to drippings in skillet. Cook over medium, stirring often, until golden brown and dry to the touch, about 8 minutes. Remove from skillet; set aside.
3. Add onion and oil to skillet over medium-high. Cook, stirring often, until browned, about 15 minutes. Add cream, salt, and pepper, stirring up browned bits on bottom of skillet. Bring to a boil over medium-high. Reduce heat to medium. Cook, stirring often, until liquid thickens, about 5 minutes. Stir in green beans. Crumble bacon over mixture, and stir to combine. Transfer to a shallow dish or platter. Sprinkle with breadcrumbs.

Sweet Potato Stacks

ACTIVE 20 MIN. - TOTAL 45 MIN.
SERVES 6

2 lb. sweet potatoes (about
4 medium), peeled
5 Tbsp. butter
2 Tbsp. fresh rosemary leaves
¼ cup cane syrup
½ tsp. ground cinnamon
1¼ tsp. kosher salt, divided
¼ cup toasted pecans, chopped

1. Preheat oven to 375°F. Cut potatoes into 48 (¼-inch-thick) rounds; set aside. (Reserve remaining potatoes for another use.) Melt butter in a small saucepan over medium-high. Stir in rosemary. Cook, stirring often, until butter is browned, about 6 minutes. Remove from heat. Remove rosemary using a slotted spoon; reserve for garnish. Stir cane syrup,

cinnamon, and ¼ teaspoon of the salt into brown butter until smooth.
2. Coat a 12-cup muffin pan with cooking spray. Place 2 potato rounds in each cup; sprinkle evenly with remaining 1 teaspoon kosher salt. Add 2 potato rounds to each cup; top each stack with 1 teaspoon brown butter mixture (reserve remaining mixture).
3. Cover pan with aluminum foil. Bake in preheated oven until potatoes are tender, 25 to 30 minutes. Remove pan from oven; discard foil. Using a small offset spatula or a spoon, remove potato stacks from the pan. Transfer to a serving platter. Drizzle with remaining brown butter mixture. Top with pecans and reserved rosemary leaves.

Roasted Carrots and Parsnips

(Photo, page 267)

ACTIVE 15 MIN. - TOTAL 50 MIN.
SERVES 8

1 lb. medium rainbow carrots,
halved crosswise and lengthwise
1 lb. medium parsnips, quartered
lengthwise
1 Tbsp. olive oil
1 tsp. kosher salt
¼ tsp. black pepper
2 Tbsp. butter, softened
1 Tbsp. finely chopped fresh flat-leaf
parsley
1 tsp. fresh thyme leaves
1 tsp. finely chopped fresh sage

1. Preheat oven to 450°F. Toss together carrots, parsnips, oil, salt, and pepper on a large rimmed baking sheet. Bake until tender and browned, turning once halfway through cook time, 40 to 45 minutes.
2. Meanwhile, stir together softened butter and herbs in a small bowl until combined. Chill until ready to serve.
3. Toss together hot vegetables and herb butter on baking sheet. Transfer vegetable mixture to a platter.

SWEET POTATO
STACKS

CORNBREAD-WILD MUSHROOM
DRESSING (PAGE 266)

CRISPY POTATO
GALETTE (PAGE 266)

BUTTERNUT SQUASH
BREAD PUDDING
(PAGE 266)

Cornbread-Wild Mushroom Dressing

(Photo, page 264)

ACTIVE 35 MIN. - TOTAL 2 HOURS
SERVES 10

- 4 large eggs, divided
- 2 (8½-oz.) pkg. corn muffin mix (such as Jiffy)
- ⅔ cup whole milk
- 8 bacon slices, cut into ½-inch pieces
- 3 (4-oz.) pkg. sliced fresh mixed wild mushrooms (such as cremini, button, oyster, and shiitake)
- 1 medium yellow onion, finely chopped (about 2 cups)
- 3 medium celery stalks, chopped (about 1¼ cups)
- 2 Tbsp. unsalted butter
- 1 cup chopped pecans
- ½ cup loosely packed fresh sage leaves, chopped, plus more for garnish
- 1 Tbsp. fresh thyme leaves, chopped
- 3 cups chicken broth
- 1½ tsp. kosher salt
- ¼ tsp. black pepper

1. Preheat oven to 400°F. Line a 12½- x 9-inch rimmed baking sheet with parchment paper, and coat with cooking spray. Lightly beat 2 of the eggs in a small bowl. Stir together beaten eggs, corn muffin mix, and milk in a large bowl. Pour batter onto prepared baking sheet. Bake until cornbread is lightly browned and a wooden pick inserted into center comes out clean, 15 to 20 minutes. Cool on baking sheet 10 minutes. (Do not turn off oven.)
2. Meanwhile, cook bacon in an ovenproof 12-inch skillet over medium, stirring often, until crisp, about 10 minutes. Transfer to a plate lined with paper towels, reserving 3 tablespoons drippings in skillet.
3. Add mushrooms to drippings in skillet. Cook over medium-high, stirring occasionally, until browned, 8 to 10 minutes. Remove from skillet; set aside. Add onion, celery, and butter to skillet. Cook, stirring often, until vegetables are tender and browned, about 6 minutes. Add pecans, sage, and thyme. Cook, stirring constantly, 2 minutes. Remove from heat.

4. Remove cooled cornbread from baking sheet; cut into 1½-inch cubes. Arrange cubes on a large baking sheet. Return to oven; bake until dried and starting to crisp, 10 to 15 minutes. Cool completely, about 20 minutes. Do not turn off oven.
5. Lightly beat remaining 2 eggs in a small bowl. Stir together eggs, cooled cornbread cubes, cooked bacon, mushrooms, onion mixture, broth, salt, and pepper in a large bowl until just combined. Spoon mixture into same skillet; let stand 15 minutes.
6. Bake in the preheated oven until top is lightly browned, 35 to 40 minutes. Garnish with additional sage leaves.

Butternut Squash Bread Pudding

(Photo, page 265)

ACTIVE 15 MIN. - TOTAL 2 HOURS, 15 MIN.
SERVES 10

- 1½ lb. butternut squash, peeled, seeded, and cut into 1-inch cubes (about 4 cups)
- 1 Tbsp. extra-virgin olive oil
- ⅛ tsp. ground nutmeg
- 2 tsp. kosher salt, divided
- ½ tsp. black pepper, divided
- 8 large eggs
- 1½ cups half-and-half
- 1½ cups chicken broth
- 2 Tbsp. Dijon mustard
- 1 Tbsp. fresh thyme leaves
- 1 tsp. chopped fresh rosemary
- ½ tsp. garlic powder
- 1 (18- to 20-oz.) challah bread loaf, cut into 1½-inch cubes (about 12 cups)
- 8 oz. Gruyère cheese, shredded (about 2 cups), divided
- 2 oz. Parmesan cheese, coarsely grated (about ½ cup), divided

1. Preheat oven to 425°F. Toss together squash, oil, nutmeg, 1 teaspoon of the salt, and ¼ teaspoon of the pepper on a large rimmed baking sheet until coated. Bake until squash is tender and starting to brown, 25 to 30 minutes. Cool on baking sheet about 10 minutes. Reduce oven temperature to 350°F.
2. Coat a 13- x 9-inch baking dish with cooking spray. Whisk together eggs, half-and-half, broth, mustard, thyme, rosemary, garlic powder, and remaining

1 teaspoon salt and ¼ teaspoon pepper in a large bowl until combined. Add bread cubes, cooled squash, 1½ cups of the Gruyère, and ¼ cup of the Parmesan; toss to coat. Spoon mixture into prepared baking dish; pour any remaining egg mixture in bowl over baking dish. Let stand at room temperature 30 minutes.
3. Sprinkle casserole evenly with remaining ½ cup Gruyère and ¼ cup Parmesan. Bake in preheated oven until it begins to brown and center is set, about 45 minutes, covering with aluminum foil after about 30 minutes to prevent excessive browning, if needed. Cool 15 minutes before serving.

Crispy Potato Galette

(Photo, page 265)

ACTIVE 25 MIN. - TOTAL 1 HOUR, 35 MIN.
SERVES 8

- ¼ cup unsalted butter
- 2 Tbsp. extra-virgin olive oil
- 2 large garlic cloves, finely chopped (about 2 tsp.)
- 2 lb. Yukon Gold potatoes, unpeeled and sliced about ⅛ inch thick (about 3 cups)
- 1 lb. russet potatoes, unpeeled and sliced about ⅛ inch thick (about 1½ cups)
- 2 large shallots, thinly sliced (about ½ cup)
- 2½ tsp. kosher salt
- ½ tsp. black pepper

1. Preheat oven to 425°F. Melt butter in a 10-inch cast-iron skillet over medium. Add oil and garlic. Cook, stirring often, until fragrant, 1 minute. Remove from heat. Transfer to a large bowl, reserving 2 tablespoons mixture in skillet. Add potatoes, shallots, salt, and pepper; toss to coat.
2. Starting in center of skillet, arrange potato and shallot slices in a circular pattern, slightly overlapping slices, until bottom of skillet is covered. Repeat process using remaining potato and shallot. Pour any remaining butter mixture in bowl over potato mixture. Press down firmly in skillet. Place skillet over high. Cook, undisturbed, until mixture begins to sizzle, 3 to 4 minutes. Remove from heat.

3. Bake in preheated oven until potatoes are tender and browned, about 50 minutes. Cool in skillet 20 minutes. Invert onto a serving platter; cut into wedges.

Stuffed Acorn Squash with Farro

ACTIVE 20 MIN. · TOTAL 45 MIN.
SERVES 8

- 4 small (1 lb. each) acorn squash, halved lengthwise and seeded
- 3 Tbsp. extra-virgin olive oil, divided, plus more for serving
- 2 tsp. kosher salt, divided
- ¼ tsp., plus ⅛ tsp. black pepper, divided
- 4 cups chicken broth
- 1⅓ cups uncooked pearled farro
- 1 medium red onion, chopped (about 1½ cups)
- 1 large garlic clove, minced (about 1 tsp.)
- ⅔ cup dried cranberries
- ⅔ cup chopped fresh flat-leaf parsley
- ½ cup toasted sliced almonds

1. Preheat oven to 450°F. Place squash halves, cut-sides up, on a large rimmed baking sheet. Drizzle evenly with 1 tablespoon of the oil; sprinkle with 1½ teaspoons of the salt and ¼ teaspoon of the pepper. Arrange squash cut-sides down. Roast in preheated oven until tender and browned, about 25 minutes. Remove from oven; turn squash cut-sides up. Do not turn off oven.
2. Meanwhile, bring chicken broth to a boil in a saucepan over high. Add farro; reduce heat to medium-low. Simmer, covered, until tender, 25 to 30 minutes. Remove from heat; drain.
3. Heat remaining 2 tablespoons oil in a large skillet over medium-high. Add onion. Cook, stirring occasionally, until beginning to brown, 4 minutes. Add garlic. Cook, stirring constantly, 2 minutes. Remove from heat. Stir in farro, cranberries, parsley, almonds, and remaining ½ teaspoon salt and ⅛ teaspoon pepper.
4. Mound about ½ cup farro mixture into cavity of each squash half. Bake in the preheated oven until heated through, about 5 minutes. Drizzle with oil, and serve.

STUFFED ACORN SQUASH
WITH FARRO

ROASTED CARROTS
AND PARSNIPS
(PAGE 262)

Thanks for the Little Things

Five of your favorite fall flavors wrapped up in adorable single-serve desserts.
No slicing—or sharing—required

MINI CHOCOLATE-PECAN
PIES (PAGE 270)

MINI APPLE CINNAMON
PIES (PAGE 270)

MINI CRANBERRY-
CHEESECAKE PIES
(PAGE 270)

MINI PUMPKIN PIES WITH
MAPLE WHIPPED CREAM
(PAGE 271)

MINI PEAR-CRANBERRY
PIES (PAGE 271)

Mini Apple-Cinnamon Pies

(Photo, page 268)

ACTIVE 1 HOUR · TOTAL 2 HOURS, 10 MIN.,
PLUS 1 HOUR COOLING
MAKES 12

¼   cup unsalted butter
11   cups chopped (about ½-inch
      pieces), unpeeled Granny Smith
      apples (about 5 large apples)
1   cup packed light brown sugar
3   Tbsp. fresh lemon juice
      (from 1 lemon)
2   tsp. ground cinnamon
1   tsp. kosher salt
2½   Tbsp. cornstarch
2½   Tbsp. cold water
2½   (14.1-oz. or 15-oz.) pkg.
      refrigerated piecrusts
      All-purpose flour, for work surface
1   large egg, lightly beaten
1½   tsp. turbinado sugar

1. Preheat oven to 375°F. Melt butter in
a large skillet over medium. Add apples,
brown sugar, lemon juice, cinnamon, and
salt. Cook, stirring often, until apples
are just tender, 12 to 14 minutes. Whisk
together cornstarch and water in a small
bowl. Stir cornstarch mixture into apples.
Cook, stirring constantly, until mixture
has thickened and apples are glazed,
1 to 2 minutes. Remove from heat; cool
completely, about 45 minutes.
2. Meanwhile, unroll piecrusts on a
lightly floured surface. Using a 5-inch
round cutter and a 4-inch round cutter,
cut crusts into 12 (5-inch) circles and
12 (4-inch) circles, rerolling dough as
needed. Place 4-inch circles in 1 layer on a
parchment paper-lined baking sheet; chill
15 minutes.
3. Meanwhile, press 1 (5-inch) circle
in bottom and up sides of each cup of
a lightly greased (with cooking spray)
12-cup muffin pan, flattening any bunches
of dough along sides.
4. Spoon filling evenly into each muffin
cup (about ⅓ cup each). Cut 1 (4-inch)
dough circle into 6 strips (just over
½-inch wide). Arrange strips in a lattice
pattern over 1 muffin cup of filling. Trim
excess dough, and press edges of lattice
to seal. Repeat with remaining 4-inch
dough circles and muffin cups. Freeze pan
for 30 minutes.
5. Remove pan from freezer. Brush each
piecrust lightly with egg, and sprinkle
evenly with turbinado sugar.

6. Bake in preheated oven until crust is
golden brown, 24 to 32 minutes. Transfer
pan to a wire rack; cool 15 minutes. Using
a small knife or offset spatula, carefully
loosen pies; transfer to a wire rack. Serve
warm, or cool completely.

Mini Chocolate-Pecan Pies

(Photo, page 268)

ACTIVE 35 MIN. · TOTAL 1 HOUR, 45 MIN.,
PLUS 1 HOUR COOLING
MAKES 12

1½   (14.1-oz. or 15-oz.) pkg.
      refrigerated piecrusts
      All-purpose flour, for work surface
¾   cup granulated sugar
¾   cup dark corn syrup
¼   cup packed light brown sugar
¼   cup unsalted butter, melted
1½   tsp. vanilla extract
¾   tsp. kosher salt
3   large eggs, beaten
2   cups pecan halves, chopped
¼   cup semisweet chocolate chips

1. Preheat oven to 350°F. Unroll piecrusts
on a lightly floured work surface. Using
a 5-inch round cutter, cut piecrusts into
12 circles, rerolling scraps as needed.
Press 1 circle in bottom and up sides
of each cup of a lightly greased (with
cooking spray) 12-cup muffin pan,
flattening any bunches of dough along
sides. Fold and crimp edges. Freeze
30 minutes.
2. Meanwhile, whisk together granulated
sugar, corn syrup, brown sugar, butter,
vanilla, and salt in a large bowl until well
combined. Whisk in eggs.
3. Remove pan from freezer. Sprinkle
pecans into piecrusts (about
2 tablespoons each). Carefully pour pie
filling over pecans (about 3 tablespoons
per piecrust).
4. Bake pies in preheated oven until filling
is set and crusts are golden brown, 24 to
28 minutes. Cool in pan on a wire rack
15 minutes. Using a small knife or offset
spatula, remove pies from pan. Transfer to
a wire rack; cool completely, about 1 hour.
5. Place chocolate in a microwavable
bowl; microwave on HIGH until melted,
about 1 minute, stirring every 30 seconds.
Drizzle melted chocolate over pies. Serve,
or let chocolate cool completely.

Mini Cranberry-Cheesecake Pies

(Photo, page 268)

ACTIVE 40 MIN. · TOTAL 50 MIN.,
PLUS 1 HOUR DRYING
MAKES 12

¾   cup fresh or thawed frozen
      cranberries, divided
2   tsp. pure maple syrup
½   cup white sanding sugar
1   tsp. grated orange zest plus
      ⅓ cup fresh juice (from 1 large
      [10 oz.] orange), plus more zest
      for garnish
1   cup, plus 2 Tbsp. granulated sugar,
      divided
2¾   cups finely crushed crisp
      gingersnap cookies (from about
      12 oz. cookies)
½   cup unsalted butter, melted
1   tsp. kosher salt, divided
2   (8-oz.) pkg. cream cheese,
      softened
¼   cup sour cream
1   tsp. vanilla extract

1. Place ½ cup of the cranberries in
a bowl; add maple syrup, and toss to
coat. Place sanding sugar in a separate
bowl. Working in batches of about
2 tablespoons each, add cranberries
to sanding sugar; toss to coat. Arrange
cranberries in 1 layer on a plate. Set aside
to dry at room temperature, at least
1 hour or up to overnight.
2. Meanwhile, stir together orange
zest, orange juice, 2 tablespoons of the
granulated sugar, and remaining ¼ cup
cranberries in a small saucepan. Bring
to a simmer over medium. Cook, stirring
occasionally and mashing cranberries
with the back of a spoon, until mixture is
slightly thickened, 4 to 5 minutes. Remove
from heat. Using a fork, mash cranberries
until mixture is almost smooth. Cool
completely, about 30 minutes. (If
needed, stir in up to 1 tablespoon water,
½ teaspoon at a time, until mixture has
consistency of loose jam.)
3. Preheat oven to 350°F. Spray a 12-cup
muffin pan with cooking spray; set aside.
Stir together gingersnap crumbs, melted
butter, ⅓ cup of the granulated sugar, and
¾ teaspoon of the salt in a bowl. Spoon
into muffin cups (about 3½ tablespoons
each); press into bottom and up sides.

4. Bake piecrusts in preheated oven until set, 12 to 16 minutes. Transfer pan to a wire rack. Use the handle of a wooden spoon to press hot crusts back into a cup shape. Cool completely, about 30 minutes.

5. Combine cream cheese, sour cream, vanilla, and remaining ⅔ cup granulated sugar and ¼ teaspoon salt in bowl of a stand mixer fitted with a paddle attachment. Beat on medium-high speed until light and smooth, 2 to 3 minutes. Transfer cheesecake mixture to a piping bag fitted with a large (¾-inch) open star tip.

6. Carefully remove cooled crusts from pan. Pipe filling into crusts (about 3 tablespoons each). Before serving, top each pie with about ½ teaspoon cranberry compote. Top with sugared cranberries and orange zest. Serve remaining compote on the side.

Mini Pear-Cranberry Pies

(Photo, page 269)

ACTIVE 40 MIN. - TOTAL 1 HOUR, 25 MIN., PLUS 1 HOUR, 20 MIN. COOLING
MAKES 12

    2   (14.1-oz. or 15-oz.) pkg.
          refrigerated piecrusts
    1   large egg, beaten
 2½   cups cubed (about ½-inch pieces)
          firm-ripe green Anjou pears
          (about 2 medium pears)
    2   cups fresh or frozen cranberries
  ½   cup granulated sugar
  ¾   tsp. kosher salt
  ¼   tsp. ground nutmeg
    6   Tbsp. all-purpose flour, divided,
          plus more for work surface
 5½   Tbsp. light brown sugar, divided
 1¼   tsp. ground cinnamon, divided
    2   Tbsp. uncooked old-fashioned
          regular rolled oats
    1   Tbsp. unsalted butter, softened
          Vanilla ice cream, for serving

1. Preheat oven to 350°F. Unroll piecrusts on a lightly floured work surface. Using a 5-inch round cutter, cut piecrusts into 12 circles, rerolling scraps as needed. Reserve remaining dough scraps. Press 1 circle in bottom and up sides of each cup of a lightly greased (with cooking

spray) 12-cup muffin pan, flattening any bunches of dough along sides. Fold over top edge; pinch to seal. Press tines of a fork at an angle to create a design in crust edge. Freeze 30 minutes.

2. Meanwhile, gather remaining dough scraps; roll to ¼-inch thickness on a clean work surface. Using 1½-inch leaf-shape cookie cutters, cut dough into 24 leaves. Using the back of a small knife, make lines resembling veins of a leaf. Place in 1 layer on a parchment paper-lined baking sheet; brush lightly with egg. Bake in preheated oven until golden brown, 10 to 14 minutes. Cool completely on a wire rack, 20 minutes. Do not turn oven off.

3. Meanwhile, combine pears, cranberries, granulated sugar, salt, nutmeg, 4 tablespoons each of the flour and the brown sugar, and 1 teaspoon of the cinnamon in a bowl; toss to coat. Let stand 10 minutes.

4. Combine oats, butter, and remaining 2 tablespoons flour, 1½ tablespoons light brown sugar, and ¼ teaspoon cinnamon in a bowl. Use fingers to rub butter into mixture until it is crumbly and butter is incorporated. Remove pan from freezer; fill each piecrust with pear mixture (about ⅓ cup each). Sprinkle with oat mixture (about ¾ teaspoon each).

5. Bake in the preheated oven until tops are golden and filling is bubbly, 26 to 32 minutes. Remove from oven; cool in pan 15 minutes. Using a small knife or offset spatula, loosen pies. Transfer to a wire rack; cool 30 minutes. Decorate with piecrust leaves. Serve warm with ice cream, or cool completely, about 1 hour.

Mini Pumpkin Pies with Maple Whipped Cream

(Photo, page 269)

ACTIVE 30 MIN. - TOTAL 1 HOUR, 45 MIN.
MAKES 12

   12   (14- x 9-inch) frozen phyllo pastry
          sheets (from 1 [16-oz.] pkg.,
          such as Athens), thawed
  ⅓   cup unsalted butter, melted
    1   (15-oz.) can pumpkin
  ¾   cup granulated sugar
  ⅔   cup whole milk
    3   large eggs
  ¾   tsp. kosher salt
  ½   tsp. ground ginger
  ¼   tsp. ground nutmeg
    1   tsp. ground cinnamon, divided,
          plus more for garnish
  ⅓   cup heavy whipping cream
    2   tsp. pure maple syrup
  ¼   tsp. vanilla extract

1. Preheat oven to 350°F. Unfold phyllo sheets; place on a work surface. Cover with plastic wrap and a damp towel. Brush top side of 1 phyllo sheet lightly with butter. Top with a second sheet. Brush top side of second sheet lightly with butter. Repeat until stack is 6 sheets thick (do not brush top side of last sheet). Cut stack into 6 (about 4½-inch) squares. Repeat with remaining sheets and butter for a total of 12 squares. Press 1 phyllo square into each cup of a 12-cup muffin pan. Cover loosely with a damp paper towel while preparing the filling.

2. Whisk together pumpkin, sugar, milk, eggs, salt, ginger, nutmeg, and ¾ teaspoon of the cinnamon in a bowl. Divide mixture among phyllo shells (about 4½ tablespoons each), and smooth tops. Bake in preheated oven until filling is almost set and phyllo is golden, 14 to 20 minutes. Cool on a wire rack 30 minutes. Remove from pan; chill 30 minutes or up to 2 days.

3. Before serving, whisk together cream, maple syrup, vanilla, and remaining ¼ teaspoon cinnamon in a bowl until stiff peaks form, 1 to 2 minutes. Transfer to a piping bag fitted with a small star tip. Pipe whipped cream onto each pie. Sprinkle with cinnamon.

The Case for Cranberry Sauce

Whether you choose canned or homemade, you've got to have it

SPICED CRANBERRY MOLD

SPRITZED CRANBERRY CHUTNEY

SPICY CITRUS-CRANBERRY RELISH

Love it or hate it, cranberry sauce is just as much a fixture on the Thanksgiving table as Nana's silver turkey platter or those Pilgrim-shaped salt and pepper shakers that get dusted off once a year. Even if you consider that little bowl of burgundy sauce as more of a decorative object than a food, you still expect it to be there.

Consider making a batch of your own from scratch this year. Whether you go for a chunky compote or a smooth jellied mold, fresh cranberry sauce is almost impossible to mess up and adds a welcome dose of acidity and color that will balance out any meal.

And if guests have strong opinions, you may have quite a conversation around the holiday table. Instead, if you're still loyal to the stuff in the can, that's okay. Just scoot those pilgrim shakers over a bit to make room for the homemade version, too, and see which dish is empty at the end of the meal.

Spiced Cranberry Mold

ACTIVE 20 MIN. - TOTAL 20 MIN., PLUS 8 HOURS CHILLING
SERVES 8

- 2 cups fresh or unthawed frozen cranberries (from 1 [10-oz.] pkg.)
- ½ cup granulated sugar
- ¼ tsp. kosher salt
- ¼ tsp. ground cinnamon
- ¼ tsp. ground cloves
- ¼ tsp. ground ginger
- 1 cup apple juice
- 1 (¼-oz.) envelope unflavored gelatin

1. Place cranberries, sugar, salt, cinnamon, cloves, and ginger in a saucepan; bring to a boil over medium-high, stirring often. Boil, stirring often, until mixture is syrupy and cranberries have released their juices but still have most of their shape, about 10 minutes.
2. Meanwhile, pour apple juice into a small bowl. Sprinkle with gelatin; let stand 5 to 10 minutes.
3. Remove cranberry mixture from heat. Whisk ½ cup hot cranberry mixture into apple juice mixture until gelatin is dissolved. Whisk apple juice mixture into remaining cranberry mixture in saucepan, stirring to lightly break down some cranberries.
4. Coat inside of a 2- to 3-cup ramekin or other mold with cooking spray. Pour cranberry mixture into prepared mold. Cool at room temperature, about 1 hour. Cover loosely, and chill until set, at least 8 hours.
5. Place mold in a shallow bowl of warm water for 1 minute. Run an offset spatula or a paring knife around edges of mold, and invert cranberry sauce onto a plate before serving. Store, covered, in refrigerator up to 1 week.

Spicy Citrus-Cranberry Relish

ACTIVE 10 MIN. - TOTAL 10 MIN., PLUS 4 HOURS CHILLING
SERVES 8

- 4 cups frozen cranberries (from 2 [10-oz.] pkg.)
- ¾ cup granulated sugar
- 1 small jalapeño chile, seeded and chopped (about ¼ cup)
- ¼ cup chopped fresh flat-leaf parsley, plus more for garnish
- 2 Tbsp. fresh orange juice (from 1 orange)
- 1 tsp. grated lime zest (from 1 lime)

Process all ingredients in a food processor until mixture is chopped and sugar has dissolved, about 30 seconds. Transfer to a bowl. Cover; chill at least 4 hours. Garnish with additional parsley, and serve. Store, covered, in refrigerator up to 1 week.

Spritzed Cranberry Chutney

ACTIVE 40 MIN. - TOTAL 40 MIN., PLUS 4 HOURS CHILLING
SERVES 8

- 4 cups fresh or frozen (unthawed) cranberries (from 2 [10-oz.] pkg.)
- 1 cup granulated sugar
- ½ tsp. kosher salt
- ½ tsp. black pepper
- 2 rosemary sprigs, plus more for garnish
- ½ cup (4 oz.) Prosecco

1. Place cranberries, sugar, salt, pepper, and rosemary in a saucepan; bring to a boil over medium-high, stirring occasionally. Boil, stirring occasionally, until cranberries begin to release their juices and sugar dissolves, about 15 minutes. Add Prosecco. Boil, stirring occasionally, until liquid is syrupy and cranberries break apart easily when mashed with a wooden spoon, 15 minutes.
2. Remove from heat, and cool to room temperature, about 30 minutes. Remove and discard rosemary. Cover chutney; refrigerate until chilled, at least 4 hours. Let come to room temperature, about 30 minutes, and serve. Store, covered, in refrigerator up to 1 week. Garnish with rosemary just before serving.

Sweet Memories of Pie

Like many African Americans with Southern roots, food writer Aaron Hutcherson believes one Thanksgiving dessert stands above all

Although many believe pumpkin to be the definitive Thanksgiving pie, sweet potato is the pie of choice for many Black people and Southerners. The history of the confection, like much of our country as a whole, can be traced back to Europe. Sweet potatoes were shipped from Peru to Western Europe as early as the 16th century, when England's Henry VIII was known to have a certain love for sweet potato tarts. His affection popularized the use of the vegetable in desserts, and the colonizers who later came to settle on North American shores brought this affinity with them.

While various types of produce such as parsnips, pumpkins, and squashes were mixed with butter, eggs, milk, and sugar and baked in open-face pies, sweet potatoes were the prevailing choice in the South thanks to agriculture. They grew easily in the region, which meant an abundance of sweet potatoes ready for Southern consumption. At the time, the main people responsible for turning those orange spuds into culinary delicacies were enslaved cooks, which explains the dessert's treasured role in African American foodways.

As such, sweet potato pie is an honored staple of my family's Thanksgiving spread. I don't think I'd even tasted pumpkin pie until I was in high school. (To me, it lacked depth in comparison.) For as long as I can remember, the person responsible for supplying said dessert has been my father.

Although my mother took care of nearly all of the day-to-day food preparation in our household, baking sweet potato pies each November is a tradition my father, Danny, upholds with pride. At some point decades ago, he made his first one, and all of our kin noted how remarkable it was. "From that point on, they just associated me with sweet potato pie," he says. It's the main thing my family members look forward to each year, with some people even putting in requests ahead of time for a pie to take home.

Some of my favorite childhood memories over the years are of me playing sous-chef for my dad as we made pie after pie. We never had an exact recipe to follow, aside from a basic outline penned in my youthful chicken scratch listing the amount of potatoes, eggs, and butter per pie along with question marks for the time and temperature. We added sugar and spices to taste. Unlike many other versions, our family recipe doesn't include any milk or cream, which results in a delightfully dense pie. I tried to recreate it on my own a few years ago with limited success, but now I've finally managed to come up with a recipe I think should make him proud. – Aaron Hutcherson

Three Flavorful Additions

ORANGE ZEST This citrus fruit is a great complement to sweet potatoes. Try adding the zest of one orange to the filling for a bit of brightness and added dimension.

SPICES My family recipe keeps it fairly straightforward with cinnamon and nutmeg, but any warming spice, such as ground allspice or cloves, would work well.

BROWN SUGAR Looking for an extra depth of flavor? Brown sugar is the answer. Use it to replace some or all of the granulated sugar in the recipe for a wonderful hint of molasses.

Hutcherson Family Sweet Potato Pie

ACTIVE 15 MIN. · TOTAL 2 HOURS, 10 MIN., PLUS 1 HOUR COOLING
SERVES 8

- 3 small (1½ lb. total) sweet potatoes
- ½ cup unsalted butter
- ¾ cup granulated sugar
- 1 tsp. vanilla extract
- ½ tsp. ground cinnamon
- ½ tsp. kosher salt
- ¼ tsp. ground nutmeg
- 1 large egg
- ½ (14.1-oz.) pkg. refrigerated piecrusts

1. Place potatoes in a large pot; add water to cover. Bring to a boil over medium-high. Reduce heat to medium-low. Simmer, partially covered, until tender, 45 minutes to 1 hour. Drain. Cool 5 minutes. Remove and discard potato skins.
2. Preheat oven to 425°F. Beat potatoes and butter using an electric mixer fitted with a whisk attachment on medium speed until smooth, about 1 minute. Beat in sugar, vanilla extract, cinnamon, salt, and nutmeg. Beat in egg until fully incorporated. Fit piecrust into a 9-inch pie plate lightly coated with cooking spray. Fold edges under and crimp. Pour potato mixture into pie shell.
3. Bake in preheated oven 20 minutes. Remove from oven; cover edges with aluminum foil to prevent overbrowning. Reduce temperature to 375°F. Return pie to oven, and bake until filling starts to brown slightly around edges, 35 to 40 minutes. Let cool about 1 hour.

The Art of the Roll

Let's start a new tradition: Make homemade bread with one foolproof recipe you can shape in three different ways

BUTTERY YEAST ROLLS

TWISTED ROLLS WITH EVERYTHING-BAGEL SEASONING

KNOT ROLLS WITH HERB BUTTER

Buttery Yeast Rolls

ACTIVE 25 MIN. · TOTAL 2 HOURS, 30 MIN.,
PLUS 1 HOUR, 30 MIN. RISING

MAKES 15

- 4 cups all-purpose flour, plus more
  for work surface
- 1½ tsp. kosher salt
- 3 Tbsp. granulated sugar, divided
- 2¼ tsp. active dry yeast
  (from 1 [¼-oz.] envelope)
- ¼ cup warm water
- 1 cup whole buttermilk, at room
  temperature
- 2 large eggs, divided
- ¼ cup, plus 2 Tbsp. unsalted butter,
  softened, divided
- 1 tsp. flaky sea salt

1. Place flour, kosher salt, and 2 tablespoons plus 2 teaspoons of the granulated sugar in bowl of a stand mixer fitted with a paddle attachment. Dissolve yeast and remaining 1 teaspoon sugar in warm water in a small bowl; let stand 5 minutes. Add yeast mixture, buttermilk, 1 egg, and ¼ cup of the butter to flour mixture. Beat on low speed until dough just comes together, about 2 minutes. Remove paddle attachment from mixer; affix a dough hook attachment. Increase mixer speed to medium; beat dough until smooth and elastic, about 7 minutes. Transfer dough to a large bowl lightly coated with cooking spray. Cover with plastic wrap, and let stand in a warm place (74°F to 80°F) until dough doubles in size, about 1½ hours.

2. Transfer dough to a lightly floured work surface. Divide dough evenly into 15 (2-ounce) pieces (A). Roll each piece into an 8-inch-long rope (B).

3. Shape each rope into a spiral, with the tip of rope in spiral center sticking up slightly. Tuck outer tip of spiral under, and pinch to bottom edge of dough to seal (C).

4. Arrange rolls 3 inches apart on 2 large baking sheets lined with parchment paper. Lightly coat tops of rolls with cooking spray. Cover loosely with plastic wrap; let stand at room temperature until rolls nearly double in size, 45 minutes to 1 hour.

5. Preheat oven to 350°F. Uncover rolls. Beat remaining egg in a small bowl; brush over rolls. Bake until rolls are golden brown, 15 to 18 minutes.

6. Microwave remaining 2 tablespoons butter in a small microwavable bowl on HIGH until melted, about 20 seconds. Brush warm rolls evenly with melted butter, and sprinkle with flaky sea salt.

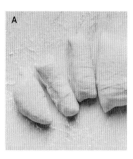

A

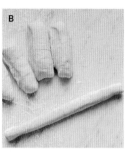

B

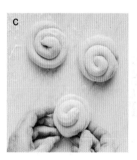

C

It's All in the Twist

Knot Rolls with Herb Butter

Proceed with Steps 1 and 2 as directed. Skip Step 3. Shape each rope into a loop, with both ends pointing down (A). Carefully stretch and pull one of the ends through the loop, making a pretzel shape (B). Tuck the ends under, making a knot (C). Proceed with Steps 4 and 5 as directed. Skip Step 6. Instead, stir together ½ cup softened **butter**, 2 Tbsp. finely chopped **fresh flat-leaf parsley**, 1 Tbsp. finely chopped **fresh rosemary**, and ¼ tsp. **black pepper** in a small bowl until combined. Spread warm rolls evenly with herbed butter.

Twisted Rolls with Everything-Bagel Seasoning

Proceed with Step 1 as directed. Proceed with Step 2, dividing dough evenly into 10 (3-ounce) pieces (each a little larger than an egg). Roll each piece into a 14-inch-long rope. Skip Step 3. Fold each rope in half so both ends point in 1 direction (A). Working with 1 rope at a time, wrap strands of rope around each other to create a twist shape (B); pinch ends together to seal (C). Proceed with Step 4 as directed. Skip Steps 5 and 6; instead, preheat oven to 350°F. Stir together 2 tsp. each **poppy seeds**, **sesame seeds**, and **dried onion flakes** and ½ tsp. **flaky sea salt** in a bowl. Uncover rolls. Beat 1 **large egg** in a bowl; brush over rolls. Sprinkle seed mixture over rolls. Bake until golden brown, 15 to 18 minutes. Brush warm rolls evenly with 2 tablespoons melted **butter**.

A

B

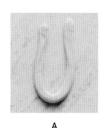

C

A

B

C

Ready for Family

Everyone loves lasagna—especially when you can make it months in advance

Butternut Squash Lasagna

ACTIVE 30 MIN. · TOTAL 2 HOURS
SERVES 10 TO 12

- 8 cups chopped butternut squash (about 3 lb.)
- 2 Tbsp. olive oil
- ¼ tsp. cayenne pepper
- ¼ cup butter, plus more for greasing
- 2 (15-oz.) containers whole-milk ricotta cheese
- 4 oz. Parmesan cheese, grated (about 1 cup)
- 3 large eggs
- ½ tsp. kosher salt
- 1 (15-oz.) pkg. frozen chopped spinach, thawed and drained well
- 1½ tsp. chopped fresh sage, plus more leaves for garnish
- 1 (9-oz.) pkg. no-boil lasagna noodles (such as Barilla Oven-Ready Lasagne)
- 1 lb. fresh mozzarella cheese, shredded (about 4 cups)

1. Preheat oven to 400°F with rack in middle position. Toss together squash, olive oil, and cayenne pepper on a large rimmed baking sheet; spread into an even layer. Bake until tender, about 35 minutes.

2. Meanwhile, cook butter in a small saucepan over medium until butter browns and has a nutty aroma, 4 to 5 minutes. Remove from heat.

3. Process ricotta, Parmesan, eggs, and salt in a food processor until well combined, about 45 seconds. Transfer cheese mixture to a medium bowl, and stir in spinach and chopped sage; set aside. Clean food processor bowl.

4. Add cooked squash to the clean food processor bowl. Process until smooth, about 1 minute, stopping to scrape sides halfway through. Add brown butter to squash, and pulse until combined, about 10 pulses. Transfer to a bowl.

5. Lightly grease a 13- x 9-inch baking dish with butter. Spread ¾ cup of the squash puree in bottom of prepared dish. Arrange 3 noodles on top. Spread 1¾ cups of the ricotta mixture over noodles, top with ¾ cup of the squash puree, and sprinkle with 1⅓ cups of the mozzarella. Repeat the layering process twice, beginning with noodles and ending with mozzarella. Cover lasagna with lightly greased aluminum foil. (If desired, wrap entire dish in plastic wrap and then in foil, and freeze up to 3 months. Thaw in refrigerator 24 hours. Remove the plastic wrap; cover with lightly greased foil before baking.)

6. Place a baking sheet lined with foil on bottom of oven to catch any cheese drips. Bake in preheated oven 30 minutes (45 minutes if baking from thawed). Uncover; bake until the lasagna is heated through and top is nicely browned, 20 to 25 more minutes. Let stand 10 minutes before serving. Garnish with additional fresh sage leaves.

COOKING (SL) SCHOOL

TIPS AND TRICKS FROM THE SOUTH'S MOST TRUSTED KITCHEN

THE CHECKLIST
Your Thanksgiving Game Plan

Spread the cooking throughout the month so you can actually enjoy the holiday

1 MONTH AHEAD

- Order a fresh turkey (or buy a frozen one) and freeze.
- Make homemade stock and gravy (without using turkey drippings), and freeze.
- Make and freeze pie dough or pecan and apple pies (see below).

3 WEEKS AHEAD

- Make and freeze unbaked rolls or biscuits.
- Make and freeze mashed potatoes.
- Make and freeze macaroni and cheese.

2 WEEKS AHEAD

- Make casseroles (such as sweet potato or green bean) without baking them, and freeze. Leave off any toppings, like breadcrumbs or cheese, until bake time.

1 WEEK AHEAD

- Thaw the frozen turkey in refrigerator. Plan on 1 day thawing per 4 pounds of turkey.
- Make and freeze soups.
- Make and chill cranberry sauce.

2 DAYS AHEAD

- Bake cornbread for dressing, and set it out so it can become dry.
- Bake and chill pumpkin pie (see below).

1 DAY AHEAD

- Prepare and chill cornbread dressing without baking.
- Thaw remaining frozen items in refrigerator.
- Brine or dry brine the turkey, if necessary.

TIME-SAVER
Jump–Start Dessert

Prepare whipped cream in advance

Chill a large bowl in freezer 10 minutes. Place 1½ Tbsp. **water** in a small bowl; sprinkle with ½ tsp. **unflavored gelatin**; let stand 3 minutes. Microwave on HIGH until gelatin dissolves, 10 seconds. Cool 5 minutes. Beat 1½ cups **heavy cream**, 1 tsp. **vanilla extract**, and 3 Tbsp. **sugar** in chilled bowl with an electric mixer on medium speed, 1 minute. With mixer running, slowly pour in gelatin mixture; beat until stiff peaks form, 2 minutes. Cover; chill up to 24 hours.

KNOW-HOW
Bake Now & Serve Later

Get a head start on three favorite pies

APPLE

Wrap unbaked pie tightly in 2 layers of plastic wrap, then in aluminum foil. Place in a zip–top plastic freezer bag; seal. Freeze up to 4 months. Unwrap pie; bake in a 425°F oven 15 minutes. Reduce temperature to 375°F; bake until filling is bubbly and crust is golden, 50 minutes to 1 hour.

PUMPKIN

Bake pie, and cool completely, about 1 hour. Wrap cooled pie tightly in plastic wrap, and refrigerate for up to 4 days. Serve chilled, or bring to room temperature before serving.

PECAN

Bake pie, and cool completely, about 2 hours. Wrap cooled pecan pie as directed for apple pie, and freeze up to 1 month. Thaw in refrigerator overnight, and then reheat in a 325°F oven for 10 to 15 minutes before serving.

WASTE NOT

Leftover Turkey's Higher Calling

Too impatient for sandwiches? Bring on the bacon, eggs, and potatoes for breakfast

Day-After-Thanksgiving Turkey Hash

ACTIVE 40 MIN. - TOTAL 40 MIN.
SERVES 4

Cook 4 **thick-cut bacon slices** in a large cast-iron skillet over medium, turning often, until crispy, about 10 minutes. Transfer bacon to a plate lined with paper towels, reserving 2 tablespoons drippings in skillet. Crumble bacon; set aside. Add 1 lb. **Yukon Gold potatoes**, unpeeled and cut into ½-inch pieces (about 3 cups) and 2 Tbsp. **canola oil** to hot drippings in skillet. Cook over medium, stirring occasionally, until potatoes are lightly browned and softened, 10 to 12 minutes. Add 1 cup chopped **yellow onion** and 1 cup chopped **red bell pepper**. Cook, stirring occasionally, until mixture is tender, about 10 minutes. Stir in 1 tsp. chopped **garlic**; cook, stirring constantly, 1 minute. Add 1½ cups torn **cooked turkey**, 2 Tbsp. **red wine vinegar**, 1 tsp. **kosher salt**, and ½ tsp. **black pepper**; toss to combine. Cook, stirring occasionally, until turkey is warmed through, 2 minutes. Top with 4 **fried eggs**; sprinkle with 2 Tbsp. sliced **scallion** and reserved crumbled bacon.

Helpful Hash Hints

SLICE POTATOES CAREFULLY
Try to make the raw potato cubes as uniform as possible so they cook evenly in the pan without any underdone or overcooked pieces.

CUT RICHNESS WITH VINEGAR
A splash of vinegar (red wine, white wine, or cider) adds a little brightness to the dish and brings out the flavors of all the other ingredients.

FINISH WITH HERBS
If you have any fresh herbs left over after Thanksgiving, sprinkle them atop the hash before serving. Almost any type (and/or sliced scallions) will taste great.

> "Slice only as much turkey as you need to serve at the time. Leave any other meat on the bone to help it stay moist in the refrigerator."

Pam Lolley
Test Kitchen Professional

TEST KITCHEN TECHNIQUE

Reheat the Right Way

Gravy is the secret to warming up leftover turkey without drying it out. Bring the gravy to a simmer in a stockpot. Then add in the turkey pieces, stir to coat, and heat until warmed through. Chicken or turkey stock or broth can be substituted.

December

It's Better with Bourbon

The South's favorite spirit also happens to pair well with chocolate, vanilla, caramel, and other sweet flavors, making dessert even more irresistible

Chocolate-Bourbon Ball Tart

Bourbon balls, ganache, and a dark chocolate crust make one incredible dessert. Remove the baked crust from its pan before filling it. Once the crust is filled, it is harder to remove from the pan.

ACTIVE 45 MIN. - TOTAL 1 HOUR, 30 MIN., PLUS 2 HOURS CHILLING

SERVES 10

BOURBON BALLS

- 1½ cups crushed vanilla wafers (such as Nilla Wafers) (from 1 [11-oz] pkg. wafers)
- ½ cup butter, softened to room temperature
- ¼ cup (2 oz.) bourbon
- ½ tsp. vanilla extract

- 2¼ cups unsifted powdered sugar, divided
- 1 cup toasted chopped pecans, divided
- ¼ cup unsweetened cocoa

CRUST

- ½ cup butter, softened to room temperature
- ⅓ cup granulated sugar
- 1 large egg yolk
- 1 cup plus 2 Tbsp. all-purpose flour
- ¼ cup unsweetened cocoa
- ½ tsp. kosher salt

GANACHE FILLING

- 1¼ cups heavy whipping cream
- 3 (4-oz.) 60% bittersweet chocolate bars, chopped
- 1 Tbsp. (½ oz.) bourbon
- 1 tsp. vanilla extract

1. Prepare the Bourbon Balls: Stir together crushed wafers, butter, bourbon, vanilla, 2 cups powdered sugar, and ½ cup pecans in a large bowl using a rubber spatula until evenly combined. Cover and refrigerate until chilled and firm, about 30 minutes.

2. Meanwhile, prepare the Crust: Preheat oven to 350°F. Beat butter and sugar with a stand mixer fitted with a paddle attachment on medium speed until smooth, about 2 minutes. Add egg yolk, flour, cocoa, and salt; beat until fully combined, about 1 minute. Transfer dough to a 9-inch tart pan lightly coated with cooking spray; press mixture evenly into bottom and up sides of pan. Freeze until firm, about 10 minutes. Place tart pan on a baking sheet. Bake until dry to the touch, 12 to 14 minutes. Transfer tart pan to a wire rack; let cool completely, about 30 minutes. Remove Crust from tart pan, and place on a cake stand or a serving platter.

3. Prepare the Ganache Filling: Microwave cream in a medium-size microwavable bowl on HIGH until just bubbling, 90 seconds to 2 minutes. Add chopped chocolate, bourbon, and vanilla; let stand, undisturbed, 5 minutes. Whisk mixture until smooth. Pour Ganache Filling into cooled Crust.

4. Finish the Bourbon Balls: Place remaining ¼ cup powdered sugar in a small bowl. Place remaining ½ cup pecans in a second small bowl. Place cocoa in a third small bowl. Remove Bourbon Ball mixture from refrigerator, and shape into about 30 (1-inch) balls. Roll 10 Bourbon Balls in powdered sugar. Roll 10 Bourbon Balls in pecans. Roll remaining 10 Bourbon Balls in cocoa.

5. Arrange desired number of Bourbon Balls in Ganache Filling in tart (store remaining balls in an airtight container in refrigerator). Chill tart until Ganache Filling is completely firm, about 2 hours. Serve cold.

CHOCOLATE-BOURBON
BALL TART

VANILLA BEAN
CUSTARDS WITH
BOURBON-
CARAMEL SAUCE

Vanilla Bean Custards with Bourbon-Caramel Sauce

These creamy custards have a kick thanks to bourbon, which pairs well with vanilla. You can substitute 1 teaspoon vanilla bean paste for the vanilla bean pod.

ACTIVE 45 MIN. - TOTAL 45 MIN.,
PLUS 4 HOURS CHILLING
SERVES 6

VANILLA BEAN CUSTARDS
2 cups whole milk
2 cups heavy whipping cream
1 vanilla bean pod
¼ cup (2 oz.) bourbon
1 cup granulated sugar
3 Tbsp. cornstarch
5 large egg yolks

BOURBON-CARAMEL SAUCE
½ cup granulated sugar
3 Tbsp. butter
¼ cup heavy whipping cream
2 Tbsp. (1 oz.) bourbon
2 Tbsp. apple juice

ADDITIONAL INGREDIENT
Sweetened whipped cream

1. Prepare the Vanilla Bean Custards: Place milk and cream in a large saucepan. Split vanilla bean pod lengthwise; scrape seeds out of pod, and add seeds and pod to milk mixture. Cook milk mixture over medium-high, stirring occasionally, until heated through, 3 to 5 minutes. Remove from heat. Remove and discard vanilla pod. Add bourbon to milk mixture; whisk to combine.

2. Whisk together sugar and cornstarch in a large bowl; whisk into hot milk mixture. Cook over medium, whisking constantly, until mixture thickens and just comes to a boil, 4 to 5 minutes. Remove from heat.

3. Whisk egg yolks in a medium bowl until smooth. Slowly drizzle one-fourth of the milk mixture into egg yolks, whisking constantly. Gradually pour yolk-milk mixture into remaining milk mixture in saucepan, whisking constantly. Cook over medium-high, whisking constantly, until mixture thickens and just begins to bubble, 3 to 5 minutes. Pour mixture evenly into 6 (1-cup) glasses. Chill until firm, about 4 hours.

4. Meanwhile, prepare the Bourbon-Caramel Sauce: Heat sugar and 3 tablespoons water in a medium saucepan over medium-high, whisking occasionally, until sugar dissolves, about 2 minutes. Bring melted sugar to a boil over medium-high (without stirring). Continue boiling, undisturbed, until sugar reaches a dark caramel color, about 7 to 10 minutes. Add butter, and whisk until melted. Add cream, and whisk until smooth. Add bourbon and apple juice. Cook over medium-high, whisking constantly, until thickened, about 3 minutes. Pour mixture into a small heatproof bowl; let cool 10 minutes. Cover and refrigerate until ready to serve.

5. To serve, spoon 1½ tablespoons Bourbon-Caramel Sauce on top of each Custard. Dollop with whipped cream. Reserve remaining Bourbon-Caramel Sauce for another use.

Bourbon-Chocolate Cake with Browned Buttercream

(Photo, page 286)

Chocolate and bourbon are already an irresistible combination, but the nutty bourbon-brown butter frosting makes this cake truly over the top. Stirring the brown butter as it chills might seem like a fussy step, but it prevents it from solidifying into separate layers and gives it a smooth texture for the frosting.

ACTIVE 35 MIN. - TOTAL 1 HOUR, 50 MIN.
SERVES 10

CAKE LAYERS
Baking spray with flour
1¾ cups granulated sugar
1¾ cups all-purpose flour
¾ cup unsweetened cocoa
1½ tsp. baking powder
1½ tsp. baking soda
1 tsp. kosher salt
2 large eggs
1 cup whole milk
½ cup canola oil
½ cup (4 oz.) bourbon
2 tsp. vanilla extract
½ cup hot water

BUTTERCREAM
2 cups butter
6 cups unsifted powdered sugar
¼ cup (2 oz.) bourbon
1 Tbsp. heavy whipping cream
½ tsp. vanilla extract

1. Prepare the Cake Layers: Preheat oven to 350°F. Coat 3 (8-inch) round cake pans with baking spray; line bottoms with parchment paper, and coat paper with baking spray. Whisk together sugar, flour, cocoa, baking powder, baking soda, and salt in a large bowl. Whisk together eggs, milk, oil, bourbon, and vanilla in a small bowl; add to flour mixture, and whisk until just combined. Add hot water to batter; whisk until combined.

2. Divide batter evenly among prepared cake pans (about 1½ cups each). Bake in preheated oven until a wooden pick inserted into centers of cakes comes out clean, 22 to 25 minutes. Cool in pans 10 minutes. Transfer Cake Layers to a wire rack; cool completely, about 45 minutes.

3. While Cake Layers bake and cool, prepare the Buttercream: Melt butter in a medium saucepan over medium, stirring often, until butter is fragrant and golden brown, 8 to 10 minutes. Remove pan from heat, and immediately pour butter into a small heatproof bowl. Let stand 15 minutes. Cover; chill until butter is cool and almost firm, about 1 hour, stirring every 15 minutes.

4. Beat chilled brown butter with a heavy-duty stand mixer fitted with a paddle attachment on medium speed until smooth and fluffy, about 3 minutes. Gradually add powdered sugar, beating on low speed until well blended and smooth, about 2 minutes. Stir together bourbon, cream, and vanilla in a small bowl. Add to butter mixture, and beat until smooth, about 2 minutes. Measure ⅓ cup Buttercream into a piping bag fitted with a star tip; set aside.

5. Spread remaining Buttercream between Cake Layers and on top and sides of cake. Pipe reserved Buttercream in piping bag around top edges of cake.

Bourbon-Praline Cheesecake

If pralines are your favorite Christmas candy, you'll love this incredible cheesecake topped with a gooey mixture of bourbon, pecans, and brown sugar. For the smoothest cheesecake, be sure to use room temperature eggs and cream cheese.

ACTIVE 30 MIN. - TOTAL 3 HOURS,
PLUS 6 HOURS CHILLING

SERVES 12

CRUST
- 2   cups graham cracker crumbs (from 1 [13½-oz.] pkg. graham cracker crumbs)
- ½   cup finely chopped pecans
- ½   cup butter, melted
- 3   Tbsp. packed dark brown sugar

FILLING
- 4   (8-oz.) pkg. cream cheese, softened to room temperature
- 1   cup granulated sugar
- ½   cup packed dark brown sugar
- 4   large eggs, at room temperature
- ¼   cup sour cream
- ¼   cup (2 oz.) bourbon
- 2   tsp. vanilla extract

PRALINE TOPPING
- ¼   cup butter
- ¼   cup packed dark brown sugar
- ¼   cup whole milk
- 2   Tbsp. (1 oz.) bourbon
- 1   cup toasted pecan halves

1. Prepare the Crust: Preheat oven to 350°F. Lightly coat a 9-inch springform pan with cooking spray. Stir together graham cracker crumbs, pecans, butter, and brown sugar in a bowl until well blended. Press mixture into bottom and 1½ inches up the sides of prepared springform pan. Bake until lightly browned, about 10 minutes. (Do not turn oven off.) Transfer Crust in springform pan to a wire rack; let cool completely, about 30 minutes.

2. Prepare the Filling: Beat cream cheese with a stand mixer fitted with a paddle attachment on low speed until smooth, about 1 minute. Add granulated sugar and brown sugar; beat until fully combined and smooth, about 1 minute. Add eggs 2 at a time, beating until just combined, about 15 seconds, stopping to scrape down sides of bowl as needed using a rubber spatula. Add sour cream, bourbon, and vanilla. Beat until just combined, about 1 minute, stopping to scrape down sides of bowl as needed (do not overbeat).

BOURBON-PRALINE
CHEESECAKE

3. Pour Filling into cooled Crust, and gently jiggle pan to smooth top. Place cheesecake in a plastic slow-cooker liner; place cheesecake in liner in a large roasting pan. (Alternatively, double wrap the springform pan with heavy-duty aluminum foil.) Place roasting pan in oven, and pour warm water into roasting pan to come halfway up sides of pan (do not let water get into slow-cooker liner). Bake in preheated oven until cheesecake center is slightly jiggly, about 1 hour. Turn oven off, and prop oven door ajar about 4 inches. Let cheesecake stand in open oven for 1 hour. Remove from oven and from slow-cooker liner. Place in refrigerator until fully chilled, at least 6 hours or up to 24 hours.

4. Meanwhile, prepare the Praline Topping: Cook butter and brown sugar in a medium saucepan over medium-high, stirring often, until melted and beginning to bubble, 3 to 5 minutes. Reduce heat to medium-low; whisk in milk and bourbon. Cook, whisking constantly, until thickened, 2 to 3 minutes. Stir in pecans. Transfer mixture to a small heatproof bowl; let cool at least 1 hour or up to 4 hours. Cover and refrigerate until ready to serve, up to 24 hours.

5. To serve, remove cheesecake from springform pan. Drizzle with Praline Topping.

BOURBON-
CHOCOLATE CAKE
WITH BROWNED
BUTTERCREAM
(PAGE 284)

Butterscotch-Bourbon Lava Cakes

Many brands of bourbon have strong notes of butterscotch, so it's no wonder the two flavors taste great together. These single-serving sweets make a great end to a dinner party or special meal. As with any lava cake recipe, timing is everything. If they overbake, they won't have rich, molten centers.

ACTIVE 20 MIN. · TOTAL 30 MIN.
SERVES 6

- ¾ cup butterscotch chips
- ½ cup butter
- 4 Tbsp. (2 oz.) bourbon, divided
- 2 tsp. vanilla extract, divided
- 1 cup plus 2 Tbsp. powdered sugar, divided, plus more for garnish
- 3 large egg yolks
- 2 large eggs
- ⅔ cup all-purpose flour
- 1 tsp. kosher salt
- ½ cup heavy whipping cream

1. Preheat oven to 450°F. Coat 6 (1-cup) ramekins with cooking spray.

2. Melt butterscotch chips and butter in a small saucepan over medium, stirring constantly, until smooth, about 2 minutes. Remove from heat; whisk in 3 tablespoons of the bourbon and 1 teaspoon of the vanilla. Transfer mixture to a medium bowl; whisk in 1 cup of the powdered sugar until smooth. Whisk in egg yolks and eggs. Fold in flour and salt using a rubber spatula until fully combined.

3. Spoon batter evenly into prepared ramekins (about ⅓ cup each). Arrange ramekins on a baking sheet. Bake in preheated oven until cake tops are golden brown and centers have a slight jiggle, 10 to 11 minutes.

4. Meanwhile, beat cream and remaining 2 tablespoons powdered sugar, 1 tablespoon bourbon, and 1 teaspoon vanilla with an electric mixer on medium-high speed until stiff peaks form, about 2 minutes.

5. Remove cakes from oven; let stand 1 minute. Gently run an offset spatula or a sharp knife around edges of each cake, and invert each onto a serving plate. (Use a kitchen towel or oven mitt to prevent burning.) Garnish cakes with additional powdered sugar; dollop evenly with bourbon whipped cream.

My Big Mama's Egg Pie

Forget sky-high desserts. For Jocelyn Delk Adams, author of the cookbook and blog *Grandbaby Cakes*, a much more sentimental and humble recipe takes center stage

My Big Mama's favorite dessert was egg pie. I didn't remember this until after my grandmother died, when I rewatched a video I'd made with her two years earlier. During our informal interview, I asked her questions about her childhood, the immense challenges of growing up and raising a family in the Jim Crow South, and—of course—how she learned to bake. We sat comfortably in her natural element, the kitchen, and chatted while I documented her history and she baked biscuits from instinct. Hunched over the stove smiling, she brushed them with butter as the scent of bread swallowed the room whole.

To know Big Mama was to adore her. Every time I hugged her, I simultaneously breathed in a whiff of her perfume and a baked good, whatever tickled her fancy to create at the time. Her skin was golden bronze melanin, and her spirit glowed even brighter. She seemed quite fragile when we had this conversation, but even at the age of 90, her memory was pristine.

When I asked her about her favorite thing to bake, the answer surprised me, and her eyes lit up as she talked about it. "I just *love* egg pie. There's nothing like it," she said. The truth was, I'd never had it before. What was egg pie? The more she talked about it, I realized how unassuming it was: simple, classic, uncomplicated. It doesn't have the grandeur of a towering coconut or caramel cake, but the magic is in its humbleness.

My Big Mama grew up during the late 1920s and 1930s in Mississippi, and her father owned a farm that her siblings worked on. Being one of the youngest children, she didn't work in the field. Instead, she prepared the meals. She cooked supper for everyone, always making sure something special and sweet also graced the table. Fresh eggs, milk, and butter were plentiful due to their glorious supply of chickens and cows, so egg pie, with its simple ingredients, became a mainstay. When supper was ready, she would ring the bell for her daddy, brothers, and sisters to run in and eat. I imagine how special a treat like egg pie must have been after they'd labored intensely in the fields all day. Its custardy, smooth filling and flaky crust made it irresistible.

Many years later, when I started baking with my Big Mama on visits to Winona, Mississippi, we focused more on making sour cream pound cakes and homemade vanilla ice cream. On Thanksgiving, sweet potato and pecan pies stole the show, and at Christmas we had Big Mama's tea cakes and my mom's 7Up cake. Egg pie unfortunately got lost in the shuffle.

But Big Mama never forgot its significance. She passed away just after Christmas two years ago, and I realized then that her favorite dessert needed a prominent place in my recipe arsenal too. Now, we make it every Christmas. The ingredients come together quickly and effectively, and small hints of vanilla and ground nutmeg give it more depth and personality. Egg pie has become my Big Mama's legacy, with each slice representing a small piece of who she was, and I will continue to serve it to honor her for years to come.

SWEET MEMORIES: JOCELYN DELK ADAMS (RIGHT) WITH HER BELOVED "BIG MAMA"

Big Mama's Egg Pie

ACTIVE 35 MIN. - TOTAL 2 HOURS, 45 MIN., PLUS 1 HOUR, 10 MIN. COOLING

SERVES 8

CRUST
- 1¼ cups all-purpose flour, plus more for work surface
- 1 tsp. granulated sugar
- ½ tsp. kosher salt
- ½ cup cold unsalted butter, cubed
- ¼ cup cold water, plus more if needed

FILLING
- 1 cup whole milk
- ¼ cup butter
- 3 large eggs, at room temperature
- 1 cup granulated sugar
- 1½ Tbsp. all-purpose flour
- 1½ tsp. vanilla extract
- ¼ tsp. ground nutmeg, plus more for garnish

1. Prepare the Crust: Whisk together flour, sugar, and salt in a bowl to combine. Add butter. Using a pastry cutter, cut butter into flour mixture until various-size crumbs form. Slowly add water, mixing with hands until dough forms, adding more water if needed until dough just comes together (there may still be some dry flour in bowl). Shape dough into a ball. Wrap tightly with plastic wrap; chill until cold, 45 to 55 minutes.

2. Meanwhile, prepare the Filling: Cook milk and butter in a saucepan over medium-low, undistorted, 10 minutes. Remove from heat. Cool to room temperature, 45 minutes.

3. Whisk together eggs, sugar, flour, vanilla, and nutmeg in a medium bowl. Whisk in cooled milk mixture. Set aside.

4. Preheat oven to 425°F. Unwrap chilled dough; place on a lightly floured work surface. Using a rolling pin, roll dough out to ¼-inch thickness. Transfer to an ungreased freezer-safe 9-inch pie plate. Press dough into bottom and up sides of plate. Crimp edges. Freeze Crust 10 minutes.

5. Remove Crust from freezer. Line with parchment paper; add pie weights. Bake in preheated oven 10 minutes. Reduce oven temperature to 325°F. Remove Crust from oven; remove weights and parchment. Cool 10 minutes.

6. Pour Filling into Crust. Bake in preheated oven until top of pie is lightly browned and center jiggles just slightly, 35 to 40 minutes. Transfer to a wire rack; cool completely, about 1 hour. Sprinkle with additional nutmeg, and serve.

Seafood Starters

Adam Evans, chef of award-winning restaurant Automatic Seafood & Oysters
shares memorable appetizers any cook can pull off

Baked Gulf Oysters with Bacon, Garlicky Greens, and Parmesan

Evans says shucking oysters is about finesse, not strength. "Secure the blade of an oyster knife into the hinge of the oyster. Then crank the handle of the knife instead of forcing the knife into the shell," he says.

ACTIVE 30 MIN. · TOTAL 1 HOUR, 15 MIN.
SERVES 6

- 8 oz. smoked bacon, diced
- 1 large onion, diced (1 ½ cups)
- 3 medium garlic cloves, chopped (1 Tbsp.)
- 3 cups thinly sliced Lacinato kale or collard greens (from 1 bunch)
- 2 Tbsp. unsalted butter
- 2 Tbsp. all-purpose flour
- 1 cup heavy whipping cream
- 2 oz. Parmesan cheese, finely shredded (about ¾ cup), plus more for garnish
- 2 Tbsp. fresh lemon juice (from 1 lemon)
- 1 tsp. crushed red pepper
- 1 tsp. kosher salt
- ½ tsp. black pepper
- 24 oysters on the half shell
- 1 (4-lb.) pkg. rock salt (ice cream salt) (such as Morton Salt)
  Lemon wedges

1. Heat a large skillet over medium. Add bacon. Cook, stirring occasionally, until crispy, 6 to 8 minutes. Add onion and garlic. Cook, stirring occasionally, until onion is translucent, about 5 minutes. Add kale or collards. Cook, stirring occasionally, until soft and tender, about 8 minutes for kale or 12 to 15 minutes for collards.

2. Add butter to skillet. Cook over medium, stirring constantly, until melted, about 20 seconds. Add flour; cook, stirring often, 1 minute. Reduce heat to medium-low. Add whipping cream and Parmesan. Cook, stirring constantly, until mixture is thick and pasty, about 45 seconds. Remove from heat; stir in lemon juice, crushed red pepper, salt, and black pepper. Transfer mixture to a medium bowl; chill until mixture is cool enough to handle and starts to firm up, about 30 minutes.

3. Preheat oven to 450°F. Spoon bacon-kale mixture evenly (1 heaping tablespoon each) onto oysters. Pour rock salt on a baking sheet; arrange oysters evenly on salt so they sit level. Bake until bacon-kale mixture is bubbly and golden brown and oyster meat has started to curl and is cooked through, 5 to 8 minutes. Remove from oven; cool 5 minutes. Garnish with additional Parmesan; serve with lemon wedges

PAN-FRIED SHRIMP ON
SEASONED CRACKERS
WITH PEPPER JELLY AND
CREAM CHEESE

Pan-Fried Shrimp on Seasoned Crackers with Pepper Jelly and Cream Cheese

Pepper jelly and cream cheese on crackers was one of Evans' favorite holiday snacks as a kid. Now, he adds pan-fried shrimp for a fancy upgrade.

ACTIVE 20 MIN. - TOTAL 50 MIN.
SERVES 8

SEASONED CRACKERS
- 1 sleeve saltine crackers (about 35)
- ¼ cup olive oil
- 1 tsp. onion powder
- 1 tsp. crushed red pepper
- ½ tsp. garlic powder
- ¼ tsp. cayenne pepper
- ¼ tsp. black pepper

PAN-FRIED SHRIMP
- 24 jumbo peeled, deveined raw shrimp (about 1 lb.)
- 1 tsp. kosher salt
- 1 tsp. black pepper
- 1 Tbsp. olive oil
- 2 Tbsp. chopped fresh flat-leaf parsley, plus more for garnish
- 2 Tbsp. fresh lemon juice (from 1 lemon)
- 1 Tbsp. chopped fresh chives, plus more for garnish
- 1 Tbsp. chopped fresh dill, plus more for garnish

ADDITIONAL INGREDIENTS
- ½ cup cream cheese, at room temperature
- ¼ cup red pepper jelly, at room temperature

1. Prepare the Seasoned Crackers: Stack crackers upright (as they are packaged in the sleeve) in an airtight container in a single layer. Whisk together oil, onion powder, crushed red pepper, garlic powder, cayenne pepper, and black pepper in a bowl; pour mixture evenly over all crackers. Secure lid on container; let stand 10 minutes. Flip container, and let stand another 10 minutes. Flip container, and let stand until oil and seasoning have soaked into crackers, about an additional 10 minutes.

2. Prepare the Pan-Fried Shrimp: Stir together shrimp, salt, and pepper in a bowl until evenly coated. Heat oil in a large nonstick skillet over medium-high. Arrange shrimp, lying flat in 1 even layer, inside skillet. Cook until shrimp just turns pink and firm, 2 to 3 minutes per side. Transfer shrimp to a large bowl; let cool slightly, about 5 minutes. Add parsley, lemon juice, chives, and dill; stir together until shrimp are evenly coated.

3. Arrange 24 seasoned crackers on a serving platter. (Reserve remaining crackers for another use.) Spread 1 teaspoon cream cheese on each cracker. Top each cracker with 1 shrimp, and spoon ½ teaspoon pepper jelly onto each shrimp. Garnish with additional parsley, chives, and dill. Serve immediately.

Meet Adam Evans

The Alabama native has made a name for himself in Birmingham and across the country for creative, comforting dishes like Gulf Shrimp Fried Rice and Duck Fat Poached Swordfish.

Creamy Smoked-Fish Dip

This rich, smoky spread is delicious served with crackers, baguette slices, and crudité, or spooned into endive leaves.

ACTIVE 20 MIN. - TOTAL 20 MIN.
SERVES 12

- 2 (8-oz.) smoked whitefish fillets or smoked salmon, skin removed
- 2 celery stalks, cut into ¼-inch cubes (about ½ cup)
- ½ cup cream cheese, at room temperature
- ½ cup thinly sliced scallions (about 5 scallions)
- ¼ cup mayonnaise
- ¼ cup chopped fresh flat-leaf parsley
- ¼ cup chopped fresh dill
- ¼ cup chopped dill pickles (from 2 pickles)
- ¼ cup fresh lemon juice (from 2 lemons)
- 1 Tbsp. drained capers, chopped
- 1 Tbsp. extra-virgin olive oil
- ½ tsp. cayenne pepper
- ½ tsp. garlic powder
- ½ tsp. onion powder
- ½ tsp. kosher salt, plus more to taste
- ½ tsp. black pepper, plus more to taste

1. Flake smoked fish into ¾-inch chunks in a medium bowl. Set aside.
2. Stir together remaining ingredients in a large bowl until smooth. Gently fold in smoked fish until incorporated, leaving some chunks intact and being careful not to overmix. Season with additional salt and black pepper to taste.

Crab Cake Bites with Old Bay Mayo

Form the crab cakes one day in advance and store them, covered, in the refrigerator. Not only does this save prep time, it ensures that they are properly chilled, which helps them hold their shape.

ACTIVE 30 MIN. - TOTAL 1 HOUR, 30 MIN.
SERVES 6

- 2 large eggs
- 1 celery stalk, cut into ¼-inch cubes (about ¼ cup)
- ¼ cup cubed (¼-inch pieces) yellow onion (from 1 small onion)
- 2 Tbsp. chopped fresh flat-leaf parsley
- 2 Tbsp. mayonnaise
- 1 Tbsp. Dijon mustard
- 2 tsp. Worcestershire sauce
- 2 tsp. Old Bay seasoning
- 1 lb. fresh jumbo crabmeat, drained and picked over
- 1 cup panko breadcrumbs
- ¼ cup canola oil
  Old Bay Mayo (recipe follows)
  Lemon wedges

1. Whisk together eggs, celery, onion, parsley, mayonnaise, mustard, Worcestershire sauce, and Old Bay seasoning in a large bowl until well combined. Fold in crabmeat and panko using a rubber spatula until well combined. Cover and chill at least 1 hour or up to 8 hours.
2. Preheat oven to 250°F. Coat a baking sheet with cooking spray. Shape crab mixture into 12 (3-inch) round cakes (about ¼ cup each) on prepared baking sheet. If crab cakes are not holding together, rechill about 30 minutes to set.
3. Heat 2 tablespoons of the oil in a large nonstick skillet over medium. Add 6 of the crab cakes, and cook until golden, 2 to 4 minutes per side. Transfer crab cakes to a rimmed baking sheet lined with paper towels. Place in preheated oven to keep warm. Repeat process with remaining oil and crab cakes. Serve immediately with Old Bay Mayo and lemon wedges.

Old Bay Mayo

Flavored with Old Bay, lemon, chives, and dill, this mayonnaise is delicious with crab cakes or any type of chilled seafood. Evans likes it on turkey sandwiches, too.

ACTIVE 5 MIN. - TOTAL 5 MIN.
MAKES ABOUT 1 CUP

Whisk together 1 cup **mayonnaise**, 1 Tbsp. chopped **fresh chives**, 1 Tbsp. chopped **fresh dill**, 1 Tbsp. grated **lemon zest** plus 2 Tbsp. **fresh juice** (from 2 lemons), and 2 tsp. **Old Bay seasoning** in a small bowl until smooth. Store, covered, in refrigerator up to 3 days.

CRAB CAKE BITES
WITH OLD BAY MAYO

The Roast with the Most

Three new ways to prepare a classic holiday centerpiece: beef tenderloin

PARSLEY-AND-CAPER-
STUFFED BEEF TENDERLOIN
WITH ROASTED VEGETABLES
(PAGE 294)

Parsley-and-Caper-Stuffed Beef Tenderloin with Roasted Vegetables

(Photo, page 293)

If this showstopping dish is on your holiday menu, you won't need to serve much more. You'll need a large cutting board or clean work surface to cut, pound, roll, and tie the meat. If you accidentally pound a hole in the beef, don't worry. Roll it as directed, and then use toothpicks to help close the hole before the meat goes into the oven.

ACTIVE 30 MIN. - TOTAL 1 HOUR, 45 MIN.
SERVES 8

- 1 (4-lb.) beef tenderloin, trimmed
- 2½ cups loosely packed fresh flat-leaf parsley leaves and tender stems (from 2 bunches)
- ¼ cup capers, drained
- 2 Tbsp. golden raisins
- 1 Tbsp. grated lemon zest (from 1 medium lemon)
- ¾ cup unsalted butter, softened and cut into ½-inch pieces
- 2½ tsp. kosher salt, divided
- 1½ tsp. black pepper, divided
- 1½ lb. baby Yukon Gold potatoes, halved
- 1 lb. small carrots, cut lengthwise into thirds
- 4 shallots, halved
- 2 Tbsp. olive oil

1. Preheat oven to 350°F. Pat beef dry, and (if it's trussed) remove string. Let stand at room temperature until ready to use. Process parsley, capers, raisins, and zest in a food processor until finely chopped, about 30 seconds. Transfer mixture to a medium bowl. Add butter, 1 teaspoon of the salt, and ½ teaspoon of the pepper, and stir into a smooth paste. Set aside.
2. Using a sharp knife, cut horizontally through center of beef, cutting to, but not through, other side using a sharp knife (cut should be within ½ inch of other side), Open flat, as you would a book. Place between 2 sheets of plastic wrap. Using the flat side of a meat mallet or the bottom of a small heavy skillet, pound to ½- to ¾-inch thickness. Spread butter mixture in an even layer over cut side of beef, leaving a ½-inch border. Roll up, jelly-roll style, starting at 1 long side; secure with kitchen twine tied at 2-inch intervals.
3. Toss together potatoes, carrots, shallots, oil, 1 teaspoon of the salt, and ½ teaspoon of the pepper. Spread mixture evenly on a baking sheet lined with aluminum foil. Place beef on top of vegetables, and sprinkle with remaining ½ teaspoon each salt and pepper. Bake in preheated oven 30 minutes. Increase oven to 450°F (do not remove beef from oven), and cook until a thermometer inserted in thickest portion of beef registers 125°F, about 18 minutes. Transfer beef to a cutting board; let rest 30 minutes.
4. Meanwhile, return vegetables to oven; continue roasting until vegetables are starting to brown and are cooked through, 10 to 15 minutes. Remove from oven. Toss vegetables with any juices on baking sheet; transfer to a serving bowl. Cover to keep warm until ready to serve.
5. Remove kitchen twine from beef. Cut beef into 1-inch-thick slices, and serve alongside vegetables.

Coffee-Rubbed Beef Tenderloin Crostini with Caramelized-Onion Butter

These savory crostini make impressive heavy hors d'oeuvres for a cocktail party, especially because several of the components can be made in advance. Don't skip the sprinkling of flaky salt at the end—it adds a delightful crunch and brings all of the flavors together.

ACTIVE 1 HOUR - TOTAL 3 HOURS, 10 MIN., PLUS 8 HOURS CHILLING
SERVES 8

- 1 tsp. ground espresso beans or finely ground coffee beans
- 1 tsp. unsweetened cocoa
- 2½ tsp. kosher salt, divided
- 2¼ tsp. black pepper, divided
- 1 (1½-lb.) center-cut beef tenderloin, tied and patted dry

COFFEE-RUBBED BEEF TENDERLOIN CROSTINI WITH CARAMELIZED-ONION BUTTER

- 1 cup unsalted butter, divided
- 1 medium sweet onion, chopped (about 1½ cups)
- 2 Tbsp. (1 oz.) dry sherry
- 2 Tbsp. canola oil
- 24 (½-inch-thick) baguette slices (sliced on an angle, from 2 [8-oz.] baguettes), toasted
- 2 cups baby arugula
- 1 Tbsp. flaky sea salt (such as Maldon)

1. Line a baking sheet with aluminum foil; set an ovenproof wire rack inside baking sheet. Stir together ground espresso, cocoa, and 2 teaspoons each of the kosher salt and pepper in a small bowl. Sprinkle mixture evenly all over beef. Place on prepared wire rack. Refrigerate, uncovered, at least 8 hours or up to 24 hours.

2. Remove beef from refrigerator; let stand at room temperature 1 hour. Meanwhile, melt ¼ cup of the butter in a small pot over low. Set aside remaining ¾ cup butter to soften. Add onion and remaining ½ teaspoon kosher salt to melted butter. Cook, stirring occasionally, until deep golden, about 30 minutes. Add sherry and remaining ¼ teaspoon pepper. Cook, stirring often, until sherry has mostly evaporated, about 2 minutes. Transfer mixture to a medium bowl. Let cool completely, about 15 minutes.

3. Cut softened ¾ cup butter into ½-inch pieces; add to cooled onion mixture in bowl, and stir gently until combined. Cover and refrigerate until ready to use. (Onion-butter mixture can be made in advance and refrigerated up to 3 days; let stand at room temperature about 20 minutes to soften before using.)

4. Preheat oven to 400°F. Heat oil in a large cast-iron skillet over medium-high. Add beef; cook until browned on all sides, about 8 minutes total. Return beef to wire rack on baking sheet. Roast in oven until a thermometer inserted in thickest portion of meat registers 115°F, 25 to 30 minutes. Let stand at least 30 minutes or up to 1 hour. Thinly slice beef on an angle.

5. Spread about 1½ teaspoons onion-butter mixture onto each toasted baguette slice. (Reserve remaining onion-butter mixture for another use.) Top each slice with 2 or 3 arugula leaves and 1 beef slice. Sprinkle evenly with sea salt. Serve immediately.

HERB-CRUSTED
BEEF TENDERLOIN

Herb-Crusted Beef Tenderloin

This crunchy-on-the-outside, tender-on-the-inside beef will go with anything else on your holiday table. When prepping the meat, trim off the thinner end and save it for another use, because it would overcook before the center is done.

ACTIVE 10 MIN. · TOTAL 2 HOURS, 30 MIN.
SERVES 8 (SERVING SIZE: 2 TO 3 SLICES)

- 1 (4-lb.) beef tenderloin, trimmed and tied
- ¼ cup Dijon mustard
- 2 Tbsp. mayonnaise
- 1 cup dry breadcrumbs
- 2 Tbsp. finely chopped fresh rosemary
- 1 Tbsp. chopped fresh thyme
- 1½ tsp. kosher salt
- 1 tsp. black pepper
- ½ tsp. garlic powder
- 2 Tbsp. olive oil

1. Line a baking sheet with aluminum foil; set an ovenproof wire rack inside baking sheet. Pat beef dry; place on wire rack, and let stand at room temperature 1 hour.

2. Preheat oven to 375°F. Stir together mustard and mayonnaise in a small bowl. Stir together breadcrumbs, rosemary, thyme, salt, pepper, and garlic powder in a medium bowl; stir in oil. Brush mustard mixture evenly all over beef. Carefully press breadcrumb mixture all over beef to fully coat.

3. Bake in preheated oven until a thermometer inserted into thickest portion of beef registers 120°F, 45 to 50 minutes. Remove from oven; let rest 30 minutes. (The beef will continue to cook as it rests.) Cut beef into ¾- to 1-inch-thick slices, and serve.

A Very Merry Brunch

Make a sweet or savory menu in advance so you can enjoy Christmas morning with your crew

POMEGRANATE
MIMOSA

CINNAMON ROLL
STRATA

THE PRETTIEST
AMBROSIA EVER

Sweet Menu Game Plan

Two days before brunch, make the yogurt mixture for the ambrosia, and cover and chill. The next day, prep and chill the mimosas (without the sparkling wine) and the strata (do not bake). Then, slice the citrus and pineapple and chill in an airtight container.

The Prettiest Ambrosia Ever

ACTIVE 20 MIN. - TOTAL 20 MIN.
SERVES 8

- 1   cup plain whole-milk Greek yogurt
- 2   Tbsp. honey, plus more for drizzling
- 2   tsp. vanilla bean paste
- ¼   tsp. kosher salt
- 4   assorted medium oranges (such as navel, Cara Cara, and blood oranges)
- 1   fresh medium pineapple, peeled and cored
- ½   cup toasted, sweetened coconut chips (such as Dang)

1. Whisk together yogurt, honey, 1 tablespoon water, vanilla bean paste, and salt in a medium bowl until smooth. (Store yogurt mixture, covered, in the refrigerator up to 2 days.)
2. Cut peel and pith from oranges; cut oranges into ¼-inch-thick rounds. Cut pineapple lengthwise into ¼-inch-thick planks; cut planks into 2-inch pieces. (Store orange rounds and pineapple pieces in an airtight container in the refrigerator up to 1 day.)
3. To assemble, spread yogurt mixture in a thick layer on a large platter. Arrange fruit over yogurt; drizzle with additional honey. Sprinkle with coconut chips (break apart any larger chips), and serve.

Pomegranate Mimosa

ACTIVE 5 MIN. - TOTAL 5 MIN.,
PLUS 4 HOURS CHILLING
SERVES 8

- 3 cups refrigerated pomegranate juice
- 1 cup (8 oz.) Aperol
- 1 (750-ml) bottle sparkling wine, chilled
    Pomegranate arils, for garnish

Stir together pomegranate juice and Aperol in a large pitcher, and chill at least 4 hours or up to 24 hours. Pour about ½ cup pomegranate mixture into each of 8 Champagne flutes, and top with chilled sparkling wine. Garnish with a few pomegranate arils.

Cinnamon Roll Strata

ACTIVE 30 MIN. - TOTAL 1 HOUR, 40 MIN.,
PLUS 4 HOURS CHILLING
SERVES 8

- 4 tsp. ground cinnamon
- 1½ cups granulated sugar, divided
- ¾ cup unsalted butter, melted
- 1 (25-oz.) pkg. frozen yeast roll dough, thawed and proofed according to pkg. directions
- 4 large eggs
- 2 cups half-and-half
- ½ tsp. kosher salt
- 1 Tbsp. vanilla extract, divided
- 4 oz. cream cheese, cut into cubes and softened
- ¼ cup whole milk
- ¼ cup powdered sugar

1. Preheat oven to 350°F. Line a 17- x 12-inch rimmed baking sheet with parchment paper, and set aside. Stir together cinnamon and 1 ¼ cups of the granulated sugar in a shallow bowl. Place melted butter in a separate small, shallow bowl. Dip each roll in melted butter, turning to coat evenly; roll in cinnamon sugar to coat evenly. Place on prepared baking sheet (rolls will be almost touching).
2. Bake in preheated oven just until puffed and cooked through, about 20 minutes. Let rolls stand until cool enough to handle, 20 to 30 minutes.
3. Lightly grease (with cooking spray) an 11-inch round or oval 2-quart baking dish. Whisk together eggs, half-and-half, salt, 2 teaspoons of the vanilla, and remaining

¼ cup sugar in a large bowl. Hold each baked roll over prepared dish, tear into bite-size pieces, and arrange in prepared dish. Pour egg mixture evenly over top. Cover with plastic wrap, gently pressing to submerge as many roll pieces in custard as possible. Chill at least 4 hours or up to 16 hours.
4. Preheat oven to 350°F. Remove plastic wrap, and let stand at room temperature while oven preheats. Bake until golden and set, 30 to 35 minutes. Set aside to cool slightly.
5. While strata bakes, combine cream cheese and milk in a small saucepan over medium. Cook, whisking constantly, until cream cheese melts and mixture is smooth, about 2 minutes. Whisk in powdered sugar and remaining 1 teaspoon vanilla until blended and smooth. Drizzle over warm strata.

Savory Menu Game Plan

The day before brunch, assemble and chill the casserole (do not bake) and bloody Mary mixer (without bourbon). Then, prepare the bacon and vinaigrette and chill in separate airtight containers, and make the croutons and store in an airtight container.

Bourbon Bloody Mary

(Photo, page 298)

ACTIVE 5 MIN. - TOTAL 5 MIN.,
PLUS 4 HOURS CHILLING
SERVES 6

- 6 cups vegetable juice (such as V8)
- 3 Tbsp. Worcestershire sauce
- 3 Tbsp. hot sauce (such as Cholula)
- 1½ Tbsp. celery salt
    Ice
- 1½ cups (12 oz.) bourbon
    Celery stalks with leaves, lime wedges, and pimiento-stuffed olives, for garnish

1. Whisk together vegetable juice, Worcestershire, hot sauce, and celery salt in a large pitcher until combined. Cover; chill at least 4 hours or up to 24 hours.
2. Pour 1 cup vegetable juice mixture into each of 6 tall glasses filled with ice. Top each with ¼ cup (2 oz.) bourbon, and stir well to combine. Garnish as desired.

Arugula Salad with Bacony Croutons and Sherry Vinaigrette

(Photo, page 298)

ACTIVE 20 MIN. - TOTAL 35 MIN.
SERVES 8

- 6 thick-cut bacon slices, chopped
- 4 cups torn sourdough bread (from 1 [8-oz.] loaf)
- 3 Tbsp. sherry vinegar
- 2 Tbsp. finely chopped shallots (from 2 medium shallots)
- 1 tsp. honey
- 1 tsp. kosher salt
- ½ tsp. black pepper
- ½ cup extra-virgin olive oil
- 5 oz. baby arugula
- 2 oz. blue cheese, crumbled (about ½ cup)
- 1 cup thinly sliced Honey Crisp apple (from 1 medium apple)
- ½ cup chopped toasted pecans

1. Preheat oven to 375°F. Cook bacon in a large skillet over medium, stirring occasionally, until crisp, 6 to 8 minutes. Remove bacon with a slotted spoon to a paper towel-lined plate and set aside, reserving drippings in skillet. Remove skillet from heat. (Bacon can be made a day ahead and stored in an airtight container in the refrigerator. Before using, place bacon on a paper towel-lined plate, and microwave on HIGH until warm, about 10 seconds.)
2. Place bread pieces in a large bowl. Pour bacon drippings from skillet over bread pieces in bowl; toss to coat. Transfer bread to an aluminum foil-lined rimmed baking sheet; spread in a single layer.
3. Bake in preheated oven until golden, about 12 minutes. Set aside to cool. (Croutons can be made a day ahead and stored in an airtight container at room temperature.)
4. Whisk together vinegar, shallots, honey, salt, and pepper in a small bowl. Slowly whisk in oil until well combined. (Vinaigrette can be made a day ahead and stored in the refrigerator. Let stand at room temperature 30 minutes to 1 hour, and whisk before using.)
5. Layer arugula, blue cheese, apple slices, pecans, croutons, and reserved bacon in a serving bowl or on a platter. Drizzle with vinaigrette just before serving.

BOURBON
BLOODY MARY
(PAGE 297)

EGGS BENEDICT
CASSEROLE

ARUGULA SALAD
WITH BACONY
CROUTONS
AND SHERRY
VINAIGRETTE
(PAGE 297)

Eggs Benedict Casserole

ACTIVE 1 HOUR - TOTAL 1 HOUR,
PLUS 8 HOURS CHILLING
SERVES 8

- 1 Tbsp. vegetable oil
- 8 oz. Canadian bacon slices, chopped
- 6 English muffins, split
- 1 bunch scallions, white and green parts separated
- 6 large eggs
- 2 cups whole milk
- ¾ tsp. black pepper
- 2 tsp. kosher salt, divided
- 1 cup unsalted butter
- 6 large egg yolks
- 2 Tbsp. fresh lemon juice (from 1 lemon)
- 1 Tbsp. Dijon mustard
- ¼ tsp. paprika, plus more for garnish

1. Heat oil in a large nonstick skillet over medium-high. Add chopped bacon.

Cook, stirring often, until lightly browned, about 4 minutes. Remove bacon with a slotted spoon to a paper towel–lined plate, reserving drippings in skillet. (Do not wipe skillet clean.) Return skillet to medium-high. Working in batches, add English muffin halves, cut-sides down, to hot drippings in skillet. Cook until toasted, about 1 minute. Let muffin halves cool slightly.

2. Chop English muffin halves into bite-size pieces, and place on bottom of a lightly greased (with cooking spray) 13- x 9-inch baking dish. Sprinkle with chopped bacon. Finely chop white parts of scallions, and sprinkle over mixture in dish. (Wrap green parts of scallions in a damp paper towel, and chill until ready to use.) Whisk together whole eggs, milk, pepper, and 1 teaspoon of the salt in a large bowl. Pour over mixture in baking dish; cover with plastic wrap. Chill at least 8 hours or up to 16 hours.

3. Preheat oven to 350°F. Let casserole stand at room temperature while oven preheats. Bake until top is browned and casserole is set, about 40 minutes.
4. While casserole bakes, make hollandaise. Melt butter in a small saucepan or skillet over medium-low. Keep butter hot over lowest heat (do not let butter brown). Process egg yolks, lemon juice, mustard, paprika, and remaining 1 teaspoon salt in a blender on medium just to combine, about 5 seconds. With blender running on medium speed, slowly and carefully pour hot, melted butter through center opening in blender lid. Process until all butter is incorporated and mixture is smooth and thick, about 1 minute.
5. Drizzle about ½ cup hollandaise over warm casserole. Finely chop reserved green scallion parts, and sprinkle over top. Lightly sprinkle with paprika, if desired, and serve with remaining hollandaise.

For the Love of Latkes

You don't have to grow up celebrating Hanukkah to become a master maker

Here's a secret I've never told anyone. It's about my grandmother, Lil Pachter. What you must know in order to appreciate it is that my Mema was a well-regarded baker among her set of friends. Her mandelbrot, the biscotti-like bar cookies studded with slivers of almonds, was particularly celebrated.

The secret was that she didn't much care for making latkes. When Hanukkah rolled around every year, hers came from the Manischewitz box.

I was simply a person who knew why Jewish people like me ate potato pancakes at Hanukkah, even though I had not experienced a particularly tasty or authentic version. After years without homemade latkes, relief came from an unlikely source. When I fell in love and married a man who is not Jewish. My family worried about whether my grandmother would accept Andrew, but when she saw that he liked Jewish foods he quickly won her over.

One night when we were newly married, I came home from work and found my guy cooking. "Surprise!" he said, as he stood in our studio apartment's kitchen grating potatoes. We couldn't make it back home that year, so he decided he'd make me from-scratch latkes. "Just like the kind your grandmother makes!" he said.

He's learning the truth as he reads this story, because I watched him work so hard to do something extraordinary for me. It takes a lot of effort to translate a food tradition that is not your own; there are no memories from which to draw. Yet there he was, grating, frying, sweating, and cursing as the aroma of frying potatoes filled the air. He was figuring out what my Mema had long ago decided was too much trouble, and he has been doing the same thing every Hanukkah for 22 years. To this day, he makes the best latkes I've ever tasted.

Andrew's Latkes

ACTIVE 40 MIN. - TOTAL 55 MIN.

MAKES 12

- 1½   lb. russet potatoes (about 3 medium potatoes), peeled and spiralized into spaghetti-shaped "noodles"
- 1½   tsp. kosher salt, plus more water
- 2   large eggs, lightly beaten
- 1   Tbsp. all-purpose flour
- ½   tsp. black pepper
- ½   cup vegetable oil, divided
  Fresh dill, for garnish (optional)

1. Preheat oven to 250°F. Line a baking sheet with parchment paper. Soak spiralized potatoes in a bowl of lightly salted cold water for 15 minutes. Drain. Using a pair of kitchen scissors or a chef's knife, cut spiralized potatoes into 1-inch-long strips. Transfer to a large bowl.
2. Whisk together eggs, flour, salt, and pepper in a small bowl until combined. Drizzle mixture over potatoes in large bowl. Gently stir to coat potatoes well.
3. Heat a large nonstick skillet over medium. Add 2 tablespoons oil, and heat until oil is shimmering but not yet smoking. Scoop 3 tablespoonfuls potato batter into skillet; flatten into a 3-inch-wide, ¼-inch-thick patty. Repeat procedure twice to form 3 latkes in skillet. Cook until golden brown on both sides, 2 to 3 minutes per side. Transfer cooked latkes to prepared baking sheet; place in preheated oven to keep warm. Repeat procedure 3 times with remaining potato batter, adding 2 tablespoons oil to skillet per batch. Garnish, if desired.

Sweeter by the Dozen

December calls for cookies, and we've got recipes for everything you have planned, whether it's baking with the kids, filling tins for gift giving, or leaving a snack for Santa

Soft Molasses–Ginger Cookies

These tender, spicy cookies have a bit of heat thanks to ground and crystallized ginger. If you don't have all of the individual spices listed in the recipe, substitute 3½ teaspoons pumpkin pie spice or apple pie spice.

ACTIVE 25 MIN. - TOTAL 1 HOUR, 25 MIN., PLUS 1 HOUR CHILLING
MAKES ABOUT 2½ DOZEN

- 1 cup unsalted butter, softened
- ½ cup packed dark brown sugar
- ⅓ cup unsulfured molasses
- 1 cup granulated sugar, divided
- 1 large egg
- 2 tsp. vanilla extract
- 2½ cups all-purpose flour
- 2 tsp. ground cinnamon
- 1½ tsp. baking soda
- 1 tsp. ground ginger
- ¼ tsp. ground cloves
- ¼ tsp. ground nutmeg
- ¼ tsp. kosher salt
- ½ cup finely chopped crystallized ginger (from 1 [3-oz.] pkg. crystallized ginger)
- 1½ cups unsifted powdered sugar
- 2 to 3 Tbsp. fresh lemon juice (from 1 lemon), as needed
  Sparkling sugar or sanding sugar

1. Preheat oven to 375°F. Line 2 baking sheets with parchment paper. Beat butter, brown sugar, molasses, and ½ cup of the granulated sugar with a stand mixer fitted with a paddle attachment on medium-high speed until smooth and fluffy, 2 to 3 minutes. Add egg and vanilla; beat until combined, about 30 seconds.
2. Whisk together flour, cinnamon, baking soda, ground ginger, cloves, nutmeg, and salt in a medium bowl until combined. Gradually add to butter mixture, beating on low speed until combined, about 2 minutes, stopping to scrape down sides of bowl as needed. Fold in crystallized ginger. Cover bowl with plastic wrap, and refrigerate until chilled, at least 1 hour or up to overnight (8 hours).
3. Remove dough from refrigerator, and unwrap. Using a 2-inch cookie scoop (about 3 tablespoons), scoop cookie dough into rounds, and roll each into a smooth ball. (You should have about 30 balls.) Place remaining ½ cup granulated sugar on a plate. Roll balls in sugar to coat, and arrange 3 inches apart on prepared baking sheets. Bake in preheated oven, in 2 batches, until cookies have crackles and edges are slightly darker in color, 10 to 12 minutes per batch. Let cool on baking sheet 10 minutes. Transfer cookies to a wire rack, and let cool completely, about 30 minutes.
4. Whisk together powdered sugar and 2 tablespoons lemon juice in a small bowl until combined and smooth; whisk in additional lemon juice 1 teaspoon at a time until reaching desired consistency. Drizzle over cooled cookies; sprinkle with sparkling sugar or sanding sugar as desired.

Benne Seed Thumbprints

Toasted benne (sesame) seeds give these treats a nice crunch to balance the sweet, sticky jam. Make the cookies easier to fill by pressing a teaspoon into the center of each again right after they come out of the oven, if needed.

ACTIVE 30 MIN. - TOTAL 1 HOUR, 15 MIN., PLUS 45 MIN. CHILLING
MAKES ABOUT 2 DOZEN

- 1 cup unsifted powdered sugar
- ¾ cup unsalted butter, softened
- 1 large egg
- 1 tsp. vanilla extract
- 2 cups all-purpose flour
- ½ cup benne seeds (sesame seeds)
- ½ cup seedless jam of choice

1. Beat sugar and butter with a stand mixer fitted with a paddle attachment on medium-high speed until light and fluffy, about 2 minutes, stopping to scrape down sides of bowl as needed. Add egg and vanilla; continue beating until combined, about 20 seconds. Add flour; beat on low speed until just combined, about 1 minute, stopping to scrape down sides of bowl as needed. Cover bowl with plastic wrap; chill until firm, about 45 minutes.
2. Preheat oven to 350°F. Line 2 baking sheets with parchment paper. Place benne seeds in a small, shallow bowl. Using a 1½-inch cookie scoop (about 1½ tablespoons), scoop cookie dough into rounds, and roll each into a smooth ball. (You should have about 24 balls.) Roll balls in benne seeds to coat, and arrange 2 inches apart on prepared baking sheets. Using your thumb or the back of a teaspoon, gently press the center of each ball to form a ½-inch-deep indentation.
3. Bake in preheated oven, in 2 batches, until bottoms are golden and benne seeds are lightly toasted, 12 to 14 minutes per batch. Remove from oven; if needed, re-press the indentation of each cookie. Transfer to a wire rack, and let cool completely, about 20 minutes. Transfer to a serving platter. Spoon 1 teaspoon jam into indention of each cookie.

Chocolate–Pecan Tassies

We gave these classic cookies an update with a rich chocolate piecrust.

ACTIVE 35 MIN. - TOTAL 3 HOURS
MAKES ABOUT 20 MINI PIES

CHOCOLATE CRUSTS
- ¾ cup unsalted butter, softened
- ⅓ cup granulated sugar
- 1 large egg yolk
- 1¾ cups all-purpose flour
- 2 Tbsp. unsweetened cocoa
- ½ tsp. kosher salt

FILLING
- 1 large egg, lightly beaten
- ¼ cup granulated sugar
- ¼ cup dark corn syrup
- 1 Tbsp. light brown sugar
- 1 Tbsp. unsalted butter, melted

Recipe continued on page 302

SOFT MOLASSES-
GINGER COOKIES

BENNE SEED
THUMBPRINTS

CHOCOLATE-
PECAN
TASSIES

HOT CHOCOLATE
BROWNIES (PAGE 303)

LINZER TREE
COOKIES
(PAGE 302)

NO-BAKE DARK CHOCOLATE-
PEPPERMINT SANDWICH
COOKIES (PAGE 302)

Recipe continued from page 300

½ tsp. vanilla extract
¼ tsp. kosher salt

ADDITIONAL INGREDIENTS

¼ cup finely chopped toasted pecans
40 pecan halves (about 1 cup)
4 oz. semisweet chocolate, chopped

1. Prepare the Chocolate Crusts: Beat butter and sugar with a stand mixer fitted with a paddle attachment on medium speed until smooth, about 2 minutes. Add egg yolk, flour, cocoa, and salt; beat until fully combined, about 1 minute. Cover bowl with plastic wrap, and chill 2 hours.
2. Coat a 24-cup mini muffin pan with cooking spray. Uncover dough, and shape into 20 (1-inch) balls; gently press each ball into bottom and up sides of 20 prepared muffin cups. Place in freezer, uncovered, until ready to use.
3. Prepare the Filling: Preheat oven to 350°F. Whisk together egg, granulated sugar, corn syrup, brown sugar, melted butter, vanilla, and salt in a glass measuring cup or a small bowl until smooth.
4. Remove Chocolate Crusts from freezer; fill each with about ½ teaspoon finely chopped pecans, and top with 2 pecan halves. Carefully drizzle Filling over pecans to come about three-fourths up the sides of each crust.
5. Bake in preheated oven until mostly dry to the touch and crust is set, about 18 minutes. Let cool 15 minutes in muffin pan. Run a small knife around edge of each crust. Lift from pan, and place on a serving platter to cool completely, about 15 minutes more.
6. Place chopped chocolate in a small microwave-safe bowl, and microwave on 50% power until melted, stirring every 30 seconds (about 1 minute total). Transfer melted chocolate to a small piping bag or a zip-top plastic bag with 1 small corner snipped off, and drizzle chocolate over cooled tassies.

Linzer Tree Cookies

(Photo, page 301)

ACTIVE 45 MIN. · TOTAL 1 HOUR, 30 MIN., PLUS 1 HOUR CHILLING

MAKES 1½ DOZEN SANDWICH COOKIES

1½ cups all-purpose flour, plus more for work surface
½ tsp. baking powder
½ tsp. ground cinnamon
¼ tsp. kosher salt
⅔ cup granulated sugar
½ cup unsalted butter, softened
2 large egg yolks
1 tsp. vanilla extract
¼ tsp. almond extract
3 Tbsp. fruit preserves or jam
2 tsp. powdered sugar

SPECIAL EQUIPMENT

Plastic or metal drinking straw

1. Whisk together flour, baking powder, cinnamon, and salt in a large bowl; set aside. Beat granulated sugar and butter with a stand mixer fitted with a paddle attachment on medium speed until light and fluffy, about 2 minutes. Add egg yolks, vanilla, and almond extract, beating until just combined, about 30 seconds (do not overbeat). Gradually add flour mixture, beating on low speed just until a dough forms, about 1 minute. Turn dough out onto a clean work surface, and divide in half. Flatten halves into 1-inch-thick disks. Wrap each disk in plastic wrap; chill 1 hour.
2. Preheat oven to 350°F. Line 2 baking sheets with parchment paper. Remove 1 dough disk from refrigerator, and unwrap. Roll to ⅛-inch thickness on a lightly floured work surface. Using a 3½-inch tree-shaped cookie cutter, cut out 18 cookies. Using a straw, poke 4 to 8 holes into each cookie, poking all the way through bottoms.
3. Arrange cookies 1 inch apart on prepared baking sheets. Bake in preheated oven, in 2 batches, until cookie edges are lightly browned, 6 to 7 minutes per batch. Cool on baking sheets about 5 minutes. Transfer cookies to wire racks; cool about 20 minutes. Repeat with remaining dough disk, but do not poke any holes in cookies. You will end up with 18 cookies with holes and 18 whole cookies.
4. Spread center of each whole cookie with about ½ teaspoon preserves, leaving a small edge around cookie without jam. Sprinkle cookies with holes evenly with powdered sugar. Place 1 cookie with holes on top of each whole cookie.

No-Bake Dark Chocolate-Peppermint Sandwich Cookies

(Photo, page 301)

Thanks to store-bought chocolate wafers, these cookies don't require any baking. If the melted chocolate mixture begins to firm up while you are dipping the cookies, microwave on HIGH for 20 seconds and stir.

ACTIVE 30 MIN. · TOTAL 30 MIN., PLUS 30 MIN. CHILLING

MAKES ABOUT 27 SANDWICH COOKIES

1 cup unsifted powdered sugar
½ cup unsalted butter
1 Tbsp. whole milk
¼ tsp. peppermint extract
Red food coloring gel
54 chocolate wafer cookies (from 2 [9-oz.] pkg.) (such as Nabisco Famous Chocolate Wafers)
2 (12-oz.) pkg. bittersweet chocolate chips
1 Tbsp. plus 1 tsp. coconut oil
Crushed hard peppermint candies

1. Beat powdered sugar, butter, milk, and peppermint extract with a stand mixer fitted with a paddle attachment on medium speed until smooth, about 1 minute. Using a wooden pick, add 1 small drop of food coloring to mixture. Beat until color is evenly distributed, about 1 minute. Beat in additional food coloring until desired color is reached. Transfer frosting to a piping bag or a zip-top plastic bag with a ½-inch corner snipped off.
2. Arrange half of the cookies upside-down on a clean work surface. Pipe a 1-inch dollop (about 2 teaspoons) frosting onto each cookie; top with remaining cookies right-side up. (Reserve any remaining frosting for another use.) Gently press sandwich cookies to push filling almost to outer edges.
3. Place chocolate chips and coconut oil in a microwavable bowl. Microwave on HIGH until fully melted and smooth, about 3 minutes, stopping to stir every 30 seconds. Dip 1 sandwich cookie into melted chocolate mixture using a fork, coating completely and letting excess drip back into bowl. Transfer dipped sandwich cookie to a baking sheet lined with parchment paper, and immediately sprinkle with crushed peppermint candies. Repeat procedure with remaining sandwich cookies, melted chocolate mixture, and crushed peppermint candies.

4. Chill dipped sandwich cookies until set, about 30 minutes. Store in an airtight container in refrigerator up to 5 days.

Hot Chocolate Brownies

(Photo, page 301)

A layer of homemade marshmallow makes these brownies outrageously good. For best results when making marshmallows, choose a dry, nonrainy day and use a candy thermometer. To save time in the kitchen, substitute your favorite boxed brownie mix.

ACTIVE 45 MIN. · TOTAL 1 HOUR, 50 MIN., PLUS 8 HOURS STANDING

MAKES 1 DOZEN

BROWNIES

Baking spray with flour
1 cup unsalted butter
2 cups semisweet chocolate chips, divided
1 cup granulated sugar
1 tsp. vanilla extract
4 large eggs, at room temperature, lightly beaten
½ cup all-purpose flour
⅓ cup unsweetened cocoa
1 tsp. baking powder
½ tsp. kosher salt

MARSHMALLOW TOPPING

⅔ cup cold water, divided
2 (¼-oz.) envelopes unflavored gelatin (from 1 [1-oz.] pkg.)
⅔ cup plus 2 Tbsp. granulated sugar
⅔ cup plus 2 Tbsp. light corn syrup
¼ tsp. kosher salt
1½ tsp. vanilla extract

ADDITIONAL INGREDIENTS

2 Tbsp. powdered sugar, plus more for cutting
1 Tbsp. unsweetened cocoa

1. Prepare the Brownies: Preheat oven to 350°F. Lightly coat a 13- x 9-inch baking pan with baking spray; line with parchment paper, leaving a 2-inch overhang on 2 sides.
2. Microwave butter and 1½ cups of the chocolate chips in a large microwavable bowl on HIGH until melted and smooth, about 90 seconds, stopping to stir every 30 seconds. Stir in sugar and vanilla until smooth. Stir in eggs until smooth. Whisk together flour, cocoa, baking powder, and salt in a small bowl; stir into chocolate mixture until just combined. Stir in remaining ½ cup chocolate chips. Spread mixture evenly in prepared baking

pan. Bake in preheated oven until just set, 26 to 28 minutes. Transfer to a wire rack; cool completely, about 1 hour.
3. Meanwhile, prepare the Marshmallow Topping: Place ⅓ cup of the cold water in bowl of a stand mixer fitted with a whisk attachment; sprinkle water with gelatin. Stir together sugar, corn syrup, salt, and remaining ⅓ cup cold water in a small saucepan. Cook over medium-high, stirring often, until a candy thermometer registers 240°F, 9 to 12 minutes (reduce heat as needed to prevent mixture from boiling over).
4. Gradually add hot sugar mixture to gelatin mixture in stand mixer bowl. Beat on medium-low speed, gradually increasing mixer speed to high, until bottom of bowl is slightly warm and mixture is very thick, 6 to 7 minutes. Stir in vanilla.
5. Working quickly, spread Marshmallow Topping over cooled Brownies; smooth with an offset spatula lightly coated with cooking spray. Stir together powdered sugar and cocoa in a small bowl. Using a fine mesh strainer, lightly dust Marshmallow Topping with powdered sugar mixture.
6. Let Brownies with Marshmallow Topping stand, uncovered, in a cool, dry place until set and dried, at least 8 hours or up to 24 hours. Slice using a knife dusted with powdered sugar after each cut.

Slice-and-Bake Sugar Cookie Bites

(Photo, page 304)

These itty-bitty cookies are meant to be eaten by the handful and look adorable packaged in a holiday tin or set out in bowls at a party. For the most even, round cookies, wrap each dough log in a sheet of parchment paper, and press the paper around it to help shape the dough.

ACTIVE 30 MIN. · TOTAL 2 HOURS, 10 MIN., PLUS 2 HOURS CHILLING

MAKES ABOUT 8 DOZEN

1 cup unsalted butter, softened
1 cup granulated sugar
1 large egg
1 tsp. vanilla extract
2¾ cups all-purpose flour
½ tsp. kosher salt
½ cup blue and white or red and green nonpareils (tiny round candy sprinkles)

1. Beat butter and sugar with a stand mixer fitted with a paddle attachment on medium speed until light and fluffy, about 2 minutes. Add egg and vanilla; beat until fully incorporated, about 1 minute. Gradually add flour and salt, beating on low speed until combined, about 2 minutes. Shape dough into 2 (12- x 1-inch) logs.
2. Place sprinkles in a small, shallow, rimmed baking sheet. Roll dough logs in sprinkles, pressing gently to adhere. (Reserve any remaining sprinkles.) Wrap each log with plastic wrap; chill until firm, at least 2 hours or up to 2 days.
3. Preheat oven to 350°F. Line a baking sheet with parchment paper. Remove 1 dough log from refrigerator, and unwrap. If needed, press some of the reserved sprinkles onto log to fully coat. Slice log into ¼-inch-thick rounds (you will have about 48 rounds). Arrange about 18 cookie rounds spaced 1 inch apart on prepared baking sheet. (Place remaining cookie rounds on a baking sheet, and place in refrigerator until ready to bake.) Bake in preheated oven, in 3 batches, until edges are light golden, 9 to 10 minutes per batch. Remove from oven; cool on baking sheet 5 minutes. Transfer cookies to wire racks; cool completely, about 20 minutes.
4. Meanwhile, remove second dough log from refrigerator, and repeat Step 3.

Red Velvet-White Chocolate Chunk Cookies

(Photo, page 304)

These cheerful cookies are made with chopped chocolate baking bars (instead of chips) to create pockets of melted chocolate throughout. For the most festive red hue, use a super red food coloring gel. To add a buttery crunch, stir in ½ cup chopped macadamia nuts into the batter with the chopped chocolate.

ACTIVE 30 MIN. · TOTAL 2 HOURS, PLUS 2 HOURS CHILLING

MAKES ABOUT 3½ DOZEN

3 (4-oz.) white chocolate baking bars
1½ cups granulated sugar
1 cup unsalted butter, softened
2 large eggs
1 tsp. vanilla extract
2⅓ cups all-purpose flour
3 Tbsp. unsweetened cocoa
1 tsp. baking powder
½ tsp. baking soda

Recipe continued on page 305

SLICE-AND-BAKE
SUGAR COOKIE BITES
(PAGE 303)

RED VELVET-WHITE
CHOCOLATE CHUNK
COOKIES (PAGE 303)

CHOCOLATE-HAZELNUT
RUGELACH (PAGE 305)

SANTA'S KITCHEN-
SINK COOKIES
(PAGE 305)

PAINTED
SHORTBREAD
COOKIES
(PAGE 306)

SPRINKLE STOCKING
COOKIES (PAGE 306)

Recipe continued from page 303

½ tsp. kosher salt
2 tsp. red food coloring gel

1. Coarsely chop 2 of the white chocolate baking bars. Set aside, and reserve for folding into cookie dough batter. Coarsely chop remaining white chocolate baking bar. Set aside, and reserve for pressing into cookie dough balls. Beat sugar and butter with a stand mixer fitted with a paddle attachment on medium speed until light and fluffy, about 2 minutes. Add eggs and vanilla; beat just until combined, about 20 seconds, stopping to scrape down sides of bowl as needed.
2. Whisk together flour, cocoa, baking powder, baking soda, and salt in a medium bowl; add to butter mixture. Beat on low speed until smooth and combined, about 2 minutes. Add food coloring; beat on medium speed until just incorporated, about 30 seconds. Fold 2 reserved chopped white chocolate baking bars into batter. Cover bowl with plastic wrap; chill at least 2 hours or up to overnight (8 hours).
3. Preheat oven to 350°F. Line 3 baking sheets with parchment paper. Remove cookie dough from refrigerator, and unwrap. Scoop 15 dough balls by heaping tablespoonfuls, and shape into 1½-inch balls. Arrange cookie dough balls 2 inches apart on 1 prepared baking sheet. (Return remaining dough in bowl to refrigerator until ready to bake.) Press one-third of the reserved chopped white chocolate baking bar into tops of dough balls. Bake until tops are crackled and edges are set, 9 to 10 minutes. Remove from oven; let cool on baking sheet 15 minutes. Transfer to a wire rack; cool completely, about 30 minutes. Repeat procedure twice with remaining dough and chopped white chocolate baking bar.

Chocolate-Hazelnut Rugelach

These rich, buttery bites remind us of chocolate-filled croissants. When kneading the dough, don't overwork it, or it will be tough and not as flaky.

ACTIVE 30 MIN. - TOTAL 1 HOUR, 40 MIN.,
PLUS 2 HOURS CHILLING
MAKES ABOUT 2 DOZEN

1½ cups all-purpose flour, plus more for work surface and dusting
2 Tbsp. granulated sugar
¼ tsp. kosher salt
4 oz. cold cream cheese, cubed
½ cup cold unsalted butter, cubed
1 large egg yolk
3 Tbsp. light brown sugar
¼ tsp. ground cinnamon
3 Tbsp. finely chopped toasted hazelnuts
2 oz. bittersweet chocolate (from 1 [4-oz.] bar), finely chopped
1 Tbsp. heavy whipping cream
1 Tbsp. sparkling sugar

1. Pulse together flour, granulated sugar, and salt in a food processor until combined, 3 to 4 pulses. Add cream cheese and butter; pulse until mixture forms large, crumbly pieces, 6 to 8 pulses. Add egg yolk; pulse until just incorporated, 3 to 4 pulses.
2. Turn dough out onto a clean work surface; knead until dough just comes together, about 1 minute. Divide in half; shape each piece into a rectangle about 5 x 3 inches. Wrap individually in plastic wrap; chill at least 2 hours or up to overnight (8 hours).
3. Stir together brown sugar and cinnamon in a small bowl. Remove 1 chilled dough rectangle from refrigerator, and unwrap. Place dough on a well-floured work surface, and lightly dust with flour. Roll into a rectangle about 12 x 6 inches. Sprinkle dough rectangle with half of the brown sugar mixture. Sprinkle half of the hazelnuts over brown sugar mixture. Sprinkle half of the finely chopped chocolate over hazelnuts. Starting at 1 long end, carefully roll dough up into a tight log. Place log, seam-side down, on a baking sheet. Repeat procedure with remaining chilled dough rectangle, brown sugar mixture, hazelnuts, and chopped chocolate. Freeze logs, unwrapped, on baking sheet 15 minutes.
4. Preheat oven to 375°F. Remove 1 dough log from freezer; cut into 12 (1-inch-thick) slices. Arrange slices, standing upright with the seam-side down, on a baking sheet lined with parchment paper. Brush tops of slices evenly with half of the whipping cream, and sprinkle with half of the sparkling sugar. Bake until rugelach are golden brown and dough is flaky, 13 to 15 minutes. Cool on baking sheet 5 minutes; transfer to a wire rack, and cool to room temperature, about 20 minutes. Repeat procedure with remaining dough log, whipping cream, and sparkling sugar.

Santa's Kitchen-Sink Cookies

Fold the candies and other mix-ins into the dough with a spatula, not the mixer, so they won't break apart.

ACTIVE 30 MIN. - TOTAL 1 HOUR, 35 MIN.,
PLUS 1 HOUR CHILLING
MAKES 3 DOZEN

1¼ cups unsalted butter, softened
1¼ cups packed dark brown sugar
1 cup granulated sugar
2 tsp. vanilla extract
2 large eggs
2 cups all-purpose flour
1¾ cups bleached cake flour
1 tsp. baking soda
1 tsp. baking powder
½ tsp. kosher salt
1 cup red and green candy-coated chocolate pieces
1 cup miniature pretzel twists, broken into pieces
½ cup semisweet chocolate chips
½ cup miniature marshmallows
Flaky sea salt

1. Beat butter, brown sugar, and granulated sugar with a stand mixer fitted with a paddle attachment on medium speed until light and fluffy, about 2 minutes. Beat in vanilla until combined. Beat in eggs 1 at a time on medium-low speed until just combined, about 20 seconds.
2. Whisk together all-purpose flour, cake flour, baking soda, baking powder, and salt in a medium bowl until combined. Gradually add to butter mixture, beating on low speed until well combined, about 2 minutes. Add candy-coated chocolate pieces, pretzels, chocolate chips, and marshmallows; fold into dough using a rubber spatula or a wooden spoon. Cover bowl with plastic wrap; chill at least 1 hour or up to overnight (8 hours).
3. Preheat oven to 400°F. Line 3 baking sheets with parchment paper. Remove dough from refrigerator, and unwrap. Scoop 12 dough balls using a 2-inch cookie scoop (about 3 tablespoons each), and arrange balls 2 inches apart on 1 prepared baking sheet. (Return remaining dough in bowl to refrigerator until ready to bake.) Bake until edges are golden, 10 to 12 minutes. Remove from oven; immediately sprinkle cookies with flaky sea salt. Let cool on baking sheets 5 minutes. Transfer cookies to wire racks; cool completely, about 20 minutes. Repeat procedure twice with remaining dough.

Painted Shortbread Cookies

(Photo, page 304)

Creative types of all ages will love decorating these simple shortbread cookies. Combine almond extract and food coloring gel to make edible "paints" that create a soft watercolor look when brushed onto dried royal icing.

ACTIVE 1 HOUR, 30 MIN. - TOTAL 4 HOURS, PLUS 2 HOURS CHILLING

MAKES ABOUT 2 DOZEN

COOKIES
- 1 cup unsalted butter, softened
- ½ cup unsifted powdered sugar
- 1 tsp. vanilla extract
- 2 cups all-purpose flour, plus more for work surface
- ¼ tsp. kosher salt

ROYAL ICING
- 1 (1-lb.) pkg. powdered sugar
- 3 Tbsp. meringue powder (such as Wilton)
- 6 to 8 Tbsp. warm water

ADDITIONAL INGREDIENTS
- Assorted food coloring gels
- Almond extract

ADDITIONAL TOOLS
- Small food-safe paintbrush

1. Prepare the Cookies: Beat butter and powdered sugar with a stand mixer fitted with a paddle attachment on medium speed until light and fluffy, about 2 minutes. Add vanilla; beat until combined, about 20 seconds. Add flour and salt; beat on low speed until a smooth dough forms, about 2 minutes.

2. Transfer dough to a lightly floured work surface, and shape into an 8-inch-long x 2-inch-wide log. Wrap with plastic wrap; chill until firm, at least 2 hours or up to 2 days.

3. Preheat oven to 350°F. Line 2 baking sheets with parchment paper. Remove dough from refrigerator, and unwrap. Slice into 24 (⅓-inch-thick) rounds. Arrange dough rounds 2 inches apart on prepared baking sheets. Bake in 2 batches until edges are golden, 11 to 12 minutes per batch. Let cool on baking sheet 5 minutes. Transfer to a wire rack, and let cool completely, about 20 minutes.

4. Prepare the Royal Icing: Place powdered sugar, meringue powder, and 6 tablespoons warm water in bowl of stand mixer fitted with a whisk attachment. Beat on medium speed until fully combined and smooth, about 1 minute, stopping to scrape down sides of bowl as needed. Increase mixer speed to high, and beat until icing is no longer glossy, about 1 minute. Stir in more warm water, 1 tablespoon at a time, until a spreadable consistency is reached. Spoon mixture into a piping bag or a zip-top plastic bag with 1 corner snipped off.

5. Pipe Royal Icing onto Cookies, using a wooden pick to fill and spread to edges of each Cookie. Let stand at room temperature until Royal Icing dries, about 1 hour.

6. Squeeze a few drops of desired assorted food coloring into separate small bowls. Add 2 teaspoons almond extract to each color, and mix together using a small paintbrush. To test your colors, paint a few practice strokes on a paper towel or a sample Cookie. (You can add more almond extract if you want your colors to be lighter.) Paint designs such as wreaths, trees, or plaid patterns onto Cookies. Let painted Cookies dry completely, about 1 hour.

Sprinkle Stocking Cookies

(Photo, page 304)

Depending on the sprinkles you choose, these stockings can be fancy or playful. However you decorate them, the key to a neat look is to dip the lower half of each iced cookie in sprinkles and then dip the top half.

ACTIVE 1 HOUR - TOTAL 2 HOURS, 30 MIN., PLUS 2 HOURS CHILLING

MAKES 3 DOZEN

- 1 cup unsalted butter, softened
- 1 cup granulated sugar
- 1 large egg
- 1 tsp. vanilla extract
- ¼ tsp. almond extract (optional)
- 2½ cups all-purpose flour, plus more for work surface
- ¾ tsp. kosher salt
- 1 (1-lb.) pkg. powdered sugar, unsifted
- 6 to 7 Tbsp. whole milk, as needed
- Assorted colors of candy sprinkles

1. Beat butter and granulated sugar with a stand mixer fitted with a paddle attachment on medium speed until light and fluffy, about 2 minutes. Add egg, vanilla, and (if using) almond extract. Beat until fully incorporated, about 30 seconds. Gradually add flour and salt, beating on low speed until combined, about 1 minute. Remove dough from bowl; shape into a flat disk about 1-inch thick. Wrap disk in plastic wrap; chill at least 2 hours or up to 24 hours.

2. Preheat oven to 350°F. Line 2 baking sheets with parchment paper. Transfer dough to a lightly floured work surface, and roll to ⅛-inch thickness. Using a 3½-inch stocking-shaped cookie cutter, cut out 36 cookies (or cut by hand using a paring knife). Arrange cookies 2 inches apart on prepared baking sheets.

3. Bake in preheated oven, in 2 batches, until cookies are slightly golden around edges but pale in the center, 6 to 10 minutes per batch, depending on the size of cookies. Do not overbake. Let cool on baking sheets 5 minutes. Transfer cookies to a wire rack, and let cool completely, about 30 minutes.

4. Beat powdered sugar and 6 tablespoons milk with a stand mixer fitted with a whisk attachment on medium speed until combined and smooth, about 1 minute, stopping to scrape down sides of bowl as needed. Beat in remaining 1 tablespoon milk 1 teaspoon at a time until desired icing consistency is reached. Place candy sprinkle colors on separate plates.

5. Spoon icing into a piping bag or a zip-top plastic bag with 1 small corner snipped off. Working with 1 cookie at a time, pipe an icing border around each cookie, and then flood cookie with icing. Using a wooden pick, spread icing to edges and corners of cookie. While icing is still wet, dip the lower portion of the stocking in 1 color of sprinkles; dip the upper portion in another color of sprinkles. Let cookies stand until set, about 1 hour.

BAKING $\boxed{\text{SL}}$ SCHOOL

KNOW-HOW

Icing and Piping Pointers

Four foolproof decorating tips from the Test Kitchen professionals

CHECK THE CONSISTENCY

Save time by using one royal icing for piping (decorating) and flooding (filling in) cookies. The icing should have the consistency of Elmer's School Glue: thick enough to hold its shape when piped, but thin enough to flow through the piping bag or tip.

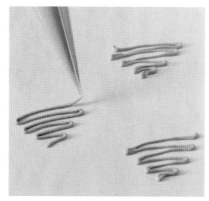

PRACTICE, PRACTICE

Start by piping a few lines and circles on parchment paper or a dry surface. If you have trouble getting the icing to flow in a smooth line, it is too thick and needs more water. If it flows out like honey and doesn't hold its shape, it is too thin.

HAVE TOOTHPICKS ONHAND

Once you have piped a border edge of icing around the cookie, flood it quickly with icing. Then use a toothpick to carefully spread icing to the border, smooth out lumps, and pop tiny air bubbles.

EMBELLISH WHEN DRY

If you want to add decorations like stripes, dots, or letters, first let the bottom layer of icing dry for at least 30 minutes. This will prevent the icings from blending together.

TEST KITCHEN TIPS

Bake Your Best Batch

Three simple tricks to improve any recipe

CHILL OVERNIGHT

Cookies made with chilled dough spread less as they bake because the fat takes longer to melt. An overnight rest in the refrigerator also helps the flour soak up liquids in the dough, making the treats taste better and bake more evenly.

USE PARCHMENT PAPER

For neater cutout cookies and less mess, roll out the dough on parchment paper. Transfer the dough (on the paper) to a baking sheet. Cut out shapes, and remove scraps.

COOL DOWN BAKING SHEETS

When making multiple batches of cookies, don't scoop raw dough onto hot baking sheets that have just been in the oven. Run cold water over the sheets between your batches.

EDITORS' PICK

Trusty Tool

A thin, flexible fish spatula makes transferring cookies off baking sheets a breeze: New Star Foodservice 43068 Wood Handle Fish Spatula.

Christmas Tradition

For *Southern Living,* it wouldn't be the holidays without a showstopping white cake, which has graced the cover of our December issue for the past 25 years. This year's coconut confection is a nod to our very first white cake, with a choice of three fillings, and topped festive sleigh.

Coconut Cake with Coconut Cream Frosting

ACTIVE 30 MIN. - TOTAL 3 HOURS
SERVES 12

FILLINGS

Whipped Chocolate Ganache Filling, Cranberry Filling, or Lemon Curd Filling (recipes, page 310

CAKE LAYERS

Baking spray with flour
1 cup (8 oz.) salted butter, softened
2 cups granulated sugar
1 Tbsp. grated lemon zest (from 2 lemons) (optional)
1 tsp. vanilla extract
½ tsp. coconut extract
3 cups (about 12 oz.) bleached cake flour (such as Swans Down)
1 Tbsp. baking powder
½ tsp. kosher salt
1 cup whole milk
6 large egg whites

COCONUT CREAM FROSTING

1 cup (8 oz.) salted butter, softened
6 oz. cream cheese, softened
2 (16-oz.) pkg. powdered sugar
¼ cup cream of coconut (such as Coco López)
2 tsp. vanilla extract
¼ tsp. coconut extract

ADDITIONAL INGREDIENTS

3 cups unsweetened shredded coconut
1 Gingerbread Sleigh Cookie (recipe, page 311)
Rosemary sprigs
Fresh cranberries
Paper banner

1. Prepare one the Fillings. Be sure to allow sufficient time for chilling the Filling before proceeding with the Cake Layers.
2. Prepare the Cake Layers: Preheat oven to 325°F. Coat 3 (8-inch) round cake pans with baking spray; set aside. Beat butter with a stand mixer fitted with a paddle attachment on medium speed until creamy, about 1 minute. Gradually add sugar, beating until light and fluffy, 3 to 4 minutes. Add lemon zest (if using), vanilla, and coconut extract; beat just until combined, about 30 seconds.
3. Sift together cake flour, baking powder, and salt in a medium bowl. Add to butter mixture alternately with milk, beginning and ending with flour mixture, beating on low speed just until combined after each addition.
4. Beat egg whites with an electric mixer on high speed until stiff peaks form (don't overbeat or they will be dry), about 2 minutes. Fold about one-third of beaten egg whites into cake batter; fold in remaining egg whites in 2 additions. Spoon batter evenly into prepared cake pans (about 2⅓ cups batter per pan).
5. Bake cakes on middle rack in preheated oven until a wooden pick inserted in center of cakes comes out clean, 23 to 25 minutes. Let cool in pans on wire racks 10 minutes. Remove cakes from pans, and place directly on wire racks. Let cool completely, about 1 hour.
6. Meanwhile, prepare the Coconut Cream Frosting: Beat butter and cream cheese with an electric mixer on medium speed until creamy, about 2 minutes. Gradually add powdered sugar, beating on low speed until combined, about 1 minute. Increase mixer speed to medium-high; gradually add cream of coconut, vanilla, and coconut extract, beating until smooth and fluffy, about 2 minutes. Let stand, covered, at room temperature until ready to use or up to 1 hour.

7. Assemble the cake: Place 1 Cake Layer on a serving plate or a cake stand. Spoon 1 cup Coconut Cream Frosting into a zip-top plastic bag. Snip a ½-inch tip off 1 bag corner. Pipe a ring of frosting around Cake Layer just inside the top edge. Spread Cake Layer with half of desired filling (if using the Whipped Chocolate Ganache Filling, spread Cake Layer with 1 cup filling), spreading to edge of piped frosting. Repeat process once with 1 additional Cake Layer, Frosting, and Filling. Top with remaining Cake Layer. (If using Whipped Chocolate Ganache Filling, discard any remaining filling.) Spread cake top and sides with a thin layer of the remaining Frosting. Refrigerate, uncovered, 1 hour. Spread remaining Frosting over top and sides of cake.
8. Gently pat shredded coconut onto top and sides of cake; top with Gingerbread Sleigh Cookie. Arrange rosemary sprigs and cranberries inside Gingerbread Sleigh Cookie and around bottom edge of cake as desired. Add paper banner to top of Gingerbread Sleigh Cookie.

Choose a Filling

Coconut pairs well with chocolate, cranberry, or lemon.
Pick your favorite flavor, and prepare the filling a day before you plan to make
the cake so that it has time to chill completely.

Whipped Chocolate Ganache Filling

ACTIVE 10 MIN. - TOTAL 10 MIN.,
PLUS 2 HOURS CHILLING
MAKES ABOUT 2⅓ CUPS

- 2 (4-oz.) semisweet chocolate baking bars, chopped
- 1 cup heavy whipping cream
- 2 tsp. vanilla extract

1. Microwave chocolate and whipping cream in a medium-size microwavable bowl on HIGH until melted and smooth, 90 seconds to 2 minutes, stopping to stir every 30 seconds. Whisk in vanilla until smooth. Cover and chill until ganache is thickened and cake is ready to be assembled, at least 2 hours or up to 8 hours.
2. When ready to assemble cake, beat ganache with an electric mixer on medium speed until soft peaks form and ganache lightens in color, 20 to 30 seconds (do not overbeat). Use immediately.

Cranberry Filling

ACTIVE 20 MIN. - TOTAL 20 MIN.,
PLUS 8 HOURS CHILLING
MAKES 1½ CUPS

- 2½ cups fresh or frozen (unthawed) cranberries
- 1 cup granulated sugar
- 2 Tbsp. fresh lemon juice (from 1 lemon)
- 2 Tbsp. water
- 1 Tbsp. cornstarch

1. Stir together cranberries, sugar, lemon juice, water, and cornstarch in a small, heavy saucepan. Bring mixture to a boil over medium; boil, stirring constantly, until berries have popped and softened and mixture has thickened, 3 to 4 minutes.
2. Remove from heat. Pour mixture into a blender. Secure lid on blender, and remove center piece to allow steam to escape. Place a clean towel over opening. Process until smooth, about 1 minute. (Alternatively, process mixture in saucepan using an immersion blender.) Return mixture to saucepan; cook over medium, stirring constantly, until very thick and slightly reduced, 4 to 5 minutes.
3. Transfer mixture to a small heatproof bowl. Place a piece of plastic wrap directly on top of mixture (to prevent a film from forming). Chill until mixture is firm and cake is ready to be assembled, at least 8 hours or up to 3 days.

Lemon Curd Filling

ACTIVE 30 MIN. - TOTAL 30 MIN.,
PLUS 4 HOURS CHILLING
MAKES 1¾ CUPS

- 6 large egg yolks
- 1 cup granulated sugar
- 1 Tbsp. grated lemon zest plus ½ cup fresh juice (from 4 large lemons)
- 1 Tbsp. cornstarch
- ½ cup (4 oz.) cold salted butter, cut into ½-in. pieces

1. Whisk together egg yolks, sugar, lemon zest and juice, and cornstarch in a small, heavy saucepan. Cook over medium, stirring constantly with a wooden spoon, until mixture is thick and coats the back of spoon, 6 to 8 minutes. Remove from heat. Whisk in cold butter until melted and smooth.
2. Pour mixture through a fine mesh strainer into a medium bowl. Place bowl in a large bowl filled with ice water; let stand, stirring often, until mixture is cool, about 20 minutes. Remove medium bowl from ice bath, and place a piece of plastic wrap directly on lemon curd. Cover and chill until curd is firm and cake is ready to be assembled, at least 4 hours or up to 3 days.

Gingerbread Sleigh Cookies

ACTIVE 40 MIN. - TOTAL 6 HOURS, 40 MIN.,
INCLUDING 1 HOUR REFRIGERATING

MAKES ABOUT 7 ASSEMBLED SLEIGH COOKIES

COOKIES

- ½ cup (4 oz.) salted butter, softened
- ½ cup granulated sugar
- 2 Tbsp. hot water
- ¼ tsp. baking soda
- ½ cup molasses
- 2¾ cups (about 11¾ oz.) all-purpose flour, plus more for work surface
- 2¼ tsp. ground ginger
- ¾ tsp. ground cinnamon
- ⅛ tsp. table salt
- ⅛ tsp. ground allspice

ROYAL ICING

- 1 (16-oz.) pkg. powdered sugar
- 3 Tbsp. meringue powder
- 6 to 8 Tbsp. warm water

ADDITIONAL INGREDIENTS

Edible glue (such as Wilton Dab-N-Hold) (optional)

1. Prepare the Cookies: Beat butter and sugar with a heavy-duty stand mixer fitted with a paddle attachment on medium speed until fluffy, about 3 minutes. Set aside.

2. Stir together hot water and baking soda in a small bowl until dissolved; stir in molasses.

3. Stir together flour, ginger, cinnamon, salt, and allspice in a large bowl. Add flour mixture to butter mixture alternately with molasses mixture in 3 additions, beginning and ending with flour mixture, beating on medium speed until incorporated after each addition. Shape mixture into a flat disk; wrap disk in plastic wrap, and refrigerate 1 hour.

4. Preheat oven to 350°F. Line 2 baking sheets with parchment paper. Roll dough to ¼-inch thickness on a lightly floured work surface. Place sleigh cookie template on top of dough; using a small paring knife, cut out dough around edges of template. (If edges of Cookies are rough from the knife, use your fingers to warm up the dough and press to smooth the edges.) Reroll scraps as needed. You should have 14 sleighs and 14 rectangles total. Be sure to cut out 2 different sides for the sleigh, not the same side twice. Cut out on side of the template, then reverse/flip over the template to get the other side. Arrange Cookies 2 inches apart on prepared baking sheets. Flip half of the sleigh Cookies to face opposite direction.

5. Bake in preheated oven, in 2 batches, until Cookie edges are lightly browned, 12 to 15 minutes. Let cool on baking sheets 2 minutes. Transfer to wire racks, and let cool completely, about 30 minutes.

6. Prepare the Royal Icing: Beat powdered sugar, meringue powder, and 6 tablespoons of the warm water with an electric mixer on low speed until combined, about 1 minute. Increase speed to medium, and beat until well combined and smooth, about 2 minutes. Beat in up to remaining 2 tablespoons warm water, ¼ teaspoon at a time, until desired consistency is reached.

7. Spoon Royal Icing into a small zip-top plastic freezer bag with a small corner snipped off (or into a piping bag fitted with a small round tip). Pipe Royal Icing onto Cookies as desired. Cover remaining Royal Icing with plastic wrap. Let Cookies stand until Royal Icing is set, about 2 hours.

8. Using edible glue or remaining Royal Icing, assemble sleigh pieces together (pieces may need to be propped as they stand to dry). Let assembled sleigh Cookies stand until set, about 2 hours.

SLEIGH COOKIE
RECTANGLE
TEMPLATE

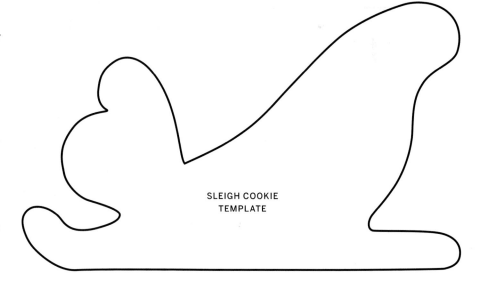

SLEIGH COOKIE
TEMPLATE

It's Tamale Time

At a *tamalada*, the cooking is as much fun as the eating

For many Southerners of Latin American heritage, Christmas means tamales: tender dumplings wrapped in leaves, like little presents. They are not particularly hard to prepare but rather involved, which makes them perfectly suited for communal cooking, especially during the holidays. These gatherings are known as tamaladas.

During my childhood, they were held at my grandmother Mita's estate, where hundreds of tamales were crafted under her direction. It was a party before the party, as there was so much camaraderie and joy in the crafting of these edible gifts.

Each one of us selected our place in an assembly line. Some of us cut,

washed, and prepped leaves; others whipped lard; some ground nixtamal corn into masa; while still others stirred bubbling sauces. Then we'd make another assembly line to shape, stuff, wrap, and tie tamales before they were steamed. It was a daylong production.

Tamale dough can be made of corn, rice, potatoes, plantains, or a mixture

TAMALE TROUBLESHOOTING
If your corn husks are too small to hold all of the dough, you have two options: Make the tamales smaller (you'll end up with a double batch), or overlap two corn husks (with their wide ends joined toward the middle) to hold the filling inside.

of root vegetables (malanga, sweet potatoes, ñame, or true white yams), depending on what country the cook is from. Some tamales are made only of dough that's often enhanced with cheese and herbs. Others are stuffed with fillings from savory (pork, turkey, chicken, beef, or seafood) to sweet (prunes, almonds, or pineapple) or a combination of both (like meat in spicy gravy with olives, capers, and raisins).

The wrappers vary, too, from dried or fresh corn husks to green tropical leaves from banana trees and the heart-shaped maxán, a plant that produces tropical flowers. You can wrap the dough into little rectangular packages tied with bows, into balls that are tied like candy wrappers, or like mine, which resemble British cardboard firecrackers.

I've taken over hosting tamaladas in my home in North Carolina, with help from my daughters, my friends, and our husbands. I prepare the sauces and dough, and cut the different wrappers. When my guests arrive, we assemble a few dozen as we talk. Some of the tamales are cooked for that evening's meal to enjoy with salads and Christmas cookies. Guests take home the rest to share with others—the perfect holiday gift, all wrapped up.

Chicken Tamales with Roasted Tomato and Dried Chile Sauce

ACTIVE 1 HOUR, 30 MIN. · TOTAL 4 HOURS
MAKES 25 TAMALES

- 1 lb. plum tomatoes (5 to 6 tomatoes)
- 1 large red bell pepper
- 2 large garlic cloves, unpeeled
- 1½ cups roughly chopped white onion (from 1 large onion)
- 3 pasilla negro chiles (dried chilaca chiles) or guajillo chiles, seeded and chopped
- ¼ cup vegetable oil or melted lard
- 2 Tbsp. kosher salt, divided
- 6 cups masa harina, plus more as needed
- 4 to 4½ cups chicken broth or water, warmed or at room temperature
- 1½ cups chilled lard or vegetable shortening

- 40 to 50 dried corn husks (from 2 [6-oz.] pkg.), soaked in warm water at least 30 minutes or up to 8 hours
- 1 lb. boneless, skinless chicken thighs, cut into 25 (2-inch) pieces
- 4 oz. queso fresco (fresh Mexican cheese) or Pecorino Romano, crumbled (about 1 cup)
- ½ cup finely chopped fresh flat-leaf parsley leaves and tender stems

1. Place tomatoes, bell pepper, and garlic in a dry cast-iron skillet, and cook over high, turning occasionally, until skins are charred and blackened, 4 to 5 minutes. Transfer charred vegetables to a bowl; peel garlic. (Skins will have blackened in spots, and garlic will be roasted within.) Working in batches if necessary, add charred vegetables, peeled garlic, onion, and dried chiles to a blender. Secure lid on blender; remove center piece to allow steam to escape. Place a clean towel over opening. Process until smooth, 30 to 45 seconds.

2. Heat vegetable oil in a large saucepan or stockpot over medium-high. Carefully pour sauce into hot oil (it will sizzle). Cook, stirring vigorously, until mixture stops splattering. Continue cooking and stirring 5 minutes. Reduce heat to low; simmer, stirring occasionally, until sauce begins to thicken, about 30 minutes. Stir in 1 tablespoon of the salt. Cool completely, about 30 minutes, and refrigerate until ready to use.

3. Whisk together masa harina and remaining 1 tablespoon salt in a large bowl. Gradually add 4 cups broth, kneading mixture with your hands until the dough comes together to form a ball. Gradually knead in up to ½ cup of broth, if necessary. The dough should be smooth and not sticky. If dough is still sticky, gradually work in more masa harina until dough is smooth.

4. Beat chilled lard in a large bowl with a stand mixer fitted with a paddle attachment on medium-high speed until fluffy, 30 seconds to 1 minute. With mixer running on medium speed, add dough in large pieces; beat until all dough has been incorporated. Continue beating until masa mixture has consistency of thick mashed potatoes and is no longer sticky, 3 to 4 minutes. Cover with plastic wrap; let stand 20 minutes.

5. Meanwhile, cut about 15 husks into 50 (½-inch-wide) strips. Set strips aside for tying tamales.

6. Gather 25 corn husks. Working with 1 husk at a time, place on a clean surface, and pat dry with a paper towel. Using an offset spatula, spread ⅓ cup of masa into a 3-inch square in middle of husk, leaving at least a 1½-inch border on all sides (the size of the husk will determine how much of a border you'll have). Place 1 piece of chicken and a heaping tablespoon of sauce in center of masa.

7. Roll 1 long side of husk over filling until filling is covered. Fold opposite side over husk, encasing filling completely. Twist ends of corn husk (like a candy wrapper), and tie ends with prepared corn husk strips. Repeat filling, rolling, and tying with 24 more corn husks, remaining masa and chicken, and about 1½ cups of the remaining sauce.

8. Fit a large stockpot with a steamer basket, and line bottom of basket with husks, completely covering bottom of basket (5 to 7 husks). Add 2 to 3 inches of water to stockpot. Place tamales flat in basket, stacking as necessary. Cover pot; bring water to a boil over high. Reduce heat to low. Steam tamales 45 minutes (replenishing water as needed). Remove from heat, and let tamales cool in pot 30 minutes.

9. To serve, remove ties, slide tamales from husks, and discard husks. Heat remaining sauce in a small saucepan over medium until hot, about 5 minutes. Place tamales on plates, ladle a bit of sauce over each serving, and sprinkle with cheese and parsley.

MAKE THEM AHEAD
After the tamales have been cooked and cooled, they can be frozen in their husks. To freeze: Place them in a single layer on a baking sheet, and freeze until solid. Transfer to a freezer-safe bag or container, and store in the freezer up to 4 months. To reheat frozen tamales, don't thaw them. Simply fit a large pot with a steamer basket, and fill the pot with 2 to 3 inches of water. Layer the tamales inside. Cover the pot, and bring the water to a boil over high heat. Reduce heat to a simmer, and steam the tamales until hot, about 30 minutes.

Pavlovas & Punch

Test kitchen pro and *Hey Y'all* host Ivy Odom is dreaming of a white Christmas.
Steal her no-snow-required planning tips

In many parts of the South, we don't know what it's like to have a white Christmas. Where I'm from, just two counties north of the Georgia–Florida line, the month of December is usually pretty warm. That's why I love this festively themed party. Decking the halls and donning apparel in a snowy scheme is a classic way to get everyone in the spirit. (And it's the one chance between Labor Day and Easter that we get to whip out a good white dress and still be fashionable.) My make-ahead vanilla Pavlovas can be a fun DIY dessert bar if you set them out with an assortment of toppings, like toasted coconut chips and sliced bananas. The Pavlovas' crackly crusts and marshmallowy centers pair well with my boozy Triple B Milk Punch. The drink gets its name from three ingredients that make up the cocktail: bourbon, brandy, and buttermilk. One cool and creamy sip will put you in a holiday mood, even if it's warm outside.

White Christmas Pavlovas

For perfectly round meringues, trace the outline of a 3½-inch cookie or biscuit cutter 6 times on 2 pieces of parchment paper. Place the parchment circle-side down on 2 baking sheets and use it as a guide for spooning the egg whites.

ACTIVE 25 MIN. · TOTAL 2 HOURS,
PLUS 3 HOURS STANDING
MAKES 12

- 1⅓ **cups granulated sugar**
- 1½ **Tbsp. cornstarch**
- 6 **large egg whites, at room temperature**
- ¼ **tsp. cream of tartar**
- ⅛ **tsp. salt**
- 1½ **tsp. vanilla extract, divided**
- 2 **cups cold heavy whipping cream**
- ⅔ **cup sour cream**
  Toppings: melted white chocolate, chopped toasted macadamia nuts, sliced banana, crumbled vanilla wafers, toasted coconut chips, sweetened flaked coconut, sliced almonds

1. Preheat oven to 225°F with racks in upper and lower third positions. Line 2 large baking sheets with parchment paper. Whisk together sugar and cornstarch in a bowl; set aside. Beat egg whites with an electric mixer fitted with a whisk attachment on medium-high speed for 1 minute. Add cream of tartar and salt; beat until combined, about 30 seconds. With mixer running on high speed, add sugar mixture 2 tablespoons at a time, beating just until glossy, stiff peaks form, and sugar is almost dissolved, about 2 minutes. (Do not overbeat.) Reduce speed to low; beat in ½ teaspoon of the vanilla.
2. Gently spoon about ⅓ cup egg white mixture onto prepared baking sheet in a 3½-inch circle. Repeat with remaining egg white mixture, creating 12 circles total on the 2 prepared baking sheets.
3. Bake in preheated oven until meringues have formed a crust, about 1½ hours, rotating baking sheets between top and bottom racks halfway through bake time.
4. Turn oven off. Let meringues stand in oven with door closed until completely cool with dry and shiny tops, at least 3 hours or up to 10 hours, depending on the humidity of your kitchen. (They should have crisp exteriors and chewy interiors.)
5. Meanwhile, chill bowl of a stand mixer and whisk attachment for 30 minutes. Pour cream into chilled bowl; beat with an electric mixer fitted with the chilled whisk attachment on medium-high speed until soft peaks form, 2 to 3 minutes. Add sour cream; beat until stiff peaks form, about 30 seconds. Beat in remaining 1 teaspoon vanilla until just combined.
6. Arrange meringues on a serving platter; top each with about ¼ cup whipped cream mixture. Garnish Pavlovas with toppings.

Triple B Milk Punch

This big-batch cocktail is made with bourbon and brandy, but you can use the same amount of one spirit if you prefer.

ACTIVE 5 MIN. · TOTAL 35 MIN.
SERVES 12

- 3 **cups cold whole milk**
- 1½ **cups (12 oz.) bourbon, chilled**
- 1½ **cups (12 oz.) brandy, chilled**
- 1½ **cups cold whole buttermilk**
- ¾ **cup honey**
- 1½ **tsp. vanilla extract**
- 4 **cinnamon sticks**
- 1 **medium-size orange, thinly sliced**
  Freshly grated nutmeg
  Ice

Whisk together milk, bourbon, brandy, buttermilk, honey, and vanilla in a half-gallon pitcher until combined. Chill at least 30 minutes or up to 1 week. Pour into a punch bowl; add cinnamon sticks and orange slices, and garnish with nutmeg. Serve over ice.

WHITE CHRISTMAS
PAVLOVAS

TRIPLE B MILK
PUNCH

COOKING SCHOOL

TIPS AND TRICKS FROM THE SOUTH'S MOST TRUSTED KITCHEN

Rule the Roast

Our best tips for prime rib, pork crown roast, and other impressive cuts of meat

CLEAN THE OVEN

Some recipes call for the meat to be cooked at a very high temperature (450°F or 500°F) at the beginning or end of the cooking process. If you're starting out with a hot oven, make sure that it is clean to prevent it from smoking up the kitchen.

SEASON WELL

The day before you plan to cook the roast, season it generously with salt and pepper and let it sit, uncovered, in the refrigerator overnight. That extra time allows the salt to permeate the meat and helps the surface dry out, which creates a nice crust.

LET IT REST

Do not transfer the meat directly from the refrigerator to the preheated oven—cold meat takes longer to heat up and cook. Instead, let the roast sit at room temperature for 30 minutes and up to two hours, depending on its size.

PULL IT EARLY

If you're cooking a roast, like prime rib, it will continue to cook once you remove it from the oven and let it rest. Use a meat thermometer, and remove the roast from the oven when it is 5 to 10 degrees shy of your desired temperature.

SUPERMARKET SMARTS

Budget Cuts, Big Flavor

Affordable alternatives to holiday favorites

IF YOU LIKE PRIME RIB, TRY:

Top Loin Roast

Also called a strip loin roast, this flavorful, well-marbled cut is where strip steaks come from.

IF YOU LIKE BEEF TENDERLOIN, TRY:

Eye of Round Roast

Similar in size and shape to a tenderloin, this lean cut of meat is tasty when roasted and thinly sliced.

IF YOU LIKE PORK CROWN ROAST, TRY:

Bone-In Pork Loin

It's half the size of a crown roast, but this rack of chops doesn't require as much fuss and is just as delicious.

"Always slice a roast against the grain. No matter the type of meat, if you cut across the fibers, it will be more tender."

—Pam Lolley, Test Kitchen Professional

Our Favorite Dessert Recipes

Saying that Southerners have a bit of a sweet tooth is like saying Bear Bryant coached a little football. Our sugar love is epic. And we're conflicted about it—not because we feel bad about it, but because we don't feel bad at all—and we know we probably should. It's our lack of guilt that we feel so guilty about. These recipes celebrate that sugar love with abandon, and with something for every season and taste—from a Lemon Coconut Cake perfect for spring celebrations to Buttermilk Peach Pudding at the height of summer to an autumnal Pumpkin-Spice Battenberg wrapped in marzipan. Tee up the holidays with a batch of Mrs. Claus' Dream Bars or a stunning Peppermint Ice Cream Cake.

CINNAMON ROULADE WITH ROASTED APPLE-CREAM CHEESE FILLING (PAGE 323)

RED VELVET CRACKLE SANDWICH COOKIES (PAGE 338)

Bread Puddings & Custards

Berry Bread Pudding

ACTIVE 20 MIN. - TOTAL 3 HOURS, 55 MIN., INCLUDING SAUCE
SERVES 6

- ½ (16-oz.) Italian bread loaf, cut into 1-inch pieces (about 6 cups)
- 3 large eggs
- 1¼ cups 2% reduced-fat milk
- 1 (12-oz.) can fat-free evaporated milk
- ¼ cup sugar
- ½ tsp. almond extract
- 6 Tbsp. seedless raspberry preserves
  Raspberry Sauce (recipe follows)

1. Place bread in 6 (8-oz.) oval-shaped cast-iron baking dishes coated with cooking spray.
2. Whisk together eggs, milk, sugar, and almond extract in a medium bowl; pour over bread in baking dishes (about ⅔ cup egg mixture each). Top each with 1 tablespoon preserves. Cover and chill 2 to 3 hours.
3. Preheat oven to 350°F. Remove baking dishes from refrigerator, and let stand 15 minutes. Bake 40 minutes or until tops are crisp and golden brown. Let stand 10 minutes. Serve with Raspberry Sauce.
Note: For a one-dish dessert, place bread in a lightly greased 11- x 7-inch baking dish. Proceed with recipe as directed in Step 2, spooning the 6 tablespoons raspberry preserves on the bread mixture. Bake at 350°F until top is crisp and golden brown, 45 to 50 minutes. Let stand 10 minutes. Serve with Raspberry Sauce.

Raspberry Sauce

ACTIVE 5 MIN. - TOTAL 35 MIN.
MAKES: ABOUT 1⅔ CUPS

- 1 (12-oz.) pkg. frozen unsweetened raspberries, thawed
- ⅔ cup sugar
- ¼ cup orange juice

Reserve 1 cup raspberries. Process remaining berries, sugar, and orange juice in a food processor until smooth. Pour raspberry mixture through a fine wire-mesh strainer into a bowl; discard pulp and seeds. Stir in 1 cup reserved raspberries. Cover and chill 30 minutes.

Blueberry Bread Pudding

ACTIVE 20 MIN. - TOTAL 9 HOURS, 20 MIN., INCLUDING CHILLING
SERVES 10 TO 12

- 1 (16-oz.) French bread loaf, cubed
- 1 (8-oz.) pkg. cream cheese, cut into pieces
- 3 cups fresh blueberries, divided
- 6 large eggs
- 4 cups milk
- ½ cup sugar
- ¼ cup butter or margarine, melted
- ¼ cup maple syrup
- 1 (10-oz.) jar blueberry preserves

1. Arrange half of bread cubes in a lightly greased 13- x 9-inch pan. Sprinkle evenly with cream cheese and 1 cup blueberries; top with remaining bread cubes.
2. Whisk together eggs, milk, sugar, butter, and maple syrup in a medium bowl; pour over bread mixture, pressing bread to absorb egg mixture. Cover and chill 8 hours.
3. Preheat oven to 350°F. Bake 30 minutes. Uncover and bake until lightly browned and set, about 30 minutes more. Let stand 5 minutes before serving.
4. Stir together remaining 2 cups blueberries and blueberry preserves in a saucepan over low heat until warm. Serve blueberry sauce over bread pudding.

Chocolate Bread Pudding with Whiskey Sauce

ACTIVE 25 MIN. - TOTAL 3 HOURS, 25 MIN., INCLUDING SAUCE
SERVES 8 TO 10

- ¼ cup unsalted butter
- 7 cups French bread cubes
- 2 cups whipping cream
- 1 cup milk
- 8 (1-oz.) bittersweet chocolate baking squares, chopped
- 5 egg yolks, lightly beaten
- ⅔ cup firmly packed light brown sugar
- 1 tsp. vanilla extract

  Whiskey Sauce (recipe follows)
  Chocolate shavings, for garnish (optional)

1. Melt butter in a large heavy skillet over medium. Add bread cubes, and cook, stirring constantly, 3 minutes or until golden. Transfer to a lightly greased 13- x 9-inch baking dish.
2. Bring whipping cream and milk to a boil over medium in skillet. Remove from heat, and whisk in chocolate until smooth. Whisk in egg yolks, brown sugar, and vanilla. Pour over bread cubes; let stand 30 minutes. Cover with foil; cut 6 small holes in foil to allow steam to escape.
3. Preheat oven to 325°F. Place baking dish in a roasting pan. Add hot water to pan to a depth of 1½ inches.
4. Bake in preheated oven until set, about 1 hour and 45 minutes. Remove baking dish from water. Cool 30 minutes on a wire rack. Serve warm with Whiskey Sauce. Garnish with chocolate shavings, if desired.

Whiskey Sauce

ACTIVE 5 MIN. - TOTAL 15 MIN.
MAKES 2¾ CUPS

- 1½ cups milk
- ½ cup butter or margarine
- 1 cup sugar
- 3 Tbsp. cornstarch
- ¼ cup water
- ½ cup bourbon

1. Cook milk, butter, and sugar in a heavy saucepan over low, stirring often, until butter melts and sugar dissolves.
2. Combine cornstarch and ¼ cup water, stirring until smooth. Add to butter mixture; stir in bourbon. Bring to a boil over medium, stirring constantly; boil, stirring constantly, 1 minute.

Buttermilk Peach Pudding

(Photo, page 321)

ACTIVE 15 MIN. - TOTAL 1 HOUR, 5 MIN.
SERVES 8 TO 10

- 1½ cups all-purpose flour
- 1 tsp. baking soda
- 1 tsp. baking powder
- 1 tsp. ground cinnamon
- ½ tsp. table salt
- ½ tsp. freshly grated nutmeg
- ½ tsp. ground ginger

3½ peaches, peeled and coarsely chopped (about 1½ lb.)
1 cup buttermilk
½ cup butter, softened
1½ cups sugar
3 large eggs
2 ripe peaches, peeled and sliced (about 1 lb.)
Vanilla ice cream

1. Preheat oven to 350°F. Sift together flour, baking soda, baking powder, cinnamon, salt, nutmeg, and ginger in a small bowl; sift again.
2. Process chopped peaches in a food processor or blender until smooth. Stir in buttermilk.
3. Beat butter and sugar at high speed with a heavy-duty electric stand mixer until fluffy. Add eggs, one at a time, beating until blended after each addition. Add peach puree; beat until well blended.
4. Layer sliced peaches in a greased 13- x 9-inch pan.
5. Fold flour mixture into butter mixture. Pour batter over sliced peaches in pan. Place pan in a large roasting pan; add boiling water to depth of 1 inch.
6. Bake in preheated oven until set, about 50 minutes. (Pudding will still be moist.) Serve warm or cold with ice cream.

Caramel Custard

ACTIVE 5 MIN. · TOTAL 4 HOURS, 15 MIN.
MAKES 1 CUSTARD

½ cup sugar
2 egg yolks
1 large egg
1 (14-oz.) can fat-free sweetened condensed milk
1 (12-oz.) can evaporated fat-free milk
3 oz. ⅓-less-fat cream cheese, softened
1 Tbsp. vanilla extract

1. Preheat oven to 350°F. Cook ½ cup sugar in an 8-inch round cake pan (with 2-inch sides) over medium, shaking pan occasionally, until sugar melts and turns light golden brown, about 5 minutes. Remove pan from heat, and let stand 5 minutes. (Sugar will harden.)
2. Process 2 egg yolks, whole egg, condensed milk, evaporated milk, cream cheese, and vanilla in a blender until smooth. Pour mixture over caramelized sugar in pan. Cover with aluminum foil.

3. Place cake pan in a broiler pan. Add hot water (150°F) to pan to a depth of ⅔ inch.
4. Bake in preheated oven until a knife inserted in center comes out clean, about 1 hour. Remove cake pan from water; cool completely on a wire rack. Cover and chill at least 3 hours.
5. Run a knife around edge of pan to loosen; invert onto a serving plate.
Banana-Caramel Custard: Prepare recipe as directed, adding 1 medium ripe banana to egg yolk mixture in blender.

Jasmine-Buttermilk-Panna Cotta with Berry Sauce

ACTIVE 15 MIN. · TOTAL 1 HOUR, 10 MIN., INCLUDING SAUCE, PLUS 1 DAY FOR CHILLING
SERVES 8

1 tsp. unflavored gelatin
1 Tbsp. cold water
2 cups heavy cream
½ cup sugar
1 (3-inch) orange peel strip, white part removed
3 jasmine tea bags
1 vanilla bean
2 cups whole buttermilk
⅛ tsp. table salt
Berry Sauce (recipe follows)

1. Sprinkle gelatin over cold water; let stand 10 minutes.
2. Meanwhile, combine cream, sugar, orange strip, and tea bags in a medium saucepan over medium. Split vanilla bean; scrape seeds into cream mixture. Add bean to cream mixture. Cook over medium, stirring constantly, just until mixture begins to boil, about 5 minutes.
3. Remove from heat; stir in gelatin mixture until smooth. Let stand 5 minutes.
4. Discard tea bags and vanilla bean. Stir in buttermilk and salt. Strain into a heatproof glass measuring cup. Divide among 8 (6-oz.) glasses. Cover and chill 24 hours. Serve with Berry Sauce.

Berry Sauce

ACTIVE 10 MIN. · TOTAL 40 MIN.
MAKES 2 CUPS

6 oz. fresh raspberries
¾ cup coarsely chopped fresh strawberries
2 Tbsp. sugar
1½ tsp. fresh lemon juice
¼ tsp. vanilla bean paste

Coarsely mash ¾ cup raspberries, the strawberries, sugar, lemon juice, and vanilla bean paste in a bowl; let stand 30 minutes. Stir in remaining raspberries just before serving.

White Chocolate-Cranberry Crème Brûlée

ACTIVE 30 MIN. · TOTAL 9 HOURS, 20 MIN., INCLUDING CHILLING
SERVES 6

2 cups whipping cream
4 oz. white chocolate
1 tsp. vanilla extract
5 egg yolks
½ cup sugar, divided
½ (14-oz.) can whole-berry cranberry sauce
Ice cubes
Fresh cranberries, for garnish (optional)

1. Preheat oven to 300°F. Combine ½ cup cream and chocolate in a heavy saucepan; cook over low, stirring constantly, 2 to 3 minutes or until chocolate is melted. Remove from heat. Stir in vanilla and remaining 1½ cups cream.
2. Whisk together egg yolks and ¼ cup sugar until sugar is dissolved and mixture is thick and pale yellow. Add cream mixture, whisking until well blended. Pour mixture through a fine wire-mesh strainer into a large bowl.
3. Spoon 1½ Tbsp. cranberry sauce into each of 6 (4-oz.) ramekins. Pour cream mixture into ramekins; place ramekins in a large roasting pan. Add water to pan to depth of ½ inch.
4. Bake in preheated oven until edges are set, 45 to 55 minutes. Cool custards in pan on a wire rack 25 minutes. Remove ramekins from water; cover and chill 8 hours.
5. Preheat broiler with oven rack 5 inches from heat. Sprinkle remaining sugar over ramekins. Fill a large roasting pan or 15- x 10-inch jelly-roll pan with ice;* arrange ramekins in pan.
6. Broil 3 to 5 minutes or until sugar is melted and caramelized. Let stand 5 minutes. Garnish, if desired.
*Test Kitchen Tip: Filling the roasting pan with ice before broiling keeps the custards cool while caramelizing the tops.

Real Banana Pudding

(Photo, right)

ACTIVE 25 MIN. - TOTAL 1 HOUR.
SERVES 8 TO 10

- ½ cup sugar
- 2 Tbsp. cornstarch
- ¼ tsp. table salt
- 2¼ cups milk
- 4 large eggs, separated
- 2 Tbsp. unsalted butter
- 1 tsp. vanilla extract
- 3⅓ cups vanilla wafers
- 4 ripe bananas, cut into ⅓-inch-thick slices
- 3 Tbsp. sugar

1. Preheat oven to 375°F. Whisk together sugar, cornstarch, and salt in a small bowl. Whisk together sugar mixture, milk, and 4 egg yolks in a medium heavy saucepan until well blended. Cook over medium, stirring constantly, until thickened, 6 to 8 minutes. Remove from heat; stir in butter and vanilla.
2. Layer half of vanilla wafers in an 8-inch square baking dish. Top with half of banana slices and half of pudding. Repeat procedure with remaining wafers, banana slices, and pudding.
3. Beat egg whites in a medium bowl with an electric mixer on high speed until foamy. Gradually add 3 tablespoons sugar, beating until sugar dissolves and stiff peaks form. Spread meringue over pudding, sealing to edge of dish.
4. Bake in preheated oven until golden, 7 to 10 minutes. Let cool 30 minutes. Serve warm, or chill an additional hour, and serve cold.

Red Velvet Soufflés with Whipped Sour Cream

(Photo, right)

ACTIVE 20 MIN. - TOTAL 50 MIN., INCLUDING WHIPPED SOUR CREAM
SERVES 6

- 1 Tbsp. butter
- 3 Tbsp. granulated sugar
- 1 (4-oz.) bittersweet chocolate baking bar, chopped
- 5 large eggs, separated
- ⅓ cup granulated sugar
- 3 Tbsp. milk
- 1 Tbsp. red liquid food coloring
- 1 tsp. vanilla extract
  Pinch of salt
- 2 Tbsp. granulated sugar
  Powdered sugar
  Whipped Sour Cream
  (recipe follows)

1. Preheat oven to 350°F. Grease bottom and sides of 6 (8-oz.) ramekins with butter. Lightly coat with 3 tablespoons sugar, shaking out excess. Place on a baking sheet.
2. Microwave chocolate in a large microwaveable bowl on HIGH until melted, 1 minute to 1 minute and 15 seconds, stirring at 30-second intervals. Stir in 4 egg yolks, ⅓ cup sugar, milk, food coloring, and vanilla. (Discard remaining egg yolk.)
3. Beat 5 egg whites and salt with a stand mixer fitted with a whisk attachment on high speed until foamy. Gradually add 2 Tbsp. sugar, beating until stiff peaks form. Fold egg white mixture into chocolate mixture, one-third at a time. Spoon into prepared ramekins. Run tip of thumb around edges of ramekins, wiping clean and creating a shallow indentation around edges of mixture. (This will help the soufflés rise.)
4. Bake in preheated oven until soufflés rise and are set, 20 to 24 minutes. (A long wooden pick inserted in centers will have a few moist crumbs.) Dust with powdered sugar; serve immediately with Whipped Sour Cream.

Whipped Sour Cream

ACTIVE 5 MIN. - TOTAL 5 MIN.
MAKES ABOUT 2 CUPS

- ¾ cup whipping cream
- ½ cup sour cream
- 2 Tbsp. sugar

Beat together all ingredients at medium-high speed with a heavy-duty electric stand mixer 45 seconds or just until lightly whipped and pourable. Use immediately.

Cakes

Layered Carrot Cake

(Photo, right)

ACTIVE 30 MIN. - TOTAL 2 HOURS
SERVES 16

CARROT CAKE BATTER
- 2 cups all-purpose flour
- ¾ cup granulated sugar
- 2 tsp. baking soda
- 1 tsp. ground cinnamon
- 1 tsp. salt
- 1 (8-oz.) can crushed pineapple in juice, drained
- ¼ cup vegetable oil
- 2 large eggs
- 2 egg whites
- 1 Tbsp. vanilla extract
- 3 cups grated carrots

CREAM CHEESE FROSTING
- ½ (8-oz.) pkg. ⅓-less-fat cream cheese
- 2 Tbsp. butter, softened
- 1 tsp. vanilla extract
- 3 cups powdered sugar
- 1 to 2 tsp. fat-free milk (optional)

1. Prepare Carrot Cake Batter: Preheat oven to 350°F. Combine flour, sugar, baking soda, cinnamon, and salt in a large bowl; make a well in center of mixture. Whisk together pineapple, oil, whole eggs and whites, and vanilla; add pineapple mixture to flour mixture, stirring just until dry ingredients are moistened. Fold in carrots. Pour Batter into 2 (8-inch) round cake pans coated with cooking spray.
2. Bake in preheated oven until a wooden pick inserted in center comes out clean, 22 to 25 minutes. Cool in pans on a wire rack 10 minutes. Remove from pans to a wire rack; cool completely, about 1 hour.
3. Prepare Cream Cheese Frosting: Beat cream cheese, butter, and vanilla in a large bowl with an electric mixer on medium speed until smooth. Gradually add powdered sugar to butter mixture; beat at low speed just until blended (do not overbeat). Beat in up to 2 teaspoons milk for desired consistency.
4. Place 1 Cake Layer on a serving plate; spread with ⅔ cup Frosting, and top with remaining Cake Layer. Spread remaining Frosting over top and sides of cake.

CLOCKWISE FROM TOP LEFT:

- BUTTERMILK PEACH PUDDING (PAGE 318)

- REAL BANANA PUDDING (LEFT)

- RED VELVET SOUFFLÉS WITH WHIPPED SOUR CREAM (LEFT)

- LAYERED CARROT CAKE (LEFT)

- RED VELVET CHEESECAKE-VANILLA CAKE WITH CREAM CHEESE FROSTING (PAGE 322)

- APPLE-SPICE BUNDT CAKE WITH CARAMEL FROSTING (PAGE 322)

- PRALINE LAYER CAKE (PAGE 323)

- PUMPKIN-SPICE BATTENBERG (PAGE 324)

Red Velvet Cheesecake-Vanilla Cake with Cream Cheese Frosting

(Photo, page 321)

ACTIVE 1 HOUR, 6 MIN. · TOTAL 13 HOURS, 24 MIN., INCLUDING 8 HOURS CHILLING

MAKES 1 CAKE

CHEESECAKE LAYERS

- 4½ (8-oz.) pkg. cream cheese, softened
- 2¼ cups granulated sugar
- 6 large eggs, lightly beaten
- 1½ cups sour cream
- ¾ cup whole buttermilk
- 4½ Tbsp. unsweetened cocoa
- 2 (1-oz.) bottles red liquid food coloring
- 1 Tbsp. vanilla extract
- 1½ tsp. distilled white vinegar

VANILLA CAKE LAYER

- ½ cup (4 oz.) salted butter, softened
- 1 cup granulated sugar
- 1½ cups bleached cake flour
- 2 tsp. baking powder
- ¼ tsp. salt
- ⅔ cup whole milk
- 1½ tsp. vanilla extract
- 3 large egg whites
- Shortening, for greasing pan

CREAM CHEESE FROSTING

- 2 (8-oz.) pkg. cream cheese, softened
- ½ cup salted butter, softened
- 1 (32-oz.) pkg. powdered sugar
- 2 tsp. vanilla extract

1. Prepare the Cheesecake Layers: Preheat oven to 325°F. Line bottom and sides of 2 (9-inch) round pans with aluminum foil, allowing 2 to 3 inches to extend over sides; lightly grease foil. Beat cream cheese and granulated sugar in a large bowl with an electric mixer on medium speed just until completely combined, about 1 minute. Add eggs, sour cream, buttermilk, cocoa, red food coloring, vanilla, and vinegar, beating on low speed just until fully combined, about 4 minutes. (Do not overbeat.) Pour batter into prepared pans.

2. Bake in preheated oven 10 minutes; reduce heat to 300°F, and bake until center is slightly jiggly, about 1 hour and 5 minutes. Turn oven off. Let layers stand in oven 30 minutes. Remove from oven; cool in pans on wire racks 1 hour. Cover and chill 8 hours.

3. Prepare the Vanilla Cake Layer: Preheat oven to 325°F. Beat butter with a stand mixer on medium speed until creamy; gradually add granulated sugar, beating until light and fluffy, about 5 minutes.

4. Stir together flour, baking powder, and salt in a bowl; add to butter mixture alternately with milk, beginning and ending with flour mixture. Beat on low speed just until blended after each addition. Stir in vanilla.

5. Beat egg whites in a clean bowl with an electric mixer on high speed until stiff peaks form; fold about one-third of egg whites into batter. Gradually fold in remaining egg whites. Pour batter into 1 greased (with shortening) and floured 9-inch round cake pan.

6. Bake in preheated oven until a wooden pick inserted in center comes out clean, 33 to 36 minutes. Cool in pan on a wire rack 10 minutes. Remove from pan to wire rack; cool completely, about 30 minutes.

7. Prepare the Cream Cheese Frosting: Beat cream cheese and butter in a bowl with an electric mixer on medium speed until creamy, about 5 minutes. Gradually add powdered sugar, beating at low speed until blended after each addition; stir in vanilla. Increase speed to medium, and beat until light and fluffy.

8. Assemble Cake: Lift Cheesecake Layers from pans, using foil sides as handles. Place 1 Cheesecake Layer, bottom-side up, on a cake plate. Place Vanilla Cake Layer on Cheesecake Layer (this layer will be slightly taller than the Cheesecake Layers; trim the top of the layer, if desired). Top Vanilla Cake Layer with the remaining Cheesecake Layer, bottom-side up. Spread a thin layer of Cream Cheese Frosting over top and sides of cake to seal in crumbs. Chill cake 20 minutes. Spread remaining Cream Cheese Frosting over top and sides of cake.

Apple-Spice Bundt Cake with Caramel Frosting

(Photo, page 321)

ACTIVE 25 MIN. · TOTAL 3 HOURS, 45 MIN.

SERVES 12

CREAM CHEESE FILLING

- 1 (8-oz.) pkg. cream cheese, softened
- ¼ cup granulated sugar
- 1 large egg
- 2 Tbsp. all-purpose flour
- 1 tsp. vanilla extract

APPLE-SPICE BATTER

- 1 cup packed light brown sugar
- 1 cup vegetable oil
- ½ cup granulated sugar
- 3 large eggs
- 2 tsp. vanilla extract
- 2 tsp. baking powder
- 2 tsp. pumpkin pie spice
- 1½ tsp. ground cardamom
- 1 tsp. kosher salt
- ½ tsp. baking soda
- ½ tsp. ground coriander
- 3 cups all-purpose flour
- 3 large Granny Smith apples (about 1½ lb.), peeled and grated
- Caramel Frosting (recipe follows)
- ⅔ cup roughly chopped toasted pecans

1. Prepare the Filling: Preheat oven to 350°F. Beat cream cheese, sugar, egg, flour, and vanilla in a bowl with an electric mixer on medium speed until smooth.

2. Prepare the Apple-Spice Batter: Beat brown sugar, oil, and granulated sugar with a stand mixer on medium speed until well blended. Add 3 eggs, 1 at a time, beating well after each addition. Stir in vanilla. Whisk together baking powder, pumpkin pie spice, cardamom, salt, baking soda, coriander, and flour in a medium bowl. Gradually add to brown sugar mixture, beating on low speed just until blended. Add apples, and beat on low speed just until combined.

3. Spoon half of the Batter into a greased and floured 14-cup Bundt pan. Spoon Filling over the apple mixture, leaving a 1-inch border around edge of pan. Swirl filling through Batter using a knife. Spoon remaining Batter over Filling.

4. Bake in preheated oven until a long wooden pick inserted in center comes out clean, 50 minutes to 1 hour. Cool in pan on a wire rack 20 minutes; remove from pan to wire rack, and cool completely (about 2 hours). Spoon Caramel Frosting over cooled cake; sprinkle with pecans.

Caramel Frosting

ACTIVE 10 MIN. · TOTAL 10 MIN.

MAKES ABOUT 1 CUP

- ½ cup packed light brown sugar
- ¼ cup heavy cream
- ¼ cup salted butter
- 1 tsp. vanilla extract
- 1¼ cups (about 5 oz.) powdered sugar, sifted

1. Bring brown sugar, cream, and butter to a boil in a 2-quart heavy saucepan over medium, whisking constantly. Boil, whisking constantly, 1 minute.

2. Remove pan from heat; stir in vanilla. Gradually whisk in powdered sugar until smooth. Gently stir until mixture begins to cool and thicken, 4 to 5 minutes. Use immediately.

Cinnamon Roulade with Roasted Apple-Cream Cheese Filling

(Photo, page 317)

ACTIVE 30 MIN. - TOTAL 1 HOUR, 50 MIN.
SERVES 10

APPLE-CREAM CHEESE FILLING

- 2 large Fuji apples, peeled and cut into ½-inch cubes (about 1 lb.)
- 1 Tbsp. granulated sugar
- 2 (8-oz.) pkg. cream cheese, softened
- 3 Tbsp. salted butter, softened
- 1 tsp. vanilla extract
- ⅛ tsp. table salt
- 1½ cups (about 6 oz.) powdered sugar

CAKE

- 4 large eggs, separated
- ¾ cup granulated sugar, divided
- 1 tsp. vanilla extract
- ¾ cup bleached cake flour
- 2 tsp. ground cinnamon
- ¾ tsp. baking powder
- ¼ tsp. table salt
- 6 Tbsp. powdered sugar, divided

1. Prepare the Apple-Cream Cheese Filling: Preheat oven to 400°F. Place apples and granulated sugar in a bowl; toss well to coat. Spread apples in a single layer on a baking sheet coated with cooking spray. Bake until tender and well browned, about 20 minutes, stirring after 10 minutes. Remove apples from pan, and cool completely.

2. Meanwhile, beat cream cheese, butter, vanilla, and salt in a large bowl with an electric mixer on medium speed until smooth, about 1 minute. Add powdered sugar; beat until smooth, about 1 minute. Fold in roasted apples. Refrigerate until ready to use.

3. Prepare the Cake: Preheat oven to 400°F. Coat a 17- x 12-inch rimmed baking sheet with cooking spray; line with parchment paper. Coat parchment with cooking spray.

4. Beat egg yolks and ½ cup granulated sugar at high speed until thick and pale, about 5 minutes. Beat in vanilla.

5. Using clean, dry beaters, beat egg whites in a separate bowl at medium speed until foamy. Increase speed to high, and beat until soft peaks form. Add remaining ¼ cup granulated sugar, 1 tablespoon at a time, beating at high speed until medium peaks form. Stir one-fourth of egg white mixture into egg yolk mixture; gently fold in remaining three-fourths egg white mixture.

6. Sift together cake flour, cinnamon, baking powder, and salt in a small bowl. Sift cake flour mixture over egg mixture, ¼ cup at a time, folding in until blended after each addition. Spread batter in prepared baking sheet.

7. Bake in preheated oven until puffed and lightly browned on top, 8 to 10 minutes. Cool 5 minutes. Sprinkle 4 tablespoons powdered sugar over top of cake. Invert cake onto a parchment paper-lined surface. Peel off top layer of parchment paper from cake. Starting at 1 short side, roll cake and bottom parchment together. Transfer to a wire rack, and cool completely, about 30 minutes.

8. Unroll Cake onto a flat surface. Spread Apple-Cream Cheese Filling over top, leaving a 1-inch border on all sides. Starting at 1 short side and using parchment paper as a guide, roll up Cake in jelly-roll fashion. Place Cake on a platter, seam-side down. Sprinkle top and sides with remaining 2 tablespoons powdered sugar. Serve immediately.

Fudge Cake

ACTIVE 15 MIN. - TOTAL 2 HOURS, 5 MIN.
SERVES 16

- 1 cup unsalted butter
- 4 (1-oz.) squares semisweet baking chocolate, finely chopped
- 1¾ cups granulated sugar
- 4 large eggs
- 1 cup all-purpose flour, sifted
  Dash of kosher salt
- 1 cup chopped toasted pecans
- 1 tsp. vanilla extract
  Powdered sugar

1. Preheat oven to 300°F. Place butter and chocolate in a large microwaveable bowl. Microwave on HIGH until completely melted, about 1 minute, stirring every 20 seconds. Add granulated sugar, and stir until well combined. Cool 10 minutes. Add eggs, 1 at a time, and stir until blended after each addition. Fold in all-purpose flour and salt. Stir in chopped toasted pecans and vanilla extract.

2. Coat a 9-inch square pan with cooking spray. Line bottom and sides of pan with parchment paper, allowing 4 to 5 inches to extend over sides. Coat parchment paper with cooking spray. Pour cake mixture into prepared pan.

3. Bake in preheated oven until a wooden pick inserted in center comes out clean, 45 to 50 minutes. Cool in pan on a wire rack 30 minutes. Lift cake from pan, using parchment paper sides as handles, and cool completely, about 30 minutes. Cut into squares, and dust with powdered sugar before serving.

Praline Layer Cake

(Photo, page 321)

ACTIVE 1 HOUR, 10 MIN. - TOTAL 2 HOURS, 55 MIN.
SERVES 10

CANDIED PECANS

- 2 Tbsp. light brown sugar
- 1 Tbsp. granulated sugar
- ¼ tsp. table salt
- 1 large egg white
- 2 cups pecan halves

CAKE

- 3 cups (about 12¾ oz.) all-purpose flour
- 1 Tbsp. baking powder
- ¾ tsp. table salt
- 2 cups granulated sugar
- 1 cup (8 oz.) unsalted butter, softened
- 3 large eggs
- 2 large egg yolks
- 1¼ cups whole milk
- 1 Tbsp. pecan liqueur
- 1 tsp. vanilla extract

FILLING

- ¾ cup packed dark brown sugar
- 6 Tbsp. (3 oz.) unsalted butter
- ¼ cup heavy cream
- 1½ cups (about 6 oz.) powdered sugar
- ¼ tsp. vanilla extract
- ½ cup finely chopped toasted pecans

Recipe continued on page 324

Recipe continued from page 323

BUTTERCREAM

- 1   cup packed light brown sugar
- 1   cup whole milk
- ½   cup (about 2⅛ oz.) all-purpose flour
- ¼   tsp. table salt
- 1   cup (8 oz.) unsalted butter, softened
- 1½ tsp. vanilla extract

1. Prepare the Candied Pecans: Preheat oven to 300°F. Whisk together 2 tablespoons light brown sugar, 1 tablespoon granulated sugar, ¼ teaspoon salt, and 1 egg white in a medium bowl until foamy. Add pecan halves; toss well to coat. Spread pecan halves in a single layer on a baking sheet lined with parchment paper. Bake until browned, 25 to 28 minutes, stirring after 15 minutes. Cool completely, about 30 minutes. (Pecans will become crisp when cool.)

2. Prepare the Cake: Increase oven temperature to 350°F. Whisk together 3 cups flour, 1 tablespoon baking powder, and ¾ teaspoon salt in a bowl. Beat 2 cups granulated sugar and 1 cup butter in a large bowl of a stand mixer at medium speed until light and fluffy, about 4 minutes. Add eggs and egg yolks, 1 at a time, beating well after each addition. Add flour mixture to butter mixture alternately with milk, in 5 additions, beginning and ending with flour mixture. Beat at low speed after each addition. Beat in pecan liqueur and 1 teaspoon vanilla. Divide batter evenly between 2 (9-inch) greased and floured round cake pans.

3. Bake in preheated oven until a wooden pick inserted in the center comes out clean, 28 to 30 minutes. Cool in pans on a wire rack 10 minutes. Remove cakes from pans; cool completely on wire rack, about 30 minutes.

4. Prepare the Filling: Combine ¾ cup dark brown sugar, 6 tablespoons butter, and ¼ cup heavy cream in a small saucepan over medium-low, and cook, stirring occasionally, until butter melts; bring to a boil. Cook, stirring constantly, 1 minute. Remove pan from heat; add powdered sugar and ¼ teaspoon vanilla. Beat at low speed until mixture thickens to spreading consistency, about 1 minute. Stir in chopped toasted pecans.

5. Prepare the Buttercream: Whisk together 1 cup light brown sugar, 1 cup milk, ½ cup flour, and ¼ teaspoon salt in a small saucepan until smooth. Place pan over medium-high, and cook, whisking constantly, until mixture is very thick and bubbly, 4 to 5 minutes. Spoon mixture into a bowl; place bowl in freezer, uncovered, until mixture is cold, about 20 minutes, stirring every 5 minutes.

6. Beat 1 cup butter in a medium bowl with an electric mixer on medium speed, using whisk attachment, until creamy and smooth, about 2 minutes. Add cold brown sugar mixture, 1 tablespoon at a time, beating well after each addition. Add 1½ teaspoons vanilla, and beat at high speed until light and fluffy, about 5 minutes.

7. Place 1 Cake Layer on a serving plate; spread Filling evenly over top, leaving a ½-inch border. Place remaining Cake Layer on top, pressing lightly. Spread Buttercream on top and sides of cake. Arrange Candied Pecans over top.

Pumpkin-Spice Battenberg

(Photo, page 321)

A Battenberg cake has two flavors of sponge cake with a layer of jam wrapped up in a thin layer of marzipan, like a present. Coat your pan with cooking spray because it will keep the parchment paper divider in place for the pretty pumpkin and vanilla layers.

ACTIVE 30 MIN. · TOTAL 2 HOURS, 10 MIN.
SERVES 10

- ⅔   cup (about 5¼ oz.) salted butter, softened
- ⅔   cup granulated sugar
- 1   tsp. vanilla extract
- 2   large eggs
- 1   large egg yolk
- 1¾ cups (about 7½ oz.) all-purpose flour
- ½   tsp. baking powder
- ½   tsp. table salt
- ¼   cup canned pumpkin
- 1   tsp. ground pumpkin pie spice
- 3   Tbsp. apricot jam
- 1   (7-oz.) pkg. marzipan
- 3   Tbsp. powdered sugar, sifted

1. Preheat oven to 325°F. Coat an 8-inch square baking pan with cooking spray. Cut a 25- x 8-inch piece of parchment paper. Fold parchment rectangle in half (short end to short end), pressing firmly on folded end to make a crease. Fold creased end over about 3 inches, pressing firmly to make another crease in parchment paper. Unfold entire piece, and turn over. Pinch and pick up middle crease, creating a 3-inch-tall divider in middle of rectangle.

Place in greased pan, pressing paper onto bottom of pan to fit as tightly as possible, and making sure divider is in the middle. Allow excess paper to extend over sides to use as handles. Coat top of parchment paper with cooking spray.

2. Beat butter, granulated sugar, and vanilla in a large bowl with an electric mixer on medium speed until well combined, about 1 minute. Beat in eggs and egg yolk. Add flour, baking powder, and salt to egg mixture; beat at medium speed until smooth, about 2 minutes. Remove 1¼ cups batter to another bowl, and stir in canned pumpkin and pumpkin pie spice. Spoon plain batter into 1 side of the parchment paper divider in prepared pan; spread until smooth. Spoon pumpkin batter into the empty side of the parchment paper divider of the prepared pan; spread until smooth.

3. Bake in preheated oven until a wooden pick inserted in center comes out clean, 30 to 33 minutes. Cool in pan 10 minutes. Lift cakes from pan, using paper sides as handles, and place on wire rack. Cool completely, about 30 minutes.

4. Remove cakes from parchment paper; trim the edges and tops of both cakes, as needed. Cut each loaf in half lengthwise, creating 4 equal strips.

5. Place jam in a microwaveable bowl; microwave on HIGH just until warm, about 30 seconds. Spread jam on tops and sides of cake strips. Gently press 1 strip of each color together at long sides; top with remaining 2 strips, alternately stacking to create a checkerboard pattern.

6. Roll marzipan on a surface sprinkled with sifted powdered sugar into a 12- x 8-inch rectangle. Place cake loaf, jam-side down, in center of marzipan rectangle with the short ends of loaf facing the long sides of rectangle. Brush remaining 3 sides of cake with jam. Wrap marzipan around cake loaf, and gently press to adhere. Trim ends and where seam meets. Place cake loaf on platter, seam-side down. Brush surface of cake lightly to remove excess powdered sugar. Lightly score top of cake in a diamond pattern with the edge of a sharp knife.

Caramel Cake

ACTIVE 10 MIN. · TOTAL 20 MIN., INCLUDING CARAMEL FILLING
MAKES 1 (2-LAYER) CAKE

- 1   cup sour cream
- ¼   cup milk
- 1   cup butter, softened

2 cups sugar
  4 large eggs
2¾ cups all-purpose flour
  2 tsp. baking powder
  ½ tsp. salt
  1 tsp. vanilla extract
  1 tsp. rum extract
    Caramel Frosting (recipe follows)

1. Preheat oven to 350°F. Combine sour cream and milk in a small bowl; set aside.
2. Cream 1 cup butter in a large bowl with an electric mixer on medium speed; gradually add 2 cups sugar, beating well. Add 4 large eggs, 1 at a time, beating well after each addition.
3. Combine flour, baking powder, and salt; add to creamed mixture alternately with sour cream mixture, beginning and ending with flour mixture. Mix after each addition. Stir in vanilla and rum extracts. Pour batter into 2 greased and floured 9-inch round cake pans. Bake in preheated oven until a wooden pick inserted in center comes out clean, 30 to 35 minutes.
4. Cool in pans 10 minutes; remove from pans, and cool on wire racks until completely cool.
5. Spread Caramel Frosting between layers and on top and sides of cake.

Caramel Frosting

ACTIVE 10 MIN. · TOTAL 10 MIN.
MAKES ENOUGH TO FROST 1 (2-LAYER) CAKE

  3 cups sugar, divided
  1 Tbsp. all-purpose flour
  1 cup milk
  ¾ cup butter
  1 tsp. vanilla extract

1. Sprinkle ½ cup sugar in a shallow, heavy 3½-qt. Dutch oven; place over medium. Cook, stirring constantly, until sugar melts (sugar will clump) and syrup is light golden brown. Remove from heat.
2. Combine remaining 2½ cups sugar and flour in a large saucepan, stirring well; add milk, and bring to a boil, stirring constantly.
3. Gradually pour one-fourth of hot mixture into caramelized sugar, stirring constantly; add remaining hot mixture (mixture will have lumps, but continue stirring until smooth).
4. Return to heat. Cover and cook over low heat 2 minutes. Uncover and cook, without stirring, over medium until a candy thermometer registers 238°F. Add

butter, stirring until blended. Remove from heat, and cool, without stirring, until temperature drops to 110°F, about 1 hour.
5. Add vanilla, and beat mixture with a wooden spoon or with an electric mixer on medium speed until frosting reaches spreading consistency.

Lemon-Coconut Cake

(Photo, page 330)

ACTIVE 25 MIN. · TOTAL 50 MIN.
SERVES 12

  1 cup butter, softened
  2 cups sugar
  4 large eggs, separated
  3 cups all-purpose flour
  1 Tbsp. baking powder
  1 cup milk
  1 tsp. vanilla extract
    Lemon Filling (recipe follows)
    3-Cup Cream Cheese Frosting
      (recipe follows)
  2 cups sweetened flaked coconut
    Fresh rosemary sprigs, gumdrops,
      for garnish (optional)

1. Preheat oven to 350°F. Beat butter in a large bowl with an electric mixer on medium speed until fluffy. Gradually add sugar; beat well. Add egg yolks, 1 at a time, beating until blended after each addition.
2. Combine flour and baking powder; add to butter mixture at low speed alternately with milk, beginning and ending with flour mixture. Beat until blended after each addition. Stir in vanilla.
3. Beat egg whites in a medium bowl with electric mixer on high speed until stiff peaks form; fold one-third of egg whites into batter. Gently fold in remaining beaten egg whites just until blended. Spoon batter into 3 greased and floured 9-inch round cake pans.
4. Bake in preheated oven until a wooden pick inserted in center comes out clean, 18 to 20 minutes. Cool in pans on wire racks 10 minutes; remove from pans, and cool completely on wire racks.
5. Spread Lemon Filling between layers. Spread 3-Cup Cream Cheese Frosting on top and sides of cake. Sprinkle top and sides with coconut. Garnish, if desired.

Lemon Filling

ACTIVE 10 MIN. · TOTAL 45 MIN.
SERVES 12

  1 cup sugar
  ¼ cup cornstarch
  1 cup boiling water
  4 egg yolks, lightly beaten
  2 tsp. grated lemon rind
  ⅓ cup fresh lemon juice
  2 Tbsp. butter

1. Combine sugar and cornstarch in a medium saucepan; whisk in 1 cup boiling water. Cook over medium, whisking constantly, until sugar and cornstarch dissolve, about 2 minutes. Gradually whisk about one-fourth of hot sugar mixture into egg yolks; add to remaining hot sugar mixture in pan, whisking constantly. Whisk in lemon rind and juice.
2. Cook, whisking constantly, until mixture is thickened, about 2 minutes. Remove from heat. Whisk in butter; let cool completely, stirring occasionally.

3-Cup Cream Cheese Frosting

ACTIVE 10 MIN. · TOTAL 10 MIN.
MAKES ABOUT 3 CUPS

  ½ cup butter, softened
  1 (8-oz.) pkg. cream cheese,
      softened
  1 (16-oz.) pkg. powdered sugar
  1 tsp. vanilla extract

Beat butter and cream cheese in a medium bowl with an electric mixer on medium speed until creamy. Gradually add powdered sugar, beating at low speed until blended; stir in vanilla.

Mama Dip's Carrot Cake

(Photo, page 330)

ACTIVE 30 MIN. · TOTAL 2 HOURS, 32 MIN.,
INCLUDING COOLING
SERVES 12

  2 cups chopped walnuts
2½ cups self-rising flour
1½ tsp. ground cinnamon
  1 tsp. baking soda
  2 cups sugar
  1 cup vegetable oil
  4 large eggs
  3 cups grated carrots

Recipe continued on page 326

Recipe continued from page 325

5-Cup Cream Cheese Frosting (recipe follows)

1. Preheat oven to 350°F. Arrange walnuts in a single layer in a shallow pan. Bake 12 minutes or until toasted and fragrant.
2. Sift together flour, cinnamon, and baking soda. Line bottoms of 3 lightly greased 9-inch round cake pans with parchment paper; lightly grease parchment paper.
3. Beat sugar and oil in a large bowl with an electric mixer on medium speed until smooth. Add eggs, 1 at a time, beating until blended after each addition. Add flour mixture, beating at low speed just until blended. Fold in carrots and 1 cup toasted walnuts. Spoon batter into prepared pans.
4. Bake in preheated oven until a wooden pick inserted in center comes out clean, 35 to 40 minutes. Cool in pans on wire racks 10 minutes. Remove from pans to wire racks; remove parchment paper, and let cakes cool 1 hour or until completely cool.
5. Spread 5-Cup Cream Cheese Frosting between layers and on top and sides of cake; press remaining 1 cup chopped walnuts halfway up sides of cake.

5-Cup Cream Cheese Frosting

ACTIVE 10 MIN. · TOTAL 10 MIN.
MAKES ABOUT 5 CUPS

- 2 (8-oz.) pkg. cream cheese, softened
- ½ cup butter, softened
- 1 (32-oz.) pkg. powdered sugar
- 2 tsp. vanilla extract

Beat cream cheese and butter in a bowl with an electric mixer on medium speed until creamy. Gradually add powdered sugar, beating until fluffy. Stir in vanilla.

Hummingbird Cake

ACTIVE 30 MIN. · TOTAL 2 HOURS, 15 MIN; INCLUDING FROSTING
SERVING 12

- 3 cups all-purpose flour
- 2 cups sugar
- 1 tsp. table salt
- 1 tsp. baking soda
- 1 tsp. ground cinnamon
- 3 large eggs, lightly beaten
- 1½ cups vegetable oil

- 1½ tsp. vanilla extract
- 1 (8-oz.) can crushed pineapple in juice, undrained
- 2 cups chopped bananas (about 4 medium bananas)
- 1 cup chopped toasted pecans
  Shortening, for greasing pans
  Cream Cheese-Vanilla Frosting (recipe follows)

1. Preheat oven to 350°F. Whisk together flour, sugar, salt, baking soda, and cinnamon in a large bowl; add eggs and oil, stirring just until dry ingredients are moistened. Stir in vanilla, pineapple, bananas, and pecans. Spoon batter into 3 well-greased and floured 9-inch round cake pans.
2. Bake in preheated oven until a wooden pick inserted in center comes out clean, 25 to 30 minutes. Cool cake layers in pans on wire racks 10 minutes; remove from pans to wire racks, and cool completely, about 1 hour.
3. Place 1 cake layer on a serving platter, and spread with 1 cup Cream Cheese-Vanilla Frosting. Repeat with second layer. Top with third cake layer, and spread top and sides of cake with remaining frosting.

Cream Cheese-Vanilla Frosting

ACTIVE 10 MIN. · TOTAL 10 MIN.
MAKES ABOUT 4 CUPS

- 2 (8 oz.) pkg. cream cheese, softened
- 1 cup butter, softened
- 2 (16 oz.) pkg. powdered sugar
- 2 tsp. vanilla extract

Beat cream cheese and butter in a bowl with an electric mixer on medium-low speed until smooth. Gradually add sugar, beating at low speed until blended. Stir in vanilla. Increase speed to medium-high, and beat 1 to 2 minutes or until fluffy.

Pineapple Upside-Down Cake

ACTIVE 35 MIN. · TOTAL 1 HOUR, 25 MIN.
SERVES 12

- 1 cup firmly packed light brown sugar
  Pinch of salt
- ½ cup butter, divided
- 1 medium peeled and cored pineapple
- 1¼ cups granulated sugar

- 2 large eggs
- 1 tsp. vanilla extract
- 1½ cups all-purpose flour
- 1 tsp. baking powder
- ¼ tsp. salt
- ½ cup sour cream
- 2 egg whites

1. Preheat oven to 325°F. Combine brown sugar, pinch of salt, and ¼ cup butter in a heavy saucepan; cook over medium, stirring occasionally, 5 to 7 minutes or until mixture bubbles and sugar melts. Pour sugar mixture into a 10-inch cast-iron skillet.
2. Cut pineapple crosswise into 6 (¼-inch-thick) rings. Arrange pineapple rings in a single layer over brown sugar mixture.
3. Beat remaining ¼ cup butter and granulated sugar in a bowl with an electric mixer on medium speed until creamy. Add eggs, 1 at a time, beating until blended after each addition. Stir in vanilla.
4. Stir together flour, baking powder, and salt; add to butter mixture alternately with sour cream, beginning and ending with flour mixture. Beat batter at low speed until blended after each addition. Beat egg whites until stiff peaks form; fold into batter. Pour batter over pineapple slices.
5. Bake in preheated oven until a wooden pick inserted in center comes out clean, 40 to 45 minutes. Cool in skillet on a wire rack 10 minutes. Carefully run a knife around edge of cake to loosen. Invert onto a serving plate; spoon any topping in skillet over cake.

Banana Snack Cake

ACTIVE 15 MIN. · TOTAL 2 HOURS, INCLUDING FROSTING AND GLAZED BANANAS
SERVES 32

- ½ cup butter, softened
- 1 cup granulated sugar
- 1 cup firmly packed light brown sugar
- 3 large eggs
- 1⅓ cups mashed very ripe bananas
- 1 tsp. vanilla extract
- 2 cups all-purpose flour, plus more for dusting
- 1 tsp. baking soda
- 1 tsp. ground cinnamon
- ¼ tsp. ground nutmeg
- ¼ tsp. table salt
- 1 cup chopped toasted pecans, divided

Shortening, for greasing pan
Cream Cheese Frosting (recipe
  follows)
Glazed Banana Slices (recipe
  follows) (optional)

1. Preheat oven to 350°F. Beat butter at medium speed with a heavy-duty electric stand mixer 1 to 2 minutes or until creamy. Gradually add sugars, beating well. Add eggs, 1 at a time, beating just until blended after each addition. Add mashed bananas and vanilla, and beat at low speed just until combined.
2. Stir together flour, baking soda, cinnamon, nutmeg, and salt in a small bowl. Gradually add flour mixture to butter mixture, beating at low speed just until blended. Stir in ½ cup pecans. Spread batter in a greased and floured 15- x 10-inch jelly-roll pan.
3. Bake in preheated oven until a wooden pick inserted in center comes out clean, 20 to 25 minutes. Cool completely on a wire rack, about 1 hour.
4. Spread cake with Cream Cheese Frosting. Top with Glazed Banana Slices, if desired. Sprinkle with remaining ½ cup chopped toasted pecans.

Cream Cheese Frosting

ACTIVE 10 MIN. - TOTAL 10 MIN.
MAKES ABOUT 3½ CUPS

Beat ½ cup **butter**, softened, and 1 (8-oz.) pkg. softened **cream cheese** in a bowl with an electric mixer on medium speed until creamy. Gradually add 4 cups **powdered sugar** and 2 tsp. **vanilla extract**, beating at low speed until blended. Increase speed to medium-high; beat 1 to 2 minutes or until fluffy.

Glazed Banana Slices

ACTIVE 15 MIN. - TOTAL 15 MIN.
MAKES ABOUT 3 CUPS

Preheat broiler with oven rack 5 to 6 inches from heat. Cut 4 ripe **bananas** in half crosswise; cut lengthwise into ¼-inch-thick slices, and place in a single layer on a lightly greased aluminum foil-lined baking sheet. Brush with 1 Tbsp. **melted butter**; sprinkle with 2 Tbsp. **light brown sugar**. Broil 4 to 5 minutes or until bubbly and just beginning to brown. (Watch to make sure they don't overbrown.)

Blueberry Coffee Cake

ACTIVE 20 MIN. - TOTAL 1 HOUR
SERVES 10

 1 large egg
½ cup fat-free milk
½ cup plain fat-free yogurt
 3 Tbsp. vegetable oil
 2 cups all-purpose flour
½ cup granulated sugar
 4 tsp. baking powder
½ tsp. table salt
1½ cups frozen blueberries
 1 Tbsp. all-purpose flour
 2 Tbsp. turbinado sugar
 2 Tbsp. sliced almonds
¼ tsp. ground cinnamon

1. Preheat oven to 400°F. Whisk together egg, milk, yogurt, and oil in a bowl.
2. Sift together flour sugar, baking powder, and salt in another bowl. Stir flour mixture into egg mixture just until dry ingredients are moistened.
3. Toss 1¼ cups blueberries in 1 tablespoon flour; fold into batter. Lightly grease a 9-inch springform pan with cooking spray. Pour batter into pan, and sprinkle with remaining ¼ cup blueberries.
4. Stir together 2 tablespoons turbinado sugar, sliced almonds, and cinnamon in a bowl; sprinkle over batter.
5. Bake in preheated oven until a wooden pick inserted in center comes out clean, 25 to 30 minutes. Cool in pan on a wire rack 15 minutes; remove sides of pan.

Chocolate Velvet Cupcakes

ACTIVE 20 MIN. - TOTAL 2 HOURS, 38 MIN., INCLUDING FROSTING
MAKES 3 DOZEN

1½ cups semisweet chocolate chips
½ cup butter, softened
 1 (16-oz.) pkg. light brown sugar
 3 large eggs
 2 cups all-purpose flour
 1 tsp. baking soda
½ tsp. table salt
 1 (8-oz.) container sour cream
 1 cup hot water
 2 tsp. vanilla extract
    Browned Butter-Cinnamon-Cream
    Cheese Frosting (recipe follows)

1. Preheat oven to 350°F. Microwave chips in a microwaveable bowl on HIGH 1 to 1½ minutes or until melted and smooth, stirring at 30-second intervals.
2. Beat butter and sugar in a bowl with an electric mixer on medium speed until well blended (about 5 minutes). Add eggs, 1 at a time, beating just until blended after each addition. Add melted chocolate, and beat until mixture is blended.
3. Sift together flour, baking soda, and salt. Gradually add to chocolate mixture alternately with sour cream, beginning and ending with flour mixture. Beat at low speed just until blended after each addition. Gradually add hot water in a slow, steady stream, beating at low speed just until blended. Stir in vanilla.
4. Place 36 paper baking cups in 3 (12-cup) muffin pans; spoon batter into cups, filling three-fourths full.
5. Bake in preheated oven until a wooden pick inserted in centers comes out clean, 18 to 20 minutes. Remove from pans to wire racks, and let cool completely, about 45 minutes.
6. Pipe frosting onto cupcakes.

Browned Butter-Cinnamon-Cream Cheese Frosting

ACTIVE 15 MIN. - TOTAL 1 HOUR, 15 MIN.
MAKES 5 CUPS

Cook ½ cup **butter** in a small heavy saucepan over medium, stirring constantly, 6 to 8 minutes or until butter begins to turn golden brown. Immediately remove from heat. Pour butter into a bowl. Cover and chill 1 hour or until butter is cool and begins to solidify. Beat butter and 2 (8-oz.) pkg. softened **cream cheese** with an electric mixer on medium speed until creamy; gradually add 2 (16-oz.) pkg. **powdered sugar**, and beat until light and fluffy. Stir in 1 tsp. **ground cinnamon** and 2 tsp. **vanilla extract**.

Lemon-Raspberry Cupcakes

ACTIVE 50 MIN. - TOTAL 2 HOURS
MAKES 2 DOZEN

 2 cups granulated sugar
 1 cup butter, softened
 2 large eggs
 1 tsp. vanilla extract
 1 tsp. fresh lemon juice

Recipe continued on page 328

Recipe continued from page 327

2½ cups cake flour
½ tsp. baking soda
1 cup buttermilk
¾ cup seedless raspberry jam
1½ (8-oz.) pkg. cream cheese, softened
¼ cup butter, softened
¼ cup fresh lemon juice
1 (16-oz.) pkg. powdered sugar, sifted
2 tsp. lemon zest
Fresh raspberries, mint leaves, for garnish (optional)

1. Preheat oven to 350°F. Place 24 paper baking cups in 2 (12-cup) muffin pans. Beat sugar and 1 cup butter in a bowl with an electric mixer on medium speed until creamy. Add eggs, 1 at a time, beating until yellow disappears after each addition. Beat in vanilla and 1 tsp. lemon juice.
2. Combine flour and baking soda; add to sugar mixture alternately with buttermilk, beginning and ending with flour mixture. Beat at medium speed just until blended after each addition. Spoon batter into baking cups, filling two-thirds full.
3. Bake in preheated oven until a wooden pick inserted in center comes out clean, 18 to 22 minutes. Cool in pans on wire racks 10 minutes. Remove from pans to wire racks, and cool completely, about 45 minutes.
4. Make a small hole in tops of cupcakes with a knife or end of a wooden spoon. Pipe or spoon about 1 teaspoon raspberry jam into centers of cupcakes.
5. Beat cream cheese and ¼ cup butter in a bowl with an electric mixer on medium speed until creamy; add ¼ cup lemon juice, beating just until blended. Gradually add powdered sugar, beating at low speed until blended; stir in lemon zest.
6. Spread cream cheese frosting on tops of cupcakes. Garnish, if desired.

Coconut-Pecan Cupcakes

(Photo, page 330)

ACTIVE 20 MIN. · TOTAL 2 HOURS, 15 MIN., INCLUDING FROSTING
MAKES 3 DOZEN

½ cup butter, softened
½ cup shortening
2 cups sugar
5 large eggs, separated
1 Tbsp. vanilla extract
2 cups all-purpose flour
1 tsp. baking soda
1 cup buttermilk
1 cup sweetened flaked coconut
1 cup finely chopped pecans, toasted
Caramel Frosting (recipe follows)
Chopped roasted salted pecans, for garnish (optional)

1. Preheat the oven to 350°F. Beat butter and shortening in a bowl with an electric mixer on medium speed until fluffy, and gradually add sugar, beating well. Add egg yolks, 1 at a time, beating until blended after each addition. Add vanilla; beat until blended.
2. Combine flour and baking soda; add to butter mixture alternately with buttermilk, beginning and ending with flour mixture. Beat at low speed just until blended after each addition. Stir in coconut and pecans.
3. Beat egg whites at high speed until stiff peaks form, and fold into batter. Place 36 paper baking cups in 3 (12-cup) muffin pans; spoon batter into cups, filling half full.
4. Bake in preheated oven until a wooden pick inserted in centers comes out clean, 18 to 20 minutes. Remove from pans to wire racks, and let cool completely, about 45 minutes.
5. Pipe Caramel Frosting onto cupcakes. Garnish, if desired.

Caramel Frosting

ACTIVE 15 MIN. · TOTAL 45 MIN.
MAKES 4½ CUPS

Microwave 1 (14-oz.) pkg. **caramels** and ½ cup **heavy cream** in a microwavable bowl on HIGH 1 to 2 minutes or until smooth, stirring at 30-second intervals. Let caramel mixture cool until lukewarm (about 30 minutes). Beat 1 cup softened **butter** in a bowl with an electric mixer on medium speed until creamy. Gradually add 5 cups **powdered sugar** alternately with caramel mixture, beating at low speed until blended and smooth after each addition. Stir in 2 tsp. **vanilla extract**.

Fresh Strawberry Meringue Cake

(Photo, page 330)

ACTIVE 1 HOUR · TOTAL 4 HOURS, 20 MIN.
SERVES 10 TO 12

1 cup chopped pecans
2 Tbsp. cornstarch
⅛ tsp. table salt
2 cups sugar, divided
7 egg whites, at room temperature
½ tsp. cream of tartar
2 (8-oz.) containers mascarpone cheese
2 tsp. vanilla extract
3 cups whipping cream
4½ cups sliced fresh strawberries
Halved fresh strawberries

1. Preheat oven to 350°F. Bake pecans in a single layer in a shallow pan 10 to 12 minutes or until toasted and fragrant, stirring halfway through. Remove from oven, and cool completely, about 10 minutes. Reduce oven temperature to 250°F.
2. Cover 2 large baking sheets with parchment paper. Draw 2 (8-inch) circles on each piece of paper. Turn paper over; secure with masking tape.
3. Process cornstarch, salt, toasted pecans, and ½ cup sugar in a food processor 40 to 45 seconds or until pecans are finely ground.
4. Beat egg whites and cream of tartar in a bowl with an electric mixer on high speed until foamy. Gradually add 1 cup sugar, 1 tablespoon at a time, beating at medium-high speed until mixture is glossy, stiff peaks form, and sugar dissolves (2 to 4 minutes; do not overbeat). Add half of pecan mixture to egg white mixture, gently folding just until blended. Repeat procedure with remaining pecan mixture.
5. Gently spoon egg white mixture onto circles drawn on parchment paper (about 1½ cups mixture per circle), spreading to cover each circle completely.
6. Bake at 250°F 1 hour, turning baking sheets after 30 minutes. Turn oven off; let meringues stand in closed oven with light on 2 to 2½ hours or until surface is dry and meringues can be lifted from paper without sticking to fingers.
7. Just before assembling cake, stir together mascarpone cheese and vanilla in a large bowl just until blended.
8. Beat whipping cream at low speed until foamy; increase speed to medium-high, and gradually add remaining ½ cup sugar, beating until stiff peaks form. (Do not overbeat or cream will be grainy.) Gently fold whipped cream into mascarpone mixture.
9. Carefully remove 1 meringue from parchment paper; place on a serving plate. Spread one-fourth mascarpone mixture (about 2 cups) over meringue; top with 1½ cups sliced strawberries. Repeat layers 2 times; top with remaining meringue, mascarpone mixture, and

halved strawberries. Serve immediately, or chill up to 2 hours. Cut with a sharp, thin-bladed knife.

Amaretto–Almond Pound Cake

ACTIVE 20 MIN. · TOTAL 3 HOURS, 5 MIN., INCLUDING GLAZE
SERVES 12

- 1¼ cups butter, softened
- 1 (3-oz.) pkg. cream cheese, softened
- 2½ cups sugar
- 3 Tbsp. almond liqueur
- 1 Tbsp. vanilla extract
- 2½ cups all-purpose flour
- 6 large eggs
- ⅓ cup sliced almonds
  Amaretto Glaze (recipe follows)

1. Preheat oven to 325°F. Beat butter and cream cheese at medium speed with a heavy-duty electric stand mixer until creamy. Gradually add sugar, beating at medium speed until light and fluffy. Add liqueur and vanilla, beating just until blended. Gradually add flour to butter mixture, beating at low speed just until blended after each addition.
2. Add eggs, 1 at a time, beating at low speed just until blended after each addition. Sprinkle almonds over bottom of a greased and floured 12-cup Bundt pan; pour batter into pan.
3. Bake in preheated oven until a long wooden pick inserted in center comes out clean, 1 hour and 5 minutes to 1 hour and 10 minutes.
4. During last 10 minutes of baking, prepare Amaretto Glaze. Remove cake from oven, and gradually spoon hot Amaretto Glaze over cake in pan. (Continue to spoon glaze over cake until all of glaze is used, allowing it to soak into cake after each addition.) Cool completely in pan on a wire rack, about 1 hour and 30 minutes.

Amaretto Glaze

ACTIVE 10 MIN. · TOTAL 10 MIN.
MAKES ABOUT 1¼ CUPS

- ¾ cup sugar
- 6 Tbsp. butter
- ¼ cup almond liqueur
- 2 Tbsp. water

Bring sugar, butter, almond liqueur, and water to a boil in a small 1-qt. saucepan over medium, stirring often; reduce heat to medium-low; boil, stirring constantly, 3 minutes. Remove from heat; use immediately.

Chocolate Pound Cake

ACTIVE 10 MIN. · TOTAL 10 MIN.
MAKES 1 (10-INCH) CAKE

- ½ cup shortening
- 1 cup margarine, softened
- 3 cups sugar
- 5 eggs
- 3 cups all-purpose flour
- ½ tsp. baking powder
- ½ tsp. salt
- ½ cup cocoa powder
- 1¼ cups milk
- 1 tsp. vanilla extract
  Creamy Chocolate Glaze (recipe follows)
  Chopped pecans, for topping

1. Preheat oven to 350°F. Cream shortening and margarine; gradually add sugar, beating until light and fluffy. Add eggs, one at a time, beating well after each addition.
2. Combine flour, baking powder, salt, and cocoa powder in a bowl; mix well. Add to creamed mixture alternately with milk, beginning and ending with flour mixture. Stir in vanilla. Pour batter into a greased and floured 10-inch tube pan.
3. Bake in preheated oven until a wooden pick inserted in center comes out clean, 1 hour and 15 minutes. Cool in pan 10 to 15 minutes; invert onto serving plate. Spoon Creamy Chocolate Glaze over top of warm cake, allowing it to drizzle down sides. Sprinkle with chopped pecans.

Creamy Chocolate Glaze

ACTIVE 10 MIN. · TOTAL 10 MIN.
MAKES ABOUT 2 CUPS

- 2¼ cups sifted powdered sugar
- 3 Tbsp. cocoa
- ¼ cup margarine, softened
- 3 to 4 Tbsp. milk

Combine sugar and cocoa, mixing well. Add margarine and milk; beat until smooth.

Strawberry Swirl Cream Cheese Pound Cake

ACTIVE 25 MIN. · TOTAL 2 HOURS, 35 MIN.
SERVES 12

- 1½ cups butter, softened
- 3 cups sugar
- 1 (8-oz.) pkg. cream cheese, softened
- 6 large eggs
- 3 cups all-purpose flour
- 1 tsp. almond extract
- ½ tsp. vanilla extract
- ⅔ cup strawberry glaze

1. Preheat oven to 350°F. Beat butter at medium speed with a heavy-duty electric stand mixer until creamy. Gradually add sugar, beating at medium speed until light and fluffy. Add cream cheese, beating until creamy. Add eggs, 1 at a time, beating just until blended after each addition.
2. Gradually add flour to butter mixture. Beat at low speed just until blended after each addition, stopping to scrape bowl as needed. Stir in extracts. Pour one-third of batter into a greased and floured 10-inch tube pan. Dollop 8 teaspoons strawberry glaze over batter, and swirl with wooden skewer. Repeat procedure once, and top with remaining one-third of batter.
3. Bake in preheated oven until a long wooden pick inserted in center comes out clean, 1 hour to 1 hour and 10 minutes. Cool in pan on a wire rack 10 to 15 minutes; remove from pan to wire rack, and cool completely, about 1 hour.

Caramel Apple Cheesecake

(Photo, page 330)

ACTIVE 30 MIN. · TOTAL 12 HOURS, INCLUDING CHILLING
SERVES 12

- 2¾ lb. large Granny Smith apples
- 1⅔ cups firmly packed light brown sugar, divided
- 1 Tbsp. butter
- 2 cups cinnamon graham cracker crumbs (about 15 whole crackers)
- ½ cup melted butter
- ½ cup finely chopped pecans
- 3 (8-oz.) pkg. cream cheese, softened
- 2 tsp. vanilla extract
- 3 large eggs
- ¼ cup apple jelly
  Sweetened whipped cream

Recipe continued on page 331

CLOCKWISE FROM TOP LEFT:

• LEMON-COCONUT CAKE (PAGE 325)

• MAMA DIP'S CARROT CAKE (PAGE 325)

• FRESH STRAWBERRY MERINGUE CAKE
(PAGE 328)

• COCONUT-PECAN CUPCAKES
(PAGE 328)

• CARAMEL APPLE CHEESECAKE
(PAGE 329)

• PEPPERMINT ICE-CREAM CAKE (RIGHT)

• APPLE-CHERRY COBBLER
WITH PINWHEEL BISCUITS (PAGE 332)

• PECAN-PEACH COBBLER (PAGE 333)

Recipe continued from page 329

1. Peel apples, and cut into ½-inch-thick wedges. Toss together apples and ⅓ cup brown sugar. Melt 1 tablespoon butter in a large skillet over medium-high heat; add apple mixture, and sauté 5 to 6 minutes or until crisp-tender and golden. Cool completely (about 30 minutes).

2. Meanwhile, preheat oven to 350°F. Stir together graham cracker crumbs, melted butter, and pecans in a medium bowl until well blended. Press mixture on bottom and 1½ inches up sides of a 9-inch springform pan. Bake 10 to 12 minutes or until lightly browned. Remove to a wire rack, and cool crust completely before filling, about 30 minutes.

3. Beat cream cheese, vanilla, and remaining 1⅓ cups brown sugar at medium speed with a heavy-duty electric stand mixer until blended and smooth. Add eggs, 1 at a time, beating just until blended after each addition. Pour batter into prepared crust. Arrange apples over cream cheese mixture.

4. Bake in preheated oven until set, 55 minutes to 1 hour and 5 minutes. Remove from oven, and gently run a knife around outer edge of cheesecake to loosen from sides of pan. (Do not remove sides of pan.) Cool cheesecake completely on a wire rack, about 2 hours. Cover and chill 8 to 24 hours.

5. Cook apple jelly and 1 teaspoon water in a small saucepan over medium, stirring constantly, 2 to 3 minutes or until jelly is melted; brush over apples on top of cheesecake. Serve with whipped cream.

Amaretto Cheesecake

ACTIVE 20 MIN. - TOTAL 9 HOURS, INCLUDING CHILLING
SERVES 12

- 1½ cups graham cracker crumbs
- 2 Tbsp. plus 1 tsp. sugar, divided
- 1 tsp. ground cinnamon
- ¼ cup plus 2 Tbsp. butter or margarine, melted
- 3 (8-oz.) pkg. cream cheese, softened
- 1 cup sugar
- 4 eggs
- 1⅓ cups plus 1 Tbsp. amaretto, divided
- 1 (8-oz.) carton sour cream
- ¼ cup sliced almonds, toasted, for garnish
- 1 (1.2-oz.) chocolate candy bar, grated, for garnish

1. Preheat oven to 375°F. Combine graham cracker crumbs, 2 tablespoons sugar, cinnamon, and butter; mix well. Press mixture into bottom and ½ inch up the sides of a 9-inch springform pan.

2. Beat cream cheese in a bowl with electric mixer on medium speed until light and fluffy. Gradually add 1 cup sugar, mixing well. Add eggs, 1 at a time, beating well after each addition. Stir in ⅓ cup amaretto; pour into prepared pan. Bake in preheated oven until set, 45 to 50 minutes. Increase oven temperature to 500°F.

3. Combine sour cream, 1 tablespoon plus 1 teaspoon sugar, and 1 tablespoon amaretto; stir well, and spoon over cheesecake. Bake in preheated oven 5 minutes. Cool cheesecake completely on a wire rack, about 2 hours. Cover and chill 8 to 24 hours. Garnish with almonds and grated chocolate.

Irish Strawberry-and-Cream Cheesecake

ACTIVE 20 MIN. - TOTAL 9 HOURS, 40 MIN., INCLUDING CHILLING
SERVES 10 TO 12

- 1 cup graham cracker crumbs
- 3 Tbsp. butter, melted
- 3 Tbsp. sugar
- 4 (8-oz.) pkg. cream cheese, softened
- 1 cup sugar
- 3 Tbsp. all-purpose flour
- 2 tsp. vanilla extract
- ¼ cup Irish cream liqueur
- 4 large eggs
- 1¼ cups sour cream, divided
- 3 Tbsp. strawberry preserves
  Whole strawberries, for garnish (optional)

1. Preheat oven to 325°F. Stir together crumbs, butter, and sugar; press mixture into bottom of a lightly greased 9-inch springform pan. Bake 10 minutes. Cool on a wire rack. Reduce oven temperature to 300°F.

2. Beat cream cheese, 1 cup sugar, and flour in a bowl with an electric mixer on medium speed until smooth. Gradually add vanilla and liqueur, beating just until blended. Add eggs, 1 at a time, beating at low speed just until blended after each addition. Add ¾ cup sour cream, beating just until blended.

3. Pour half of batter into prepared crust. Dollop strawberry preserves over batter;

gently swirl batter with a knife to create a marbled effect. Top with remaining batter.

5. Bake in preheated oven 55 minutes or until edges of cheesecake are set. (Center of cheesecake will not appear set.) Turn off oven; let cheesecake stand in oven 15 minutes. Remove cheesecake from oven; gently run a knife around edge of cheesecake to loosen. Cool completely on a wire rack. Cover and chill 8 hours.

6. Release and remove sides of pan. Spread remaining ½ cup sour cream evenly over top of cheesecake; garnish, if desired.

Peppermint Ice-Cream Cake

(Photo, left)

ACTIVE 1 HOUR, 40 MIN. - TOTAL 38 HOURS, INCLUDING FREEZING
SERVES 10 TO 12

CHIFFON CAKE LAYERS
- 2 cups sifted cake flour
- 2½ tsp. baking powder
- ½ tsp. table salt
- 1¼ cups granulated sugar, divided
- ½ cup canola oil
- ½ cup milk
- 1 tsp. vanilla extract
- 4 large egg yolks
- 8 large egg whites
- 1 tsp. cream of tartar

PEPPERMINT ICE CREAM LAYERS
- ½ gal. vanilla ice cream, softened
- 1 cup finely crushed hard peppermint candies (about 40 pieces)

WHIPPED CREAM FROSTING
- 3 cups heavy cream
- 1 tsp. vanilla extract
- ½ cup powdered sugar
  Crushed hard peppermint candies, for garnish

1. Prepare Chiffon Cake Layers: Preheat oven to 325°F. Lightly grease bottoms of 4 (8-inch) round disposable aluminum cake pans with cooking spray; line bottoms with wax paper, and lightly grease.

2. Whisk together flour, baking powder, salt, and 1 cup sugar in bowl of a heavy-duty electric stand mixer.

3. Whisk together oil, milk, vanilla, and egg yolks; add to flour mixture, and beat at medium speed 1 to 2 minutes or until smooth.

4. Beat egg whites at medium speed until foamy. Add cream of tartar; beat at high

Recipe continued on page 332

Recipe continued from page 331

speed until soft peaks form. Gradually add remaining ¼ cup sugar, 1 tablespoon at a time, beating until stiff peaks form and sugar dissolves. Gently stir one-fourth egg white mixture into flour mixture; gently fold in remaining egg white mixture. Divide batter among prepared pans, spreading with an offset spatula. Sharply tap pans once on counter to remove air bubbles.

5. Bake in preheated oven until a wooden pick inserted in center comes out clean, 14 to 16 minutes. Cool in pans on wire racks 10 minutes. Remove from pans to wire racks; discard wax paper. Cool completely. Wrap layers in plastic wrap, and freeze 12 hours.

6. Meanwhile, prepare Peppermint Ice Cream Layers: Line 3 (8-inch) disposable aluminum cake pans with plastic wrap, allowing 6 to 8 inches to extend over sides. Stir together ice cream and candies in a large bowl. Divide mixture among prepared pans (about 2½ cups per pan), spreading to within ½ inch of sides of pans. (The cake layers shrink a little as they cool, so this helps ensure the ice cream layers will be the same size.) Cover with plastic wrap; freeze 12 to 24 hours.

7. Assemble Cake: Remove plastic wrap. Place 1 Cake Layer on a serving plate; top with 1 Ice Cream Layer. Repeat with remaining Cake and Ice Cream, Layers, ending with Cake Layer. Wrap entire cake with plastic wrap, and freeze 12 to 24 hours.

8. Prepare Whipped Cream Frosting: Beat cream and vanilla in a bowl with an electric mixer on medium speed until foamy. Increase speed to medium-high; gradually add powdered sugar, beating until stiff peaks form. (Do not overbeat or cream will be grainy.) Remove cake from freezer. Spread top and sides with Whipped Cream Frosting. Garnish, if desired. Serve immediately, or freeze up to 12 hours. Store in freezer.

Easy Mocha Chip Ice Cream Cake

ACTIVE 20 MIN. - TOTAL 5 HOURS, 15 MIN. INCLUDING GANACHE
SERVES 8 TO 10

- 1 pt. premium dark chocolate chunk-coffee ice cream, softened
- 3 sugar cones, crushed
- ⅓ cup chocolate fudge shell topping
- 1 (14-oz.) container premium chocolate-chocolate chip ice cream, softened
- 6 cream-filled chocolate sandwich cookies, finely crushed
  Mocha Ganache (recipe follows)
  Chocolate-covered coffee beans, for garnish (optional)

1. Line an 8- x 5-inch loaf pan with plastic wrap, allowing 3 inches to extend over sides. Spread chocolate chunk-coffee ice cream in pan. Sprinkle with crushed cones, and drizzle with shell topping. Freeze 30 minutes.
2. Spread chocolate-chocolate chip ice cream over topping. Top with crushed cookies, pressing into ice cream. Freeze 4 hours or until firm.
3. Lift ice cream loaf from pan, using plastic wrap as handles; invert onto a serving plate. Discard plastic wrap. Prepare Mocha Ganache, and slowly pour over ice-cream loaf, allowing ganache to drip down sides. Freeze 10 minutes. Garnish, if desired. Let stand at room temperature 10 minutes before serving.

Mocha Ganache

ACTIVE 5 MIN. - TOTAL 5 MIN.
MAKES ABOUT ½ CUP

- 1 (4-oz.) semisweet chocolate baking bar, chopped
- 1 tsp. instant espresso
- 4 Tbsp. whipping cream, divided

Microwave semisweet chocolate, espresso, and 3 Tbsp. whipping cream in a microwavable bowl on HIGH 1 minute or until melted and smooth, stirring at 30-second intervals. Whisk in an additional 1 Tbsp. whipping cream until smooth. Use immediately.

Cobblers & Tarts

Apple-Cherry Cobbler with Pinwheel Biscuits

(Photo, page 330)

ACTIVE 1 HOUR - TOTAL 1 HOUR, 15 MIN.
SERVES 8 TO 10

APPLE-CHERRY FILLING
- 8 large Braeburn apples, peeled and cut into ½-inch-thick wedges (about 4½ lb.)
- 2 cups granulated sugar
- ¼ cup all-purpose flour
- ¼ cup butter
- 1 (12-oz.) pkg. frozen cherries, thawed and well drained
- 1 tsp. lemon zest
- ⅓ cup fresh lemon juice
- 1 tsp. ground cinnamon

PINWHEEL BISCUITS
- 2¼ cups all-purpose flour
- ¼ cup granulated sugar
- 2¼ tsp. baking powder
- ¾ tsp. salt
- ¾ cup cold butter, cut into pieces
- ⅔ cup milk
- ⅔ cup firmly packed light brown sugar
- 2 Tbsp. butter, melted
- ¼ cup finely chopped roasted unsalted almonds
  Sweetened whipped cream (optional)

1. Prepare Apple-Cherry Filling: Preheat oven to 425°F. Toss together apples, sugar, and flour in a large bowl. Melt ¼ cup butter in a large skillet over medium-high; add apple mixture. Cook, stirring often, 20 to 25 minutes or until apples are tender and syrup thickens. Remove from heat; stir in cherries, lemon zest and juice, and cinnamon. Spoon apple mixture into a lightly greased 3-qt. baking dish. Bake apple mixture 12 minutes, placing a baking sheet on oven rack directly below baking dish to catch any drips.
2. Prepare Pinwheel Biscuits: Stir together 2¼ cups flour, sugar, baking powder, and salt in a large bowl. Cut cold butter pieces into flour mixture with a pastry blender or fork until crumbly; stir in milk. Turn dough out onto a lightly floured surface; knead 4 to 5 times. Roll dough into a 12-inch square. Combine brown sugar and

2 tablespoons melted butter; sprinkle over dough, patting gently. Sprinkle with almonds. Roll up, jelly-roll style; pinch seams and ends to seal. Cut roll into 12 (1-inch) slices. Place slices in a single layer on top of apple mixture.

3. Bake in preheated oven 1 or until biscuits are golden, 15 to 17 minutes. Serve with whipped cream, if desired.

Banana Bread Cobbler

ACTIVE 15 MIN. · TOTAL 1 HOUR, 5 MIN., INCLUDING TOPPING
SERVES 8

- 1 cup self-rising flour
- 1 cup sugar
- 1 cup milk
- ½ cup butter, melted
- 4 medium ripe bananas, sliced
  Streusel Topping (recipe follows)
  Vanilla ice cream

1. Preheat oven to 375°F. Whisk together flour, sugar, and milk just until blended; whisk in melted butter. Pour batter into a lightly greased 11- x 7-inch baking dish. Top with banana slices, and sprinkle with Streusel Topping.

2. Bake in preheated oven until golden and bubbly, 40 to 45 minutes. Serve with ice cream.

Streusel Topping

ACTIVE 10 MIN. · TOTAL 10 MIN.
MAKES 3½ CUPS

- ¾ cup firmly packed light brown sugar
- ½ cup self-rising flour
- ½ cup butter, softened
- 1 cup uncooked regular oats
- ½ cup chopped pecans

Stir together brown sugar, flour, and butter until crumbly, using a fork. Stir in oats and pecans.

Pecan-Peach Cobbler

(Photo, page 330)

ACTIVE 45 MIN. · TOTAL 1 HOUR, 41 MIN.
SERVES 10 TO 12

- 12 to 15 fresh peaches, peeled and sliced (about 16 cups)
- ⅓ cup all-purpose flour
- ½ tsp. ground nutmeg
- 3 cups sugar
- ⅔ cup butter
- 1½ tsp. vanilla extract
- 2 (15-oz.) pkg. refrigerated piecrusts
- ½ cup chopped pecans, toasted
- 5 Tbsp. sugar, divided
  Sweetened whipped cream, for serving

1. Preheat oven to 475°F. Stir together peaches, flour, nutmeg, and 3 cups sugar in a Dutch oven. Bring to a boil over medium; reduce heat to low, and simmer 10 minutes. Remove from heat; stir in butter and vanilla. Spoon half of mixture into a lightly greased 13- x 9-inch baking dish.

2. Unroll 2 piecrusts. Sprinkle ¼ cup chopped pecans and 2 tablespoons sugar over 1 piecrust; top with other piecrust. Roll to a 14- x 10-inch rectangle. Trim sides to fit baking dish. Place pastry over peach mixture in dish.

3. Bake in preheated oven until lightly browned, 20 to 25 minutes. Unroll remaining 2 piecrusts. Sprinkle 2 tablespoons sugar and remaining ¼ cup pecans over 1 piecrust; top with remaining piecrust. Roll into a 12-inch circle. Cut into 1-inch strips, using a fluted pastry wheel. Spoon remaining peach mixture over baked pastry. Arrange pastry strips over peach mixture; sprinkle with remaining 1 tablespoon sugar. Bake 15 to 18 minutes or until lightly browned. Serve warm or cold with whipped cream.

Strawberry-Rhubarb Crisp

ACTIVE 25 MIN. · TOTAL 35 MIN.
SERVES 15

- 3 cups fresh stalks or frozen sliced rhubarb, thawed
- 1 qt. fresh strawberries, mashed
- 2 Tbsp. lemon juice
- 1 cup sugar
- ⅓ cup cornstarch
- 2¾ cups all-purpose flour, divided
- 1¾ cup sugar
- 1 tsp. baking powder
- 1 tsp. baking soda
- ½ tsp. salt
- 1 cup butter or margarine
- 1½ cups buttermilk
- 2 large eggs, lightly beaten
- 1 tsp. vanilla extract
- ¼ cup butter or margarine, melted

1. Preheat oven to 350°F. Combine rhubarb, strawberries, and lemon juice in a saucepan; cook over medium 5 minutes.

2. Combine 1 cup sugar and cornstarch; gradually stir into rhubarb mixture. Bring mixture to a boil, stirring constantly; boil 1 minute. Remove from heat; set aside.

3. Combine 2 cups flour, 1 cup sugar, baking powder, baking soda, and salt; cut in 1 cup butter with a pastry blender until mixture is crumbly. Add buttermilk, eggs, and vanilla; stir with a fork until dry ingredients are moistened.

4. Spread half of batter into a greased 13- x 9-inch baking dish. Spoon rhubarb mixture evenly over batter; drop remaining batter by tablespoonfuls over filling.

5. Combine melted butter, remaining ¾ cup flour and ¾ cup sugar; sprinkle mixture over batter.

6. Bake in preheated oven 40 to 45 minutes. Cool on a wire rack. Cut into squares.

Lemon-Almond Tarts

ACTIVE 30 MIN. · TOTAL 3 HOURS
SERVES 6

VANILLA WAFER CRUSTS
- 75 vanilla wafers
- ¼ cup powdered sugar
- ½ cup butter, melted

LEMON-ALMOND FILLING
- 1 (7-oz.) pkg. almond paste
- 2 large eggs
- ¼ cup granulated sugar
- 2 Tbsp. melted butter
- ⅔ cup lemon curd
- 2 (6-oz.) pkg. fresh raspberries
  Fresh mint sprigs, for garnish (optional)

1. Prepare Crusts: Preheat oven to 350°F. Pulse vanilla wafers in a food processor 8 to 10 times or until finely crushed. Stir together crushed wafers, powdered sugar, and butter in a bowl. Press crumb mixture on bottom and up sides of 6 lightly greased 4-inch tart pans with removable bottoms. Place on a baking sheet.

2. Bake in preheated oven until lightly browned, 10 to 12 minutes. Transfer to a wire rack. Let cool completely, about 30 minutes.

3. Meanwhile, prepare Filling: Reduce oven temperature to 325°F. Beat almond paste, eggs, sugar, and butter with an

Recipe continued on page 334

Recipe continued from page 333

electric mixer on medium speed until well blended. Pour mixture into crusts.

4. Bake in preheated oven until set and just beginning to brown around edges, 18 to 20 minutes. Let cool on a wire rack 30 minutes. Spread 1½ tablespoons lemon curd onto each tart. Cover and chill 1 to 24 hours. Remove tarts from pans, and top with raspberries just before serving. Garnish, if desired.

Strawberry-Orange Shortcake Tart

ACTIVE 20 MIN. - TOTAL 1 HOUR, 25 MIN.
SERVES 8

- 1¾ cups all-purpose flour
- ¼ cup plain yellow cornmeal
- 2 Tbsp. sugar
- ¾ tsp. baking powder
- ½ tsp. salt
- 6 Tbsp. cold butter, cut into pieces
- 1 large egg, lightly beaten
- ⅔ cup buttermilk
- 1 Tbsp. orange marmalade
- 1 (16-oz.) container fresh strawberries, cut in half
- ½ cup orange marmalade
- 2 cups heavy cream
- 2 Tbsp. sugar
  Fresh mint sprigs, sweetened whipped cream, for garnish (optional)

1. Preheat oven to 425°F. Place flour, cornmeal, sugar, baking powder, and salt in a food processor. Process 20 seconds or until mixture resembles coarse sand. Transfer to a large bowl.
2. Whisk together egg and buttermilk; add to flour mixture, stirring just until dry ingredients are moistened and a dough forms. Turn dough out onto a lightly floured surface, and knead 3 to 4 times. Press dough on bottom and up sides of a lightly greased 9-inch tart pan.
3. Bake in preheated oven until golden and firm to touch, 20 to 22 minutes.
4. Microwave 1 tablespoon marmalade on HIGH 10 seconds; brush over crust. Cool 45 minutes.
5. Stir together strawberries and ½ cup marmalade.
6. Beat heavy cream with 2 tablespoons sugar in a bowl with an electric mixer on medium speed until soft peaks form. Spoon onto cornmeal crust; top with strawberry mixture. Garnish, if desired.

Sweet Tea Icebox Tart

ACTIVE 25 MIN. - TOTAL 6 HOURS, INCLUDING GINGERSNAP CRUST
SERVES 12

- 2 Tbsp. unsweetened instant iced tea mix
- 1 (14-oz.) can sweetened condensed milk
- ½ tsp. orange zest
- ½ tsp. lime zest
- ⅓ cup fresh orange juice
- ¼ cup fresh lemon juice
- 2 large eggs, lightly beaten
  Gingersnap Crust (recipe follows)
- 1 cup heavy cream
- 3 Tbsp. sugar
  Orange slices, fresh mint sprigs, for garnish (optional)

1. Preheat oven to 350°F. Stir together iced tea mix and 2 tablespoons water in a large bowl. Whisk in sweetened condensed milk, zests, juices, and eggs until blended. Place Gingersnap Crust on a baking sheet; pour in milk mixture.
2. Bake in preheated oven just until filling is set, 20 to 25 minutes. Cool completely on a wire rack (about 1 hour). Cover and chill 4 to 24 hours. Remove tart from pan, and place on a serving dish.
3. Beat cream and sugar in a bowl with an electric mixer on medium speed until stiff peaks form. Pipe or dollop on top of tart; garnish, if desired.
Note: 2 (4-oz.) packages ready-made mini graham cracker piecrusts may be substituted. bake this tart in a 14- x 4-inch tart pan with removable bottom; increase bake time to 25 to 28 minutes or until filling is set.

Gingersnap Crust

ACTIVE 7 MIN. - TOTAL 7 MIN.
MAKES 1 (9-INCH) CRUST

- 1½ cups crushed gingersnap cookies
- 5 Tbsp. butter, melted
- 2 Tbsp. light brown sugar
- ¼ tsp. ground cinnamon

Stir together all ingredients. Press mixture into a 9-inch tart pan with removable bottom.

Vanilla-Buttermilk Tarts

ACTIVE 30 MIN. - TOTAL 4 HOURS, 30 MIN.
MAKES 8 TARTS

- ⅔ cup sugar
- ¼ cup all-purpose flour
- 1½ cups buttermilk
- 3 large eggs
- 2 tsp. vanilla bean paste
- 1 (8- or 10-oz.) pkg. frozen tart shells
  Fresh fruit, fresh basil sprigs, for topping

1. Whisk together sugar and flour in a 3-quart heavy saucepan; add buttermilk and eggs, and whisk until blended. Cook over medium, whisking constantly, until pudding-like thickness, 7 to 8 minutes. Remove from heat, and stir in vanilla bean paste. Cover and chill 4 to 24 hours.
2. Meanwhile, bake frozen tart shells according to pkg. directions, and cool completely, 30 minutes. Spoon custard into shells; top with desired toppings just before serving.

Red Velvet Cake-Berry Trifle

(Photo, page 345)

ACTIVE 20 MIN. - TOTAL 1 HOUR, 15 MIN.
SERVES 6 TO 8

- 1 Tbsp. cornstarch
- 1¼ cups sugar, divided
- 6 cups assorted fresh berries
- ½ cup butter, softened
- 2 large eggs
- 2 Tbsp. red liquid food coloring
- 1 tsp. vanilla extract
- 1¼ cups all-purpose flour
- 1½ Tbsp. unsweetened cocoa
- ¼ tsp. table salt
- ½ cup buttermilk
- 1½ tsp. white vinegar
- ½ tsp. baking soda

1. Preheat oven to 350°F. Stir together cornstarch and ½ cup sugar. Lightly grease an 11- x 7-inch baking dish with cooking spray. Toss berries with cornstarch mixture; spoon into dish.
2. Beat butter in a bowl with an electric mixer on medium speed until fluffy; gradually add remaining ¾ cup sugar, beating well. Add eggs, 1 at a time, beating just until blended after each addition. Stir in red food coloring and vanilla.
3. Combine flour, cocoa, and salt in a small bowl. Stir together buttermilk,

vinegar, and baking soda in a 2-cup liquid measuring cup. (Mixture will bubble.) Add flour mixture to butter mixture alternately with buttermilk mixture, beginning and ending with flour mixture. Beat at low speed until blended after each addition. Spoon batter over berry mixture.

4. Bake in preheated oven until a wooden pick inserted in center comes out clean, 50 to 50 minutes. Cool on a wire rack 10 minutes.

Cookies & Bars

Caramel-Filled Chocolate Cookies

(Photo, page 345)

ACTIVE 15 MIN. - TOTAL 1 HOUR, 30 MIN.
MAKES 4 DOZEN

- 1 cup butter, softened
- 1 cup plus 1 Tbsp. granulated sugar, divided
- 1 cup firmly packed brown sugar
- 2 large eggs
- 2 tsp. vanilla extract
- 2¼ cups all-purpose flour
- ¾ cup unsweetened cocoa
- 1 tsp. baking soda
- 1 cup chopped pecans, divided
- 6 (2-oz.) pkg. chocolate-caramel cookie bars, cut into 1-inch pieces

1. Preheat oven to 375°F. Beat butter in a bowl with an electric mixer on medium speed until creamy; gradually add 1 cup granulated sugar and brown sugar, beating until blended. Add eggs, 1 at a time, beating until blended after each addition. Beat in vanilla.
2. Combine flour, cocoa, and baking soda in a medium bowl; gradually add flour mixture to butter mixture, beating at low speed until blended after each addition. Stir in ½ cup pecans. Shape 1 Tbsp. dough around each candy piece, covering completely, to form balls.
3. Combine remaining ½ cup pecans and remaining 1 Tbsp. sugar. Gently press the top of each ball into pecan mixture. Place balls, pecan sides up, 2 inches apart on parchment paper-lined baking sheets.

4. Bake in preheated oven, in batches, 7 to 10 minutes. Cool on baking sheets 2 minutes. Transfer to wire racks, and cool completely, about 30 minutes.

Chocolate Chip Pretzel Cookies

ACTIVE 30 MIN. - TOTAL 1 HOUR, 15 MIN.
MAKES ABOUT 5 DOZEN

- ¾ cup butter, softened
- ¾ cup granulated sugar
- ¾ cup firmly packed dark brown sugar
- 2 large eggs
- 1½ tsp. vanilla extract
- 2¼ cups plus 2 Tbsp. all-purpose flour
- 1 tsp. baking soda
- ¾ tsp. table salt
- 1½ (12-oz.) pkg. semisweet chocolate chips
- 2 cups coarsely crushed pretzel sticks

1. Preheat oven to 350°F. Beat butter and sugars at medium speed with a heavy-duty electric stand mixer until creamy. Add eggs and vanilla, beating until blended.
2. Combine flour, baking soda, and salt in a small bowl; gradually add flour mixture to butter mixture, beating just until blended. Beat in chocolate chips and pretzel sticks just until combined.
3. Drop dough by tablespoonfuls onto parchment paper-lined baking sheets.
4. Bake in preheated oven, in batches, 10 to 14 minutes or until desired degree of doneness. Transfer to wire racks, and cool completely, about 5 minutes.

Chunky Cherry-Double Chip Cookies

(Photo, page 345)

ACTIVE 30 MIN. - TOTAL 1 HOUR, 25 MIN.
MAKES ABOUT 5 DOZEN

- ½ cup dried cherries
- ¾ cup butter, softened
- ¾ cup granulated sugar
- ¾ cup firmly packed dark brown sugar
- 2 large eggs
- 1½ tsp. vanilla extract
- 2¼ cups plus 2 Tbsp. all-purpose flour
- 1 tsp. baking soda
- ¾ tsp. table salt

- 1 (12-oz.) pkg. semisweet chocolate chunks
- 1 cup white chocolate chips
- ⅓ cup slivered toasted almonds

1. Preheat oven to 350°F. Microwave 1 Tbsp. water and dried cherries in a glass bowl on HIGH 30 seconds, stirring once. Let stand 10 minutes.
2. Beat butter and sugars in a bowl with an electric mixer on medium speed until creamy. Add eggs and vanilla, beating until blended.
3. Combine flour, baking soda, and salt in a small bowl; gradually add flour mixture to butter mixture, beating until blended. Stir in semisweet chocolate chunks, white chocolate chips, almonds, and cherries.
4. Drop dough by tablespoonfuls onto lightly greased (with cooking spray) baking sheets.
5. Bake in preheated oven, in batches, until edges are just light golden brown, 8 to 10 minutes. Transfer to wire racks, and cool completely, about 20 minutes.

Cranberry-Pistachio Cookies

ACTIVE 8 MIN. - TOTAL 30 MIN.
MAKES 3½ DOZEN

- 1 cup butter, softened
- ¾ cup granulated sugar
- ¾ cup firmly packed light brown sugar
- ½ tsp. almond extract
- 2 large eggs
- 2¼ cups all-purpose flour
- 1 tsp. baking powder
- 1 tsp. table salt
- 2 cups chopped fresh cranberries
- 1 cup roasted coarsely chopped shelled raw pistachios
  Cookie Frosting (recipe follows)

1. Preheat oven to 375°F. Beat butter in a bowl with an electric mixer on medium speed until creamy; gradually add sugars, beating until blended. Add almond extract and eggs, beating until blended.
2. Combine flour, baking powder, and salt in a medium bowl; gradually add flour mixture to butter mixture, beating at low speed until blended after each addition. Stir in cranberries and pistachios.
3. Drop dough by rounded tablespoonfuls onto ungreased baking sheets.
4. Bake in preheated oven, in batches, 9 to 11 minutes. Transfer to wire racks, and cool completely, about 20 minutes.

Recipe continued on page 336

Recipe continued from page 335

5. Spread cookies with frosting, and sprinkle with additional chopped pistachios and dried cranberries.

Cookie Frosting

ACTIVE 10 MIN. - TOTAL 10 MIN.
MAKES 1 CUP

Beat 2 Tbsp. softened **butter** in a bowl with an electric mixer on medium speed until creamy; gradually add 2 cups sifted **powdered sugar**, beating until blended. Add 2 Tbsp. **milk**, and beat until smooth. Tint with food coloring as desired.

Pecan Pie Cookies

ACTIVE 20 MIN. - TOTAL 2 HOURS, 45 MIN.
MAKES 4½ DOZEN

- 1¼ cups butter, softened, divided
- ½ cup granulated sugar
- ½ cup plus 3 Tbsp. dark corn syrup, divided
- 2 large eggs, separated
- 2½ cups all-purpose flour
- ½ cup powdered sugar
- ¾ cup finely chopped pecans

1. Beat 1 cup butter and sugar with an electric mixer on medium speed until light and fluffy. Add ½ cup corn syrup and egg yolks, beating until blended. Gradually stir in flour; cover and chill 1 hour.
2. Melt ¼ cup butter in a heavy saucepan over medium heat; stir in powdered sugar and 3 tablespoons corn syrup. Cook, stirring often, until mixture boils. Remove from heat. Stir in pecans; chill 30 minutes. Shape into ¼-inch balls (about ¼ teaspoon mixture per ball); set aside.
3. Preheat oven to 375°F. Shape dough into 1-inch balls; place 2 inches apart on lightly greased (with cooking spray) baking sheets. Beat egg whites until foamy; brush on dough balls.
4. Bake in preheated oven, in batches, 6 minutes. Remove from oven, and place pecan balls in center of each cookie. Bake until lightly browned, 8 to 10 minutes more. Cool on baking sheets 5 minutes. Transfer to wire racks, and cool completely, about 30 minutes. Freeze up to 1 month, if desired.

Mississippi Praline Macaroons

ACTIVE 20 MIN. - TOTAL 1 HOUR, 20 MIN.
MAKES ABOUT 3 DOZEN

- 3 large egg whites, at room temperature
- ¼ tsp. cream of tartar
  Pinch of table salt
- 1 cup firmly packed light brown sugar
- 1 cup toasted coarsely chopped pecans
- 36 pecan halves

1. Preheat oven to 325°F. Beat egg whites, cream of tartar, and salt with a heavy-duty electric stand mixer using whisk attachment at high speed, until foamy; gradually add brown sugar, beating until stiff peaks form and sugar dissolves. Gently fold in toasted chopped pecans.
2. Drop batter by heaping teaspoonfuls 1 inch apart onto lightly greased (with cooking spray) aluminum foil-lined baking sheets. Press 1 pecan half into each cookie, flattening slightly.
3. Bake in preheated oven, in batches, until pecan halves are toasted and cookies are lightly browned, 33 minutes. Cool on baking sheets 1 minute; transfer to wire racks, and let cool 20 minutes. (Cookies will crisp while cooling.)

Lemon Meltaways

ACTIVE 30 MIN. - TOTAL 2 HOURS
MAKES ABOUT 3½ DOZEN

- ¾ cup plus 2 Tbsp. butter, softened
- 1½ cups powdered sugar, divided
- 1 Tbsp. loosely packed lemon zest
- 2 Tbsp. fresh lemon juice
- 1½ cups all-purpose flour
- ¼ cup cornstarch
- ¼ tsp. table salt

1. Beat butter at medium speed with a heavy-duty electric stand mixer until creamy. Add ½ cup powdered sugar; beat at medium speed until light and fluffy. Stir in zest and juice. Whisk together flour, cornstarch, and salt. Gradually add flour mixture to butter mixture, beating at low speed just until blended. Cover and chill 1 hour.
2. Preheat oven to 350°F. Using a 1-inch cookie scoop, drop dough by level spoonfuls 2 inches apart onto parchment paper-lined baking sheets.

3. Bake in preheated oven, in batches, 13 minutes or until lightly browned around edges. Cool on baking sheets 5 minutes.
4. Toss together warm cookies and remaining 1 cup powdered sugar in a small bowl. Transfer to wire racks, and cool completely, about 15 minutes.

Outrageous Peanut Butter Cookies

ACTIVE 10 MIN. - TOTAL 40 MIN.
MAKES 8 COOKIES

- ¼ cup all-purpose flour
- ⅛ tsp. baking soda
- ¼ cup firmly packed dark brown sugar
- 2 Tbsp. butter, softened
- 2 tsp. well-beaten egg
- ¼ tsp. vanilla extract
- ⅓ cup extra-chunky peanut butter
- 1½ Tbsp. uncooked regular oats
- ½ (1.8-oz.) chocolate-coated caramel-peanut butter-peanut candy bar, chopped
- 1 Tbsp. granulated sugar

1. Preheat oven to 325°F. Combine flour and baking soda in a small bowl.
2. Beat brown sugar, butter, egg, and vanilla in a bowl with an electric mixer on low speed 1 minute or until blended. Add peanut butter, and beat 20 seconds. Add flour mixture; beat 30 seconds or until blended. Stir in oats and chopped bar.
3. Drop dough by heaping tablespoonfuls 2 inches apart onto a parchment paper-lined baking sheet. Flatten dough slightly with bottom of a glass dipped in granulated sugar.
4. Bake in preheated oven until lightly browned, 15 to 20 minutes. Cool on baking sheet 2 minutes. Transfer to wire rack, and cool completely, about 15 minutes.

Strawberry Shortcake Sandwich Cookies

(Photo, page 345)

ACTIVE 30 MIN. - TOTAL 2 HOURS, 20 MIN.
MAKES ABOUT 1¼ DOZEN

COOKIES
- ½ cup butter, softened
- 1 cup granulated sugar
- 1 large egg
- 1 tsp. vanilla extract
- 1 tsp. loosely packed lemon zest
- 2 cups all-purpose flour

½ tsp. baking soda
¼ tsp. table salt
½ cup sour cream
Coarse sanding sugar

MERINGUE FILLING
½ cup granulated sugar
⅓ cup light corn syrup
⅛ tsp. table salt
2 large egg whites
¼ tsp. cream of tartar
½ tsp. vanilla extract

REMAINING INGREDIENT
1 cup seedless strawberry jam

1. Prepare Cookies: Preheat oven to 375°F. Beat butter in a bowl with an electric mixer on medium speed until creamy; gradually add granulated sugar, beating until fluffy. Add egg, beating until blended. Beat in vanilla and lemon zest.
2. Combine flour, baking soda, and salt in a medium bowl; gradually add flour mixture to butter mixture alternately with sour cream, beating at low speed just until blended after each addition.
3. Drop dough by rounded tablespoonfuls 2 inches apart onto parchment paper-lined baking sheets. Sprinkle generously with sanding sugar.
4. Bake in preheated oven until puffed and lightly browned around edges, 11 to 13 minutes. Cool on baking sheets 5 minutes. Transfer to wire racks, and cool completely, about 30 minutes.
5. Prepare Meringue Filling: Bring sugar, corn syrup, salt, and 3 tablespoons water to a boil in a small, heavy saucepan over medium-high, stirring just until sugar dissolves. Cook, without stirring, until a candy thermometer registers 240°F, about 4 minutes. Beat egg whites and cream of tartar in a bowl with an electric mixer on high speed until soft peaks form. Gradually pour hot sugar syrup into egg white mixture, beating first at medium speed and then at high speed; beat in vanilla. Continue beating 5 minutes or until mixture is thick, glossy, and the texture of marshmallow fluff.
6. Spoon filling into a piping bag fitted with a medium star tip; pipe onto bottoms of cookies. Spoon 1 tablespoon jam onto filling on half of frosted cookies. Top with remaining frosted cookies to create a sandwich. Let stand 1 hour or until filling is set.

Toasted Coconut Cookies

ACTIVE 20 MIN. - TOTAL 1 HOUR, 15 MIN.
MAKES 4 DOZEN

¼ cup butter, softened
¼ cup shortening
1 cup sugar
1 large egg
½ tsp. coconut extract
1½ cups all-purpose flour
1 tsp. baking powder
½ tsp. baking soda
½ tsp. table salt
1 cup sweetened flaked coconut
½ cup crispy rice cereal
½ cup uncooked regular oats

1. Preheat oven to 325°F. Beat butter and shortening in a bowl with an electric mixer on medium speed until creamy; gradually add sugar, beating until blended. Add egg and coconut extract, beating until blended.
2. Combine flour, baking powder, baking soda, and salt in a small bowl; gradually add flour mixture to butter mixture, beating until blended after each addition. Stir in coconut, cereal, and oats.
3. Drop dough by heaping teaspoonfuls onto lightly greased (with cooking spray) baking sheets.
4. Bake in preheated oven, in batches, until golden brown, 12 to 14 minutes. Cool on baking sheets 5 minutes. Transfer to wire racks, and cool completely, about 20 minutes.

Tropical White Chocolate Cookies

(Photo, page 345)

ACTIVE 15 MIN. - TOTAL 50 MIN.
MAKES ABOUT 4 DOZEN

¾ cup butter, softened
¾ cup firmly packed brown sugar
¾ cup granulated sugar
1 tsp. vanilla extract
2 large eggs
1½ cups sweetened flaked coconut
1 Tbsp. loosely packed lime zest
2 Tbsp. fresh lime juice
2½ cups all-purpose flour
1 tsp. baking soda
½ tsp. table salt
1 (12-oz.) pkg. white chocolate chips
½ cup chopped macadamia nuts

1. Preheat oven to 375°F. Beat butter, sugars, and vanilla with an electric mixer on medium speed until creamy. Add eggs, beating until blended. Add coconut, lime zest, and lime juice, beating until blended.
2. Combine flour, baking soda, and salt in a small bowl; gradually add flour mixture to butter mixture, beating until blended. Stir in white chocolate chips and macadamia nuts.
3. Drop dough by rounded tablespoonfuls onto ungreased baking sheets.
4. Bake in preheated oven, in batches, until lightly browned, 10 to 12 minutes. Transfer to wire racks, and cool completely, about 20 minutes.

Orange Palmiers

ACTIVE 20 MIN. - TOTAL 1 HOUR, 25 MIN.
MAKES ABOUT 3½ DOZEN

¾ cup Demerara sugar
1 tsp. ground cinnamon
1 (17.3-oz.) pkg. frozen puff pastry sheets, thawed
⅔ cup orange marmalade

1. Combine sugar and cinnamon in a small bowl. Sprinkle ¼ cup sugar mixture over a 12-inch square on a work surface. Unfold 1 pastry sheet on top of sugar, and roll sheet into a 12- x 9-inch rectangle. Spread ⅓ cup marmalade over dough, leaving a ½-inch border around edges. Starting with 1 long side, roll up pastry, jelly-roll style, to center of pastry sheet. Roll opposite side to center. (The shape will resemble a scroll.) Wrap in plastic wrap, and freeze 20 minutes. Repeat procedure with ¼ cup of the sugar mixture and remaining pastry sheet and ⅓ cup marmalade.
2. Preheat oven to 375°F. Remove 1 pastry roll from freezer, and cut into ½-inch-thick slices; place 2 inches apart on a parchment paper-lined baking sheet. Sprinkle each slice with a small amount of the remaining sugar mixture.
3. Bake in preheated oven until light golden brown on bottom, 14 to 16 minutes. Remove from oven, and carefully turn each cookie over. Return to oven, and bake until crisp and golden brown, 8 to 10 more minutes. Transfer cookies to a wire rack, and cool completely, about 30 minutes. Repeat procedure with the remaining pastry roll.

Key Lime Tassies

(Photo, page 345)

ACTIVE 45 MIN. - TOTAL 4 HOURS, 45 MIN.

MAKES 60 COOKIES

CURD

2	cups granulated sugar
½	cup salted butter, softened
4	large eggs, at room temperature
1	cup bottled Key lime juice, at room temperature

CREAM CHEESE PASTRY

1	(8-oz.) pkg. cream cheese, softened
1	cup salted butter, softened
¼	cup granulated sugar
3½	cups all-purpose flour

ADDITIONAL INGREDIENTS

Powdered sugar

Lime zest, for garnish (optional)

1. Prepare the Curd: Beat 2 cups granulated sugar and ½ cup butter in a bowl with an electric mixer on medium speed until blended. Add eggs, 1 at a time, beating just until blended after each addition. Gradually add Key lime juice to butter mixture, beating at low speed just until blended after each addition. (Mixture may separate at this stage but will emulsify as it is heated and whisked.)

2. Transfer mixture to a heavy 4-quart saucepan. Cook over medium-low, whisking constantly, until mixture thickens and just begins to bubble, 14 to 16 minutes. Remove saucepan from heat, and cool curd 30 minutes. Place heavy-duty plastic wrap directly on surface of warm curd (to prevent a film from forming), and chill until firm, about 4 hours. Refrigerate in an airtight container up to 2 weeks.

3. Prepare the Cream Cheese Pastry: Beat cream cheese, 1 cup butter, and ¼ cup granulated sugar with a heavy-duty electric stand mixer on medium speed until creamy. Gradually add flour to butter mixture, beating at low speed just until blended after each addition. Shape dough into 60 (1-inch) balls, and place on a baking sheet; cover and chill 1 hour.

4. Preheat oven to 400°F. Place 1 chilled dough ball into each cup of lightly greased miniature muffin pans; press dough into bottoms and up sides of cups, forming shells.

5. Bake in preheated oven until lightly browned, 10 to 12 minutes. Remove shells from pans to wire racks, and cool completely, about 20 minutes.

6. Spoon about 1½ teaspoons of the Curd into each pastry shell. Cover filled shells, and chill until ready to serve. Just before serving, sprinkle filled shells evenly with powdered sugar and, if desired, garnish with lime zest.

Note: You will have leftover curd. It is great spread on warm biscuits or scones, as a topping for pound cake, or as a dip for fresh fruit.

Peppermint Pinwheels

ACTIVE 30 MIN. - TOTAL 4 HOURS

MAKES ABOUT 5 DOZEN

1	cup salted butter, softened
1½	cups granulated sugar
1	large egg
1	tsp. peppermint extract
1	tsp. vanilla extract
2½	cups all-purpose flour
1½	tsp. baking powder
¼	tsp. salt
	Red food coloring paste or gel

1. Beat butter with a heavy-duty stand mixer on medium speed until creamy, about 2 minutes; gradually add sugar, beating well. Add egg and extracts, beating until combined.

2. Stir together flour, baking powder, and salt in a small bowl. Gradually add to butter mixture, beating on low speed just until blended.

3. Divide dough in half; add desired amount of red food coloring to 1 portion, and knead until color is distributed. Shape dough halves into disks; wrap in plastic wrap, and chill until firm, about 1 hour.

4. Divide each half of dough into 2 equal portions. Roll out each portion on floured wax paper into an 8-inch square, trimming edges if necessary.

5. Invert 1 white dough square onto 1 red dough square; peel wax paper from white dough. Tightly roll up dough, jelly-roll fashion, peeling wax paper from red dough as you roll. Repeat with remaining dough squares. Wrap rolls in plastic wrap, and chill 2 hours.

6. Preheat oven to 350°F. Remove dough from refrigerator, and cut into ¼-inch-thick slices; place slices 2 inches apart on parchment paper-lined baking sheets. (Keep unbaked dough chilled while baking cookies.)

7. Bake in preheated oven, in batches, until bottoms are lightly browned, 10 to 12 minutes. Remove cookies from pans to wire racks, and cool completely.

Red Velvet Crackle Sandwich Cookies

(Photo, page 317)

ACTIVE 30 MIN. - TOTAL 40 MIN.

MAKES 21 SANDWICH COOKIES

3	oz. semisweet baking chocolate, chopped
¼	cup unsalted butter
1	cup granulated sugar
2	large eggs
1	Tbsp. red liquid food coloring
2	cups all-purpose flour
2	Tbsp. unsweetened cocoa
1	tsp. baking powder
½	tsp. baking soda
½	tsp. kosher salt
2	cups powdered sugar, divided
4	oz. cream cheese, softened

1. Preheat oven to 375°F with oven racks in the top third and bottom third of oven. Melt chocolate and butter in a large microwavable glass bowl on MEDIUM until melted, about 1½ minutes, stirring every 30 seconds. Whisk in granulated sugar, eggs, and food coloring until smooth.

2. Whisk together flour cocoa, baking powder, baking soda, and salt in a bowl; add to butter mixture, stirring just to combine.

3. Place 1 cup of the powdered sugar in a small bowl. Drop dough by tablespoonfuls into powdered sugar, rolling to coat, and place 1 inch apart on parchment-lined baking sheets. Gently flatten domed tops of dough. Bake in preheated oven until cookies are almost set and crackled, 10 to 11 minutes. Transfer pans to wire racks, and cool completely, about 30 minutes.

4. Beat cream cheese and remaining 1 cup powdered sugar in a bowl with an electric mixer on medium speed until smooth; spread 1½ teaspoons filling onto flat side of half of each cookie. Cover with remaining cookies, flat side down.

Bourbon Balls

ACTIVE 30 MIN. - TOTAL 53 MIN.

MAKES ABOUT 5 DOZEN

1	(12-oz.) pkg. vanilla wafers, finely crushed
1	cup chopped pecans, toasted
¾	cup powdered sugar
2	Tbsp. unsweetened cocoa
½	cup bourbon
2½	Tbsp. light corn syrup
	Powdered sugar

1. Stir together crushed vanilla wafers, pecans, powdered sugar, and cocoa in a large bowl until well blended.

2. Stir together bourbon and corn syrup until well blended. Stir together bourbon mixture and wafer mixture. Shape into 1-inch balls; roll in powdered sugar. Cover and chill up to 2 weeks.

Cane Syrup Slice 'n' Bakes

(Photo, page 345)

ACTIVE 35 MIN. · TOTAL 3 HOURS, 10 MIN.
MAKES ABOUT 5 DOZEN

2	cups butter, softened
¾	cup granulated sugar
¼	cup cane syrup*
1½	tsp. kosher salt
2	tsp. vanilla extract
4	cups all-purpose flour
1	large egg, lightly beaten
½	cup turbinado sugar

1. Beat butter, sugar, syrup, salt, and vanilla with an electric mixer on medium speed 2 to 3 minutes or until creamy.

2. Add flour; beat until blended. Divide dough into 4 portions, and shape each portion into an 8- x 2-inch log. Wrap each log in plastic wrap, and chill 1 hour.

3. Whisk together egg and 1 tablespoon water. Unwrap logs, and brush with beaten egg. Sprinkle turbinado sugar over logs, pressing to adhere, and rewrap. Chill 30 minutes.

4. Preheat oven to 350°F. Cut logs into ¼-inch-thick slices; place 1 inch apart on 2 parchment paper-lined baking sheets. Bake 10 to 14 minutes or until edges are lightly browned, switching pans halfway through. Cool on baking sheets 5 minutes. Transfer to wire racks, and cool.

*Sorghum or honey may be substituted.

Black-Tie Benne Slice 'n' Bakes: Prepare recipe as directed, reducing butter to 1½ cups and adding ½ cup each tahini and white sesame seeds to butter, sugar, cane syrup, salt, and vanilla in Step 1. Substitute ¾ cup black sesame seeds for turbinado sugar.

Gingersnap Slice 'n' Bakes: Prepare recipe as directed, reducing salt to 1¼ teaspoons and adding 2 teaspoons ground cinnamon, 1 teaspoon. ground cardamom, and ¼ teaspoon each ground allspice, ground cloves, and ground nutmeg to butter, sugar, cane syrup, salt, and vanilla. Stir in ½ cup chopped crystallized ginger after adding flour.

Fruitcake Slice 'n' Bakes: Soak 1 cup candied fruit, 1 teaspoon. firmly packed orange zest, and 1 teaspoon loosely packed lemon zest in ¼ cup spiced or dark rum 30 minutes. Prepare recipe as directed, stirring fruit mixture into dough after adding flour. Substitute ¾ cup chopped walnuts for turbinado sugar.

Lemon-Rosemary Slice 'n' Bakes: Prepare recipe as directed, omitting egg and turbinado sugar and adding 1 Tbsp. lemon zest and 2 teaspoons minced fresh rosemary butter, sugar, cane syrup, salt, and vanilla. Reduce flour to 3½ cups, and add ½ cup cornmeal with flour. Toss together warm cookies and 2 cups powdered sugar.

Easiest Peanut Butter Cookies

ACTIVE 20 MIN. · TOTAL 35 MIN.
MAKES ABOUT 30 COOKIES

1	cup peanut butter
1	cup sugar
1	large egg
1	tsp. vanilla extract

1. Preheat oven to 325°F. Stir together peanut butter, sugar, egg, and vanilla in a bowl until combined; shape dough into 1-inch balls. Place balls 1 inch apart on ungreased baking sheets, and flatten with tines of a fork. Bake 15 minutes. Remove to wire racks to cool.

2. Evenly press 1 cup of your desired addition, such as chocolate chips, chocolate-coated toffee bits, or chopped peanuts, onto the top of prepared cookie dough on baking sheets; bake as directed.

Peanut Butter-and-Chocolate Cookies: Divide peanut butter cookie dough in half. Stir 2 melted semisweet chocolate baking squares into half of dough. Shape doughs into 30 (1-inch) half peanut butter, half chocolate-peanut butter balls. Flatten gently with a spoon. Proceed as directed.

Pecan Crescents

ACTIVE 40 MIN. · TOTAL 2 HOURS, INCLUDING CHILLING
MAKES ABOUT 5 DOZEN

1	cup pecan halves, toasted
1	cup butter, softened
¾	cup powdered sugar, sifted
2	tsp. vanilla extract
2½	cups sifted all-purpose flour
	Powdered sugar

1. Preheat oven to 350°F. Pulse pecans in a food processor until they are coarse like sand.

2. Beat butter and ¾ cup powdered sugar in a bowl with an electric mixer on medium speed until creamy. Stir in vanilla and ground pecans. Gradually add flour, beating until a soft dough forms. Beat at low speed just until combined. Cover and chill 1 hour.

3. Divide dough into 5 portions; divide each portion into 12 pieces. Roll dough pieces into 2-inch logs, curving ends to form crescents. Place on ungreased baking sheets.

4. Bake in preheated oven until lightly browned, 10 to 12 minutes. Cool 5 minutes. Roll warm cookies in powdered sugar. Cool completely on wire racks.

Peppermint Candy Shortbread

ACTIVE 45 MIN. · TOTAL 1 HOUR, 10 MIN.
MAKES 2 DOZEN

1	cup butter, softened
⅓	cup sugar
2½	cups all-purpose flour
4	(2-oz.) vanilla bark coating squares
⅔	cup crushed hard peppermint candy

1. Preheat oven to 350°F. Beat butter in a bowl with an electric mixer on medium speed until creamy; gradually add sugar, beating well. Add flour, beating just until blended.

2. Divide dough into 3 equal portions. Place 1 portion of dough on an ungreased baking sheet; roll into a 6-inch circle. Score dough into 8 triangles. Repeat procedure with remaining 2 portions of dough.

3. Bake in preheated oven until almost golden, about 25 minutes. Cool on baking sheets 5 minutes. Remove disks to wire racks to cool completely.

4. Separate disks into wedges, working very carefully.

5. Melt bark coating in top of a double boiler over hot water. Remove from heat. Carefully dip wide edges of shortbread in melted coating; place shortbread on wax paper. Sprinkle crushed candy over coated edges. Let stand until coating is firm.

Raisin-Oatmeal Cookies

ACTIVE 10 MIN. - TOTAL 8 HOURS, 22 MIN., INCLUDING CHILLING

MAKES 2 DOZEN

- 1 cup butter or margarine, softened
- 1 cup sugar
- 1 cup firmly packed brown sugar
- 2 large eggs
- 2 cups self-rising flour
- 2 tsp. ground cinnamon
- 3 cups uncooked regular oats
- 1 cup raisins
- 1 cup chopped pecans

1. Preheat oven to 400°F. Beat butter and sugars with an electric mixer on medium speed until fluffy. Add eggs, beating until blended. Gradually add flour and cinnamon, beating at low speed until blended. Stir in oats, raisins, and pecans. Cover and chill dough 8 hours.
2. Divide dough into 2 equal portions. Roll each portion into a 12-inch log. Cut each log into 1-inch-thick slices. Place slices on ungreased baking sheets.
3. Bake in preheated oven until golden brown, about 12 minutes; remove to wire racks to cool.

Soft Coconut Macaroons

Using clear vanilla extract will keep the macaroons pearly white, but if you don't have it, regular vanilla will work fine.

ACTIVE 10 MIN. - TOTAL 30 MIN.

MAKES 2½ TO 3 DOZEN

- 4 egg whites
- 2⅔ cups sweetened flaked coconut
- ⅔ cup sugar
- ¼ cup all-purpose flour
- ½ tsp. clear vanilla extract
- ¼ tsp. salt
- ¼ to ½ tsp. almond extract

1. Preheat oven to 325°F. Stir together all ingredients in a large bowl, blending well. Drop dough by teaspoonfuls onto lightly greased baking sheets.
2. Bake in preheated oven 18 to 20 minutes. Remove to wire racks to cool.

Tea Cakes

ACTIVE 20 MIN. - TOTAL 1 HOUR, 40 MIN.

MAKES 3 DOZEN

- 1 cup butter, softened
- 2 cups sugar
- 3 large eggs

Sugar Cookies

ACTIVE 30 MIN. - TOTAL 41 MIN.

MAKES ABOUT 7 DOZEN

- 1 cup butter, softened
- 1 cup powdered sugar
- 1 cup granulated sugar
- 2 large eggs
- 1 cup vegetable oil
- 2 tsp. vanilla extract
- 1 Tbsp. fresh lemon juice
- 5¼ cups all-purpose flour
- 1 tsp. cream of tartar
- 1 tsp. baking soda
- ¼ tsp. salt
  Colored sugar

1. Preheat oven to 350°F. Beat 1 cup butter in a bowl with an electric mixer on medium speed until fluffy; add sugars, beating well. Add eggs, vegetable oil, vanilla, and lemon juice, beating until blended.
2. Combine flour cream of tartar, baking soda, and salt; gradually add to sugar mixture, beating until blended.
3. Shape dough into 1-inch balls; roll in colored sugar, and place about 2 inches apart on lightly greased baking sheets.
4. Bake in preheated oven, in batches, 9 to 11 minutes or until set. (Do not brown.) Remove to wire racks to cool.

Chocolate Kiss Cookies: Omit colored sugar. After baking, immediately place 1 unwrapped milk chocolate kiss in center of each cookie, and cool.

Peanut Butter Cup Cookies: Omit colored sugar. After baking, immediately place 1 unwrapped miniature peanut butter cup in the center of each cookie, and cool.

Lemon Cookies: Omit vanilla and colored sugar. Increase lemon juice to ¼ cup, and add 1 tsp. grated lemon rind to dough. Proceed as directed.

Lemon Thumbprint Cookies: Prepare Lemon Cookies, and press thumb in center of each cookie to make an indentation. Bake and cool as directed. Spoon ½ tsp. raspberry jam in each indentation.

- 1 tsp. vanilla extract
- 3½ cups all-purpose flour
- 1 tsp. baking soda
- ½ tsp. salt

1. Preheat oven to 350°F. Beat butter in a bowl with an electric mixer on medium speed until creamy; gradually add sugar, beating well. Add eggs, 1 at a time, beating until blended after each addition. Add vanilla extract, beating until blended.
2. Combine flour, soda, and salt in a medium bowl; gradually add flour mixture to butter mixture, beating at low speed until blended after each addition.
3. Divide dough in half; wrap each portion in plastic wrap, and chill 1 hour.
4. Roll half of dough to ¼-inch thickness on a floured surface. Cut out cookies with a 2½-inch round cutter, and place 1 inch apart on parchment paper-lined baking sheets.
5. Bake in preheated oven until edges begin to brown, 10 to 12 minutes; let stand on baking sheet 5 minutes. Remove to wire racks to cool. Repeat with remaining dough.

Ultimate Chocolate Chip Cookies

ACTIVE 30 MIN. - TOTAL 44 MIN.

MAKES ABOUT 5 DOZEN

- ¾ cup butter, softened
- ¾ cup granulated sugar
- ¾ cup firmly packed dark brown sugar
- 2 large eggs
- 1½ tsp. vanilla extract
- 2¼ cups plus 2 Tbsp. all-purpose flour
- 1 tsp. baking soda
- ¾ tsp. salt
- 1 (12-oz.) pkg. semisweet chocolate chips

1. Preheat oven to 350°F. Beat butter and sugars in a bowl with an electric mixer on medium speed until creamy. Add eggs and vanilla, beating until blended.
2. Combine flour, baking soda, and salt in a small bowl; gradually add to butter mixture, beating well. Stir in chocolate chips. Drop by tablespoonfuls onto lightly greased baking sheets.
3. Bake in preheated oven 8 to 14 minutes or until desired degree of doneness. Remove to wire racks to cool completely.

Peanut Butter-Chocolate Chip Cookies: Decrease salt to ½ tsp. Add 1 cup creamy peanut butter with butter and sugars. Increase flour to 2½ cups plus 2 tablespoons. Proceed as directed. (Dough will look a little moist.)

Oatmeal-Raisin Chocolate Chip Cookies: Reduce flour to 2 cups. Add 1 cup uncooked quick-cooking oats to dry ingredients and 1 cup raisins with chips. Proceed as directed.

Pecan-Chocolate Chip Cookies: Add 1½ cups chopped toasted pecans with chocolate chips. Proceed as directed.

Almond-Toffee Chocolate Chip Cookies: Reduce chocolate chips to 1 cup. Add ½ cup slivered toasted almonds and 1 cup almond toffee bits. Proceed as directed.

Simple Brownies with Chocolate Frosting

(Photo, page 345)

ACTIVE 15 MIN. · TOTAL 2 HOURS
MAKES 4 DOZEN BARS

- 1 (4-oz.) unsweetened chocolate baking bar, chopped
- ¾ cup butter
- 2 cups sugar
- 4 large eggs
- 1 cup all-purpose flour
  Shortening, for greasing pan
  Chocolate Frosting (recipe follows)
- 1½ cups toasted coarsely chopped pecans

1. Preheat oven to 350°F. Microwave chocolate and butter in a large microwaveable bowl on HIGH 1 to 1½ minutes or until melted and smooth, stirring at 30-second intervals. Whisk in sugar and eggs until blended. Whisk in flour. Pour mixture into a greased 13- x 9-inch pan.
2. Bake in preheated oven until a wooden pick inserted in center comes out with a few moist crumbs, 25 to 30 minutes.
3. Pour Chocolate Frosting over warm brownies, and spread to edges. Sprinkle with pecans. Cool in pan on a wire rack, about 1 hour. Cut into squares.

Chocolate Frosting

ACTIVE 15 MIN. · TOTAL 15 MIN.
MAKES ABOUT 1 CUP

Place ½ cup **butter**, ⅓ cup **sugar**, and 6 Tbsp. **unsweetened cocoa** over medium heat in a large saucepan; cook, stirring constantly, 4 to 5 minutes or until butter is melted. Remove from heat, and beat in 1 tsp. **powdered sugar** and 1 tsp. **vanilla extract** with an electric mixer on medium speed until smooth.

Cappuccino-Frosted Brownies

ACTIVE 20 MIN. · TOTAL 1 HOUR
MAKES 1 DOZEN

- 4 (1-oz.) unsweetened chocolate baking squares
- ¾ cup butter
- 2 cups sugar
- 4 large eggs
- 1 cup all-purpose flour
- 1 tsp. vanilla extract
- 1 cup semisweet chocolate chips
  Cappuccino-Buttercream Frosting (recipe follows)

1. Preheat oven to 350°F. Microwave chocolate squares and butter in a large microwaveable bowl on HIGH 1½ minutes or until melted and smooth, stirring at 30-second intervals. Whisk in sugar. Add eggs, 1 at a time, whisking just until blended after each addition. Whisk in flour and vanilla. Add chocolate chips, stirring to combine. Pour mixture into a lightly greased (with cooking spray) 13- x 9-inch baking pan.
2. Bake in preheated oven until a wooden pick inserted in center comes out clean, 30 to 35 minutes. Cool completely in pan on a wire rack, about 1 hour.
3. Spread Cappuccino-Buttercream Frosting evenly on top of cooled brownies, and cut into squares. Cover and chill, if desired.

Cappuccino-Buttercream Frosting

ACTIVE 10 MIN. · TOTAL 10 MIN.
MAKES ABOUT 3 CUPS

Dissolve 1 (1.16-oz.) envelope **instant mocha cappuccino mix** in ¼ cup hot **milk** in a small cup, stirring to combine; cool completely. Pour milk mixture into a large bowl; add ½ cup softened **butter**, and beat with an electric mixer on medium speed until blended. Gradually add 1 (16-oz.) pkg. **powdered sugar**, beating until smooth and fluffy.

Peanut Butter Mississippi Mud Brownies

(Photo, page 348)

ACTIVE 20 MIN. · TOTAL 2 HOURS, 15 MIN.
MAKES ABOUT 2½ DOZEN

- 4 (1-oz.) unsweetened chocolate baking squares
- 1⅓ cups butter, softened and divided
- 2½ cups granulated sugar, divided
- 4 large eggs
- 2 cups all-purpose flour, divided
- 1 tsp. vanilla extract
- ½ cup creamy peanut butter
- ½ cup firmly packed light brown sugar
- 2 large eggs
- 1 tsp. baking powder
- 3 cups miniature marshmallows
- 1½ cups lightly salted roasted peanuts
  Chocolate Frosting (recipe follows)

1. Preheat oven to 350°F. Microwave chocolate in a microwave-safe bowl on MEDIUM 1½ minutes or until melted and smooth, stirring at 30-second intervals.
2. Beat 1 cup butter and 2 cups granulated sugar with an electric mixer on medium speed until light and fluffy. Add 4 eggs, 1 at a time, beating just until blended after each addition. Add melted chocolate, beating just until blended. Add 1 cup flour, beating at low speed just until blended. Stir in vanilla. Spread half of batter in a greased and floured 13- x 9-inch pan.
3. Beat peanut butter, brown sugar, and remaining ⅓ cup butter and ½ cup granulated sugar in a bowl with an electric mixer on medium speed until light and fluffy. Add 2 eggs, 1 at a time, beating just until blended after each addition. Stir together baking powder and remaining 1 cup flour, and add to peanut butter mixture, beating at low speed just until blended.
4. Spoon peanut butter mixture over brownie batter; top with remaining brownie batter, and swirl together.
5. Bake in preheated oven until a wooden pick inserted in center comes out with a few moist crumbs, 45 to 55 minutes. Remove from oven to a wire rack; sprinkle with marshmallows and peanuts.
6. Prepare Chocolate Frosting, and drizzle over brownies. Cool completely.

Chocolate Frosting

ACTIVE 15 MIN. · TOTAL 15 MIN.
MAKES ABOUT 2 CUPS

Cook ¼ cup **butter**, 3 Tbsp. **unsweetened cocoa**, and 3 Tbsp. **milk** in a saucepan over medium, whisking constantly, 4 minutes or until slightly thickened; remove from heat. Whisk in 2 cups **powdered sugar** and ½ tsp. **vanilla extract** until smooth.

Peanut Butter-Candy Bar Brownies

ACTIVE 25 MIN. · TOTAL 2 HOURS
MAKES 1½ DOZEN

- Shortening, for greasing pan
- 1 (16-oz.) pkg. peanut-shape peanut butter sandwich cookies, crushed
- ½ cup butter, melted
- 1 (14-oz.) can sweetened condensed milk
- ½ cup creamy peanut butter
- 1 Tbsp. vanilla extract
- 5 (1.5-oz.) pkg. chocolate-covered peanut butter cup candies, coarsely chopped
- 2 (2.1-oz.) chocolate-covered crispy peanut butter candy bars, coarsely chopped
- 1 cup semisweet chocolate chips
- ½ cup honey-roasted peanuts
- ½ cup sweetened flaked coconut

1. Preheat oven to 350°F. Line bottom and sides of a 13- x 9-inch baking pan with aluminum foil, allowing 2 to 3 inches to extend over sides; grease foil with shortening.
2. Combine crushed cookies and butter in a medium bowl. Press crumb mixture into bottom of prepared pan.
3. Bake in preheated oven 6 to 8 minutes. Do not turn oven off.
4. Combine sweetened condensed milk, peanut butter, and vanilla in a medium bowl, stirring until smooth.
5. Sprinkle peanut butter cup candies, chopped candy bars, chocolate chips, peanuts, and coconut over crust. Drizzle condensed milk mixture over coconut.
6. Bake in preheated oven until lightly browned, 27 minutes. Cool completely in pan on a wire rack, about 1 hour. Lift brownies from pan, using foil sides as handles. Remove foil, and cut into bars.

Apple-Butterscotch Brownies

ACTIVE 15 MIN. · TOTAL 2 HOURS
MAKES ABOUT 2 DOZEN

- 1 cup chopped pecans
- 2 cups firmly packed dark brown sugar
- 1 cup butter, melted
- 2 large eggs, lightly beaten
- 2 tsp. vanilla extract
- 2 cups all-purpose flour plus more for dusting pan
- 2 tsp. baking powder
- ½ tsp. salt
- 3 cups peeled and diced Granny Smith apples (about 1½ lb.)
- Shortening, for greasing pan

1. Preheat oven to 350°F. Bake pecans in a single layer in a shallow pan 8 to 10 minutes or until toasted and fragrant, stirring halfway through.
2. Stir together brown sugar butter, eggs, and vanilla in a large bowl.
3. Stir together flour , baking soda, and salt in a small bowl; add to brown sugar mixture, and stir until blended. Stir in apples and pecans. Pour mixture into a greased and floured 13- x 9-inch pan; spread evenly.
4. Bake in preheated oven until a wooden pick inserted in center comes out clean, 35 to 45 minutes. Cool completely, about 1 hour. Cut into bars.

Apple Hello Dolly Bars

ACTIVE 15 MIN. · TOTAL 2 HOURS
MAKES ABOUT 2 DOZEN

- 2 cups graham cracker crumbs
- ½ cup butter, melted
- ½ (12-oz.) pkg. semisweet chocolate chips
- ½ (12-oz.) pkg. butterscotch chips
- 1 cup sweetened flaked coconut
- 2 cups peeled and finely chopped Granny Smith apples (about 1 lb.)
- 1½ cups coarsely chopped pecans
- 1 (14-oz.) can sweetened condensed milk

1. Preheat oven to 350°F. Stir together graham cracker crumbs and butter; press onto bottom of a lightly greased (with cooking spray) 13- x 9-inch pan. Layer chocolate and butterscotch chips, coconut, apples, and pecans in prepared pan; drizzle with condensed milk.

2. Bake in preheated oven until golden brown, 40 to 45 minutes. Cool completely on a wire rack, about 1 hour.

Lemon-Cheesecake Bars

ACTIVE 20 MIN. · TOTAL 9 HOURS, 35 MIN.
MAKES 9 BARS

- ⅓ cup butter, softened
- ¼ cup firmly packed dark brown sugar
- ¼ tsp. table salt
- ¼ tsp. ground mace or nutmeg
- 1 cup plus 2 Tbsp. all-purpose flour, divided
- 1 cup 1% low-fat cottage cheese
- 1 cup granulated sugar
- 1 Tbsp. loosely packed lemon zest
- 3½ Tbsp. fresh lemon juice
- ¼ tsp. baking powder
- 1 large egg
- 1 large egg white

1. Preheat oven to 350°F. Beat butter, sugar, salt, and mace in a bowl with an electric mixer on medium speed until smooth. Add 1 cup flour, beating at low speed until blended. Press mixture onto bottom of a lightly greased (with cooking spray) 8-inch square pan.
2. Bake in preheated oven 20 minutes.
3. Meanwhile, process cottage cheese in a food processor 1 minute or until smooth, stopping to scrape down sides as needed. Add granulated sugar, remaining 2 tablespoons flour, lemon zest and juice, baking powder, whole egg, and egg white; process 30 seconds or until blended. Pour filling over crust.
4. Bake in preheated oven until set 25 minutes. (Edges will be lightly browned.) Cool 30 minutes. Cover and chill 8 hours. Cut into bars.

Mrs. Claus' Dream Bars

(Photo, page 348)

ACTIVE 20 MIN. · TOTAL 1 HOUR, 45 MIN.
MAKES ABOUT 2 DOZEN BARS

- 2 cups gingersnap crumbs
- ½ cup butter, melted
- Shortening, for greasing pan
- 1 (14-oz.) can sweetened condensed milk
- 1 (6-oz.) pkg. peanut butter chips
- ¾ cup miniature candy-coated chocolate pieces

1 cup sweetened flaked coconut
(optional)
½ cup chopped pecans

1. Preheat oven to 350°F. Combine
gingersnap crumbs and melted butter in
a medium bowl; press onto bottom of a
greased 13- x 9-inch pan. Carefully spread
condensed milk over crumb mixture.
2. Combine peanut butter chips,
chocolate pieces, coconut (if using),
and pecans in a medium bowl. Sprinkle
mixture evenly over condensed milk, and
gently press mixture down.
3. Bake in preheated oven until lightly
browned, 25 to 30 minutes. Cool in pan on
a wire rack, about 1 hour. Cut into squares.

Orange Dreamsicle Crispy Treats

ACTIVE 20 MIN. · TOTAL 1 HOUR, 50 MIN.
MAKES 32 BARS

¼ cup plus 6 Tbsp. butter, softened, divided
1 (10-oz.) pkg. miniature marshmallows
1¾ tsp. vanilla extract, divided
½ cup orange cake mix
6 cups crisp rice cereal
1 (12-oz.) pkg. white chocolate chips
3 cups powdered sugar
6 Tbsp. fresh orange juice
¼ tsp. orange extract
Peach food coloring gel

1. Melt ¼ cup butter in a large Dutch oven
over medium-low; cook 2 minutes or until
butter is melted. Add marshmallows;
cook, stirring constantly, 3 minutes or
until melted. Remove from heat.
2. Stir in 1½ teaspoons vanilla. Add
orange cake mix, stirring until blended.
Add cereal and white chocolate chips,
stirring until well coated. Spread mixture
into a lightly greased (with cooking spray)
13- x 9-inch pan. Cool completely, about
30 minutes.
3. Meanwhile, stir together powdered
sugar, remaining 6 tablespoons butter,
orange juice, remaining ¼ teaspoons
vanilla extract, orange extract, and
desired amount of peach food coloring
gel. Spread over cereal mixture. Let stand
1 hour before cutting into bars.

Salted Caramel–Pecan Bars

(Photo, page 348)

ACTIVE 25 MIN. · TOTAL 1 HOUR
MAKES 4 DOZEN BARS

12 graham cracker sheets
1 cup firmly packed brown sugar
¾ cup butter
2 Tbsp. whipping cream
1 tsp. vanilla extract
1 cup toasted chopped pecans
¼ tsp. kosher salt

1. Preheat oven to 350°F. Line a
15- x 10-inch jelly-roll pan with aluminum
foil; lightly grease foil with cooking
spray. Arrange graham crackers in a
single layer in prepared pan, slightly
overlapping edges.
2. Bring sugar, butter, and cream to a
boil in a medium heavy saucepan over
medium heat, stirring occasionally.
Remove from heat, and stir in vanilla
and pecans. Pour mixture over graham
crackers, spreading to coat. Bake in
preheated oven until lightly browned
and bubbly, 10 to 11 minutes.
3. Immediately sprinkle with salt. Transfer
bars (on aluminum foil) to wire racks, and
cool completely, about 30 minutes.

Peach Melba Shortbread Bars

ACTIVE 20 MIN. · TOTAL 2 HOURS, 20 MIN.
MAKES ABOUT 1½ TO 2 DOZEN BARS

2 cups all-purpose flour
½ cup sugar
¼ tsp. table salt
1 cup cold butter
1 cup peach preserves
6 tsp. raspberry preserves
½ cup sliced almonds
Sweetened whipped cream, for garnish

1. Preheat oven to 350°F. Combine flour,
sugar, and salt in a medium bowl. Cut
butter into flour mixture with a pastry
blender or fork until crumbly. Reserve
1 cup flour mixture. Press remaining flour
mixture onto bottom of a lightly greased
(with cooking spray) 9-inch square pan.
2. Bake in preheated oven until
lightly browned, 25 to 30 minutes.
3. Spread peach preserves over crust
in pan. Dollop ¼ teaspoon raspberry
preserves over peach preserves. Sprinkle
reserved 1 cup flour mixture over
preserves. Sprinkle with sliced almonds.

4. Bake in preheated oven until golden
brown, 35 to 40 minutes. Cool in pan
1 hour on a wire rack. Cut into bars.
Garnish with sweetened whipped cream.

Strawberry–Lemon Shortbread Bars

ACTIVE 20 MIN. · TOTAL 8 HOURS, 10 MIN.
MAKES 4 DOZEN BARS

2 cups all-purpose flour
½ cup powdered sugar
¾ tsp. loosely packed lemon zest, divided
¾ cup cold butter
2 (8-oz.) pkg. cream cheese, softened
¾ cup granulated sugar
2 large eggs
1 Tbsp. fresh lemon juice
1 cup strawberry preserves

1. Preheat oven to 350°F. Combine flour,
powdered sugar, and ½ teaspoon lemon
zest in a medium bowl; cut in butter with
a pastry blender until crumbly. Press
mixture onto bottom of a lightly greased
(with cooking spray) 13- x 9-inch pan.
2. Bake in preheated oven until
lightly browned, 20 to 22 minutes.
3. Meanwhile, beat cream cheese and
granulated sugar in a bowl with an electric
mixer on medium speed until smooth.
Add eggs, 1 at a time, beating just until
blended after each addition. Stir in fresh
lemon juice and remaining ¼ teaspoon
lemon zest, beating until blended.
4. Spread preserves over crust. Pour
cream cheese mixture over preserves,
spreading to edges. Bake 28 to 32 more
minutes or until set. Cool in pan 1 hour on
a wire rack; cover and chill 4 to 8 hours.
Cut into bars. Garnish with sweetened
whipped cream.

Ginger–Lemon Bars with Almond Streusel

ACTIVE 20 MIN. · TOTAL 1 HOUR, 50 MIN.
MAKES 4 DOZEN

2 cups all-purpose flour
½ cup powdered sugar
½ tsp. baking soda
¼ tsp. salt
¾ cup cold butter
¾ cup slivered almonds

Recipe continued on page 344

Recipe continued from page 343

Shortening, for greasing pan
1 (10-oz.) jar lemon curd
3 Tbsp. finely chopped crystallized ginger
Powdered sugar, for garnish (optional)

1. Preheat oven to 350°F. Combine flour, sugar, baking soda, and salt in a large bowl; cut in butter with a pastry blender until crumbly. Toss in almonds; reserve 1 cup flour mixture. Press remaining flour mixture onto bottom of a lightly greased 13- x 9-inch pan.
2. Bake in preheated oven until lightly browned, 15 to 20 minutes. Spread lemon curd over crust, leaving a 1/4-inch border. Sprinkle with ginger and reserved flour mixture. Bake 15 to 20 minutes or until lightly browned. Let cool 1 hour on a wire rack. Garnish, if desired.

Tequila-Lime-Coconut Macaroon Bars

ACTIVE 20 MIN. · TOTAL 2 HOURS, 5 MIN.
MAKES 3 DOZEN

Shortening, for greasing foil
2 cups all-purpose flour, divided
2 cups sugar, divided
1/2 cup cold butter, cut into pieces
4 large eggs
1 1/2 cups sweetened flaked coconut
1 tsp. lime zest
1/3 cup fresh lime juice
3 Tbsp. tequila
1/2 tsp. baking powder
1/4 tsp. salt
Powdered sugar and lime peel curls, for garnish (optional)

1. Preheat oven to 350°F. Line bottom and sides of a 13- x 9-inch pan with heavy-duty aluminum foil, allowing 2 inches to extend over sides; lightly grease foil.
2. Stir together 1 3/4 cups flour and 1/2 cup sugar. Cut in butter with a pastry blender or fork until crumbly. Press mixture onto bottom of prepared pan.
3. Bake in preheated oven until lightly browned, 20 to 23 minutes.
4. Meanwhile, whisk eggs in a bowl until smooth; whisk in coconut, lime zest and juice, tequila, and remaining 1 1/2 cups sugar. Stir together baking powder, salt, and remaining 1/4 cup flour in a bowl; whisk into egg mixture. Pour over hot crust.

5. Bake in preheated oven until filling is set, 25 minutes. Let cool 1 hour on a wire rack. Lift from pan, using foil sides as handles. Remove foil, and cut into bars. Garnish, if desired.

Raspberry-Lime Swirl Bars

ACTIVE 40 MIN. · TOTAL 4 HOURS, 40 MIN., INCLUDING 4 HOURS CHILLING
MAKES 2 DOZEN

1 (10-oz.) pkg. shortbread cookies, finely crushed (about 2 cups)
6 Tbsp. (3 oz.) salted butter, melted
1 Tbsp. powdered sugar
1 cup granulated sugar
3/4 cup fresh lime juice (from 5 to 6 limes)
1/4 cup cornstarch
3 large egg yolks
2 large eggs
1/2 cup (4 oz.) cold salted butter, diced
1/4 cup seedless raspberry jam

1. Line a 9-inch square metal baking pan with aluminum foil, allowing 2 to 3 inches to hang over sides. Spray the sides and bottom of the prepared pan with cooking spray. Process the crushed shortbread cookies, melted butter, and powdered sugar in a food processor until finely ground, about 20 seconds. Press the mixture evenly into the bottom of the pan; cover and chill 2 hours.
2. Preheat the oven to 350°F. Combine the granulated sugar, lime juice, cornstarch, egg yolks, and eggs in a medium saucepan. Cook over medium, whisking constantly, until the mixture comes to a boil, about 5 minutes. Boil 1 minute, whisking constantly. Remove from heat, and whisk in the cold butter until incorporated.
3. Remove the shortbread crust from the refrigerator. Pour the lime curd evenly over the shortbread crust. Dot with the jam, and use a wooden spoon or chopstick to create jam swirls.
4. Bake in preheated oven until the filling is set, about 25 minutes. Let cool in pan on a wire rack to room temperature, about 1 hour. Cover and chill until set, 2 hours or up to overnight. Remove from pan. Remove and discard foil; cut into bars.

Lemon Drop Squares

ACTIVE 10 MIN. · TOTAL 1 HOUR, 30 MIN.
MAKES ABOUT 2 DOZEN

2 1/2 cups all-purpose flour
1 cup butter, cubed
2/3 cup granulated sugar
1/2 cup uncooked quick-cooking oats
1/3 cup firmly packed brown sugar
2 (10-oz.) jars lemon curd

1. Line bottom and sides of a 13- x 9-inch pan with heavy-duty aluminum foil or parchment paper, allowing 2 to 3 inches to extend over sides; lightly grease foil.
2. Preheat oven to 350°F. Beat flour, butter, granulated sugar, oats, and brown sugar with an electric mixer on medium speed until crumbly and mixture resembles wet sand. Reserve 1 1/4 cups mixture. Press remaining mixture onto bottom of prepared pan.
3. Bake in preheated oven 20 to 22 minutes until light golden brown.
4. Meanwhile, microwave both jars of lemon curd at the same time on HIGH 1 minute or until pourable. Spread lemon curd over hot baked crust, and sprinkle with reserved crumb mixture.
5. Bake in preheated oven 30 minutes or until bubbly and brown. Let cool in pan on a wire rack 30 minutes. Lift from pan, using foil sides as handles. Cool completely on a wire rack (about 30 minutes). Remove foil, and cut into squares.

Luscious Lemon Bars

ACTIVE 20 MIN. · TOTAL 2 HOURS, 5 MIN.
MAKES ABOUT 2 DOZEN

2 1/4 cups all-purpose flour, divided
1/2 cup powdered sugar
1 cup cold butter, cut into pieces
4 large eggs
2 cups granulated sugar
1 tsp. lemon zest
1/3 cup fresh lemon juice
1/2 tsp. baking powder
Powdered sugar

1. Preheat oven to 350°F. Line bottom and sides of a 13- x 9-inch pan with heavy-duty aluminum foil, allowing 2 to 3 inches to extend over sides; lightly grease foil.
2. Stir together 2 cups flour and 1/2 cup powdered sugar. Cut in butter using a pastry blender or fork until crumbly. Press mixture onto bottom of prepared pan.

Recipe continued on page 346

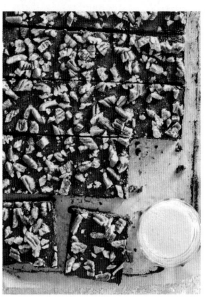

Recipe continued from page 344

3. Bake in preheated oven 20 to 25 minutes or until lightly browned.
4. Meanwhile, whisk eggs in a large bowl until smooth; whisk in granulated sugar, lemon zest, and lemon juice. Stir together baking powder and remaining ¼ cup flour in a small bowl; whisk into egg mixture. Pour mixture over hot baked crust.
5. Bake in preheated oven 25 minutes or until filling is set. Let cool in pan on a wire rack 30 minutes. Lift from pan, using foil sides as handles. Cool completely on a wire rack, about 30 minutes. Remove foil, and cut into bars; sprinkle with powdered sugar.

No-Bake Fudgy Toffee Bars

ACTIVE 30 MIN. · TOTAL 4 HOURS, 30 MIN., INCLUDING 4 HOURS CHILLING
SERVES 16

  Salted butter, for greasing paper
1½ cups heavy cream
 3 Tbsp. powdered sugar
 3 (4-oz.) semisweet chocolate baking bars, finely chopped
 1 tsp. vanilla extract
 2 (11-oz.) pkg. caramels
 ⅓ cup evaporated milk
 17 graham cracker sheets
 2 (1.4-oz.) chocolate-covered toffee candy bars (such as Heath), coarsely chopped

1. Line a 9-inch square baking pan with parchment paper, allowing parchment to extend over sides of pan. Grease paper.
2. Combine cream and powdered sugar in a small saucepan. Bring to a simmer over medium-low, stirring occasionally. (Do not bring to a boil.) Place chopped chocolate in a medium bowl. Pour cream mixture over chocolate; let stand 1 minute. Gently stir until chocolate melts and mixture is smooth. Stir in vanilla.
3. Combine caramels and evaporated milk in a saucepan over medium-low. Cook, stirring often, until caramels melt and mixture is smooth, 9 to 10 minutes. Remove from heat; let stand 10 minutes.
4. Place 1 layer of graham cracker sheets in prepared pan, breaking crackers to fit as needed. Pour one-third of the caramel mixture over crackers. Using an offset spatula, smooth caramel to edges of pan. Pour one-third chocolate mixture over caramel; smooth chocolate to edges of pan. Repeat layers 2 times with remaining graham cracker sheets, caramel mixture, and chocolate mixture, ending with chocolate. Sprinkle chopped toffee candy over top. Chill, uncovered, 4 hours or overnight.
5. Lift toffee bar mixture from pan using parchment. Trim edges if necessary. Cut into 16 pieces. Serve chilled.

Oven-Baked Churros

ACTIVE 15 MIN. · TOTAL 30 MIN.
MAKES 3 DOZEN

 1 (17.3-oz.) pkg. frozen puff pastry sheets, thawed
 ¼ cup sugar
 1 tsp. ground cinnamon
 ¼ cup melted butter

1. Preheat oven to 450°F. Unfold and cut puff pastry sheets in half lengthwise, and cut each half crosswise into 1-inch-wide strips. Place strips on a lightly greased parchment paper-lined baking sheet. Bake 10 minutes or until golden brown.
2. Meanwhile, combine sugar and cinnamon. Remove pastry strips from oven, and dip in butter; roll in cinnamon-sugar mixture. Let stand on a wire rack 5 minutes or until dry.

Pies

Key "Light" Pie

ACTIVE 10 MIN. · TOTAL 1 HOUR, 20 MIN.
SERVES 8

 1 (14-oz.) can fat-free sweetened condensed milk
 ¾ cup egg substitute
 2 tsp. lime zest (about 2 limes)
 ½ cup fresh lime juice
 1 (6-oz.) reduced-fat ready-made graham cracker piecrust
  Thawed fat-free frozen whipped topping, lime wedges, lime rind curls, for garnish (optional)

1. Preheat oven to 350°F. Process condensed milk, egg substitute, lime zest and juice in a blender until smooth. Pour mixture into piecrust.
2. Bake in preheated oven until set, 10 to 12 minutes. Let pie cool completely on a wire rack, about 1 hour. Garnish, if desired.

Caramel Apple Blondie Pie

(Photo, page 348)

ACTIVE 40 MIN. · TOTAL 4 HOURS, 30 MIN.
MAKES 8 TO 10 SERVINGS

 6 large Granny Smith apples (about 3 lb.)
 2 Tbsp. all-purpose flour
 2 cups firmly packed light brown sugar, divided
 1 cup butter, divided
1½ cups all-purpose flour
1½ tsp. baking powder
 ½ tsp. table salt
 3 large eggs, lightly beaten
 3 Tbsp. bourbon
 ¾ cup coarsely chopped toasted pecans
 ½ (14.1-oz.) pkg. refrigerated piecrusts
  Apple Cider Caramel Sauce (recipe follows)

1. Peel 6 large Granny Smith apples, and cut into ¼-inch-thick wedges. Toss with 2 tablespoons flour and ½ cup brown sugar in a large bowl. Melt ¼ cup butter in a large skillet over medium-high; add apple mixture, and sauté 15 minutes or until apples are tender and liquid is thickened. Remove from heat; cool completely (about 30 minutes).
2. Meanwhile, preheat oven to 350°F. Melt remaining ¾ cup butter. Stir together flour, baking powder, and salt in a large bowl. Add eggs, bourbon, ¾ cup melted butter, and remaining 1½ cups brown sugar, stirring until blended. Stir in pecans.
3. Fit piecrust into a 10-inch cast-iron skillet, gently pressing piecrust all the way up sides of skillet. Spoon two-thirds of apple mixture over bottom of piecrust, spreading and gently pressing apple slices into an even layer using the back of a spoon. Spoon batter over apple mixture; top with remaining apple mixture.
4. Place pie on lower oven rack. Bake in preheated oven until a wooden pick inserted in center comes out with a few moist crumbs, 1 hour and 10 minutes to 1 hour and 20 minutes. Remove from oven; cool pie completely on a wire rack.
5. Drizzle cooled pie with ⅓ cup Apple Cider Caramel Sauce. Serve with remaining sauce.

Apple Cider Caramel Sauce

ACTIVE 15 MIN. - TOTAL 15 MIN.
MAKES ABOUT 1½ CUPS

- 1 cup apple cider
- 1 cup firmly packed light brown sugar
- ½ cup butter
- ¼ cup whipping cream

Cook cider in a 3-qt. saucepan over medium heat, stirring often, 10 minutes or until reduced to ¼ cup. Stir in brown sugar, butter, and cream. Bring to a boil over medium-high, stirring constantly for 2 minutes. Remove from heat, and cool completely. Refrigerate up to 1 week. To reheat, microwave on HIGH 10 to 15 seconds or just until warm; stir until smooth.

Salted Caramel-Chocolate Pecan Pie

ACTIVE 25 MIN. - TOTAL 1 HOUR, 20 MIN.
SERVES 8

CHOCOLATE FILLING
- 1½ cups sugar
- ¾ cup butter, melted
- ⅓ cup all-purpose flour
- ⅓ cup 100% cacao unsweetened cocoa
- 1 Tbsp. light corn syrup
- 1 tsp. vanilla extract
- 3 large eggs
- 1 cup toasted chopped pecans
- 1 (9-inch) unbaked deep-dish piecrust shell

SALTED CARAMEL TOPPING
- ¾ cup sugar
- 1 Tbsp. fresh lemon juice
- ⅓ cup heavy cream
- 4 Tbsp. butter
- ¼ tsp. table salt
- 2 cups toasted pecan halves
- ½ tsp. sea salt

1. Prepare Filling: Preheat oven to 350°F. Stir together sugar, butter, flour, cocoa, corn syrup, and vanilla in a large bowl. Add eggs, stirring until well blended. Fold in chopped pecans. Pour mixture into crust.
2. Bake in preheated oven 35 minutes. (Filling will be loose but will set as it cools.) Remove from oven to a wire rack.
3. Prepare Topping: Bring sugar, lemon juice, and ¼ cup water to a boil in a medium saucepan over high. Boil, swirling

occasionally after sugar begins to change color, 8 minutes or until dark amber. (Watch carefully as the sugar could burn quickly once it begins to change color.) Remove from heat; add cream and butter. Stir constantly until bubbling stops and butter is incorporated (about 1 minute). Stir in table salt.
4. Arrange pecan halves on pie. Top with warm caramel. Cool 15 minutes; sprinkle with sea salt.

Tennessee Whiskey-Pecan Pie

(Photo, page 348)

ACTIVE 30 MIN. - TOTAL 3 HOURS, 10 MIN.
SERVES 8

CRUST
- ½ tsp. butter
- ¼ cup finely chopped pecans
  Pinch of kosher salt
- 1¼ cups all-purpose flour
- 2 Tbsp. granulated sugar
- ½ tsp. table salt
- ¼ cup cold butter, cubed
- ¼ cup cold shortening, cubed
- 3 to 4 Tbsp. buttermilk

FILLING
- 1 cup dark corn syrup
- ½ cup granulated sugar
- ½ cup firmly packed light brown sugar
- ¼ cup Tennessee whiskey*
- 4 large eggs
- ¼ cup butter, melted
- 2 tsp. plain white cornmeal
- 2 tsp. vanilla extract
- ½ tsp. table salt
- 2½ cups lightly toasted pecan halves

REMAINING INGREDIENTS
  Whiskey Whipped Cream (recipe follows) (optional)

1. Prepare Crust: Melt butter in a small skillet over medium heat, swirling to coat sides of pan. Add pecans, and sauté 2 minutes or until fragrant and lightly toasted. Sprinkle pecan mixture with a pinch of salt. Remove pecans from skillet, and cool completely. Reserve for use in Step 4.
2. Pulse flour, sugar, and salt in a food processor until well combined. Add cubed butter and shortening; pulse until mixture resembles coarse meal. Drizzle 3 tablespoons buttermilk over flour mixture, and pulse just until moist clumps form. (Add up to 1 tablespoon buttermilk,

1 teaspoon at a time, if necessary.) Shape dough into a flat disk, and wrap tightly with plastic wrap. Chill dough at least 1 hour.
3. Meanwhile, prepare Filling: Place corn syrup, sugars, and whiskey in a large saucepan, and bring to a boil over medium, whisking constantly. Cook, whisking constantly, 2 minutes; remove from heat. Whisk together eggs, butter, cornmeal, vanilla, and salt in a bowl. Gradually whisk about one-fourth of hot corn syrup mixture into egg mixture; gradually add egg mixture to remaining corn syrup mixture, whisking constantly. Stir in pecan halves; cool completely (about 30 minutes).
4. Preheat oven to 325°F. Unwrap dough, and roll into a 13-inch circle on a lightly floured surface. Sprinkle dough with sautéed pecans. Place a piece of plastic wrap over dough and pecans, and lightly roll pecans into dough. Fit dough into a lightly greased (with cooking spray) 9-inch pie plate. Fold edges under, and crimp. Pour cooled filling into prepared crust.
5. Bake in preheated oven until set, 50 to 55 minutes. Cool completely on a wire rack, about 2 hours. Serve with Whiskey Whipped Cream, if desired.
*Water or apple juice may be substituted.

Whiskey Whipped Cream

ACTIVE 5 MIN. - TOTAL 5 MIN.
MAKES ABOUT 1½ CUPS

Beat 1 cup **heavy cream** and 1 tsp. **Tennessee whiskey** in a bowl with an electric mixer on medium-high speed until foamy. Gradually add 3 Tbsp. **powdered sugar**, beating until soft peaks form.

CLOCKWISE FROM TOP LEFT:

- PEANUT BUTTER MISSISSIPPI MUD BROWNIES (PAGE 341)

- SALTED CARAMEL-PECAN BARS (PAGE 343)

- MRS. CLAUS' DREAM BARS (PAGE 342)

- CARAMEL APPLE BLONDIE PIE (PAGE 346)

- PIÑA COLADA ICEBOX PIE (RIGHT)

- CRANBERRY-APPLE PIE WITH PECAN SHORTBREAD CRUST (RIGHT)

- PEANUT BUTTER-BANANA CREAM PIE (RIGHT)

- TENNESSEE WHISKEY-PECAN PIE (PAGE 347)

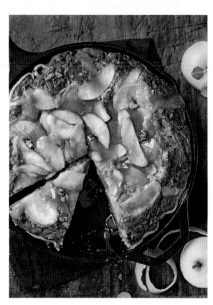

Cranberry-Apple Pie with Pecan Shortbread Crust

(Photo, left)

ACTIVE 30 MIN. - TOTAL 4 HOURS
SERVES 12

CRUST

1	cup finely chopped pecans
1½	cups butter, softened
¾	cup powdered sugar
3	cups all-purpose flour

FILLING

3	lb. Gala apples
1	cup firmly packed light brown sugar
¾	cup sweetened dried cranberries
¼	cup all-purpose flour
1	tsp. ground cinnamon
2	Tbsp. butter, melted
	Toasted pecan halves, powdered sugar, for garnish (optional)

1. Prepare Crust: Preheat oven to 350°F. Bake pecans in a single layer in a shallow pan until lightly toasted and fragrant, stirring halfway through, 4 to 5 minutes. Cool completely, about 20 minutes.
2. Meanwhile, beat butter in a bowl with an electric mixer on medium speed 1 minute or until creamy; add powdered sugar, beating well. Gradually add flour, beating at low speed until mixture is no longer crumbly and starts to come together into a ball. Stir in pecans. Shape one-third of dough into an 8-inch log; wrap in plastic wrap, and chill until ready to use. Press remaining dough on bottom and up sides of a 9-inch springform pan. Cover and chill crust.
3. Prepare Filling: Peel apples. Cut into ¼-inch-thick wedges. Toss together apples, brown sugar, cranberries, flour, and cinnamon. Spoon mixture into prepared crust. Drizzle with melted butter.
4. Cut reserved dough log into 8 (1-inch) pieces. Gently shape each piece into a 6- to 8-inch rope. Lightly press each rope to flatten into strips. Arrange strips in a lattice design over filling.
5. Bake in preheated oven until juices are thick and bubbly, crust is golden brown, and apples are tender when pierced with a long wooden pick, 1 hour to 1 hour and 10 minutes, covering with aluminum foil during last 30 minutes to prevent excessive browning. Cool completely in pan on a wire rack. Remove sides of pan. Garnish, if desired.

Peanut Butter-Banana Cream Pie

(Photo, left)

ACTIVE 35 MIN. - TOTAL 5 HOURS, 45 MIN.
SERVES 8

22	peanut butter sandwich cookies
½	cup lightly salted dry-roasted peanuts
¼	cup butter, melted
½	cup granulated sugar
¼	cup cornstarch
2	cups half-and-half
4	large egg yolks
3	Tbsp. butter
2	Tbsp. creamy peanut butter
2	tsp. vanilla extract, divided
2	medium bananas
2	cups heavy cream
½	cup powdered sugar
	Halved peanut butter sandwich cookies, chopped lightly salted dry-roasted peanuts, for garnish (optional)

1. Preheat oven to 350°F. Process cookies and peanuts in a food processor about 1 minute or until finely chopped. Stir together cookie mixture and melted butter. Lightly grease a 9-inch pie plate with cooking spray. Press crumb mixture on bottom, up sides, and onto lip of pie plate.
2. Bake in preheated oven until lightly brown, 10 to 12 minutes. Transfer to a wire rack, and cool completely, about 30 minutes.
3. Whisk together granulated sugar and cornstarch in a large, heavy saucepan. Whisk together half-and-half and egg yolks in a medium bowl. Gradually whisk half-and-half mixture into sugar mixture, and bring to a boil over medium, whisking constantly. Boil, whisking constantly, 1 minute; remove from heat.
4. Stir butter, peanut butter, and 1 teaspoon vanilla into sugar mixture. Place heavy-duty plastic wrap directly on warm custard (to prevent a film from forming), and cool 30 minutes.
5. Cut bananas into ½-inch-thick slices; place in a single layer on bottom of crust. Spoon custard over bananas; cover and chill 4 to 48 hours.
6. Beat cream in a bowl with an electric mixer on high speed until foamy; gradually add powdered sugar and remaining 1 teaspoon vanilla, beating until soft peaks form. Top pie with whipped cream. Serve immediately, or chill up to 4 hours. Garnish, if desired.

Piña Colada Icebox Pie

(Photo, left)

ACTIVE 25 MIN. - TOTAL 6 HOURS, 20 MIN.
SERVES 8

2	cups pecan shortbread cookie crumbs (about 16 cookies)
1	cup sweetened flaked coconut
¼	cup butter, melted
⅓	cup sugar
2	Tbsp. cornstarch
1	(8-oz.) can crushed pineapple in juice
1	(8-oz.) pkg. cream cheese, softened
1½	cups cream of coconut, divided
2	large eggs
1	cup whipping cream
	Lightly toasted shaved coconut, pineapple wedges, fresh pineapple mint sprigs, for garnish (optional)

1. Preheat oven to 350°F. Lightly coat a 9-inch pie plate with cooking spray. Stir together cookie crumbs, coconut, and butter; firmly press on bottom and up sides of pie plate. Bake until lightly browned, 10 to 12 minutes. Transfer to a wire rack; cool completely, about 30 minutes.
2. Stir together sugar and cornstarch in a small heavy saucepan; stir in pineapple. While stirring constantly, bring to a boil over medium-high; cook, stirring constantly, until thickened, about 1 minute. Remove from heat; cool completely, about 20 minutes.
3. Beat cream cheese at medium speed with a heavy-duty electric stand mixer, using whisk attachment, until smooth. Gradually add 1 cup cream of coconut, beating at low speed just until blended. (Chill remaining ½ cup cream of coconut until ready to use.) Add eggs, 1 at a time, beating just until blended after each addition.
4. Spread cooled pineapple mixture over bottom of piecrust; spoon cream cheese mixture over pineapple mixture.
5. Bake in preheated oven until set, 38 to 42 minutes. Cool completely on a wire rack, about 1 hour. Cover and chill 4 hours.
6. Beat whipping cream at high speed until foamy. Gradually add remaining ½ cup cream of coconut, beating until soft peaks form; spread over pie. Garnish, if desired.

Baking at High Altitudes

Liquids boil at lower temperatures (below 212°F), and moisture evaporates more quickly at high altitudes. Both of these factors significantly impact the quality of baked goods. Also, leavening gases (air, carbon dioxide, water vapor) expand faster. If you live at 3,000 feet or below, first try a recipe as is. Sometimes few, if any, changes are needed. But the higher you go, the more you'll have to adjust your ingredients and cooking times.

A Few Overall Tips

- Use shiny new baking pans. This seems to help mixtures rise, especially cake batters.
- Use butter, flour, and parchment paper to prep your baking pans for nonstick cooking. At high altitudes, baked goods tend to stick more to pans.
- Be exact in your measurements (once you've figured out what they should be). This is always important in baking, but especially so when you're up so high. Tiny variations in ingredients make a bigger difference at high altitudes than at sea level.
- Boost flavor. Seasonings and extracts tend to be more muted at higher altitudes, so increase them slightly.
- Have patience. You may have to bake your favorite sea-level recipe a few times, making slight adjustments each time, until it's worked out to suit your particular altitude.

Ingredient/Temperature Adjustments

CHANGE	AT 3,000 FEET	AT 5,000 FEET	AT 7,000 FEET
Baking powder or baking soda	Reduce each tsp. called for by up to ⅛ tsp.	Reduce each tsp. called for by ⅛ to ¼ tsp.	Reduce each tsp. called for by ¼ to ½ tsp.
Sugar	Reduce each cup called for by up to 1 Tbsp.	Reduce each cup called for by up to 2 Tbsp.	Reduce each cup called for by 2 to 3 Tbsp.
Liquid	Increase each cup called for by up to 2 Tbsp.	Increase each cup called for by up to 2 to 4 Tbsp.	Increase each cup called for by up to 3 to 4 Tbsp.
Oven temperature	Increase 3° to 5°	Increase 15°	Increase 21° to 25°

Metric Equivalents

The recipes that appear in this cookbook use the standard United States method for measuring liquid and dry or solid ingredients (teaspoons, tablespoons, and cups). The information on this chart is provided to help cooks outside the U.S. successfully use these recipes. All equivalents are approximate.

METRIC EQUIVALENTS FOR DIFFERENT TYPES OF INGREDIENTS

A standard cup measure of a dry or solid ingredient will vary in weight depending on the type of ingredient. A standard cup of liquid is the same volume for any type of liquid. Use the following chart when converting standard cup measures to grams (weight) or milliliters (volume).

Standard Cup	Fine Powder (ex. flour)	Grain (ex. rice)	Granular (ex. sugar)	Liquid Solids (ex. butter)	Liquid (ex. milk)
1	140 g	150 g	190 g	200 g	240 ml
¾	105 g	113 g	143 g	150 g	180 ml
⅔	93 g	100 g	125 g	133 g	160 ml
½	70 g	75 g	95 g	100 g	120 ml
⅓	47 g	50 g	63 g	67 g	80 ml
¼	35 g	38 g	48 g	50 g	60 ml
⅛	18 g	19 g	24 g	25 g	30 ml

USEFUL EQUIVALENTS FOR LIQUID INGREDIENTS BY VOLUME

¼ tsp.					=	1 ml		
½ tsp.					=	2 ml		
1 tsp.					=	5 ml		
3 tsp.	=	1 Tbsp.		=	½ fl oz.	=	15 ml	
		2 Tbsp.	=	⅛ cup	=	1 fl oz.	=	30 ml
		4 Tbsp.	=	¼ cup	=	2 fl oz.	=	60 ml
		5⅓ Tbsp.	=	⅓ cup	=	3 fl oz.	=	80 ml
		8 Tbsp.	=	½ cup	=	4 fl oz.	=	120 ml
		10⅔ Tbsp.	=	⅔ cup	=	5 fl oz.	=	160 ml
		12 Tbsp.	=	¾ cup	=	6 fl oz.	=	180 ml
		16 Tbsp.	=	1 cup	=	8 fl oz.	=	240 ml
1 pt.	=	2 cups			=	16 fl oz.	=	480 ml
1 qt.	=	4 cups			=	32 fl oz.	=	960 ml
						33 fl oz.	=	1000 ml	=	1 l

USEFUL EQUIVALENTS FOR DRY INGREDIENTS BY WEIGHT

(To convert ounces to grams, multiply the number of ounces by 30.)

1 oz.	=	1/16 lb.	=	30 g
4 oz.	=	¼ lb.	=	120 g
8 oz.	=	½ lb.	=	240 g
12 oz.	=	¾ lb.	=	360 g
16 oz.	=	1 lb.	=	480 g

USEFUL EQUIVALENTS FOR LENGTH

(To convert inches to centimeters, multiply the number of inches by 2.5.)

1 in.						=	2.5 cm	
6 in.	=	½	ft.			=	15 cm	
12 in.	=	1	ft.			=	30 cm	
36 in.	=	3	ft.	=	1 yd.	=	90 cm	

USEFUL EQUIVALENTS FOR COOKING/OVEN TEMPERATURES

	Fahrenheit	Celsius	Gas Mark
Freeze Water	32°F	0°C	
Room Temperature	68°F	20°C	
Boil Water	212°F	100°C	
Bake	325°F	160°C	3
	350°F	180°C	4
	375°F	190°C	5
	400°F	200°C	6
	425°F	220°C	7
	450°F	230°C	8
Broil			Grill

Recipe Title Index

This index alphabetically lists every recipe by exact title

Month-by-Month Index

This index alphabetically lists every food article and accompanying recipes by month

General Recipe Index

This index lists every recipe by food category and/or major ingredient.

MEREDITH CONSUMER MARKETING
Director, Direct Marketing-Books: Daniel Fagan
Marketing Operations Manager: Max Daily
Assistant Marketing Manager: Kylie Dazzo
Content Manager: Julie Doll
Senior Production Manager: Liza Ward

WATERBURY PUBLICATIONS, INC.
Editorial Director: Lisa Kingsley
Associate Editor: Tricia Bergman
Creative Director: Ken Carlson
Associate Design Director: Doug Samuelson
Production Assistant: Mindy Samuelson
Contributing Copy Editor: Linda Wagner
Contributing Proofreader: Mike Olivo
Contributing Indexer: Mary Williams

Recipe Developers and Testers: Meredith Food Studios

MEREDITH CORPORATION
Executive Chairman: Stephen M. Lacy

In Memoriam: E.T. Meredith III (1933–2003)

Library of Congress Control Number: 2020931335

ISBN: 978-1-4197-5061-8

First Edition 2020
Printed in the United States of America
10 9 8 7 6 5 4 3 2 1
Call 1-800-826-4707 for more information.

Distributed in 2020 by Abrams, an imprint of ABRAMS.
Abrams® is a registered trademark of Harry N. Abrams, Inc.

ABRAMS The Art of Books
195 Broadway, New York, NY 10007
abramsbooks.com

Pictured on front cover:
Coconut Cake with Coconut Cream Frosting, page 309